GU01018134

Selected Pol

The Great Moving Right
Show and Other Essays

Selected Political Writings:

The Great Moving Right Show and Other Essays

Stuart Hall

*Edited by Sally Davison, David Featherstone,
Michael Rustin and Bill Schwarz*

Lawrence and Wishart
London 2017

Lawrence and Wishart Limited
Central Books Building
Freshwater Road
Chadwell Heath
RM8 1RX

ISBN 9781910448656

British Library Cataloguing in Publication Data.
A catalogue record for this book is available from the British Library

Printed and bound by ImprintDigital.com, UK

Contents

Part 3: Neoliberalism

INTRODUCTION:
Redefining the political

THE POLITICAL ESSAY has a long and honourable history: indeed the essay as a literary form is peculiarly suited to politics. The essay is for-the-moment, composed to address a particular historical configuration, capturing emergent histories as they come into sight. Or, as Stuart Hall was fond of conceiving of his own essays, they are *interventions*, often with foes to be dispatched to the left and to the right. The political essay is seldom dispassionate. The essay-form is not an innocent medium. It is combative, working to organise intellectually its constituency of readers.

This is certainly true of the political essays in this collection. But the essay form was also ideally suited to Hall's more theoretical preoccupations, since one of his abiding concerns was to tease out the complex contours of significant political moments and to get a sense of what was shaping them. In most of the essays gathered here we can see him trying to identify the nature of the specific shifts and currents that have coalesced into the moment he is analysing. This is a clearly discernible characteristic of even his earliest essays, but, as we outline below, Hall later theorised this way of writing as 'conjunctural' analysis. The wide range of elements he draws on in his writing is central to Hall's unique contribution as a political theorist.

Hall's essays also embody a more philosophical or abstract purpose, which nevertheless remains focused on real-world concerns: they continually return to the question of what politics is and where it happens. This abstract question is worked into the interstices of his concrete political analyses. His work thus represents a striking refusal of the prevailing codifications of what politics entails and where it is to be located; his appropriation of Gramsci's conception of hegemony enlarged the conception of what constitutes class politics;[1] and he also contended that emergent political forces did not always look 'political'

1

in the orthodox manner. They might not traverse the landscape of conventional politics at all. Think of the dynamics of feminism, for example, with its insistence on the personal as political. From such a viewpoint the domain of what counts as 'politics' expands radically.

It has been suggested that Hall could be regarded as a Gramscian before he had ever read Gramsci. Many elements of what we think of as a Gramscian approach are present in some form in his work before his encounter with Gramsci ever took place: Hall wrote on the educative functions of the state (on 'moral and intellectual leadership'); on the complexity of the networks that bind political society to civil society; on the material force of 'philosophies' (of various sorts) on the political stage, and on the embodiment of specific ideologies in the disparate figures of the intellectual (again of various sorts); on the political conception of the idea of the people as a necessarily contingent formation; and on his methodological commitment to a politics of the 'concrete'. It is clear, though, that when – belatedly – Gramsci arrived, he was to prove a revelation.

Gramsci and conjunctural analysis

Hall's encounter with Gramsci did much to crystallise his notion of conjunctural analysis. The promise of such an approach lay in its potential for identifying key elements in the movement of political forces, and for isolating the properties of emergent social forms. This engagement with the dynamics of particular conjunctures was strikingly apparent in his writing in *Policing the Crisis* and 'The great moving right show'. In these texts he was seeking to identify the forces that were driving the unravelling of the social democratic settlement and its replacement by a populist authoritarianism.[2] Hall's understanding of an emerging conjuncture was central to his analysis of the complexities of a political moment, which he saw as composed of, and constituted by, the complex interaction of condensed elements from competing historical times.

Hall arrived conceptually at the idea of conjuncture through Louis Althusser's 1962 essay 'Contradiction and Overdetermination', which itself drew on Lenin and Gramsci.[3] Althusser's reading of Lenin alerted Hall to the theoretical usefulness of apprehending the displacements that lie at the heart of politics. It was Lenin's contention that the revolutionary situation in Russia had occurred not because the contending forces fell neatly into two opposing camps, in which the underlying class interests, immediately and transparently, determined the domain of politics. On the contrary, the revolutionary moment had only come about, in Lenin's mesmerising formulation because:

> as a result of an extremely unique historical situation, *absolutely dissimilar currents, absolutely heterogeneous* class interests, *absolutely contrary* political and social strivings have *merged*, and in a strikingly 'harmonious' manner.[4]

Althusser, in his interpretation of this passage, named such a conjunctural situation as 'overdetermined'. Time and again Hall returned to Lenin's words and to Althusser's concept.

Gramsci saw the political as a live, decentred, disorderly domain, composed of myths and passions as much as of rational doctrines. For him, Machiavelli's gift was his ability to craft a formal philosophy that could grasp these dimensions of political reality. According to Gramsci, Machiavelli's philosophy 'gives political passions a more concrete form'. Neither formally systematised nor made up of 'pedantic classification', it sees politics as an arena for the making of a 'concrete phantasy'.[5] To think in these terms adds a further layer of meaning to the idea of 'the concrete', for it alerts us to the relations between politics and the subjective forces of human passion. It endeavours to hold together, in a single moment, the objective and the subjective in their mutual constitution of 'the political'.[6] This, too, marked a necessary component of conjunctural analysis.

Hall was convinced that any social analysis of value would recognise the centrality of *difference* in the making of social life. This is what underlies the deconstructive drive in his political essays. In order to grasp the endless movements of difference in the social world, the overarching meta-theories that have been devised to bring societies within the orbit of human thought need themselves to be deconstructed, to ensure that they do not also – in the very instant that they set out to explain the world – override and obliterate difference. A principle of deconstructive thought, for Hall, was precisely the need to recognise difference and to provide difference with the analytical weight it requires. In this sense Lenin's formulations cited above – '*absolutely dissimilar currents, absolutely heterogeneous* class interests, *absolutely contrary* political and social strivings' – are of the greatest significance.

Yet in order to think politically there is an inevitable moment when the practice of deconstruction has to be halted, at least temporarily. This was not, for Hall, a matter of formal logic, or of a paramount conceptual consistency. It was, rather, the moment when politics intruded onto the terrain of theory, driven by the need to mobilise abstraction in order to grasp the unpredictabilities of the historical world. For Hall politics was never only a question of contingency or of a chaos of spiralling indeterminacy. Emergent historical forces, even when radically unpredictable, were never without their social determinations. Indeed they gave them shape, and enabled them to enter the historical stage. It was in this sense that Hall never finally vacated the theoretical terrain of Marxism.

It was through Gramsci that Hall was able to alight upon this theoretical movement that enables an understanding (and deconstruction) of the ways in which contrary social forces could, through political practice, 'merge'. Conjuncture provided a methodological means to hold deconstruction at bay. (In a different dimension of his theoretical vocabulary, articulation plays this same role.) Deconstruction is intrinsic to the work of theory, but politics has to pause and inquire how the 'absolutely dissimilar' can be brought into a provisional, practical unity.[7]

Combating orthodoxy

From the 1950s onwards Hall's work had broadly two orthodoxies in his sights, and they remained with him, in varying forms, throughout his life.

The first masqueraded – and still masquerades – as no orthodoxy at all: it presents itself, *sotto voce*, as the reasonable, sensible acknowledgement of how in Britain politics just *is*. This is a mentality disciplined by the institutional horizons of Westminster, as if these provide all that needs to be known about how politics operates. Such sentiments can be heard from representatives of the political parties; from accredited figures in the academy; and, often in most concentrated form, in the utterances of the media commentators.

For Hall the fundamental fault-line was between a politics that was constrained by the norms of Westminster and one capable of embracing the breadth and complexities of human life as it was lived day by day. The dominating concern was with the deeper forms and presuppositions of politics rather than its institutional content; with how the field of politics was to operate rather than with the instrumental objectives enshrined in the party manifestos; with ensuring that the relation between state and citizen was perpetually regarded as a contingent, open-ended *question*, rather than focused on the choices dictated by the constitutional-electoral system – placing your cross against candidate X or Y. This is not to say that it did not matter to Hall who voted for whom. It did of course. But the problem that continually remained in the foreground of his field of political vision was the broader question of *the terms* on which the relations between people and state were organised.

The second orthodoxy Hall held in his sights was a redundant and lost version of Marxism. In Britain in the years before 1956 this cut deeper in political life than is, in our own times, easily recognised. There were always dazzlingly talented intellectuals working inside the political world of Marxism, and it is these thinkers that register most readily in the collective memory. But the reflexes of a mechanical orthodoxy ran deep in some sections of the pre-1956 left. From the very beginning Hall understood his encounters with Marxism to be conducted in the slipstream of a necessary but unprogrammed, and yet-to-be worked out, revisionism: in a bid, in other words, to rejuvenate Marxism in order that it could work for the historical imperatives of the mid-twentieth century. 1956 brought Khrushchev's denunciations of Stalinism, followed by the Soviet invasion of Hungary. These events generated a momentous fracture in the international Communist movement and there followed substantial collateral damage for the authority of official, state-sanctioned Marxisms. From this point on Hall located himself historically as of the political generation of '56: as a principled, self-styled, unapologetic revisionist. In this story Marxism had a constant if uneasy role to play, as it continued to do until the end of his life. Hall's engagement with politics cannot be fathomed without acknowledging this long presence of Marxism in his thought.[8]

But such affiliations proved anything but straightforward. As he was later to explain, he found himself 'dragged backwards into Marxism, against the tanks in Budapest'.[9] He embraced a (contrary) version of

Marxism just as the dominant, most conspicuously visible codifications were being universally vilified – properly so – for transmogrifying into a vehicle for the justification of Soviet colonialism. So, to imagine himself as having been 'dragged backwards into Marxism' depended on a vision of history in which political events were formed by their own – chaotic, unpredictable, asymmetrical, multiple – determinations. Abstract categorisations, such as the relations of production, the class struggle, the falling rate of profit, while they might be potentially appropriate conceptual tools, could not in themselves begin to explain the complex, contradictory and contingent terrain of politics, which was always the consequence of many determinations.

The limitations of both the forms of orthodoxy outlined above were apparent in their response to Hall's reading of Margaret Thatcher's Conservatism: the leading commentators of the day derided the thought that Thatcherism was in the business of pursuing an ideological or cultural programme, with its own underlying philosophies, let alone that it could be construed as a historic bid for hegemony. It was therefore revealing that in the run of obituaries which followed Hall's death in 2014 such views had silently disappeared from the media landscape. The notion that there had once existed a Thatcherite project, driven by a new generation of Tory *philosophes*, had emerged – by default – as uncontroversial. It had become, belatedly, the new common sense.

An expanded view of politics

This collection reflects Hall's engagement with shifting political conjunctures over a long period of time, from the 'First New Left' of the post-1956 period to the contemporary epoch of the ascendancy and 'crisis' of the neoliberal project. The essays collected here give a sense of the extraordinary range of political interventions made by Hall, but also point to some of the important continuities in his work – in analytical approach, political commitment, sensibility and tone.

His attention to diverse articulations of the political is a central feature of these essays. But committing himself to an expanded idea of what politics comprises did not mean that he supposed that 'everything *is* politics', always and in perpetuity. This would be to signal an unwarranted inflation of the domain, whereby any social act could be deemed 'political', allowing for the invocation of too easy an alibi for radical political activity. It is not that everything always is politics. The ground keeps shifting. That is the point. The crucial issue is that any site in the social formation, in any particular moment, *can become* the condensation of political antagonisms; the site of evolving, potential political forces; and the terrain on which political allegiances are made or unmade. How this occurs, or where the terrain is to be located, is a contingent matter that no formal theory of politics can stipulate or anticipate. In this sense, the place of politics is frequently *displaced*, meaning that what is significant politically may not inhabit, or only partially inhabit, the institutional arrangements of formal politics.

It is of course apparent, as Michael Rustin points out in his afterword to this collection, that if any social practice, in any sphere of social life, has the potential for becoming the site for political rupture, to segregate a portion of Hall's writings under the rubric 'political' may at first sight seem a perilous endeavour. Our aim, however, is to showcase the richness and diversity of Hall's articulations of the political in his interventions on key issues within the public arena of politics – and his constant endeavours to expand what we might think of as belonging in this arena.[10] This means that the writings collected here are primarily rooted in engagements with British political contexts, developments and relations, but, as with the work of other major intellectuals, for example Gramsci's writings on Italy, they speak to broader political issues and problematics. They were intended as, and should be read as, part of an ongoing intellectual endeavour to expand our notions of what constitutes the political, in which studying a specific context produces insights that in turn feed back into new forms of theoretical understanding.

Hall's work was characterised by an ever increasing attention to the displacements which operated in the field of politics. A reading of politics emerged in which the 'subjects' addressed by political forces were seen as operating through an unsteady amalgam of psychic investments, which conventional politics was unsuited to explain. This is an interpretation which locates the displaced elements of political life at the centre of things. This approach is perhaps most directly expressed in this collection by a 1966 essay on 'Political commitment', which is a less well-known essay and works at a relatively higher level of abstraction than the other articles collected here. It is in this essay that Hall was most explicit in his critique of the reduction of politics to its technological and institutional practices and to its attendant discursive forms: the absolutism of opinion polls, for example, or of the more elaborate intellectual apparatus of psephology. This is what he had in mind when he invoked politics 'in the narrow sense'. As he shows in an extraordinarily prescient aside, in 1960s Britain the privatisation of politics was already underway and could be named as such. Connected to this was his apprehension that a peculiar quality of the established political system was its capacity to *depoliticize* politics itself, an argument which has striking resonances with contemporary debates about 'post-politics'. Hall writes of a constitutional arrangement which sought to elevate, in place of 'the people', an electoral calculus in which 'the electorate', as a malleable and passive force, subsumed the forces of the unruly, unpredictable multitude.

In order to counter and to recast such conceptions of politics Hall was persuaded that the relations of political representation should be understood as 'active and transformative'. They were of the *first* importance. For significant structural change to occur, mass popular support was the precondition. 'The people' needed to be mobilised. 'Political consciousness', wrote Hall, 'is closely linked with the sense which a society makes of its own life, actions, experiences, history: with social consciousness, and with the dominant structure of feeling and attitude which prevails at any particular time.' The dynamic by which latent human needs were expressed in political terms had to be brought out into the open and integrated in the daily practices of political struggle.

Hall indicates two instances from his own experience when such moments of 'political creativity' had been realised: the launch of the New Left in 1956 and – connected but distinct – the early years of the Campaign for Nuclear Disarmament (CND). Underwriting each was not only the making of a new radicalism, but the expansion of the domain of politics: of what counts as 'politics'. As Hall writes in his reflections on 'The First New Left' (the only non-contemporaneous piece in this collection), 'the New Left' itself had a project to broaden the politics of CND: 'to "educate", in Gramsci's sense, the moral impulse which brought most people to the peace movement into a wider politics of the left'.

A distinctive element in Hall's political disposition was his commitment to a radical populism. This was a practice informed by, but not reducible to, class politics. It is a way of imagining politics that is instinctively suspicious of the imperatives of class reductionism, in which every dimension of political life was perceived through the exclusive optic of class.[11] Thinking in terms of populism – in terms of the people rather than in terms of a class – gave scope for the emergence of a broader, more expansive conception of the range of social groups which could act as agents for democratic change.

It was an unwelcome ruse of history that, from Hall's view, in the 1970s and 1980s it was the *Thatcherites* who moved most confidently onto the terrain of 'the popular' and actively sought to create a popular dimension to the pre-existing norms of constitutional politics. This is Hall reflecting on the populist elements of Thatcherism, in 'The empire strikes back' (see p203):

> By 'populism' I mean something more than the ability to secure electoral support for a political programme, a quality all politicians in formal democracies must possess. I mean the project, central to the politics of Thatcherism, to ground neo-liberal policies directly in an appeal to 'the people'; to root them in the essentialist categories of commonsense experience and practical moralism – and thus to construct, not simply awaken, classes, groups and interests into a particular definition of 'the people'.

The passage makes explicit Hall's deepening allegiance to a discursive understanding of political struggle. It presupposes that on the political terrain 'the people' – or indeed, the working class, or women, or any number of such social groupings – has no prescribed collective identity, ready and waiting to be summoned into action. 'The people' is not an already-existing, integral and unified social entity. It is a discursive construct, coming into being *in the process of political activity* itself.[12]

'The political', as a noun, increasingly came to assume a greater analytical presence for Hall. The term conveyed the expansive arena of political practice, as opposed to a narrow focus on the dominant institutions of political society. 'The political' is the arena where collective identifications are made, or not; where they accrue political leverage, or not; where political forces are made and unmade. The discursive work of politics is to discover a means by which such shared identifications can come into conscious political life, and sustain social agents in embarking upon the pursuit of the historic tasks which have befallen them. Or, as Hall has it, the strategic objective of politics is not to 'awaken' social actors, as if they are dormant and only awaiting the summons from on high, but to create the contexts in which they can discursively *'construct'* themselves as a collective political force – in which they can become political agents of their own making. In Hall's reading this long and complex process, often working at some remove from the conventional terrains of political life, is how politics happens.

Hall saw the time of CND's first surge of radicalism, from 1958 to 1964, as one such significant point of political rupture. In his own political life there occurred a further two movements that required a wholesale reconsideration of how politics was constituted. These were the mobilisations which exploded around feminism, and sexual politics more generally, and around 'race'.

Hall frequently despaired of mainstream politics: he was puzzled by the depth of the insulation of the bulk of professional politicians, even those of radical temperaments, from what was new or emergent in British life. What was especially striking for him was the profound incomprehension of the nation's leaders at what was happening before their very eyes in terms of sexual and black politics from the late 1960s onwards. For Hall, however, the speed with which the inherited practices of everyday life were in the process of being turned inside out, and exposed to incessant scrutiny, was something to applaud, take solace from, and marvel at.

The seriousness of these interventions as politics derived in part from their insistence that difficult, exacting questions – uncomfortable questions about the deepest dynamics of one's own selfhood – should be placed on the political agenda.

We publish here the lecture which took for its title 'Racism and reaction', and we include also an extract from *Policing the Crisis*, that extraordinary account of the deepening reflexes of authoritarianism which from the 1970s came to infiltrate both political and civil society.[13] What remains remarkable about both these texts is the degree to which 'race' works as the decisive explanatory concept that gives form and meaning to Hall's readings of authoritarian populism and the exceptional state. Without *Policing the Crisis* there could have been no analysis of Thatcherism in 'The great moving right show'. There was virtually no other figure at the time who was centrally reading the crisis of the British state, in its most general manifestations, through the lens of 'race'. It is instructive to remember that *Policing the Crisis* began life in the backstreets of Handsworth in Birmingham, a place radically removed from the established locales of British political business. It is in this sense a vindication of the decision to read the transformations in the state at an angle and at some distance from the dominant institutions where power was most concentrated.

Mapping the shifts

Hall's 'The great moving right show', which develops the arguments about authoritarian populism first made in *Policing the Crisis*, stands as a model of conjunctural analysis. It was an interpretation of the making of the new conjuncture *as it was happening*. That this was so underwrites the degree of uncertainty which occurs at one point in the essay. 'There is still some debate', he noted, 'as to whether [Thatcherism] is likely to be short-lived or long-term, a movement of the surface or something more deeply lodged in the body politic'. At the start of 1979 he couldn't be sure. By the time he died, in 2014, he was in a position to see more clearly the deeper reach of the historical movements. By then it was apparent that Thatcherism had marked the first stirrings of something larger, and more deeply globalised, than had been visible at the end of the 1970s. In retrospect it could be seen as signalling the making of a new political order which was to have epochal consequences. In it were the lineaments of what can now be named as the neoliberal revolution. It is this globalised order which inescapably defines our own historical present.

The essays from the 1980s are unflinching in their assessment of the Thatcherite facility for moulding popular conceptions of politics and common sense, but they are equally as tough-minded in their engagement with the deficits of left strategy. Essays such as 'The crisis of Labourism', for example, reflect on the longstanding limitations of the Labour Party's conception of politics. Hall argues, for example, that Neil Kinnock, the UK Labour Party's leader from 1983 to 1992, had 'no feel for the language and concerns of the new social movements', and that was dangerous for the party. The failure of the Labour leadership during the 1984-85 miners' strike to generalise at the national level the issues of class that the party claimed to represent significantly contributed to the failure of the strike, and doomed it 'to be fought and lost as an old rather than as a new form of politics'.

This was 'doubly unbearable' because, in 'the solidarity it displayed, the gigantic levels of support it engendered, the unparalleled involvement of the women in the mining communities, the feminist presence in the strike [and] the breaking down of different social interests which it presaged', the miners' strike 'was instinctually with the politics of the new'. Hall lamented Labour's failure to adopt the strategy of a 'war of position' – the struggle 'for leadership and mastery over a whole number of different fronts in the course of making itself the focal point of popular aspirations, the leading popular political force'.

The expansive imagination of the left envisioned by Hall here should caution against a reading of Hall's writings as in any sense responsible for the way his insights were taken up by New Labour and Blairism.[14] The New Times project, as it was elaborated by Hall and other colleagues at *Marxism Today*, sought to engage with a terrain that had been changed by the fundamental political, economic and cultural restructuring of the 1980s, including Hall's essay on 'The meaning of new times'. In this the project was undeniably influential on New Labour trajectory. But Hall himself drew very different conclusions from this analysis. He was committed to a 'modernising' project for the Labour Party and the wider left, but on very different terms from those adopted by Blair and New Labour.

In 'The state: socialism's old caretaker', he sees how Ken Livingstone's Greater London Council (GLC) is 'so exciting, so prefigurative for the left': 'one begins to see here and there a glimmer of a local state transforming the ways in which it "represents" society politically; being more dependent on the passage of power into the state from constituencies outside it than on monopolising power'. He welcomed this pluralism – a phenomenon that was very different from the party management of New Labour – and hoped that it would become a permanent feature of the socialist scene. But, as Doreen Massey recalls, the 'sneering' attitude towards this left project, which was 'feminist, anti-racist and anti-homophobic as well as challenging to capital', came as much from traditional elements within the Parliamentary Labour Party as from the Conservatives.[15]

One of Hall's enduring contributions was his engagement with the political articulations of multiculturalism(s). Rather than seeing multiculturalism as a state strategy, operating from above, he adopted a more open understanding of how multiculturalism worked, and how it was reconfiguring political and social relations. But he was also keenly aware of political efforts to mobilise opposition to pluralism and difference. As he argues in 'Our mongrel selves': 'In the face of the proliferation of cultural difference, and the multi-ethnic character of the new Britain, and threatened on the other side by ... an emerging European identity, we have seen over the past decade a particularly defensive, closed and exclusive definition of "Englishness" being advanced as a way of warding off or refusing to live with difference'. He engaged consistently with such exclusivism and later what he termed the 'multi-cultural drift' that characterised New Labour.[16]

Hall's antipathy to Blairism and the New Labour project is made clear in the final essays collected here. 'The great moving nowhere show', published in 1998, argued that the Blair project was still 'essentially framed by and moving on terrain defined by Thatcherism'. As Michael Rustin notes in his afterword here, Hall regarded the 1997 election victory for Labour as a huge missed opportunity, and was profoundly critical of the intellectual underpinning of the Blair project, especially its notion of the 'Third Way', which he saw as 'hot on the responsibilities of individuals', while 'those of business are passed over with a slippery evasiveness'.

The final two essays in the collection come from *Soundings*, the journal which Hall co-founded with Doreen Massey and Michael Rustin in 1995, with the aim of continuing the analysis and questioning of left politics that had been associated with *Marxism Today*. Its positioning statement, 'Uncomfortable times', made clear that the project sought to continue the expansive understanding of the political that had shaped Hall's work; it argued that 'change can be achieved in many social spaces besides that which is normally designated as political'.[17]

'New Labour's double shuffle' takes as its problematic the failure of New Labour to offer a radical alternative to Thatcherism despite the huge electoral mandate it had received in 1997. Hall traces the way that New Labour had adapted to rather than challenged the neoliberal terrain, as well as analysing the significant and distinctive terms on which it made this adaption. 'The neoliberal revolution' offers an assessment of the 2010-15 Coalition project, and the dynamics of the post financial crisis conjuncture more generally, and engages with the mutations and articulations of neoliberalism as they had been negotiated and refracted through political debate. Hall contended that this was 'arguably the best prepared, most wide-ranging, radical and ambitious of the three regimes which since the 1970s have been maturing the neoliberal project'. He laments neoliberalism's ability to reproduce itself in the wake of the 2008 crisis, noting that 'in terms of laying foundations and staging the future on favourable ground, the neoliberal project is several stages further on'.

These essays represent the final instalments of Hall's charting of the shifting formations of neoliberalism, to be read alongside the *Soundings* Kilburn Manifesto project, which he co-edited and contributed to, though he died before it was completed.[18] The way this Manifesto has inspired and engaged new audiences demonstrates the continued relevance of the style of political engagement and analysis that Hall developed.

***

The publisher and editors are grateful to the estate of Stuart Hall for permission to republish the essays contained here. We would like to thank for Nick Beech for allowing us to consult his invaluable bibliography of Stuart Hall's writings. We are particularly grateful to Catherine Hall.

Sally Davison, David Featherstone and Bill Schwarz

Notes

1. Gramsci's work was very important to Hall. For an introduction to Gramsci's work, including the concept of hegemony, see Roger Simon, *Gramsci's Political Thought: An Introduction*, third edition, Lawrence & Wishart 2015.
2. See in particular chapter 9 in this book, '1970: Birth of the law and order society', which is an extract from Hall et al, *Policing the Crisis: 'Mugging', the State and Law and Order*, Macmillan 1978; and chapter 10, 'The great moving right show'.
3. See Louis Althusser, 'Contradiction and Over-determination', in *For Marx*, Penguin 1969. See also, in this book, pp257–8 in 'The Meaning of New Times', and p346–7 in Afterword.
4. V.I. Lenin, 'Letters from Afar' in Lenin, *Collected Works, Vol 23*, Progress Publishers 1964, p306.
5. Antonio Gramsci, *Selections From the Prison Notebooks*, Lawrence and Wishart 1971, p126.

6. In his final labours Hall was much preoccupied with the question of how the objective and the subjective played out within the domain of politics. He returned to Freud and Foucault in order establish a degree of clarification on the issue of subjectivity. For earlier formulations, see particularly Stuart Hall, 'Fantasy, Identity, Politics', in Erica Carter, James Donald and Judith Squires (eds), *Cultural Remix. Theories of Politics and the Popular*, Lawrence and Wishart 1995. And a text crucial for him in these matters was Judith Butler, *The Psychic Life of Power: Theories in Subjection*, Stanford University Press 1997.

7. We draw here from observations by Wendy Brown at a roundtable on Stuart Hall at the Townsend Center for the Humanities at Berkeley in March 2016.

8. See also Afterword, p342–7.

9. Stuart Hall, 'Cultural Studies and its theoretical legacies', in David Morley and Kuan-Hsing Chen (eds), *Stuart Hall: Critical Dialogues in Cultural Studies*, Routledge 1996, p264.

10. Other collections of Hall's work are planned in the near future that are organised around other themes.

11. Important for Hall here was the publication of Ernesto Laclau, *Politics and Ideology in Marxist Theory: Capitalism, Fascism, Populism*, Verso 1977.

12. These sentences are based on an unpublished manuscript of Hall's.

13. See chapter 9, '1970: Birth of the law and order society', extracted from *Policing the Crisis*, and chapter 8, 'Racism and reaction'.

14. For Hall as critic of New Labour, see chapter 19, 'The great moving nowhere show' and chapter 20, 'New Labour's double-shuffle'.

15. Doreen Massey, *World City*, Polity 2007.

16. Stuart Hall, 'Conclusion: the multi-cultural question', in B. Hesse (ed), *Un/settled Multiculturalisms: Diasporas, Entanglements, Transruptions*, Zed Books 2000, p231.

17. Stuart Hall, Doreen Massey and Michael Rustin, 'Uncomfortable times', *Soundings* 1, November 1995.

18. Stuart Hall, Doreen Massey and Michael Rustin (ed), *After neoliberalism: The Kilburn manifesto*, Lawrence & Wishart 2015 (download for free at https://www.lwbooks.co.uk/book/after-neoliberalism-kilburn-manifesto).

Note on the text

The language in some of the earlier essays has been occasionally modernised, and most essays have been very lightly copy-edited. For reasons of space, four essays have been also been slightly abridged – this is indicated with an asterisk in the list below and on the title page. A few explanatory footnotes have been added to give context, but there is also information on historical figures on p354, which is linked to the index. For the purposes of ease of reading, no distinction has been made between references from the original texts and additional notes for this book. Similarly, we have not added in ellipses to show where abridgements have been made. Our aim has been to produce a book that is easy to read rather than a heavily annotated scholarly edition.

Places of first publication

'The new Conservatism and the old', *Universities & Left Review*, Vol 1, No 1, spring 1957, pp21-4

'A sense of classlessness', *Universities & Left Review*, No 5, winter 1958, 26-32

'The supply of demand', in E.P. Thompson (ed), *Out of Apathy*: New Left Books/Stevens and Sons, London 1960, 56-97*

'The Cuban crisis: Trial-run or steps towards peace?', *War & Peace: The CND Quarterly*, Vol 1 No 1 January-March 1963, 2-16*

'Political commitment', in Lawrence Bright and Simon Clements (eds), *The Committed Church*, Darton, Longman and Todd, London 1966, 3-25

'A world at one with itself', *New Society*, No 403, 1970, 1056-8

'Racism and reaction: A public talk arranged by the British Sociological Association and given in London on 2 May 1978', in *Five Views of*

Multi-Racial Britain Commission for Racial Equality, London 1978, 23-35

'1970: Selsdon man: birth of the law and order society', 273-282, from Chapter 9 of *Policing the Crisis: 'Mugging', the State and Law and Order*, Macmillan, London 1978 (with Chas Critcher, Tony Jefferson, John Clarke and Brian Roberts)

'The great moving right show', *Marxism Today*, Vol 23 No 1 January 1979, 14-20

'The "Little Caesars" of social democracy', *Marxism Today*, Vol 25 No 4, April 1981, 11-15

'The empire strikes back', *New Socialist*, July-August 1982

'The crisis of Labourism', in James Curran (ed.), *The Future of the Left*, Polity Press/Basil Blackwell, Cambridge/Oxford 1984 (text for this book is based on revisions Hall made in 1988)*

'The State: socialism's old caretaker', *Marxism Today*, Vol 28 No 11, November 1984, 24-29

'Blue election, election blues', *Marxism Today*, Vol 38 No 7, July 1987, 30-35

'The meaning of new times', in Stuart Hall and Martin Jacques (eds) *New Times*, Lawrence & Wishart, London 1989

'The first New Left: life and times', in Oxford University Socialist Discussion Group (eds), *Out of Apathy: Voices of the New Left Thirty Years On*, Verso 1989*

'And not a shot fired: the end of Thatcherism?', *Marxism Today*, Vol 42 No 12, December 1991, 10-15

'Our mongrel selves', *New Statesman*, June 1992 (based on the 1992 Raymond Williams Memorial Lecture)

'The great moving nowhere show', *Marxism Today* (special issue), November-December 1998, 9-14

'New Labour's double-shuffle', *Soundings*, No 24, summer 2003, 10-24

'The neoliberal revolution', *Soundings*, No 48, summer 2011, 9-28

* indicates essay has been abridged in this edition

PART 1: THE NEW LEFT AND AFTER

The new Conservatism and the old

1957

THE DISORDERLY THRUST of political events disturbs the symmetry of political analysis. Before Suez, one would have been tempted to speak of contemporary British Conservatism as a brand-new thing.[1] Fashioned by tough-minded political savants and intellectuals for the new world that is post-welfare Britain – thriving, lively, realistic, with its feet firmly planted in the political middle ground, its fingers on the pulse of the expanding middle classes, its winning smile on the faces of the 'new men of power' and future safe behind the glass doors of the giant oligopolies – the 'new Conservatism' offered itself as a going concern with a gilt-edged future, a safe investment for the politically uncommitted. Forced to re-examine the 'new' Conservatism in the light of recent events, most socialists would be tempted to say that it is merely the 'old Toryism' writ large. They could certainly muster an impressive case. One would have to go back to the heyday of imperialism – to plunge back several decades, behind two world wars – to discover the sources of the assumptions which appear to have governed the Conservative government's policy in the Middle East. If this is the 'new Conservatism' in action, it is not merely 'old' – it is prehistoric, dislocated from and insensitive to its environment, ranging abroad like a mastodon in Kensington Park.

But it seems closer to the truth to say that contemporary Conservatism is an unstable blend of the new and the old. The process by which it remained in business – the process of public theft and private accommodation by which the new Tories snatched up the welfare state and roped in the middle classes – is an unfinished process, and precisely because it is unfinished, it has had a disastrous effect on the party and its public philosophy. The scope of the party has expanded, but its character has not radically altered. Within its structure, conflicting tendencies are held together in a state of comparative disequilibrium.

The left and the right of the party are not two distinct groups. Each assuages its prejudices by selecting symbols in the other's camp. The new middle-class recruits to the party are the most aggressively nationalist: the defenders of capital punishment promote defence cuts; the advocates of bipartisanship, turn out, under pressure, to be militantly anti-American. Mr Angus Maude, whose *The English Middle Classes* (with Roy Lewis) is one of the classic defences of 'enlightened' Toryism, is discovered as one of the ordering minds behind the Suez Group.[2] The party is held together, not by a coherent social philosophy, but by an unquestioning allegiance to the most rootless archetypal images. It subscribes to a confused rhetoric: 'Britain's prestige abroad' is a phrase which covers the Suez debacle; 'the incentives of free enterprise' appear compatible with a widening dollar-gap and shrinking markets; a 'property-owning democracy' supports the plea for 'realistic rents'; our 'responsibilities to the Commonwealth' covers our wilful disregard for the imperatives of Commonwealth opinion. Party policy is consequently the pawn of irrational forces and the prey to disguised and muted pressures. Behind the facade of Butskellism and bipartisanship, the old prejudices wax, the old interests play, the old neuroses govern.

'Liberal conservatives', who distrust Mr Butler's ambivalences, like to think that he was not necessary to them. This view is factually incorrect. Between 1945 and 1954, it was the rhetoric and the persona of Mr Butler which worked such wonders for the party. His success was due in large measure to the skill with which he assessed the electoral consequences of Labour's 'peaceful revolution'. But the party has, for the moment at least, taken his measure: his 'philosophy' still provides the party with its public front, but in a moment of crisis, it seeks its leadership elsewhere.

It is necessary to summarise briefly the main trends in that 'peaceful revolution', in order to comprehend the altering shape of latter-day Conservatism, and the shifts in popular opinion which sustain it.

The period 1945 to 1951 can be regarded as the focal point in a challenging new-style middle-class revolution. It was a revolution with two distinct phases, and the Labour Party was responsible for only one of these, and even there it could not or did not wholly assess its social and political implications.

The limited revolution

The welfare state – with its three main planks, social security, income redistribution and nationalisation – had valid but limited objectives. It sought to redistribute wealth towards the middle, and buttress the structure of 'opportunity' from below. It tried to redress the balance of social forces in the community – but not to alter the relationship of one group to another, within the still hierarchical structure of British society. The social pivot of the revolution of 'welfare' was consequently located somewhere about the middle of the social scale. The consequences of increased assistance were to swell the ranks of the middle classes, and to validate what may be called 'middle' virtues in British society. As Angus Maude and Roy Lewis put it:

> A great part of the strength and of the value of the middle classes in English political life has been their ability to set off, within themselves, intellect against money, common sense against intellect, and a tradition of gentility against all three (p72).

And later, perhaps more revealingly:

> They are what they are by virtue not of trade but of organization, not of property but of independence; not by virtue of government; not solely because they wanted to have but because of what they wanted to be … 'What shall we do to be received?' the new middle classes have cried, and in every generation the retort has come – from above and below – 'Learn to behave like gentlemen! (p69)

As Alistair Cook observed, at the time of the 1955 general election, the result would depend on how many working-class men, looking into their mirrors, saw middle-class faces. The Conservative victory was reply enough.

It is difficult to see what else could have been expected. So long as the general pattern of the society remained inegalitarian, social mobility implied the gradual assumption of middle-class ways of life and middle-class values by the promoted. The economy remained, at base, capitalist in character: and because of the manner in which a capitalist economy functions and grows, an unequal structure of wealth – and hence of social power and position – was a necessary feature. Over and above the cost of social welfare, the imperatives of growth in a capitalist economy had to be obeyed. The welfare state consequently established its own norms: given the logic of the economic structure, there were 'natural' levels beyond which redistributive taxation could not go, 'realistic' costs below which health and housing could not be permitted to fall. These were the unspoken checks and balances of the mixed economy with a massive private sector. And although that two-headed monster was spawned in the no-man's-land between the two parties, the cumulative pressure from the private sector tailored Mr Butler, rather than Mr Gaitskell, to the job.

It was reasonable to assume, therefore, that the Conservative Party, refurbished from the left, would continue to govern innocuously on the basis of a negative vote of confidence from those whom mobility had dislodged from their natural political allegiance. But the climate of post-war Britain, and the character of the support behind the Conservative Party in the country, was considerably affected by other, deeper changes in the society, with their roots not so much in the welfare state as in the capitalist sector of the economy.

Logic of social change

The most important of these changes reflect mutations in the capitalist system itself. The growth of management – the proliferation of supervisory jobs in industry – marked the expanding scale of capitalist production itself. It was a witness to the growth in the scope of the service, distributive and supervisory functions in large-scale production, which had been taking place since the turn of the century. The private sector consequently offered the most attractive opportunities, guaranteeing wealth, power and prestige. The young men of talent, particularly from the lower-middle class, promoted by the mechanism of the state, found themselves drawn into positions of power, demanding loyalty and responsibility, in private industry. This was another stage in the logic of social change in a mixed economy.

To find the legitimate satisfaction of their ambitions in the upper ranks of management implied the gradual – if difficult – acceptance of the whole philosophy of a private economy. In a limited sense at least, this assumption of new status undermined their allegiance to several of the cardinal principles of the welfare state. Taxation became a public enemy: the guarantee of full employment, limited controls, the cost of state assistance – these were re-interpreted as restraints and hindrances to growth and prosperity. When the authoritative voices of the *Economist* and the *Financial Times* called for 'the removal of restraints', for an imaginative release from 'the rigid state', for a 'modest dash for freedom', they spoke as much for the new as for the old industrial elites.

The pressure for the removal of restraints was buttressed from below by the general sense, pervading the middle classes, that further redistribution of wealth could proceed only at the expense of their own social and economic prospects. These fears found release through a profound sense of irritation against the whole panoply of state assistance, and particularly against the encumbrances of the bureaucracy in government circles. No doubt these attitudes were to be found in their most aggressive form in the small but articulate group which had benefited most. But they had become in a sense the thrusting spearhead of the middle-class revolution, and their responses to the conditions of post-war Britain had very soon eaten back into and undermined the whole morale of the society.

These various phases of the 'peaceful revolution' must be seen in the context of the cold war, and in the light of Britain's declining prestige abroad. A world of divided, hostile camps placed intolerable strains on a society undergoing profound social change. While the very fabric of the society was being rewoven, the dictates of foreign policy grew more rigid and insistent. Because of the role which Britain had chosen – as the pivot of the North Atlantic alliance – it was committed to defence expenditure far beyond its means, and implicated in policies in Asia and the Middle East totally beyond its capacities. Its failures to adjust to the dramatic changes in the world beyond Europe witnessed, not merely to the disintegration of the 'morality' of the welfare state, but – more simply – to a failure of nerve and realism. The pursuit of prestige by a second-rate power in a nuclear age is a disturbing phenomenon to observe. Caught up by virtue of its weakness and dependence in the web of American diplomacy, Britain worked consistently against its best interests. It took such steps as the re-armament of Germany, calculated to intensify the cold war, ignoring the more difficult but more rewarding path towards a military detente.

The logic of cold war politics was rigid, implacable and inhibiting. It forced restraints upon Britain in a period in which it should have been seeking a greater freedom of range and movement. Instead it conspired merely to maintain the polarity of power in the world. Its desire to retain – if not restore – its crumbling imperial heritage fettered its freedom. And this reckless, half-hearted pursuit of prestige abroad was conducted under the compelling shadow of nuclear weapons, in a world in which fear itself has become the prime factor in stability.

Ethos of discontent

The consequence of these pressures, exerted upon the society from several quarters, was a state of muted, but at times extreme, moral confusion. The society was an open arena, in which conflicting forces from without and within had free play. The political apathy which characterised the period between 1951 and 1955 had its source, not in disinterest, but in bewilderment. The economy had to reconcile within itself the opposing claims of the welfare state and a refurbished capitalism: it had to balance off the cost of social security against the driving and persistent pressure for private capital accumulation. The widening dollar-gap, the prospect of shrinking markets, increased international competition, the burden of defence and of 'diplomatic' assistance to the 'uncommitted' world, were constant irritants. At home, the society tried to accommodate a profound social revolution within the constraining limits of a mixed economy and a hierarchical social structure. It sought to satisfy the stimulated ambitions of the middle classes within the traditional social framework, and to establish an arbitrary community of interests between the groups whose power derived from consumer power and those whose power depended directly or indirectly on increasing profits. The morale of the society was beset by the play of unsatisfied ambitions, unfocused irritation, spurious dissatisfactions and uncertainties. For the 'peaceful revolution' appeared to have brought only the encroachment of bureaucracy, with its distancing effects upon intelligent and spontaneous participation in the life of the community: and the end of the war had brought only a self-perpetuating state of armed peace.

But the most common reward today for success achieved through the legitimate, taxable channels is to find a boot crunching firmly on one's presumptuous head; and the boot belongs not to a member of the aristocracy, keeping presumption in its place, but to the Socialist state, the revolutionaries' state, the state of blessed opportunity.

And so here we are, with our degrees and our posh education, our prideful positions in the public service, our ambitious names in print, trying to get on with the work brought home in the bulging brief-case, while the baby cries in the next room or even in the same room, or while the mortgage slowly and respectfully strangles the life, the love, the adventure and the talent out of us.[3]

Mr George Scott's *Time and Place*, from which this passage is taken, is an unpleasant but representative document of this period. It catches in an authentic form the suffocated, thwarted ambition, the explosively inverted class prejudice, the rooted self-interest of the new men of power manqué. It is through the 'salon poujadism' of *Time and Place*, the disabled romanticism of *Look Back In Anger*, or the conspicuously anti-romantic amorality of the Lucky Jim 'archetype', that the temper and tone of the post-welfare generation found their legitimate expression.

'Democracy v. Liberty'

In the end, it is the informing spirit of the 'peaceful revolution' which, despite the remarkable achievements of social security, has not been satisfied. It is this spirit, in repressed forms, which is the source of the strange motions that disturb the ordered universe of post-welfare Britain, and which has urged the Conservative Party into irrational and dangerous paths.

Through its attempt to capture the 'revolution', the Conservative Party made itself the guardian of a state which had preserved only the external forms of stability and ordered growth.

... this vast and elaborate structure, which has come into existence as the end product of the activities of myriads of men seeking security as well as truth, may produce in single individuals feelings of powerlessness, loneliness, ultimately of revolt and destructiveness.[4]

It was, surprisingly enough, two 'new Conservatives' who glimpsed this prospect: and the same observation was given a more pointedly personal validation in George Scott's autobiography: 'Whether they know it or not, and I fancy they do not, the revolutionaries have bred a generation of counter-revolutionaries'. Mr Butler, it is true, seemed to believe that he was grooming merely a generation of realists. But there was evidence enough of an alien and irrational spirit abroad – not least of all in the ranks of the so-called 'moderates'. It is they, for example, who helped to fashion the ideology of presumption and prescription which assumed the status, during the party's first term of office, of a new official philosophy. Professor Oakeshott – the party's latter-day Bagehot – reminded them that 'political activity comes first and a political ideology comes after'. And in fact, the new ideology was in no sense a social or moral philosophy: it was a kind of academic mythology. It was hostile to the study of politics by reason and intelligence; it was sceptical of the moral basis of political action: 'government by the people', literally interpreted, was a form of 'democratic tyranny', because it was 'contrary to our political tradition and principles', and part of a dangerous tradition of thought which was purported to run 'through the mystical clap-trap of Robespierre, St Just, Lenin and Stalin'.[5] (Mr Worsthorne, the source of these quotations, is a leader writer for the influential organ of establishment opinion, *The Daily Telegraph*: indeed, it is fascinating to watch the ideas in Professor Oakeshott's *Inaugural Lecture* gain wider and wider currency, as they filter through the 'higher' journalism of the weeklies and monthlies to the 'daily newspaper world'.) This ideology was significant precisely because – in its popularised and degenerated forms – it prepared the ground for a disorderly retreat from reason. How the old prejudices must have flared and flourished when Mr Utley – who is one of the liveliest and most intelligent minds on the right today – could go so far as to whoop, 'Democracy is out', in the first sentence of a *Spectator* leader (January 1955). This kind of language persistently undermined democratic sentiments in the community: it eroded the foundations for the just and responsible conduct of public affairs; it created the ethos within which irresponsibility could thrive. The image of Britain's prestige abroad was *hoisted* as the unifying factor – and perhaps the only one – in the conflicting amalgam of political forces: and this image was pursued with remarkable 'flair' and 'vigour', quite beyond the reasonable limits by which policy must necessarily be constrained in the contemporary world.

Suez: the moment of truth

It would be wrong to see Suez in isolation. It is part of the pattern of six years of disastrous and misguided government. But it takes an event as traumatic as Suez to strip away the masks of rhetoric, and to expose the repressed sources of Britain's policy and its consequences. It is clear now that we have connived against both the welfare of the Arab peoples and the stability of the state of Israel, for the sake of the 'national interest': and that we have used the obsolete weapons of power and intrigue to secure it. While the British and French troops remained in Port Said, we were, on an even calculation, about twelve hours away from a third world war. It is clear, too, that Britain has identified itself everywhere with policies calculated to thwart the colonial and national revolutions. It should be clear, for example, that, in Cyprus, Britain has been waging what amounts to an imperialist war, and that – through Suez – it came perilously close to involving the British people with the hysteria of French reaction. It should be clear – with Hungary and Poland to point the moral – that Britain's cold war policy represented a dramatic failure of responsibility to Eastern as well as Western Europe: and that nothing can redeem these blunders, except patient and persistent work towards a military detente and a settlement in Europe. It is clear above all that the future of Britain depends upon the strengthening of a sense of responsibility to international organisations: that the 'prestige' of Britain is a phantom, which can only be pursued at the expense of the fate of the world itself.

The Suez debacle mirrors, as well, the moral failure of the left. The shortcomings of the 'peaceful revolution' on the one hand, and the deformations of socialism in Eastern Europe on the other, should serve to convince us that the socialist reconstruction of society demands an imaginative experimentation with forms of democratic control and responsibility hitherto undreamt of in 'welfare' philosophy. The events of recent months should be enough to persuade the left that the whole raison d'être of British foreign policy – and particularly the role of Britain between East and West – deserves complete re-examination. The whole philosophy of 'strategic containment and military alignment' – which are the keystones of American diplomacy – is bankrupt and dangerous to continue. The problem of a European settlement is pressing and immediate, but it must be solved on other moral and political grounds than these.

When we take recent trends in domestic politics into consideration, it is clear that the Labour Party should see itself not merely as the passive agent of the parliamentary system, but – in a genuine sense – as the bulwark of democratic practice and the defenders of the tradition of reason, responsibility and patience in politics. It is the tradition of reason which has suffered extreme pressure during the past decade, from the reactionary right and the reactionary left alike. There is, when all is said and done, too much, rather than too little, left for the Labour Party to do. The fact is that Britain can no longer afford the irresponsibility and instability which has become a characteristic feature of contemporary Conservatism. The whole ideology is obsolete and dangerous. Conservatism has disappeared into the wilderness of unreason, and it should be left there to sing among the nightingales.

Notes

1. The Tories returned to power in 1951, apparently now modernised and accepting the broad outlines of the postwar settlement. Butskellism, an amalgamation of the names of leading Tory R.A.B. Butler and Labour's Hugh Gaitskell, referred to this apparent consensus across the two main parties. But in 1956 the Conservatives apparently reverted to type when they invaded Suez, after Egypt's President Nasser announced the nationalisation of the Suez Canal. This was seen by the British government, already hostile to the Nasser regime, as a serious threat to its interests in the region.
2. Angus Maude and Roy Lewis, *The English Middle Classes*, Penguin 1950.
3. *Time and Place*, George Scott, Staples 1956, p191.
4. *English Middle Classes*, p66.
5. The quotations are from Peregrine Worsthorne, 'Democracy v. Liberty', *Encounter*, January 1956.

A sense of classlessness

1958

... the more that distinctions are broken down, the more exquisite they become.

William Whyte, *The Organization Man*

CLEARLY, THERE HAS been a major shift in the patterns of social life in this country. How deep they go, and whether they alter our older notions of 'class' is difficult to tell (see endnote 1: The post-war boom). The drawing of distinctions is made more difficult by the fact that such changes are taking place at a remarkably uneven pace – the old crowding in upon the new and blurring the points of transition. The focal centres of this process are the large cities – and the new urban concentrations we are making: though the spread of these patterns of life into smaller cities and throughout the country may be swifter than we suppose. (Given the predominance of the London metropolis over other centres in our cultural life, and its concentration of the channels of communication, the pace of change should not surprise us.) But even in large urban centres, the unevenness of development makes analysis difficult. In the area of south London where I live, old and new physical environments coexist within a single borough. Here are the old two-storey brick dwellings of a working-class suburb, row after row in a dark street butting straight into the warehouse, lumber yard or factory gate: there are the new eight-storey flats of an LCC housing estate, enclosed in a grass-and-concrete jigsaw, offering the beginnings of a 'contemporary' urban facade. Along the Brixton Road, the barrow boys are hawking goods outside a 'utility' style British version of the supermarket. Some of the local children go to school at a Dickensian brick building constructed – and hardly retouched – since the 1880s: but not far away is the glass-and-steel compound of the local comprehensive, not yet completed.

It is not only a matter of new physical surroundings. The post-war prosperity and the high levels of employment have made possible new spending habits amongst working people. A local housewife in a new town whom we talked to said, apologetically, 'Yes, we've got a small car – if that's what you can call it'. Fifteen years ago a car would have been considered a luxury: today, she is looking forward to the day when she can exchange the second-hand model for a small new family car. This attitude towards a whole range of consumer goods has altered, of course, even within the interiors of older-style working-class districts: but the change is to be seen most sharply where exteriors have changed as well – where 'home- making' and 'interior decoration' are newly acquired interests, part of the shift into new housing estates and new towns – part of a new style of urban life. The recent induced spread of hire-purchase is, of course, one way of stimulating a semi-stagnant economy: it is also, however, an attempt – on the part of the banks and finance houses who are best equipped to do so – to catch up with and sustain a current of domestic spending on furniture, household goods and appliances, and TV sets, which has been growing, with certain lapses, since the war. At the same time, the older working-class homes survive, much as Hoggart described in *The Uses of Literacy* – warm, cluttered living rooms, impervious to *House and Garden*.[1] Bits and pieces of chain-store furniture have penetrated, but not sufficiently to upset the pattern of life or to destroy the sense of familiar congestion. Where does the old end, and where does the new – the real not the superficially new – begin, in this maze of gradual accommodations?

The third and perhaps most crucial change can be observed in the rhythm and nature of industrial work. Here again, the pace of development offers a picture of extraordinary imbalance. In certain kinds of work, and, consequently, in certain regions of the country, things are much as they were. I am thinking particularly of the heavy industries and of mining. Even here, there have been technological innovations: but these offer themselves very much as modifications of traditional skills in the life of a working man. He is still engaged in labouring directly upon the means of production, in factories where safety regulations may have been improved by legislation, but where factory layout and the work processes have altered little since the last century. Yet side by side with this pattern of industrial labour as Engels and Marx wrote of it, have grown up the 'technological' industries

– the manufacturing industries based upon chemical and automative processes. Here the very nature of work itself, the rhythm and skills involved, have changed out of all recognition.

Of course, the growth in volume of consumer goods or the council house do not – in themselves – transform a working class into a bourgeoisie. 'The working class does not become bourgeois by owning the new products, any more than the bourgeois ceases to be bourgeois as the objects he owns change in kind'.[2] It is a matter of a whole way of life, of an attitude towards things and people, within which new possessions – even a new car, a new house or a TV set – find meaning through use. The drive towards a higher standard of living is a legitimate materialism, born out of centuries of physical deprivation and want. It becomes a form of social envy – a desire to become 'middle-class' in style of life – only in certain peculiar circumstances. The central distinction between working-class and middle-class styles of life has always been, as Raymond Williams points out, a distinction 'between alternative ideas of the nature of social relationship', embodied, as it were, in typical working-class institutions (the trade union, the friendly and co-operative societies) as well as in a hundred shared habits, and local, particular responses to life (see endnote 2: Low life and high theory). The crucial difference is that between the bourgeois notion of society as a stage upon which each individual tries to 'realise' himself through personal effort and competitiveness; and the working-class notion of society as a co-operative entity – where 'the primary affections and allegiances, first to family, then to neighbourhood, can in fact be directly extended into social relationships as a whole, so that the idea of a collective democratic society is at once based on direct experience, and is available, as an idea, to others who wish to subscribe to it'.[3] This serves as a broad generalisation about bourgeois and working-class attitudes to life – in spite of the fact that, in the late nineteenth century, the bourgeois classes tempered the drive to individualism by a certain liberal and paternal ideal of duty and service; and in the twentieth century, the notion of 'collective service' in the trade unions has been blunted by a bureaucratic structure of leadership.

Nevertheless, a way of life cannot be sustained without a certain pattern of social relationships, and outside of certain physical, economic and environmental pressures. Working-class culture, as we have experienced it, grew up as a series of defences against the encroachments – economic and social – of bourgeois society. The sense of solidarity which developed through work, in the family and the older communities, and which sustained men and women through the terrors of a period of industrialisation – liberating as it was for many – was also, for many, harsh and oppressive. It remained, for all its strengths, a 'class' life, a pattern of – in some cases – hastily erected personal and collective barricades. Solid as the old working-class communities were, they were often, of necessity, defensive or aggressive towards other communities, other national and racial groups, towards the 'queer' fellow and the 'odd man out', towards the 'scholarship boy', or even, sometimes, the militant. This is not a matter of praise or blame. It is a matter of the economic and social system within which an industrial proletariat, with its own values and attitudes, matured and grew. Marx understood this. He saw the new social relationships growing within the womb of the old society, he saw them transforming society itself, as men forced themselves out of the constraints which the old industrial ghettos and factories imposed, until the separate communities became a single community, and – in this sense at least – the bourgeois world was 'proletarianised'. (I am not thinking of enforced collectivisation!) Marx saw an industrial working class not merely *surviving into*, but *itself creating*, conditions of prosperity and abundance.

Class consciousness

The central problem concerns the different objective factors which shaped and were in turn shaped and humanised by an industrial working class; the subjective ways in which these factors grew to consciousness within the minds and lives of working people: and the degree to which these shaping factors have changed or are in process of changing. To lump these together as 'the economic base' is not enough, though that formulation is broadly true as a proposition, understood over a comparatively long period of history. But we need to break the 'economic base' down into constituent factors, permitting a much freer play in our interpretation between 'base' and 'superstructure' (see endnote 3: Consciousness and the heavy industrial base). This is necessary because we are concerned with a changing pattern of life, attitudes and values – particular responses to a particular situation – many of which can best be seen and isolated in what has so far been considered, in vulgar-Marxist interpretations (rather patronis-ingly), as the 'ideological superstructure'.

Though Marx himself became more deeply involved with objective factors as he elaborated the labour theory of value (an emphasis which Engels was at pains to modify – cf the well-known letter to Bloch, *Selected Works*, Vol. 2, pp443-4, but also the letters to C. Schmidt, pp441, 448-50, and to H. Starkenburg, pp457-9), a reading of *Capital* will not reveal the clean separation of subjective from objective factors in the growth of the working class. (The early chapters on 'Commodities', for example, must be seen in relation to the earlier work on alienation in the *Economic & Philosophical Manuscripts of 1844* and the *German Ideology*.) The early industrial working class matured within early entrepreneur capitalism. The key points in this system, for our purposes, were the nature of private property, the accumulation of capital and the exploitation of labour (profits and wages), the alienation of the worker from his labour in the 'working day', and his alienation from the products which he made (the 'commodity' relationship, where; 'the more the worker expends himself in work, the more powerful become the world of objects which he creates in fact of himself, the poorer he becomes in his inner life, the less he belongs to himself'.[4]

New factors

These were the primary factors which shaped the 'consciousness of class' amongst working people, and which made it possible for an industrial proletariat to become the base for an active and conscious political movement. Now it is clear that these primary factors have changed radically with the development of capitalism, at least in those sectors of the system which have expanded and been most susceptible to technological and institutional change. They have also changed 'subjectively' – i.e. as they present themselves to the consciousness of working people. With the growth of the joint stock firm or corporation, the whole nature of private property has been revolutionised. It can no longer be identified or personalised in the shape of the single industrial magnate, the 'robber baron' or even the entrepreneur family. This does not mean to say that there are no rich men left. But their riches – their pieces of property – are held largely in the form of pieces of corporate property, shares in the anonymous, complex, modern industrial firms which spawn their way across the face of modern business. 'Property' has gone underground, it has been institutionalised and incorporated, vested nominally in the person of an abstract company or firm. The maximisation of profit has passed from the personal responsibility of the businessman or financier, and is now established as the institutional motive of the firm. Further, as the spread of different jobs and functions within a modern firm multiplies, it is difficult for anyone outside to see exactly who is responsible for what. Where do decisions (e.g. to raise prices, alter models, lay off redundant labour, fix salaries and wages) now originate? In the drawing office? In the boardroom? With the advertising agent or the salesman? At the Ministry of Labour or the Board of Trade? Responsibility is difficult to localise. And many young men, drawn into the lower ranks of management, feel that part of the responsibility, at least, is theirs: they 'discover' a responsibility to the firm itself, and, eventually, are drawn into the whole ideology of big corporation business. The spirit which prevails in the multi-product firms, like ICI, Unilever, Tube Investments, United Steel, Vickers, London Tin, etc, has been justly described as the spirit of 'organised irresponsibility'.

Secondly, where profits and wages are concerned ('the rate of exploitation'), there have been some significant changes, though here the uneven development of which I spoke earlier is more noticeable. Certainly in times of prosperity, wages and living standards have been seen to rise – if not continuously, and in many particular spots – as a general trend throughout the society. That is at least the general feeling in the minds of many working people: as such, it gives rise to a different set of emotional responses to 'big business' and to 'wage disputes' – it is part of the new 'class consciousness'. It makes people more responsive to managerial patter about 'productivity' and 'the responsibility of the firm', and thus leads even the organised trade union movement to a greater involvement with 'keeping the firm competitive', with business unionism as practised in the United States, than would have been possible under the conditions which Marx foresaw – an increase in the rate of exploitation, a continual decline in real wages, longer working hours, and the proletarianisation of the middle class.

People's capitalism

The accumulation of capital and the maximising of profits are still, of course, the organising principle of the modern large firm.

Accumulation, however, is performed in an altogether new way, progressively less through the open money market and more through retained profits (except for large share issues): and although the banks, finance houses and insurance companies are deeply involved in the funding of expansion, this is done more through the 'anonymous' structure of interlocking directorships rather than in the open market. The maximisation of profit is still the driving motive behind the system: but because of the stability of the large firm, it can be considered to take place over a much longer period of 'growth': further, it has been tempered by the post-Marx recognition on the part of management that if goods are to be sold, effective domestic demand must be kept up, and the domestic market remain buoyant, provided profit levels can also be maintained. At the present time, for example, where lower and lower prices are being paid to the primary producing countries for raw materials, so that the overseas demand for our goods is falling off, the large firms will be seen to indulge in more 'give-away' schemes, and the banks in 'cloth-cap' accounts, and the finance houses in 'bonus' hire purchase offers. These are the mechanisms of a 'people's capitalism'.

Marx described the alienation of labour thus:

> the work is *external* to the worker ... it is not a part of his nature ... consequently he does not fulfil himself in his work but denies himself, has a feeling of misery, not of well-being, does not develop freely a physical and mental energy, but is physically exhausted and mentally debased. The worker therefore feels himself at home only during his leisure, whereas at work he feels homeless.

Now I am sure that, for many kinds of industrial work still performed, this feeling is still true. This would hold, for example, for the steel worker and the miner. But a subtle change of attitude is engendered in those industries where mechanisation and automation can and have been applied. In the first place, the work is not necessarily physically arduous, though it is probably mentally exhausting and repetitive. In many automation processes, even the repetitiveness has gone. The line between the skilled worker and the minor technologist is breaking down, particularly in industries based on chemical processes. Here the work is of a higher order, demanding skills of comparison of readings, compiling of data for 'programmes', etc; though machines take over the skills which used to depend on personal craft and individual judgement. This is what J.M. Domenach describes as 'work on work' (see *Esprit* November 1957), employing new technological skills. The gross 'means of production' – I mean the physical landscape of wheels and machines and exposed conveyor belts which provide the visual and psychological background of a film like Eisenstein's *Strike* – have disappeared in the technological industries. It is not that 'work' is any less external, but that the externality of work may itself, because of the 'higher' skills demanded, and the higher order of human cooperation involved, be accepted as a part of the necessary technical development of the means and skills of industrial labour. It may have been just possible to 'humanise' a nineteenth-century textile shop: it is impossible to 'humanise' a computing machine. The transformation of the technical base itself has done its work. Of course, automated work demands a higher level of culture, education and consciousness on the part of a skilled labour force: in this sense the development of the means of production must in turn raise the level of human consciousness, and may make possible, and in turn create, the demand for greater participation in all the human activities – the 'social relations of production' – associated with work. This is the shift which Reisman remarks on as a shift 'from the hardness of materials to the softness of men'. This change is itself beginning to take place in industry. But whereas Marx saw the 'humanisation' of work coming through direct participation and control, including control over ownership, from below, the development in capitalism is towards the 'personalisation' of work, through guided participation, excluding ownership, from above. Thus the spread of the ideology of 'human relations' and 'personnel management' in industry – a conception of worker-management relations which has invaded the more advanced points of British industry (cf the ICI schemes, and their persistent advertising campaign on this subject, which soften up public and workers as well). In the circumstances of which Marx wrote, a brutalised working class within a severe work-discipline were unconscious of the nature of their alienation: today, alienation of labour has been built-in to the structure of the firm itself. 'Joint consultation' and 'personnel relations' is a form of false consciousness, part of the ideology of consumer capitalism, and the rhetoric of scientific management.

The habit of consumption

Marx also spoke of the relationship between the worker and the objects which he produces – the 'fetishism of commodities', where 'the more powerful becomes the world of objects which he creates in fact of himself'. Iris Murdoch has remarked that Marx's economic theory was the last one which was based on labour and *production*: since then we have had economic theories based on *consumption* (see 'A House of Theory', *Conviction*). Now this is true, but the reasons for this development are to be found, not in the independent development of a body of economic theory, but in the way in which the capitalist system itself, which bourgeois economics had perforce to explain, had itself developed. The factor which Marx fixed upon was the *creation* of alien objects – commodities – which took on an independent life of their own, apart from their usefulness – in the commodity market. The worker, because of his low spending power, had little to do with these commodities apart from their production. Today, because of increased purchasing power, the commodities which the worker as *producer* makes at the factory, he purchases back as a *consumer* in the shops. Indeed, consumption has been so built into capitalism that it has become the most significant relationship between the working class and the employing class.[5] The worker knows himself much more as consumer than as producer: prices now appear a cleaner form of exploitation than wages. This is the role in which the capitalist system has annexed an entire class to itself: so much so that it appears to the working class now enjoying a higher level of consumption than ever before, that to break the system at the point of production (e.g. to reintroduce the concept of production for usefulness) would be to cut off his nose to spoil his face – as a consumer. The purpose of a great deal of advertising, for example, is to condition the worker to the new possibilities for consumption, to break down the class resistances to consumer-purchase, which became part of working class consciousness at an earlier period. This is known in the world of advertising as 'sales resistance'. ('When you buy your second car, make sure it's a Morris'.)

Status value

Further, in an era of expanded consumer demand, the alienation of commodities has gone a stage further than Marx foresaw. Not only have objects produced taken on an existence independent from their production as economic things in the market; not only has the working class been built into the market itself: but commodities – things-in-themselves – have accumulated a social value as well. They have become insignias of class and status. Through the purchase and display of certain kinds of consumer goods, which have gathered for themselves status value, a working-class family can define its social standing in relation to other families (if they live in a neighbourhood where such things matter): they can even – so the advertisers suggest – raise their class position by buying the right kinds of goods. Of course, in relation to the new managerial groups which have grown up in industry (see Peter Shore's 'In The Room At The Top', *Conviction*), or the owners of industrial property, the gap between exploited and exploiters may well be the same – or at least not substantially altered. But the sense of difference has been blunted – partly because there are now more opportunities for people to work within big business in positions of limited responsibility (what is now referred to as 'middle management'). Thus in their lives and their work, working-class and lower middle-class people can realise themselves through the possession (on hire purchase perhaps) of 'alien things'. Capitalism as a social system is now based upon consumption. Both in consumption and production, the working class is gradually becoming a factor in its own permanent alienation.

Whilst it may have been true, in the past, as Raymond Williams argues, that 'the working class does not become bourgeois by owning the new products', that working-class culture is a 'whole way of life', not reducible to its artefacts, it may now be less and less true, because the 'new things' in themselves suggest and imply a way of life which has become objectified through them, and may even become desirable because of their social value. In those places in welfare Britain where the working class has been put directly in touch with 'the new opportunities', the 'whole way of life' is breaking down into several styles of living (this is the language of the furnishing advertisements), each imperceptibly, but, as William Whyte says, 'exquisitely', differentiated one from another. The very fact that it is sometimes difficult to disentangle one 'style' from another (e.g. what 'style' is one purchasing when one buys, for example, Times Furnishings, C&A styles, or Marks & Spencer's, where the prices are comparatively low but the fashions are up-to-the-minute?) adds to the general sense of class-confusion.

The more clearly we grasp the particular ways in which the sense of solidarity and community sustained life in the older working-class localities, the more sharply will we see the degree of anxiety and confusion which attends the new 'classlessness'. When the old sense of class begins to break up, and while a new pattern of class emerges, the society is not merely fluid – it can be made to appear more free and 'open'. The working-class boy must find his way through a maze of strange signals. For example, the 'scholarship boy' who retains some sense of allegiance to his family and community has constantly to draw the distinction within himself between the just motive of self-improvement (which took him to university in the first place) and the false motive of self-advancement ('room at the top'). This is because culture, education and learning, like the other 'commodities' of our society, have accreted to themselves a social value in a hierarchy of status symbols. To learn or to read is no longer a process through which the individual broadens and deepens his experience for its own sake (processes which, when they grow out of a genuine community, a 'whole way of life', are perfectly compatible with a working-class way of life): they are, in themselves, modes of propulsion up the status ladder. Books imply different – and 'exquisitely' differentiated – styles of living. Thus, instead of the continuous broadening out of culture, as living standards improve and the means of production are technically developed, there is a cultural discontinuity in the community – a gap between an increasingly skilled working class and the riches of culture, which now properly belong to that class – which the creep of social opportunity cannot bridge.

Creeping up the ladder

For once the working class has set tentative feet on the status ladder, once the notion of the ladder itself has entered its consciousness as a necessary part of life, there is nothing left but perpetual forms of striving – not the open, brutal struggle of the period of primary *accumulation* – a Morgan against a Rockefeller – but the blander, more inner, nervous inconspicuous struggle of a period of public consumption – a Smith against a Jones. The ladder sorts out the community into a series of separate, competing individuals: for a class *as a class* cannot advance by means of it. We must each go it alone. And, even when there are more opportunities for self-advancement around, they can only be seized at the expense of someone else. By means of the image of a social ladder, the other images of bourgeois life – individualism, privacy, 'the spirit of healthy competition', 'cultivating one's own garden' (Mr Crosland's metaphor for happiness), 'a property owning democracy' – finally enter working-class consciousness. As many working-class men and women said to us, when we enquired about the growth of community life in the new towns – 'What do you have a home for, if you don't stay in it?'. Or, as a skilled maintenance operative who had moved to a new town from South London remarked – 'I wanted a house and a bit of space around it: after all, that's what we came for. People are too close to you – breathing down your necks ...'. And we thought of Bethnal Green. The image of a 'property owning democracy', and the complex of emotions contained in that contradictory phrase, is now the point of deepest conflict today within the working class (individual opportunity against the concept of the improvement of the whole community).

When, in his extraordinarily perceptive chapter at the end of *Culture and Society* (in the section 'The Development of a Common Culture'), Raymond Williams speaks of 'the conversion of the defensive element of solidarity into the wider and more positive practice of neighbourhood', he is thinking of a genuine broadening out of the idea of working-class solidarity, and its development in an ever widening 'community' which would eventually embrace the whole society. Nevertheless, one should be careful about the concept of 'neighbourhood' as it is customarily projected in a consumer capitalist society. For intense personal rivalries over status and 'style of life' can flourish and bloom within the 'neighbourhood' idea as it has grown up in the United States: where there may be 'neighbourhood' facilities to be 'consumed' by all, where there is no sharp sense of class, but where there are 'exquisite' distinctions of status. Something of this kind appears to be happening where the shift in consciousness from production to consumption is heightened by a change or improvement in neighbourhood; for example, in new towns, in the expanding suburbs and dormitory towns, and on the large housing estates in welfare Britain. 'Homemaking' and 'gardening' are not community skills, but subtle modes of status differentiation and striving, a new kind of individualism which enters working-class lives, so to speak, 'with the new furniture, *Woman's Realm* and *The Practical Householder*'. In the subtlest and more complicated ways, the new capitalism recognises and tries to cater for, at least in form, the human problems of industrial society, which in substance socialism first named. But these are only falsely attended to, resulting in a false consciousness in working-class people, making the real problems not only more difficult to solve but more difficult to see. Thus, while the large corporations have not replaced competition by cooperation, they are preoccupied with the 'spirit of collectiveness'. The human need for participation and control in industry has been sublimated into the practice of 'human relations'. And since a common culture and a genuine community has not been permitted to develop, the genuine human needs which have hitherto been expressed through these terms have been watered down into 'the need for neighbourliness' (what Riesman calls 'the glad hand' – but what, in an English new town was described as 'a cheery good morning'), 'the sense of belonging' (to whom? for what?), 'togetherness'. This is part of the same process of cultural degeneration which Hoggart describes in the *Uses of Literacy* ('Unbending the Springs of Action'): from a genuine sense of tolerance to a false sense of 'freedom' (from 'live and let live' to 'anything goes'), from a genuine sense of community to a false identification with the group (from 'everybody mucks in' to 'the gang's all here'), from a true sense of the present to a false sense of the 'contemporary' (from 'enjoy y'self while y'can' to 'we've never had it so good'). The process is far advanced in Britain: and what I have been trying to argue is that, since its roots are only in part to be discovered in changes in working-class culture, and can also be seen in the social and economic system within which culture grows, this process of degeneration has deeper sources than has so far been discovered.

Of course the sense of class confusion which I have been describing does not mean that there are no classes left. But where the subjective factors determining 'class consciousness' alter radically, a working class can develop a false sense of 'classlessness'. The true class picture, which so skilfully conceals itself behind the bland face of contemporary capitalism, is broadly speaking that which C. Wright Mills describes in *The Power Elite*.[6] It consists, on the one hand, of a number of interpenetrating elites or narrow oligarchies, whose functions within capitalism are different, but who share a common 'style of life', a common ideology and a common economic interest through the 'mutual care' of corporate private property: and, on the other hand, a permanently exploited, permanently alienated 'mass' of consumers (consuming goods and culture equally). This 'mass' has been, if you like, 'proletarianised' – not, as Marx thought *downwards* towards minimum wage levels, but *upwards* towards roughly middle-class styles of living. In the process, however, the old middle class and the old industrial proletariat are, gradually, ceasing to exist. (There are important distinctions, both in structure and habits, between the British and the American 'power elites', which deserve studies of their own.)

A series of life styles

Both Hoggart and Williams rightly protest against the use of the terms 'mass' and 'masses' (see Culture & Society, pp297-312). 'Masses', as Williams argues, is a kind of formula for progressive manipulation of anonymous groups of people – 'our listeners', 'our readers', 'viewers'. 'There are in fact no masses: there are only ways of seeing people as masses' (p300). But what we need to ask is not 'who are the masses?' but 'why is it necessary in our society for people *to be seen, and be persuaded to see themselves* as 'the masses'? It is necessary because this sense of classlessness, which can only be engendered by the persuasive use of a formula, must exist before people will accept their own cultural and economic exploitation. They have to be made accessories after the fact. This is the context in which we should understand the discussion about 'the mass media', about advertising and culture. Every form of communication which is concerned with altering attitudes, which changes or confirms opinions, which instils new images of the self, is playing its part. They are not peripheral to the 'economic base': they are part of it. (It is significant that some of the most important recent technological advances have been made in what is now called 'the communications industry', and that this side of big business is where the labour force is expanding most rapidly.) That fact in itself should make us seriously rework our ideas of the ways in which (as Engels, that arch-revisionist, put it) the superstructures 'exercise their influence upon the course of the historical struggles' and the conditions within which 'the economic movement finally asserts itself as necessary' (Letter to Bloch, see above).

The break-up of a 'whole way of life' into a series of life-styles (so-called 'lower-middle class' unfolding into 'middle-middle class', and so on, upwards) means that life is now a series of fragmented patterns for living for many working-class people. One cannot organise militantly to keep up with the Joneses. Moreover, many must feel a personal repugnance against involving themselves with a series of interlocking rat-races. But what else can they do? Self-improvement and self-advancement are now parts of the same process. That is the message of the capitalism of the proletariat. That is the tragic conflict within a working class which has freed itself only for new and more subtle forms of enslavement.

The fact that these forms of enslavement are mental and moral as well as material: the fact that they are taking shape at a period when greater leisure and comparative improvements in living standards are becoming possible – these point to the central paradox of contemporary capitalism with which socialists have now to deal. Marx suggested that complete alienation of man would not take place until the means of complete freedom themselves existed within the womb of society. In my view – and I would reiterate the discontinuity in the experience of classlessness between different regions and different industries of which I spoke at the very beginning – we are on the edge of some such moment in history. (The gap between some countries and the rest in this matter is, of course, the greatest human challenge of the age: but it deserves detailed treatment of its own.) Within the industrial countries, the material and technological means for complete human freedom – a freedom within which man could develop a true individuality and a true consciousness of himself and his possibilities – are almost to hand. But the structure of human, social and moral relationships are in complete contradiction and have to be set over against our material advances, when we are reckoning them up. Until we can throw over the system within which these relationships take place, and the kind of consciousness which feeds the system and upon which it feeds, the working class will be men as things for other people, but they can never be men for themselves.

Endnotes

1: The post-war boom

It is often said that the phenomena I am discussing are part of a false period of prosperity connected with the post-war boom: that it will fall off, and be overtaken by a series of economic crises of the old kind. I have heard 'the coming slump' predicted on four occasions by so-called militants since coming to England (1951). I am not impressed. I do not mean by that that I consider contemporary capitalism to be completely insulated against economic crisis. But I think it is time that we learned to reckon with the remarkable growth of stability and concentration within the system: the fact that it can and has changed in the light of periodic slumps in the past – the reasons for which, paradoxically enough, were most effectively pointed out by socialists: and the fact that the new power elites in Britain and the United States are probably the smartest and most far-seeing that have ever been in the business. Furthermore, the attitudes and changes which I discuss here are structural and institutional changes within capitalism: they have been running parallel to, they have been fed by – but they are different from – the 'welfare state' itself, considered as a system of social security – a structure which could admittedly, and indeed has already begun to, break up either through political malice on the part of a ruling class, or in response to a downturn in economic activity. Contemporary capitalism may disappear if the welfare state disappeared: at least, people's consciousness of economic matters would certainly be affected by a long period of hardship. But if what I have been arguing is true, if the working class has itself, to some degree, been seduced into playing a complementary role to capitalism, then the changes in social attitudes run deeper than talk about a 'temporary period of prosperity' would suggest. One is not any less against the system because one suggests that, in many important respects, it has changed. That smear is a form of subtle political blackmail.

2. Low life and high theory

To my mind, there has always been this kind of connection – under-stressed by Marx – between the life which working-class people made for themselves in an industrial society, and the body of socialist theory which grew out of it. This interpenetration of experience and theory is what really lies behind much of the talk about 'theory and practice'. It can best be seen in the somewhat cloudy but centrally important realm of 'humanist values'. There is no space at this point to trace out in detail what the connection has been: it is to be found, at least in part, in those sections of *The Uses of Literacy* which many socialists have discounted as 'not political enough'. The important point is this: that socialism cannot develop as a set of ideas or as a programme without a matrix of values, a set of assumptions, a base in experience, which gives them validity. There have to be some points of 'recognition' – where the abstract planning meets sharply with human needs as people experience them in the here and now. That is why it is not possible to postpone the problem of socialism until after the revolution. Socialism has always existed within capitalist society – at least in so far as working-class life offered itself as a set of alternate values, as a different image of the community, as a critique, to bourgeois life. We are making the socialism of tomorrow today: it is potential in the lives of ordinary people – working-class and others – who resist and reject, both intellectually and in experience, the values of a capitalist society. Unless the values of working-class experience can find new forms and thrive in the new conditions of consumption and prosperity which we have been discussing, socialist ideas will eventually dry up and disappear. Every day, in our own lives, in our personal relations with people, and our impersonal relations to things, we are making and destroying socialism itself.

3. Consciousness and the heavy industrial base

The model of 'base and superstructure' is – or ought to be – at the heart of every 'rethinking' and 'revisionist' controversy. It seems clear to me, on the one hand, that the simplistic economic-determinist reading of this formula has now to be discarded: it means that too much of importance has to be left out of our analysis. It is too blunt and imprecise an instrument. On the other hand, it is clear that some such organic relationship exists between 'the way we make our life' and 'the way we see ourselves' – and that, without such a framework of understanding, we may get a series of brilliant socialist programmes (perhaps), but no kind of socialist humanism. This article is, in part, an attempt to use the interpenetration of base and superstructure as an analytic framework for a discussion of some tendencies in contemporary capitalism. But the ideological discussion needs to go much further. Clearly, there are points at which 'ideas', or 'a structure of assumptions', directly impinge upon and affect, if not the nature of the 'economic base', then certainly the way it behaves, and even its development over fairly long periods of history. Furthermore, there are periods when cultural alienation and exploitation become so ramified and complex that they take on an independent life of their own, and need to be seen and analysed as such. What is more, there is a large area of personal choice, of conscious moral decisions made in certain moral situations – questions which E.P. Thompson refers to as concerning 'agency and choice' (See *New Reasoner* 5) – which we cannot slip or slide over by means of some convenient theory of economic inevitability.

I think the confusion is, in part, due to certain ambiguities which attend Marx's use of this analytic tool, in different parts of his work and at different periods of his life. The concept certainly took on, in the later years, a rigidity – due, in part, to the fact that he was dealing specifically with economic facts and causes – which is not to be found in his earlier work. Certainly there is no simplicity of analysis in *The Eighteenth Brumaire* or the *History of the Class Struggles in France*. It would be of immense value if the whole body of the earlier studies – particularly the untranslated and, one suspects, unfashionable *Economic and Philosophical Manuscripts* – were restored to their proper place. At least in the earlier writings on 'alienation' we need to give a different weight or emphasis to 'superstructure' than we would imagine simply from a study of *Capital*.

My plea is, at least, that 'revisionism' should begin with this concept, and that it should start in Marx's work itself, which is a body of analytic concepts and not a sealed house of theory. Engels plays, in the development of the base-superstructure controversy, a most significant 'revisionist' role. E.g. '... According to the materialist conception of history, the *ultimately* determining element in history is the production and reproduction of real life. More than this neither Marx nor I have ever asserted. Hence, if somebody twists this into saying that the economic element is the *only* determining one, he transforms that proposition into a meaningless, abstract, senseless phrase' ... 'We make our history ourselves, but, in the first place, under very definite assumptions and conditions' (Letter to Bloch, passim). The letter ends – a timely warning – 'Marx and I are ourselves partly to blame for the fact that the younger people sometimes lay more stress on the economic side than is due to it. We had to emphasise the main principle vis-a-vis our adversaries ... Unfortunately, however, it happens only too often that people think they have fully understood a new theory and can apply it without more ado from the moment they have mastered its main principles, and even those not correctly. And I cannot exempt many of the more recent "Marxists" from this reproach, for the most amazing rubbish has been produced in this quarter too' (*Selected Works*, Vol. 2, p 443-4).

Notes

1. Richard Hoggart, *The Uses of Literacy*, Chatto and Windus 1957.
2. Raymond Williams, *Culture and Society*, Chatto & Windus 1958, p324.
3. Raymond Williams, 'Working Class Culture', *ULR* 2 summer 1957.
4. *Economic and Philosophic Manuscripts 1844*, translated in Karl Marx, *Selections*, Bottomore & Rubel (eds), London 1961, p70.
5. This involves the working class capitulating to the root self-image of man in capitalist society. See Charles Taylor, 'Alienation and Community', *ULR* 5, Autumn 1958.
6. C. Wright Mills, *The Power Elite*, Oxford University Press 1958. See the chapter on *The Mass Society*.

The supply of demand

1960*

The old-fashioned Conservative is one who looks out at the comforts made achievable by rising incomes and the hire-purchase revolution, and who feels vaguely that the workers are unfairly luckier than he was as a boy – that they are getting above their station. The modern Conservative should be one who looks up at the television aerials sprouting above the working-class homes of England, who looks down on the housewives' tight slacks on the back of the motor-bicycle and family sidecars on the summer road to Brighton, and who sees a great poetry in them. For this is what the deproletarianisation of British society means; and the changes in social and industrial attitudes of mind which it could bring with it are immense.

'The Unproletarian Society', *The Economist*, 16 May 1959

Thus *The Economist*.

I do not, of course, mean that the whole of the working class can now afford these luxuries – far from it. So far this is only a trend – we are still only at the threshold of the new era of abundance; and there are many workers on £7 or £8 a week, and even more social service beneficiaries, who are still acutely worried by the problem of subsistence. But the trend is now quite definite; and it is significant that even these poorer workers are themselves peering across the threshold; they have accepted the new standards as the social norm, and are already thinking of the day when they too will acquire these goods. All this must have a profound effect on psychology of the working class ... There are clear political implications here for the Labour Party, which would be ill advised to continue making a largely proletarian class appeal when a majority of the

47

population is gradually attaining a middle-class standard of life, and distinct symptoms even of a middle-class psychology.

'The Search for Equality', *The Future of Socialism*, A. Crosland

Thus the 'new thinking'.

These passages plunge us deep into the sludge and confusion and cross-fire of the no-man's-land of British politics today. Who could have imagined that the leader-writers of *The Economist* – those sour-faced Bagehots of yesterday – would have become the popularisers and myth-makers of the 1960s? And yet here they are, remarking in a voice choked with emotion, the 'revolution of the deproletarianised consumer'. Outside the homestead, television aerials flourish like weeds, motor-bicycles and family sidecars slither into place; around the working-class housewife, 'mechanical slaves on the hire-purchase have sprung up ... as she works in the non-telly hours'; average workers have overcome the enormous technical problems of 'getting their own families on to wheels'. Then, 'in the middle of this roaring decade, something began to happen in the field of consumer goods that can only be called a breakthrough'. As the journal brushed away the cobwebs of the 1950s from before its eyes, it looked out across the vast plain of capitalism, beheld the sheep, each in his station, grazing comfortably, and was satisfied. We have nothing to fear, save smugness itself! (The quotes are from 'Farewell To The Fifties', *The Economist*, 26 December 1959.)

And what is happening in the back garden of the most impressive Labour ideologue of them all? Mr Crosland's workers, too, are 'peering across thresholds' and accepting new standards as the social norm. Prosperity! Capitalism, by an infinite dialectic of its own, works silently towards its own reform. We have only to watch, amazed, as the economy, with the skill of an acrobat, doubles itself: and then, before you can say 'Heathcoat Amory!' we shall have sailed into the calm waters of the Second American Age.

Mr Crosland's picture of mid-century Britain rests upon the assumption that the class basis of the society has at last been worn down. Over the decades, the beetles of reform have been at work, eating away the scaffolding. The 'income revolution', the social wage of welfare, the growth in consumer power, the breaking up of the old working-class communities, state intervention, the humanisation of the system by the managerial revolution and the withering away of ownership: these have been the agencies of change. Mr Crosland himself admits that, subjectively, strong class feelings survive: that, objectively, there are wide gaps in income, power and style of life. But he takes comfort from the fact that 'greater equanimity of class relations does not necessarily lead to a pro-rata diminution in class consciousness, or even a blurring of class lines'. His emphasis remains that class distinctions *are* breaking down, and will continue to do so with another round of prosperity.

Public and private priorities

In what sense are we prosperous? We spend, as a society, nearly two-thirds as much on advertising as we spend on education: as much on packaging as on industrial research. We have undertaken, over the next two years, a greater expansion programme in the motor-car industry than ever before (including direct loans from the government to the motor firms) – although the roads are choked, and the accident rate for pedestrians higher than it has ever been. For the purposes of prestige, it is true, we have driven one or two 'clearways' across fields: other than that the road programme is a series of stupid squiggles on a map. In the centres of cities the private developers and land speculators throw up one office slab after another: typists and clerks are herded into these dense, overcrowded urban canyons – yet there has been only *one* new hospital built since the war. The out-patients departments, the waiting-rooms, the mental hospitals, are often squalid and ill equipped: many railway waiting rooms and labour exchanges are still peeling and dismal.

This is the age, we are told, of the 'teenage revolution'. Very well. In 1944, the McNair Committee recommended that the permanent body of trained youth leaders ought to be between 5000 and 6000, with an intake of 300 per year: recent surveys show that in 1956 the total was closer to 1000, and the Labour Party Report on *The Younger Generation* suggests that, by 1959, it had declined to 700. Public expenditure on the Youth Service has never passed beyond the £3,000,000 mark.

Yet, with a flick of the wrist at the last Budget, the Chancellor turned back £63,000,000 to industry by way of cuts in the income tax rate: that is a sum which exceeds, by about £13,000,000, the total spent on all building projects for primary and secondary education in the same year. The *Financial Times* reported (12 December 1958) that Sir Frank Spriggs had been paid £75,000 in compensation for loss of office as a managing director of the Hawker-Siddeley Group: that sum is about equal to the annual national budget of the Workers' Educational Association. In their essays in *Conviction*, Peter Townsend and Brian Abel-Smith documented the 'double standards' which prevail in welfare throughout the 'welfare state'. These contrasts are not incidental: they run right through the economy. They are almost the defining principles of the welfare state in its mid-century form.

Even when we look at these contrasts, we find ourselves often imprisoned within the existing framework. We rarely throw ourselves beyond the limits of what exists, and ask questions (now labelled 'Utopian') about what *could* exist. If we find an old people's home where there are carpets on the floor, we think – 'Good: this is what it should be like'. But is it? Suppose we stopped and asked: 'Is this good enough: is *that* what old age is like for the thousands in our institutions?' 'Why are they still so miserably furnished, so institutional, in the bad sense?' And, beyond the proportion of the population who are genuinely on the poverty line – the 5 million retirement pensioners, the 500,000 widows on special benefit, the 250,000 receiving industrial injuries and disablement allowances, the 2 million men and women dependent on unemployment benefit – what about the average skilled working-class family? Where is the expansion in community provision here to match the surge in consumer goods? The play centres for the kids, the new youth clubs (not the hastily converted schoolroom with desks) for the teenagers, the crèches for the children of the increasing number of working mothers, the new ante-natal centres and baby clinics, the special schools for the mentally and physically disabled? Where is the great advance in the period of post-war prosperity?

The expansion has *not* come. In the midst of plenty, the government has convinced us that 'we simply cannot afford' many of these things.

Perhaps we are *moving* towards prosperity in these fields? But that is not true either. The recipient is paying *more* for health and dental care, for school meals and spectacles – not less. The number of council-built dwellings has fallen from 244,916 at the peak period (1953) to 143,283 (in 1958). Yet in 1956, the LCC were obliged to tell the 165,000 families on its waiting list (53,000 of whom were in the urgent' A' category) that only 2000 would be rehoused by 1959 (*Labour Research*, March 1959). At the same time, as a result of the government withdrawal of subsidies and the increase in the interest rates to municipal authorities, the cost of a £2000 council house is now £7,148, of which £5,148 is in interest repayments over sixty years (as of July 1959). This is another way of saying that an extra £1 a week has been added to the rent of a new council house.

As a result of the Block Grant system, expenditure on local health services will rise by only 3.6 per cent in 1960 (as compared with an average rise of 7 per cent between 1950 and 1959). Local expenditure on child care will rise by only 1.8 per cent – a rate which will be more than offset by the rise in prices over the same period. Any expenditure by local councils above these estimates will have to come from the ratepayers.

The government has cut back public transport and extended the modernisation period of the railways. But the government has allowed (and *helped*) the motor manufacturers to expand, and protected privately owned road transport. Yet we cannot 'afford' to pay railwaymen a living wage. It is coal which has subsidised private industry (by selling fuel at absurdly low prices to manufacturers) and steel which has failed the nation (by failing to expand and keeping the economy in short supply):[1] yet the pits are closing in many areas, the NUM is signing redundancy agreements, and the profits of the steel companies continue to expand. What are these absurd priorities to which we appear, in spite of ourselves, to be harnessed? How can we say, on the one hand, that there are so many things 'which we cannot afford', and yet assert that 'we have never had it so good'? It does not make sense.

Yet Mr Crosland and Mr Gaitskell seem to accept, with little qualification, the Conservative claim that 'Tory Freedom Works!' (Works for *whom*?) If it *does* work, then Mr Gaitskell should accept, as well, the current apathy of the electorate. If the situation is good, the trends healthy, the auguries auspicious, then 'apathy' is no problem, and there is very little left for the Labour Party to *do*. We should therefore extend a warm welcome to apathy – the outward and visible sign of an inward spiritual and material grace. The only problem, as Tory freedom wipes out one black spot after another, will be to get the electorate to vote *at all*. Think of Mr Macmillan and Mr Amory, going on and on in the House, lacerated each week by Bernard Levin in the *Spectator*, unable to get back to their directorships, unable to move on the overcrowded roads, as the electorate busily travels from one seaside pier to the next!

Faults in the structure

Of course, the problems sketched above are not simply capitalism's 'little local difficulties'. They are central to the system itself: they are *structural* faults and weaknesses which have survived the managerial and corporate 'revolution' in capitalism, and come out on the other side, unresolved. They remain, because the new managers who shape and balance the policies of the large firms, the heirs and beneficiaries of 'stability' and 'expansion' and 'growth', are the subalterns and NCOs of the system of private appropriation and accumulation. They have altered the techniques of the capitalist system: they have not changed its function.

If the new capitalists do not 'own' it all personally, as the nineteenth-century captains of industry did, it is because the size of the territory is now too great. Even a small corner of an industrial empire like Unilever is enough to bring enormous wealth (through capital gains as much as dividends) to the new large shareholder. The most lucrative source of wealth in the economy is industrial property: and, in spite of the development of management, the owners of large pieces of corporate property are still in control of the policies of the firm.[2] They are the generals of the system, relying on the efficiency and devotion of the managers, who serve it also, share in its benefits and reap rewards through salaries and perks on the firm. And the system is *still* driven by the need – over longer periods, it is true, but taking one year with another – to generate as much surplus wealth as it can. Regardless of the personal feelings of the new capitalists and their lieutenants, the system, moved by profit, establishes the priorities: and the priorities give rise to the myths.

And so the ritual of prosperity begins to unfold in quite new ways. To explain the power of these myths we need to understand – not why we have so much, but why we feel satisfied with what we have. We have only to take a slightly different position from Mr Crosland's – as Mr Strachey does in *Contemporary Capitalism* – to come up with a significantly different picture of what is going on in the economy: the growth of the large corporations; the stability of the managerial and propertied classes, whose social power is now equidistant with any of the provinces of the market which they command; the increasing obsolescence of the market in conditions of oligopolistic competition; the concentration of power; the two or three commanding giants in each sector, fixing prices, quietly salting away to reserves, watching the needle of capital gains shudder and leap, deciding the annual pay-off to the scattered small shareholders, carving up, amalgamating, buying out, taking over.[3] Here is 'last stage capitalism', with reluctant Labour pitted against the power of corporate Capital: the sand in the machine, the Past in front of the Future of Socialism.

It is capitalism in stalemate with which we are dealing: inflation without balanced growth, investment sprees (1954-55) followed by widespread industrial stagnation (1956-58).[4] It is also a capitalism of startling contrasts: the Shell tower watching you from the South Bank and the empty space where the National Theatre ought (surely by now!) to be: the white settlers of capitalism in the Surrey hills and the worried 'savages' of Preston and South Shields: the new look of industry at Dagenham and the old feel of the coal face at Barnsley: North and South. Pockets of prosperity, where the consumer goods industries have blossomed: patches of stagnation in Lancashire, where the last threads of the cotton industry are spinning out. If some pits are closing, it is not because we have finally admitted that coal mining is an inhuman form of labour in an age of technological advance; but because the miners are to be allowed to bear the brunt of the unplanned advance of other industries (oil and atomic energy), and we cannot yet plan the use of fuel or cope with the major human readjustments which would be created by planned change on this scale.

The car industry in the Midlands is booming: but the motor firms can scarcely get their lorries through to the ports, because the roads are crowded, and the harbours full and unreconstructed; the shipbuilding industry is in semi-stagnation, and the railway system is obsolete, with its modernisation plans in cold storage. Certainly there is prosperity: but we are often so mesmerised by it that we cannot get far enough away to take an *overall* look – a look at the unplanned chaos of it all, and the false targets to which we subscribe.

Contemporary capitalism has two distinct faces, but they belong to the same coin. In the economic sphere, where the economy has life, capitalism goes ahead (the car and consumer goods industries), leaving behind the whole question of balanced growth (enough steel? modern railways? decent roads?) and the human needs which stem from that advance (what do the miners do *now*?). In the social sphere, we suffer public squalor (in welfare, education, urban development and so on) for the sake of private splendour (the new TV set, the washing machine, the small car): whereas the real question *should* be how we can manage as a society to provide every housewife with a washing machine *without* at the same time starving the children of a decent education; how we can provide for everyone adequate transport for living and for leisure *without* having the children or the old folk run down on the narrow streets.

Capitalism – even where it is 'delivering the goods' – appears unable to make the transition from one century to another human or bearable. Industrial technology, automation and so on, under a system of unplanned private enterprise, are going to take the same toll from society – in terms of misery, unemployment, the interruption of secure patterns of life, the loss of skills – as the first industrial revolution did. In terms of human and social priorities, we are no further forward. The public sector lives in retirement, like a gentlewoman in 'straitened circumstances' to whom the 'affluent' uncle sends the occasional grudging cheque. The society is not going to pass smoothly into a genuine, balanced and lasting prosperity for all: it is going to jerk, spasmodically, towards prosperity for some – the devils of 'efficiency' and profit, all the time, lopping off the hindmost.

The limits of reform

Even if we allow for Mr Strachey's bleak optimisms – the 'countervailing' power of the unions and the intervention of the state, he suggests, will keep the welfare state intact and employment 'full' – we are still left with an economy which, at best, is able to hold things together, its back to the wall. The idea of a labour movement strong enough to make demands, to set the standards, to pitch forward the aspirations of a new skilled working class, to re-order the priorities, is (has to be) absent from his picture. It is capitalism which sets the priorities: and the priorities accurately reflect the inner contradictions of capitalism itself: the contradiction between production for profit and production for use. From Mr Strachey's point of view, a strong labour movement may *prevent* the development of classic crises of production such as we had in the past: but can it force capitalism to tackle crisis in its new form – inflation and recession? Labour can perform a defensive role in the economy – and increasingly appears to do so, as simply one more vested interest: it cannot go ahead to set new priorities for the community. The contradiction between production for *use* and production for *profit* remains.

In the post-1950 period, that contradiction has been resolved in favour of *profit*. After the Butskell honeymoon, the mixed economy has unmixed itself, and the private sector has once again taken the lead. And now, as profits in some sectors drive the economy forward, the contradictions unfold into politics and popular mythology: a revival of confidence in the business class, the spread of the business ethos in the shadow of the large firms, and three successive Tory victories. Capitalism has created a new context of social power.

Can Mr Strachey's 'countervailing power of Labour' graft public and human priorities on to a profit-dominated system of production? There are no signs that this is happening. Labour itself has capitulated before some of the powerful myths of the system. Suppose that we wanted to assert that education was more important than advertising – indeed, that the £400,000,000 which is spent on advertising undermines the very educational purposes for which we spend £670,000,000 – how would we go about it? Haven't we been told that 'advertising has helped to raise our standard of living and brought us the good things of life'? Can we touch advertising, which, by creating wants, keeps the economy ticking over, without endangering the economy itself?

If we tax the rich more, we shall damage the circuit of energy – accumulation, profits and investment – which keeps the wheels of capitalism turning: yet if we tax them less, we shall have to cut back the welfare state. If we tried to dismantle our armoury of dangerous weapons – on the grounds that £1,514,000,000 is too much to spend on a nuclear defence policy which provides no defence – we would induce a serious disequilibrium in our whole economy: yet if we continue to make them, we shall increase the probability that they will be used.

Suppose that we were to decide to assist the 'underdeveloped' countries in a serious way. We should be obliged to guarantee, over long periods, stable markets for their primary products with periodical review of prices: but then we should have to plan industry in a more rational way.[5] 'We should also have to prevent capital from seeking, as it has done over the last decade, its 'natural' and 'quick' return on profits: we should have to insist that capital should be available at low rates of interest and over long periods. We should have to prevent private capital flowing, as it has done, to the already developing countries (Australia, Canada, South Africa), and direct it to the needy areas (India, Malaya, Central Africa, Burma and Ceylon). But that would be to strike at the heart of capitalism itself.

Labour, brought to these frontiers of control after 1945, lost its nerve and turned back without trying to cross. Since then, it has been obliged to work within the framework, accepting the capitalist hierarchy of priorities as 'given', learning to put up with the imbalance and jerkiness of the economy, with a society of startling contrasts. In place of its *own* order of priorities, Labour has followed along the trail which consumer capitalism opened up, making do as it went along. So that today, it is Labour – trapped into a defensive posture – which has to try to make the system work, careful not to ask for too much, nodding when the newspapers say that 'taxation is too high' – even to the point of trying to fight an election on this platform! The vision of community responsibility and common ownership has been abandoned. The new aspirations of a skilled working class have been diverted into the satisfaction of personal wants: they have never been given social or political urgency. The 'dream' is broken up. As Mr Gaitskell said, in his speech to the Blackpool Conference:

> We have long ago come to accept, we know very well, for the foreseeable future, at least in some form, a mixed economy; in which case, if this is our view – as I believe it to be of 90 per cent of the Party – had we better not say so instead of going out of the way to court misrepresentation?

The 'foreseeable future' is a long, long vista. So far as the Labour Party is concerned, it might as well get used to the idea of living inside capitalism for ever.

Is it any wonder that the whole movement of politics has become increasingly sluggish, shuttling between half-believed platitudes and contrasting 'images'? It is because deep down we know the true state of the nation, but *cannot see a political way forward*, that we have drifted into an acceptance of the disquieting mythologies of prosperity. It is because this stalemate has been lost sight of in the 'revolution in consumer goods', that the thing is tolerable at all – that 'breakthrough' in the middle of 'this roaring decade' about which the *Economist*, Mr Crosland, Mr Gaitskell and Mr Macmillan all rejoice to concur.

Consumer versus taxpayer

At the heart of the rituals of affluence lies the 'consumer'. He is the folk-hero of corporate capitalism, and the god in the works. A bland, half-thing of a man, peering nervously at the frontiers of consumption and taste. That he makes with his skill, masters the machine with his craft, learns and adapts to the applied techniques of science, manages with his mind, experiences with his senses, and suffers with the rest of us, is incidental to the routines of consumer capitalism. He *buys*: he has the feel of the packaged goods: his choices are 'free'. Before the bargain counter, we are all equal.

Of course, he is not free. If he were, capitalism would not spend £400,000,000 a year persuading him to buy, jogging his spending arm, and another £400,000,000 wrapping it all up with 'impact' and 'sales appeal', employing the salesmen and the ad-men, greasing the palm of the hard hand behind the soft sell. If the consumer were free, an irrational phrase like 'whiter than white' would never have entered our vocabulary. If he were all-powerful, the corporations could not fix and maintain prices behind his back. If he were sovereign, there would be *one* usable detergent on the market, not fifteen with (almost) the same ingredients.

But the primacy of the consumer is supported in several other significant ways. In the first place, the very structure of the mixed economy counterposes the private possession of consumer goods to the public services of welfare and community spending. You cannot go shopping for a better education (unless to the public schools) or a better hospital, or an adequate transport system. You cannot *choose* – via the market – to spend less on advertising and more on hospitals, to delay the office block in the centre for the sake of the council housing estate round the corner. These 'social' decisions are fixed elsewhere, beyond the reach of the 'consumer'. They have been taken right away from the direct intervention and control of the ordinary citizen, into those secluded places where the market *in fact* operates: in the boardroom and the bank manager's suite of offices. Community services do not appear to belong to the same category – to come from the same source, to be social capital in the same sense, to be governed by targets publicly established. Eventually the consumer *does* begin to feel 'free' to decide about detergents in a way in which he is not 'free' to decide the education of his children. Education, health, welfare, housing and so on, therefore, assume the status of 'unnecessary and wasteful spending'.

What is more, we begin to feel that our interests as 'consumers', as 'taxpayers', are being jeopardised by too much public spending; we start to reckon the cost of every new school in terms of the number of TV sets of which it has deprived us: even though, in another capacity (it sometimes seems, in another life) we too shall need medical care, and our children will go to the schools, and we shall live in the council house, and we shall travel on public transport. Indeed, when people *do* encounter public squalor they feel immediately the human irritations of the system, the absurdity of the priorities, without quite knowing who is to blame, or in what direction to project their frustration, their complaints. Hence the paradox: it is often the man who is the most aggressive defender of his status as a consumer who is most bitter about the state of the public services. 'The trains are late! The tubes are full!' 'They' are getting at us again … (as indeed they are: but do we see it?). As the vision of a socialist *community* disappeared, as cheeseparing became the hallmark of public services in the last days of Labour and the early years of Tory rule, the labour movement began to lose its sense of how working people could (and had to) provide *for themselves*, as a community. The society was forced, by the very driving pressure from the consumer industries themselves, as they began to be the providers of life and the givers of good things, to think of prosperity almost entirely in terms of the things which it could purchase, possess, and enjoy as private individuals. We had entered, as separate consumers, directly into the mythology of prosperity. 'Prosperity' had become much more a question of how people could be made to see themselves (in terms of their generalised feelings about how things worked) and much less a solid affair of genuine wealth and well-being.

In that sense, consumer capitalism did genuinely – about the middle of the roaring fifties – break through some kind of sound barrier in public consciousness. Not, as has been supposed, into the 'American' pattern (or what we imagine it to be like: Galbraith gives quite a different picture in *The Affluent Society*), where working people genuinely began to savour the joys of personal display and status through the possession of goods; but rather, into a more muted, more confusing pattern, where we defined our interests as human beings in terms of the things we *might* – or others might – conceivably possess, although we did not seem to have very many of them *yet*. And for those people who were genuinely worried about the vast tracts of our life which were being seriously neglected, there was also the comforting subsidiary myth, that we had only to let prosperity take its course. That, in the next wave, capitalism would suddenly begin to sweep the streets, build working-class flats, reform the secondary modern nightmares, limit the growth of office blocks, of its own sweet accord.[6] Indeed, this is a view still popularly held and successfully put about. It too is part of the religion of the rise of the consumer goods industries.

The drive of the consumer goods industries, coupled with the mythologies of affluence, corrupted our sense of the *usefulness* of things. The second-hand car, the washing machine or the telly did not become 'status symbols' in the American sense – providing the working class with the insignias of social position, and smoothing out the way into the middle class. But they acquired, in consciousness, a social importance out of all proportion to their *use*, or our needs. The 'sovereign consumer' blotted out the man who was also a father, a lorry driver, a pedestrian, a pensioner, a victim in a car crash wanting urgent attention at the out-patient's, a miner whose pit is to be closed, a family man on the 'short list' for a council flat, a near-sighted bank clerk, an underpaid teacher with a mother-in-law to keep, or a building worker with bad teeth. The consumer goods industry did not, to any significant extent, give us the goods: instead, it gave us a definition of the Good Life.

And all this, as the welfare state began to shrink in influence (also in the roaring fifties) and the umbrella of the firm began to open out in its place. It is one of the paradoxes of prosperity that the very 'humanisation' of capitalism and the firm, of which Crosland and others speak so glowingly, is one of the root causes of the decline in community responsibility in the last decade. It may be that ICI is a good firm to work for. But this process places a limit to our social thinking. The responsibility of the firm – no matter how well discharged – ends at the frontier of the firm. There are many things which the most humane private corporation cannot do. It can look after its own workers, but only partly and paternalistically – setting them off as favoured citizens against their less well-off fellows. The welfare-minded firm can 'afford' substantial grants to public schools and private schemes for the education of managerial children: what it cannot do is to reduce the average size of the classes from forty to thirty for *all* children. That is because 'looking after its own' may well be one of the firm's priorities: giving managerial children an elite education, or increasing the science-training capacity of the public schools is something from which, in the short run, the corporation can expect to benefit directly. Beyond that frontier, the most responsible firm (to its employees) becomes irresponsible (when seen from the point of view of the community).

Gradually, throughout the 1950s, these barriers to social thinking have become higher, the citadel of private responses and private interests and tastes more and more impregnable. As much as anything, this was due to the fact that the Labour Party had ceased to be alive, in any active sense, to the human and revolutionary priorities which a proper understanding of the words 'welfare' and 'community' would have given. For sooner or later, if the party had understood why these things were the essence of socialism, what had to be done to get the priorities right, they would have had to confront directly the revival of capitalism and the refurbishing of capitalist ideology and culture. This would have brought us back to common ownership, to the participation of individuals in determining the priorities of the society and how they work out, to control over our economic and social environment. Instead of which 'community responsibility' and 'welfare' and 'common ownership' have become the current platitudes of political thinking: they have been reduced to the status of careful accounting and social administration, forced to subscribe to the criterion of economic 'efficiency'.

There has not been, so far, a thrusting, confident celebration of the new capitalism on the part of the majority of people in this country. There has been, rather, a slow, sullen, suspicious acquiescence in a future in which no one quite believed – a mood of cautious watchfulness. It is one of the attitudes which the merchants of 'prosperity' cannot forgive the British working class. 'Don't they know when they are well off?' 'Don't they know they haven't had it so good?' But the majority of working people maintained a silence of disbelief.' All that good? Well. In a prosperity state, could the old age pensioners live on £3 a week? In the leisure age, could the unions still be reluctant to fight for the 40-hour week? Occasionally, a specific case gives them a whiff of capitalism at work, a look in at the back-stairs deals, the private washing of bonds, the capital gains, the conferences at the Bank of England, the cryptic telegrams to Hong Kong, the 'working parties' on the grouse-moors in Scotland, night and day, the tasks of capitalism being attended to. One of the things which Mr Macmillan will never understand about working people in Britain is that they are *still* just that bit defensive when they say, 'I'm all right Jack'.

Producing the consumer

> I do not think of my relatives, friends, neighbours, colleagues as masses; we none of us can or do. The masses are always the others, whom we don't know, and can't know.
>
> Raymond Williams, *Culture and Society*, p299

Nevertheless, in 'consumer capitalism', communication increasingly takes the form of the persuasive manipulation of one (unknown) group by another.

> There are, in fact, no masses, there are only ways of seeing people as masses ... The fact is, surely, that a way of seeing other people which has become characteristic of our kind of society has been capital-ised for the purposes of political or cultural exploitation. What we see, naturally, is other people, many others, people unknown to us. In practice, we mass them and interpret them according to some convenient formula.
>
> *Culture and Society*, p300

Think of the consumer again, the folk-figure of the tale. Seen as such. Thought of as such, and catered for. Restricted within a certain framework to the circle of his private grudges and dreams, wishes, longings, his stifled aspirations, his desire to get on a little, to know a little. Of course, *people* are not like that at all. But the relationship between the 'consumer' and the 'provider of all good things', the universal bread-basket, is essentially a limiting, distorting one, reducing the individual from a complex and contradictory human being to the sum of his private urges and aggressions. And, where this 'consumer' relationship obtains, the different forms of social communication are increas-ingly closed to public and social appeals of any kind; more dependent upon persuasive formulations (to counter the 'sales resistance' of the customer); less and less open to reasoned thinking and stubborn criti-cism (what is the reasoning behind 'whiter than white?'); and – for that very reason – less and less a rational form of discourse at all (advertising is a debased art of this kind of society – half way between degraded salesmanship and bastard poetry).

People, then, have to be *massed* in some way to become 'available'. 'The masses'. 'Readers'. 'Viewers'. 'The Floating Vote'. 'Four-and-a-half homes out of every five in the country have …' 'Six million house-wives!' 'Seven million teenagers!' And so on. The relationship is not a static, but a moving one – moving towards persuasion. Audiences are 'won', readers 'captured', the electorate 'convinced', the floating vote 'brought round to our way of thinking', teenagers 'civilised'. The cate-gories, like animated packages, begin to move. The Labour Party gives up on policy and begins to concentrate on its 'image'. Mr Macmillan, explaining away the Devlin Report, has at least (cold comfort) 'a pleasing television personality'.[7] The *content* of the thing falls away: the formal, impersonal *approach* is everything. It is the *form* of Michael Foot's radicalism, the shape and sound of Gilbert Harding's institu-tionalised bellyache that get us – not what they are radical or bellyaching *about*. (Mr Harding is on about his dyspepsia again.) So that even politics ceases to be the open clash of opposing views and interests, smoothed down into a depressing grey of accommodating half-agreements and washed by the 'charm of politics' itself. At such a time the 'floating vote' holds the pass between the political parties and the seat of government only because we are living through the age of floating politicians.

This debased art of persuasion also makes use of 'projection' of the marketable side of our character – our 'personality'. The key concepts are 'impact' and 'drive' and 'the hard sell'. Television reaches through the screen into the homes of millions … 'You can become the woman in the frame … Take *True Romances* into your life'. Your life. You. It is almost as if the screen were already almost two-way, as if, behind a thin film, the persuader could almost see you folks out there, with your little wishes in your little homes beside your little fires. He is willing to come in and get you … On the other hand, you might just like to step outside and meet *him!*

When we speak of 'communications' in a consumer society, we have to think less of how we speak to one another, and more of how other people speak *at* us. This process is by no means limited to advertising. Persuasion is not simply persuasion to spend: it is often, also, invitations to *live* – in an odd, limited sort of way. And here we are on different ground. Think how rapidly the *language* of advertising breaks into the language of common speech (the language with which we communicate, among other things, pleasure, pain, love and distress). Where does the advertising copy end and the 'Woman's Column' begin? What is the frontier between the 'Cunard way of life' advert, and the 'exclusive' interview, or the glamorised, quick-Cook's-tour of the pick of the high spots with Group-Captain Townsend? Life begins to fade into the picture … In these constantly circulating images and suggestions, we are beginning to indulge in a secular dream-life: a half-life into which we are invited to project, not ourselves, but little bits of ourselves – mostly that nasty little bit that wants just to see how other people get on and up. Not much more, but that is enough. 'Living in the picture' is never possible, for the gap between fantasy and life is too sharp. But 'living *near* the picture' becomes a habit which makes constant calls on the attention and emotions.

The culture, in its many forms, throws out perpetually a bewildering plethora of suggestions and invitations – 'Get On, Get Up, Get Out, Climb In, Look at That, Feel Sorry! Feel Tempted? Come over here where it's warm …'. The victim is dazzled by a maze of popular distractions, just close enough to life to be 'real', just enough out of reach to be 'far out'. But where does the circle begin and end? Who does what to whom? Who is responsible? We are not to blame, says Unilever, we are just protecting our interests: besides we are giving people what they want. We are not to blame, says the *Daily Mirror*, our job is to run a newspaper: besides aren't we giving the people what they want? THIS IS A DEMOCRACY. 'Success for us', writes Mr Cecil King of the *Mirror* and *Sunday Pictorial*, 'involves the closest contact with our readers and a sensitivity to atmosphere as it changes'. What follows, he goes on, arises 'from the appetite of the reader, not from any lack of virtue on the part of the proprietor'.

The home-centred society

The media of information are constantly using up the direct sentiments and emotions of people, projecting into our lives normative and desirable values, often with a commercial twist. And even when these attitudes are rejected in their more blatant forms, they often leave a scatter of doubts in their trail – with important political results. It is true that the swing away from Labour in the last election, serious though it was as part of a continuing trend, was not a landslide, reflecting a major and irreversible social trend. On the other hand, the celebration of 'prosperity' and capitalism has only just begun: and Labour shows no signs of comprehending exactly what is taking place, and appears to lack the will to meet the challenge. If that trend does develop, 'prosperity' will have gathered, by 1964, a head of steam that will be capable of blowing Mr Gaitskell and his band of men right through into the wild blue yonder. That is because, in the absence of a real political alternative, the dissenting Labour vote *could* become a reckless, burn-the-controls, all-out-for-Jack rout, capable of sustaining a permanent Tory majority.

Why? Because the straight play for ambition and status which the press and the mass media make reflects certain real elements in the social pattern of post-war Britain. This reality, which the media distort, is less a matter of consumer goods than we think, and more a matter of our social thinking, our attitude towards ourselves and our society.

The working-class teenage generation which has an annual spending power today of £900,000,000 has not become middle-class: they dress differently, they are more sophisticated and casual – but they are still resolutely, unchallengeably 'working-class'. Why should that be so? Isn't it because they are still, as a social group, wage-earners rather than salary-drawers? Their social consciousness still affected by the place of work (though less so than before), where the relationship between employer and employee remains a stubborn fact of life? They have used their independence to become less conformist in an adult sense, less servile to authority, liking to be petted and pushed and fed and fixed *less* rather than more? They would like to get on: money assumes a central place in their thinking: the radiogram or the motor-cycle is as important a key in their lives as the motor-car or the telly has become in the working-class home. But few of them *identify* themselves with middle-class youngsters of the same age, or share their tastes, or talk in the same way, or feel they have access to the same ends of our culture. Social attitudes in a class-stratified culture are more firmly placed, and cannot be blurred simply by a plethora of 'good things'. Similarly, the new skilled working class in the new town is still a *working* class. The new house may absorb more time and energy, holidays may be more frequent, more regular, take the family farther afield: but the central pattern of life holds together through these major changes in income and environment.

It seems ridiculous, then, to speak of the working class as if it was becoming 'bourgeois', without qualifying that judgment. But the qualifications are substantial, and lead us in a different direction.

If it is true that the skilled worker is becoming part of what Mark Abrams recently called 'The Home-centred Society', the loss is not a loss of a good man 'to the other side', but a loss in the quality of the new working-class community itself. A pride in the home is a just and proper human value, and one, incidentally, central to working-class culture: but a *home-centred* society will be one driven in upon itself to a dangerous degree, and involving a general loss to the community life as a whole. It depends upon the emphasis, and we must be careful how we reckon up gain and loss in this process. The working-class 'community' was a warm, friendly place, familiar, with concrete relationships between the home and the neighbourhood: it was also, often, a cluttered, cramped, inconvenient slum, without light or change, a limiting and narrowing place in which to bring up one's children. There have been gains as well as losses.

The urgent question – cultural in form but, ultimately, political in implication – is whether the values and virtues of the old communities can be transposed into the new physical environments. The prospects are, rather, that, as the sharper divisions of class disappear, the society will grade itself out into a series of status groups, involving the loss of the old community sense without anything more satisfying or rewarding to take its place. And where these changes are going through, what should be taking our attention is not the smooth shift to middle-class attitudes, but the coarsening and loss of working-class values when faced with the appeals to individualism and selfishness of a revived, status-conscious capitalism. What is *there* is not 'the distinct symptoms even of a middle-class psychology' – but a loss of any social psychology at all – any coherent picture of where people *are* and so what values they can affirm: a crisis in the psychology of the working class itself, and therefore, in extension of that, a crisis in the labour movement.

The politics of life

It is important to get this right, because this is the changing social background to politics today. It is also important because there has always been a deep, if complex, relationship between working-class attitudes and the conscious movement towards socialism. The central subjective distinction between the two 'interests' in society has been the distinction, beginning in experience and extending into political action, between the working-class attitude to sharing and community, and the bourgeois attitude to competition: the one fed into and gave meaning to such political concepts as co-operation and common ownership: the other gave rise to the veneration of the market, individualism and 'equality of opportunity'.

In so far, then, as the 'ladders of success' and the notion of 'getting on' in its bourgeois form *do* reach into working-class life, and we use education and other social processes to clamber over one another, so the 'springs of action' in the working-class communities, new or old, are weakened. If education is simply, as *The Sunday Times* puts it, a series of 'Ladders Of Opportunity', then we shall have yielded up one of our central values – the concept that education is to enlarge our capacities as *people* – and taken over a more meretricious attitude towards education, as a process for personal advancement, another form of status-striving.

It has always been *politics* in this largest sense, which was able to convert 'ways of life' into forms of social living. In this sense, the labour movement – for all its weaknesses – has in the past *stood in place of* the finest of these attitudes, caught up and carried through all that was *best* in the *worst* of the working-class communities, giving 'the best in all of us' a consciously worked-out vision of how the society *as a whole* could be better, and what we would have to do to make it so. In that sense, socialism has always been a *vision* which began in *experience*, and politics has been the form of the link between the two.

> The real business of Socialists is to impress on the workers the fact that they are a class, whereas they ought to be Society.
>
> William Morris, *Commonweal*, July 1885

Once again, as the society adjusts to changing, shaping forces, the task for socialism is to take up, in a concrete way, and give political expression to the 'best that is in us'. In that sense, the changes in working-class life and attitudes are *gains*, not losses, in the main: and where there has been loss, in quality, in direction, in emphasis, the task of the labour movement is to challenge and confront at the source the substitutes and blandishment which we are offered. The labour movement ought to be open now to the expanding horizons which working people have fought for by their own struggle, speaking in the name of those changes, standing in their place. But instead what we have is this:

> In short, the changing character of labour, full employment, new housing, the new way of life based on the telly, the fridge, the car and the glossy magazines – all have their effect on our political strength.
>
> Mr Gaitskell, Blackpool Conference

The *way of life* based on the telly and the glossy magazines? Life? Has the labour movement, through the fire and brimstone of the last fifty years, to lie down and die before the glossy magazines? Has Labour no sense of the capacities, the potential of a society, more various, more skilled, more literate, less cramped and confined, less beaten down and frustrated? So that now, we are going to fade away in front of the telly and the fridge?

What we have before us in Mr Gaitskell's speech is nothing short of a tragic failure in political imagination. For without the movement of politics to give the new aspirations of the new groups in society direction and clarity, the danger is that the society, unable to cross the social barriers raised before it by capitalism, will harden into a mediocre meritocracy. Gradually, the elites will draw more and more from within their own ranks: the ways to the top will sift and separate us according to our talents, helping to develop the acquisitive, self-aggrandising instincts, shutting off the generosities of our culture, our social responses to life. The whole notion of community responsibility one for another could, with another round of *this* kind of prosperity, disappear from politics as a force. We should be left, then, with competing political firms, shuffling out the same goods, expending vast sums of money to achieve what the detergent manufacturers call 'marginal differentiation in the product'. That is not where we *are*: but it is certainly where we are going.

Only in projecting a new kind of community, a new kind of social consciousness, can the Labour Party offer anything distinctive and positive. It may take a long time, and some may be impatient for power and therefore restive. But, short of ruin or folly, this is the only way in which the Labour Party can now ever win, and it is not after all anything out of the tradition that is being offered: Labour came into existence, not as an alternative party to run this society, but as a means of making a different society. Experience teaches, and we may have to wait some time, though the present balance is in fact quite delicate and could easily be disturbed. But, short or long, the use of the future is evident: basic analysis, basic education, basic democratic organisation.[8]

The only question is whether we can do it in time.

Notes

1. See John Hughes, 'Steel Nationalisation and Political Power', *New Reasoner*, 1958.
2. See K. Alexander, 'Power at the base', in E.P. Thompson (ed), *Out of Apathy* [the book in which this essay also first appeared]; see also 'The Insiders: Michael Barratt Brown on "The Controllers"', in *ULR 5, 6, 7*; and Peter Shore's 'Room at the Top' in *Conviction*.
3. John Strachey *Contemporary Capitalism*, Gollancz 1956.
4. See K. Alexander and J. Hughes, *A Socialist Wages Plan*, New Left Booklet 1959, Chaps. 1 and 2.
5. See Peter Worsley, 'Outside the whale', also in E.P. Thompson (ed), *Out of Apathy*.
6. Secondary-modern schools were the schools attended by students (the

great majority) who had not passed the selection test for grammar schools (the '11-plus' examination). These schools were less well funded than the grammar schools and students attending them were regarded as 'not academic'.

7. The Devlin Commission was set up by the Macmillan government to inquire into events in Nyasaland (now Malawi) in 1958, after heavy repression by the colonial authorities against those opposed to the imposed federation with Rhodesia. The report was very critical of the government, and, in turn, the government rejected its findings.

8. Raymond Williams, 'Class and Voting in Britain', *Monthly Review*, January 1980.

The Cuban crisis: trial run or
steps towards peace?

1963*

WAS THE CUBAN crisis the trial-run for a thermonuclear war, or the sort of war-by-other-means which leaves the two contestants more anxious to reach a settlement?[1] Now that the crisis has receded somewhat, and the missiles are dismantled and the bombers on their way home, that is the most serious question of all – how will the crisis be *read*?

In itself, the crisis was disastrous – a naked confrontation of power, directly involving the nuclear deterrent, which moved twice within the space of a week towards the unthinkable. Neither the retrospective nonchalance of Mr Khrushchev nor the coolness of the Kennedy 'high command' is enough to convince one that the crisis was wholly under control. Yet the most significant thing about Cuba may turn out to be its *timing*. For Cuba occurred at a time when basic, profound revisions of strategy are being undertaken by both the Americans and the Soviet Union. In the summer, the US formally adopted the 'counterforce strategy'; after a protracted debate, we appear to be moving rapidly now towards the creation of a third nuclear force in Europe.[2] The Soviet Union must soon decide what its response to this rapidly changing strategy is to be. Meanwhile, Berlin, East Germany and the India-China dispute hang fire. These decisions will shape the whole conduct of the Cold War for the next five years. The Cuban shadow has lengthened over them. Either something yields – or we are heading for a showdown in the mid-1960s.

The Cuban crisis was not, in essence, a military, but a political confrontation. As seen from Washington, the Castro regime was 'unacceptable' long before the Soviet missiles arrived. Latin America is, after all, traditionally regarded as the 'back garden' of the US. It has intervened more than once in the last decade to preserve its special

70

interests in the hemisphere. The Cuban revolution was a break in the chain, a challenge to American prestige in the continent, a potential threat to 'stability'. Indeed, ever since the break between Castro and the US, and months before Castro discovered that he was a Marxist, or Soviet technicians arrived in Havana, the US has pursued two objectives in relation to Cuba: (1) to bring down the Castro regime, and (2) to ward off the threat to the other Latin American states.

The US has pursued this line with considerable consistency. It survived a change in Administration – the first invasion was planned under Eisenhower and executed under Kennedy. The construction of Soviet missile sites was *predated* by a new Cuban 'scare', which began to develop again at the beginning of the summer. As early as September, *Time* magazine suggested that the US 'could support military action against Cuba by anti-Communist nations in Latin America … Or – and it may come to this – it could get the job done itself, once and for all'. In this it was rehearsing a theme which had already become respectable in certain American circles. Precisely the same estimates of American policy were made to me when I was in Cuba at the beginning of the year. When we consider why the Cubans should have requested military assistance from the Soviet Union on such a massive scale, we are apt to forget the disastrous invasion at the Bay of Pigs, and the stated American intention to achieve the same end by more effective means.

Soviet missiles *added* a nuclear dimension to an already simmering political crisis. American objectives were then reversed: the aims became (1) to remove the missile threat, and (2) to bring down Castro. The guarantees against invasion which the US was obliged to give in order to get the missiles dismantled have therefore only masked the true nature of the crisis. As *Time* put it again to the President in the week following the crisis, 'as long as he (Castro) is in power, there will be a Caribbean crisis'. Any *real* solution to the Cuban affair, then, must deal with both the short-run and the long-term aspects.

From the Soviet point of view, Cuba is both an opportunity and a challenge. Until the break between Castro and the US, Soviet penetration of the hemisphere had not made much progress. Cuba provided a point of entry into Latin America. But it also offered a dramatic challenge to the strategy of the Khrushchev leadership.

The Chinese 'line' on countries like Cuba is that the Communist powers must take every means, including war if necessary, to extend their influence, and undermine the position of the 'imperialist' powers, via the worldwide nationalist revolutions. Support for these movements, the Chinese argue, should be massive, direct and military. There is no point supporting 'bourgeois nationalists' like Nehru. The strategy is to forward revolutionary movements in the 'Chinese' way – by wars of liberation. Mr Khrushchev argues, however (and he won his point at the meeting of eighty-one Communist Parties in Moscow), that the Communist bloc is now so strong that it can throw its protective nuclear shield across any country struggling to be free. While the Soviet deterrent holds the imperialist challenge at bay, country after country will be detached from Western influence, and the West will be progressively undermined. But Mr Khrushchev is also convinced that nuclear war is too risky to use directly as part of his strategy – though he is willing to match the United States in the use of it as a political threat.

In Cuba, Mr Khrushchev was forced to show how his strategy would work in practice. (At the same moment, the Chinese were giving a cool demonstration of their line in action – the deliberately limited military probe in the Indian highlands.) If the Americans invaded Cuba again, as has seemed inevitable since the reversal at the Bay of Pigs, which policy would be most effective?

Everything turned on Mr Khrushchev's ability to deliver the goods. But could he? At this point, the Cuban crisis 'escalated' into the nuclear sphere, and the question of the 'balance of nuclear power' between East and West played a vital role.

The fact is that, at the moment, Khrushchev does not have the goods. No true nuclear 'balance' exists. It seems quite certain now that the Soviet Union adopted, sometime in the late 1950s, the 'minimum deterrent' position – a purely retaliatory nuclear role, based on a limited strike force, and bolstered by a gigantic space programme. Mr Kennedy, however, rode to power partly on the crest of the widespread fear that a 'missile gap' had been allowed to develop under President Eisenhower. The missile gap, like the bomber gap before it, turned out to be a manufactured illusion. In both delivery and destructive capability, the Americans are well ahead, and have been since the arms race began in earnest. Yet, partly under pressure from the 'military-industrial' complex, Mr Kennedy increased his military budget in 1961-2 (an increase of $3000 million, and, later in the year, another $4000 million), and the 1963 appropriations reveal yet a new leap forward.

In global terms, the Soviet limited deterrent is now under severe pressure. It is small in comparison with the US capacity. Most of its sites are 'soft' – i.e. exposed to military intelligence and U2 overflights. No invulnerable second strike weapon, such as the Polaris sub, has been developed. Faced with what must now seem like a determined American crash programme to keep the lead, the Soviet Union has taken several steps to correct the imbalance, short of creating a huge Inter-Continental Ballistic Missiles force. Thus it brought the U2 flights to a halt, expanded its space programme, rigidly opposed inspection of a Test Ban for fear of espionage, and recently tested weapons in a very high megaton range. But these do not add up to anything remotely approaching nuclear parity.

Locally in the Caribbean, the only way to make good Soviet claims was to bring in to play the only missile weapons which it has in any numbers – Intermediate Range Ballistic Missiles (IRBMs) – and to site them as close to their targets as it could get – in Cuba itself. Hence the hasty construction of missile sites, the clumsy lying of Mr Gromyko to President Kennedy. Hence also the military panic in Washington: the US was at last face to face with a Soviet deterrent threat which, in military terms, really meant something. And so to the crisis itself – quarantine and blockade, threat of invasion and bombing, flash-point.

As well as its political and military significance, the Cuban crisis also had *global* importance. Its repercussions were general and world-wide, as all nuclear crises are. Such a crisis travels like an electrical impulse through the entire circuit of the Cold War. At precisely the same moment as Soviet and American fleets were steaming towards a confrontation on the high seas, Chinese troops were probing the Indian border. Had Mr Khrushchev succeeded in restoring the balance by slipping 40 IRBMs under the net of the Early Warning System, to within striking distance of Washington, Omaha or Cape Canaveral, there is no doubt that this lever would have been used to bring back into the arena of negotiation Berlin and the status of East Germany.

From another point of view, the Cuban crisis had direct repercussions throughout the NATO alliance. In spite of Cabinet pique at the fact that the quarantine decision had been taken without consultation, Proteus [a US nuclear submarine] sailed from its Holy Loch berth 'for an unknown destination', and Strategic Air Command (SAC) bases in Europe were put on first alert. Within the terms of the Alliance, European NATO powers like Britain were directly implicated in the President's actions.

The involvement of the NATO allies in the Cuban crisis was defined by the letter of the North Atlantic Treaty; but it was also a necessary extension of the nuclear logic. Had the interception of the Russian fleet on the high seas developed into a general war, every country with nuclear bases would have been high on Mr Khrushchev's target list. An attempt to forestall attack by a first strike would have involved a Soviet strike at bases in Britain, Turkey, Spain and Morocco *simply because they exist*.

The Cuban crisis had direct repercussions in the Caribbean, but it also, it is clear, enveloped the whole globe. It demonstrated the precise nature of Britain's commitment in its role as a base for the American deterrent and as a junior partner in the Alliance. That commitment, in turn, implied British support for a logically tendentious American policy. For, as the *Economist* pointed out, the US seemed to be arguing that 'a ground-to-ground missile sited with Soviet connivance in the Western hemisphere is "offensive" … whereas an American-controlled missile sited in the Eastern hemisphere is a normal defensive precaution, which the Russians must live with'. Walter Lippman pointed out that America was defending its right to maintain *both* the Monroe Doctrine (which excluded European intervention in the Western hemisphere) *and* the Truman Doctrine (the right to contain Soviet power along the periphery of the Communist world). Britain, and the NATO allies, were, as Lippman remarked, upholding America's right to enforce both doctrines at once, one in each hemisphere.

II

What are the signs that either Mr Kennedy or Mr Khrushchev are taking such steps, in the light of the Cuban affair, as would severely limit the world's exposure to nuclear war?

There are none. Indeed, the pointers are all the other way. After their much-publicised 'baptism of fire', the Kennedy team seem to have adopted a stance of tough-minded realism. The President is still speaking critically of the 'synthetic hard line' which some sections of the press are pushing; but his own outlook, and that of his high command, appears to be (to use his own phrase) 'sombre'. Undoubtedly Mr Gromyko's prevarication did much to destroy what basis of mutual trust might have existed. But the psychological climate is not encouraging. In Europe, the pace seems to have been stepped up. There is a general air of 'business as usual', and a sense of bustle and haste: every day brings a new pronunciation on some aspect of Western strategy, the latest being the Polaris deal.

Last summer, after a protracted debate, the Secretary for Defence, Mr McNamara, announced the adoption of the 'counterforce' strategy. This means that, in the weapons field, not only is Cuba to be followed by a development in the *scale* and *instability* of the deterrent (a first-strike strategy), but also by the *spread* of weapons and the creation of a third nuclear force. Meanwhile nothing whatsoever has moved in relation to the proposed Draft Disarmament Treaty (the only hope of scaling down the deterrent), and the positions of the two sides in relation to a Test Ban appear, after Cuba, unchanged.

Nor has there been any approach made to the points of political tension. The idea of Disengagement in Central Europe – the only way of lifting the pressure from Europe *without* European nuclear rearmament – has been dropped. Indeed, for the first time since the Rapacki Plan was proposed, the British Government has come out openly against the proposal.[3] No further approach has been made on the question of Berlin since the President's meeting with Dr Adenauer. Now that the Kennedy policy of 'negotiation from strength' seems, in Washington, to have paid off, no move on Berlin will be made – until Mr Khrushchev begins to worry at the problem, like a dentist with a loose tooth, some time next year.

The post-Cuba situation, then, gives absolutely no sign of an opening towards a *detente*, in either the political or military sphere. What we face instead this winter is a series of decisions which will harden the position all round – the prospect of a new splurge in the arms race, the spread of nuclear weapons to Europe, a possible resumption of the crisis in the Caribbean, a certain confrontation in Central Europe next year, with the two adversaries geared up for an exchange on the basis of first-strike strategies. An exceedingly bleak outlook.

III

The conflict between East and West seems to move with a certain established rhythm. Each crisis is followed by basic revisions of policy and strategy – and each time the intensity of the struggle is revised *upwards.* After the Berlin Air-Lift, the American 'crash programme' on the hydrogen bomb; after Korea, the doctrine of 'massive retaliation'; now, after Cuba, the era of 'counterforce'. The problem is that those who are opposed to this consistent escalation of the level of danger are never precise enough about their proposals, do not direct their challenge to the particular decisions which are about to be taken. Suppose, then, we were to pose a precise alternative route which might take us away from a nuclear show-down in the mid-1960s. What would our demands be?

The advantage of this kind of programmatic approach is that it enables public opinion generally, and the peace movements in particular, *to confront directly* the decisions which political and military establishments make. The precondition of such an approach, however, is that we see it as a process – slow, perhaps, and dangerous at each stage: but *less* dangerous as the process gathers momentum, rather than more dangerous, which is the actual prospect which we face now.

I. The first priority is to prevent a new spiral in the arms race, and to get instead some immediate reduction in the level at which the nuclear 'balance' is maintained. The only prospect of doing this seems to be through a First Stage Disarmament agreement, with proper inspection and control guarantees. This seems a good way off, but it will be even more difficult once the counterforce strategy has been adopted in full by both sides. Thus what we need is *an enforced pause* in the build-up, a postponement of the counterforce crash programme, and the maintenance by both sides of a *limited deterrent* posture, at least until the chances of a Disarmament Agreement can be further explored. The object here is *not* to stabilise the deterrent, but to bring the two sides into line, at a fairly low deterrent level, so that agreed disarmament is easier to reach and quicker to begin. It would be excellent if U Thant, as Secretary General of the body to which the Disarmament Subcommittee is directly responsible, could point out the way in which the counterforce strategy is likely to sabotage the chances at Geneva: and if he could mobilise, for this purpose, a precise expression of world opinion.

2. The most important corollary of the adoption of a limited deterrent position by the two sides is that a strict embargo must be placed on the spread of weapons to Europe, in either a NATO or European deterrent form. Thus the President should be strengthened in his opposition to the spread of weapons to Europe. Here, the role of the European

allies is *crucial* – especially Britain. A measure of unilateral disarmament by Britain – the abandonment of its militarily inconsequential national deterrent – would be one step which could be taken unilaterally against spread. The strong and active opposition by Britain to the creation of a third nuclear force in Europe would be another. The French are less likely to play, but they will not have a delivery system of any scale until the late 1960s, by which time an agreed Disarmament Treaty might be in force: and France cannot create a credible deterrent by itself, or with West Germany, without American assistance, or British know-how, though General De Gaulle seems to think he can.

3. The two proposals made so far would have the effect of enforcing a pause in the nuclear build-up; reducing the level of weapons; and confining, in the first stage, nuclear weapons to the two major powers. To complete the confinement of weapons on a minimum deterrent basis, and to deal with what, from the point of view of the Soviet Union, must be one of the essential bargaining points, it would be necessary to begin to phase out overseas strategic nuclear bases. A minimum deterrent force does not require the scatter of nuclear bases which the US at present maintains: it has enough inter-continental range delivery capacity to maintain the limited deterrent from the American heartland. Further, if we have learned anything from the Cuban episode, it is that foreign nuclear bases, whether strategic (such as SAC bases in Britain and Jupiter missiles in Turkey), intermediate (such as Soviet missiles in Cuba) or tactical (such as the tactical nuclear equipment of Soviet troops stationed in East Germany), constitute a real and present threat to peace. If strategic nuclear bases were phased out, it would mean a withdrawal of the retaliatory strike capacity of both sides to the heartland of America and the Soviet Union, pending disarmament measures. One of the problems involved in such a move is that the two strategies of the major powers involved are asymmetric – the Soviet Union is strong on the ground in Europe, but weak in inter-continental hardware; for the Americans the situation is precisely the reverse. But a rational quid-pro-quo system could be worked out – with an American conventional strength maintained in Europe *for a time* while strategic bases go, in return for the withdrawal of tactical nuclear weapons from the Soviet forces which remain outside of the territory of Russia itself.

4. This would leave unresolved the problem of the defence of Western Europe. But this is where the question of Disengagement in

Central Europe comes in. From the Soviet viewpoint, the threat in Europe arises from the strategic bases on its periphery. But if these are to go progressively, then, from the American and European point of view, the Russians will be left with an overwhelming conventional strength in Europe. The only way, then, to complete the pause, would be to establish, along the lines of the Eden, Gaitskell or Rapacki Plans, a Zone of Controlled Disengagement, with effective United Nations inspection and guarantees, in Central Europe. From both a political and a military point of view, Disengagement is the *pivot* of the whole scheme. This Zone would be both non-nuclear and demilitarised – i.e. involving the withdrawal of Soviet ground forces to the heartland of the Soviet Union.

If the price for this is the maintenance, for a time, of a *conventional* American force in, say, France or Britain, to match Soviet strength confined to Russia, then we should be willing to pay it. In fact, the Russians might well be willing to consider, at the same time as military withdrawal from Central Europe is being undertaken, a cut in conventional strength in return for an American limited deterrent posture: its proposals for the reduction of conventional armies in the First Stage of its Draft Disarmament Treaty is higher than that proposed by the US – a reduction to 1.7 million, as against 2.1 million – in spite of its acknowledged strength in this field.

5. The major outstanding problem in the way of an agreement to disengage in Central Europe is, of course, Berlin. Any such settlement must, inevitably, involve a new approach to the Berlin problem. With the withdrawal of American and Soviet forces from Central Europe, certain precise guarantees must be given in relation to Berlin. This can only be by way of a UN guarantee for the freedom of West Berlin, perhaps by a UN presence in the city, with the right of access to the city guaranteed by four power-plus-UN-plus East and West German agreement. This would involve not only the de facto recognition of the East German Government, as a party to the agreement, but, more sensibly, the admission of the two Germanies to full member status of the guaranteeing authority, the UN.

6. If we could move towards some such a pause in the political and military build-up, it would then be possible, in more gradual stages, to keep nuclear weapons out of the rest of the world. Here again, the approach would have to be two-fold. Primarily, there is the question of China's nuclear capability. There may be no way now of stopping the

creation of a Chinese nuclear force, but it will take some time for it to develop a delivery capability. What we have been envisaging here is a gradual approach towards a *detente* in Europe and a First Stage Disarmament Treaty agreement. There is certainly no way of making such a Disarmament agreement hold, unless it is global in its effect: and no way of making it global, and subject to UN inspection and control, unless China can be a party to it – i.e. unless and until it is a full member of the UN. It is not perhaps cynical to comment that we can judge the seriousness of American intentions in the disarmament field by its maintained opposition to the entry of China to the UN. While the US opposes this, it *cannot* believe that 'general and complete' disarmament is anything but a propaganda phrase.

More generally, there is the question of keeping the rest of the world – much of it facing the task of industrialisation – free from the nuclear burden. Here the general climate would be considerably improved if, within the framework of the UN, the denuclearisation of those parts of the globe not directly implicated in the East-West conflict could be negotiated. Proposals already exist in relation to some areas: Latin America (the Brazil proposal); Scandinavia (the Unden Plan); the Balkans (the Yugoslavs have made suggestions here); the Southern Hemisphere (the Australian Labour Party once proposed a comprehensive plan); and Africa (see the Accra Assembly proposals). Both Draft Treaties propose the neutralisation of Outer Space. Other areas – the Middle East, South-East Asia – could be considered. This would be a more gradual extension of the terms of a *detente*, but vital for those areas which are now threatened with nuclear penetration.

IV

What we have done so far is to sketch, in relation to the existing contingencies of the global conflict after Cuba, the areas in which negotiations are vital, and the kinds of steps which would *limit* rather than *extend* the nuclear conflict. We have tried to relate these proposals to the actual decisions which, if we read the signs correctly, are about to be taken in the pursuit of the Cold War. We have tried to make those demands as precise as possible, since this is, in our view, the only effective way to 'speak truth to power', the only kind of opposition to the military thinking of the two camps which makes sense. We have envisaged them as steps in a process. They represent *less* than we could hope for, but *more* than we can reasonably expect, given the post-Cuba climate. We point again and again to the crucial fact – that winter and spring 1962-3 is a period of basic revision and decision, and that what matters most now is *which alternative we can force governments to choose*: the path, via 'counterforce', the arms race and Berlin, towards nuclear holocaust, or the alternative route towards agreed disarmament. This is a fateful transition period in the Cold War: only the force of popular opinion, and the most intensive study and analysis, can sway the balance. What is most urgently needed is the general mobilisation of public opinion behind the *second* alternative, and a direct engagement between the peace movements and the military-political establishments of both the Soviet and the Western Alliances. Our job is to enforce a pause, and to turn the tide. The demands must be concrete, specific and precise. The mobilisation of opinion and pressure must be international. The opportunity is limited, and the time for action is *now*.

Specifically, how does this proposal relate to Britain? What are the chances, for example, of action on some of these steps from the British government? The answer seems to be – very little. The government accepted its subordinate role in Cuba with ill grace: but it followed blindly along the path laid down by the terms of the NATO Alliance. The British deterrent, which was designed to 'prevent us from going into the conference chamber naked' was not a strong enough weapon of diplomacy during the Cuban crisis, as Mr Grimmond remarked, even to get us *into* the conference chamber. Yet the British government seems wedded to the deterrent – in fact, willing, as the price of entry into Europe, to consider merging the British effort with the French and the West Germans in a European nuclear force.

What of the Labour Party? Here the situation is different, and the balance is changing. The Common Market dispute has placed on the agenda several questions of foreign and defence policy which the party hoped it had ditched for ever with the defeat of the unilateralists at Scarborough. Thus, in his Common Market speech, Mr Gaitskell again and again used the phrase 'independent foreign policy' – though he has nowhere made that term precise in its application. Apparently, the Labour Party is still opposed to the British national deterrent. They seem now, after the NATO Parliamentarians meeting, also opposed to a third European nuclear force. In his exchange with Mr Heath, Mr

Gaitskell expressed great concern at the hardening of the government's attitude towards Disengagement in Europe. The feeling in the party leadership seems to have crystallised against a close European political and military alignment. All these are straws in the wind. The leadership is woolly in relation to each of them, perhaps for electoral reasons: they have never been gathered together into a programme of *related demands*, a programme around which support could be actively mobilised. That is certainly a task for those within the party who are seriously concerned about the post-Cuba turn of events. It is not necessary for CND, as it did four years ago, to become embroiled in an inner-Labour-Party fight. But it would be nothing short of a disaster if, because of its experience at Scarborough, CND should abdicate the political struggle for a more marginal role, at precisely the time when such crucial political decisions are being taken.

The fragmentary and hesitant approach of the Opposition to these questions is matched in public opinion generally. But Cuba undoubtedly gave the more complacent or the less rigid a severe jolt. Thus, to judge simply from the press response, *some* of the steps outlined above would meet with moderate support from certain sections of the public, if only CND were willing to make common cause, from its own independent and non-aligned position, with them. For the first time, during the crisis, the *Sunday Times* accepted CND's pessimistic interpretation of a policy based on the deterrent. In that same week, the *Observer* called, in an extended editorial, for several of the 'steps towards peace' which we have outlined above. *The Times*, surprisingly, responded critically towards the idea of a European deterrent. Again, these are straws in the wind; the serious British press is notoriously cautious – the only really critical comment on the new counterforce strategy came from James Cameron in the *Herald*. The other papers sanctimoniously recorded Mr McNamara's views, including the incredible welcome which he gave to another round of Soviet rearmament. Yet the very uncertainty of press comment reflects, in our view, an increasing awareness of the present nuclear dangers, and, in the light of Cuba, a break-up of the traditionally hostile attitude towards the Campaign. We must go out to meet this body of opinion, and seek to mobilise support within it for the limited steps which we propose to counter the race towards the brink.

What, specifically, are we asking *Britain* to do, to ensure that steps are made towards peace along the lines of our proposals? In certain cases, there are unilateral measures which Britain could take to facilitate and hasten the *detente*. In other cases, British pressure could be vital. In any event, it is essential to clarify the imprecise phrase, 'an independent foreign policy'.

Unilaterally, Britain could (1) abandon its independent national deterrent, as a step towards the limitation of nuclear weapons to the US and the USSR and as a move to prevent the spread of weapons to Europe; (2) oppose the creation of a third nuclear force, either in a European or a NATO form; (3) oppose the maintenance of strategic nuclear bases and installations in Britain, as a way of enforcing upon the US a more limited nuclear posture. By way of direct pressure, Britain could (1) give every support to the idea of Disengagement in Central Europe, including precise proposals; (2) strongly oppose the full adoption of a counterforce policy by the United States; (3) support a solution to the Berlin problem along the lines suggested above. These, at any rate, are concrete objectives to work for – objectives which the peace movement and CND must take the initiative in popularising. But active British support for such steps implies a degree of independence which, the Cuban crisis suggests, does not at the moment obtain. The crisis revealed once again the conflict between our obligations to the UN under the Charter, and our obligations under the NATO alliance. Many of us believe that conflict to be both ineradicable and dangerous, and would choose the UN even if it meant withdrawal from the Alliance. Many others, who go with us some of the way, would not go so far. But what is necessary is agreement on certain limited steps which can be taken now. What we can surely all agree upon is that, in any given case, our obligations to the UN take precedence over our commitments to our alliances, pacts or treaties. We must define much more precisely what the area of independent action is, given our Treaty obligations: and take steps to ensure that the Alliance, which asks of us simply a sleeping role during a crisis, does not prevent us taking an active and independent role in *creating the conditions for peace*. Thus, if we must choose between supporting Disengagement and maintaining the harmony of the alliance with West Germany, Disengagement has first priority. If we are implicated in a crisis at the behest of the American President, we will act, as the 42 neutral nations did during Cuba, to strengthen the hand of the Secretary General of the UN, not tacitly support rash action on the high seas. This reordering of priorities is the precondition of an independent foreign policy.

An independent initiative for peace is what is most needed, not simply in general terms, but to counteract the particular trend which shows active life since the Cuban crisis. Such an initiative is not a matter for political leaders, but for the whole community of publics which constitute the nation. To mobilise such an overwhelming pressure of public opinion, the case must be understood, the fateful procession of events precisely prejudged, the support for *particular measures* clear and sharp. We must build bridges to every support in the country – taking them step by step with us as far as they are willing to go. If *The Times* cold-shoulders every proposal we make *except* the opposition to a European deterrent, then even such limited support is to be welcomed. On the basis of these precise points, and the logic which lies behind them, we have to challenge and confront every group, organisation and individual in the country. On the basis of these proposals, we can make common cause with the other non-aligned peace movements which have begun to grow – with the American peace movement in our opposition to counterforce, with the German Easter marchers in our support for a solution to Berlin, with the Poles on Disengagement, with the Africans and the Scandinavians on Denuclearised Zones. That is what 'government by default' means today. The danger is that, while we stand on the sidelines waving our slogans hopefully, with the best will in the world, the nuclear parade is passing us by.

Notes

1. The US government were hostile to the leadership of Cuba after the revolution of 1959, and this pushed the Cuban government towards alliance with the Soviet Union. The Soviet Union saw an opportunity to base nuclear missiles within striking distance of the US, as tit-for-tat for US missiles based near its own borders in Europe. When the US government realised that missiles were being based in Cuba they imposed a naval blockade on Cuba, in October 1962, to enforce a 'quarantine' on all offensive military equipment under shipment to Cuba. At this point there were global fears of a nuclear war breaking out, but in the end Kennedy and Khrushchev came to an agreement based on the missiles being removed and Kennedy promising not to invade Cuba.

2. A counterforce strategy is one that is based on targeting the enemy's military capacity rather than its population. Previously deterrence had been centred wholly on Mutually Assured Destruction (MAD). One implication of counterforce strategy was a willingness to engage in a first strike. Robert McNamara was the pioneer of this strategy, and it was also linked to the idea of a European deterrent, either within NATO or based on French and British nuclear weapons.

3. The Rapacki Plan was for a denuclearised zone in parts of Eastern Europe.

Political commitment

1966

I AM NOT GOING to make a case for political commitment. There is
no simple 'case' of this kind to make. To formulate the question in
this way is to suggest that arguments can be advanced in favour of one
political party within an already clearly-defined pattern of political
interests. But what is at issue just now is not so much the clash of
clearly defined political positions but, rather, the formation of political consciousness itself. 'Political man' in the old sense is a
fast-disappearing species. This is not a matter of politics in the narrow
sense. Political consciousness is closely linked with the sense which a
society makes of its own life, actions, experiences, history: with social
consciousness, and with the dominant structure of feeling and attitude which prevails at any particular time. It is with this relationship,
primarily, that this paper will be concerned.

There is no point in trying to answer the question about commitment by reference to the policies adopted by political parties,
since the role of political parties in the formation of consciousness
(as opposed to the struggle for electoral succession) has itself become
one of the problematic issues of our time. Nor will it do to take refuge
in some unrevised ideology, since this is the age of the reversal of the
great ideologies, the transvaluation of political world-views. On the
other hand, there is no point in trying to get behind the issues by
speaking in personal terms, without allowing for the fact that a giving
of the whole self to politics, the harnessing and orchestrating of one's
life around a political commitment, is a stance adopted by fewer and
fewer people – least of all by full-time politicians: it is a personal style
which runs against the grain of contemporary feeling and attitudes.

We have to start by trying to define the political sensibility of the
period. Or rather, the absence of a political sensibility. There seems to
me several good reasons why political consciousness should prove so
elusive at this time.

First, there is the rapidly changing social and economic background of society. About this, contradictory things can be said, and contradictory inferences drawn. But, undeniably, changes in social life have unhinged the older forms of political consciousness, while illusions about what has actually happened as a result of those changes have as yet prevented the formation of a new political awareness.

The second factor I have mentioned already: namely the transformation of the great ideologies of the past, and the conditions within which they flourished. One has only to think of the contortions which ideologists of 'the west' go through in order to make the realities of welfare capitalism fit the old rhetoric of liberalism to understand how powerfully events have transformed the great bourgeois ideologies of the past. The development of 'polycentrism' in the east, the Sino-Soviet dispute, and – on a more ideological plane – the separation which has been taking place between 'marxism' and 'Soviet society', point to the same phenomenon in communist societies. And the revival of nationalism in the third world has upset most ideological calculations.

The third factor is, undoubtedly, the dominance in recent history of two major camps east and west of the iron curtain: and, more precisely, the fact that these camps have constituted groupings in the politico-economic, the military and the ideological senses. In the old world, ideas followed trade and trade followed the flag. In the new world, it could be said that political ideas have clustered around the weapons systems. All the factors which, until the impact of the revolutions in the third world, kept these military-economic groupings together have also served to keep the politics of the two blocs in straitjackets.

The fourth factor is the transformation of the nature of politics itself in the advanced capitalist societies. This is sometimes defined in terms of the maturing of mass political parties – though it could also be interpreted as their decline. It is also sometimes defined in terms of the collapse or the breakdown of the recognised agencies of change.

The fifth factor is related to this change in the character of politics in the 'advanced' world: it might be called the rise of the 'new issues' in politics – issues which are 'new' in the sense that they appear, falsely, as 'non-political'; or cannot be interpreted as arising directly from the clash of traditional social interests. Such an issue is the issue of race in advanced societies; such a new interest group is the group loosely designated as 'youth'.

The sixth factor is what has been described as the ideology of the end-of-ideologies. This is different from the very real sense which people might have that none of the old ideological pictures now offer an acceptable image of how modern societies work. It is, rather, the belief that there is something inherently wrong in seeking ideological models and explanations at all: that modern technological society renders all ideology obsolescent. Within this framework of thinking, ideologies are always described as holistic, millenarian, violent, apocalyptic: whereas politics is practical, pragmatic, middle-ranged, the art of the possible. In some ways, this attempt to drive a wedge between politics and political theory, between piecemeal engineering and social revolution, is the most dynamic ideology we have in 'the west'.

One of the most striking developments of the end-of-ideology ideology in recent years is the attempt to sociologise out of existence the political sensibility. I do not mean the fact that in the journals, the press, and the media of comment, it is now *de rigeur* to refer political events to their sociological background. Provided this does not become an intellectual fetish, it is a perfectly proper procedure. I mean the process by which politics is degutted and neutered by always being presented as a form of social inquiry. Nowadays, for example, university students, who are often chary of overt political commitment, are only too willing to run a survey instead. I am not despising facts, or the discovery of facts. Provided they are selected with a sense of relevance, facts can be revolutionary things. But they are seldom revolutionary in a vacuum. And although one can understand why young people who find themselves in a confused social situation will want to learn to describe their society more accurately, there isn't much to be said for continually throwing up descriptions of the society which never lead into social or political action. What is more, the social inquiry approach has a strong tendency to make people the objects rather than the agents of change. By demoting the role of human agency, it robs the situation of its historical dimensions and of its potential for change. To use the distinction drawn in a recent article by David Cooper ('Violence In Psychiatry,' *Views*, Summer 1965), this approach is characteristic of a whole group of disciplines in the field of social explanation, which make human behaviour 'explicable', but not 'intelligible in terms of what people are actually doing to each other'. Consequently, for all the refinement of measurement involved, the descriptions of our society accumulated in this way lack agency, historical perspective, existential meaning, or a proper subjectivity. Instead what seems to reign as a dominant mood in the whole intellectual climate just at present is a spurious search for 'objectivity', a bogus pseudo-scientism. Such an intellectual climate – especially when mediated to an even wider public by the press and the journals – is one covertly hostile to politics.

A more direct expression of the same trend is the reduction of political issues to the psephological equation. Again, we are told that this represents a sophistication of method – and so it does. But every methodological advance has its ideological content. It is one thing to be able to test more accurately the balance of political forces at any one time. It is quite another thing to allow this technique so to dominate the scene that politics itself becomes a question of 'sampling' the state of public opinion as it exists, an elaborate process of echoing back to the electorate what it already knows – sugared, of course, by effective methods of presentation, and the right party 'image'. The point about this model of politics is that it omits the praxis of politics – the whole dynamic by which latent human needs are expressed in political terms and, by being formulated, become the conscious demands of a section of the society, around whom a political agitation can be built, maintained, and carried. Of course this is the radical model of politics: it is the conservative model which, on principle, believes that politics means manoeuvring the status quo. But it is precisely because this conserving model of politics has come, in the last decade, to be the dominant model of political action, among both conservative and radical groupings in society (and especially in the political parties), that potential agitations continually wind their way harmlessly out into the sands, and the Labour Party, especially, finds itself confined and constrained by the whole framework of assumptions. Psephology itself is not responsible for this change in the character of politics. But it is part of a mosaic of influences, all of which appear to have the effect of legitimising the change – of making it seem inevitable, and, because inevitable, right.

The phrase 'the absence of political sensibility' is not intended just as a descriptive comment. It is part of the logic of the model of politics which both sides in the party political game have decided to work. I am trying to indicate something more active than merely a general withdrawal from political engagement. After all, people do still support and work for good causes, and most of the good causes are, in the long run, good political causes. But it is not their political character which attracts the support. Quite the reverse. The politics of what I have called the 'new issues' is the politics of the unpoliticised. It is not unfair to cite the Oxfam campaign (since the organisation itself is acutely aware of the problem) as an example of a good cause which has won significant support, both in terms of money and of mobilised energies (and voluntary service overseas and Freedom From Hunger are parts of the same structure of feeling), but which attracts support partly because it treats a political issue (the gap between the rich and poor nations) in a non-political way. Objectively this kind of campaign has done a great deal of good. It has also helped, in a subtle way, to de-politicise for some part of the British people the issue of poverty in the third world.

It is the de-politicisation, the defusing, of hot issues which is so striking. Take an instance of the same process in a different sphere. Radicals are always trying to define the 'establishment' bias of the media, especially BBC television, in terms of partiality to Conservative as against Labour spokesmen. In most cases this version of the argument is hard to substantiate. The fact is that the bias of the media is in favour of 'the system' – to which both political parties now belong. It operates most effectively against any manifestation or development which cannot be contained within this framework of organised neutrality. One instance of this is the reporting in the press (with the notable exception, on occasions, of the *Guardian*) of the activities of the Campaign for Nuclear Disarmament. These are presented either as an aspect of 'Easter madness' or in terms of the number of Labour MPs who have spoken from CND platforms (that is with reference to the existing modus vivendi). Operating on the basis of this bias, it isn't unfair to suggest that the British press would have missed such events as the formation of the Labour Party in the 1890s, on the grounds that nothing of real political significance could possibly be happening outside the Tory-Liberal seesaw. An even better – because subtler – example is the BBC television programme *Gallery*. Here is an excellent programme of its kind, serious, informed, purposeful, under Ian Trethowan's capable chairmanship. It is only in relation to issues outside the formalised political game that his touch is less sure: the most notorious example being his crude partisanship over the matter of the Vietnam 'teach-ins'.

The rigidity with which the existing body of 'workable' assumptions controls the flow and formation of opinion, and hence the formation of consciousness, is peculiarly an aspect of politics in the industrialised world. In the emergent societies every issue is a political issue, and all sections of the community – revolutionaries and reactionaries alike – are aware of how immediately every opinion, attitude, every nuance of class, status and economic interest, can be cashed in the political arena. These are societies of instant politics. This is not to say that there is always a true and meaningful disclosure of the political interests at play. But one problem these societies do not seem to have is how to keep the political instinct alive.

Not infrequently, at this point, people tend to fall back on an easy romanticisation of the past. They speak as if we have left behind a golden age when the majority of people were fully and continuously politicised. In fact, in the nineteenth century, from which so much of this imagery is drawn, political consciousness was neither stable nor 'given'. It was made – made, changed, remade – from one period to another, and in the praxis of men. True, it is in this period that we can for the first time speak of the formation of the working class: but we cannot speak of the formation of the working-class consciousness. That consciousness changed as industrialisation and the social system of industrial society itself changed; it changed in line with its own human traditions, its own kinds of organisation, its own culture. We can see particular historical moments when a certain kind of consciousness was achieved, partly in the lived experience of men, partly because of the active minority. We can see the confrontations between this and the hostile consciousness of the opposing classes and interests – confrontations when the issue could have gone either way. We can see the conflicts fought through. And, the 'moment' having passed, we can see the apparent disengagement of the forces of struggle, and the dissolving of that form of consciousness, its surpassing by the 'real movement of history'. Such forms of consciousness are never permanent – now it is with the Jacobins of the clubs and the corresponding societies, now with the men of the charter, now with the utopians and co-operators, now with the militants of the sects, now with the new unionists. Such forms of consciousness did not 'happen'. They were achieved, carried at great personal cost, sometimes lost amidst great personal distress, in the active lives of men and women. The record of one such historical 'moment' has recently been given in E.P. Thompson's *The Making of The English Working Class*.[1] That moving account alone should do something to dissolve the mechanistic manner in which forms of consciousness and of struggle are commonly discussed today, on every side of the political fence (not excluding the far left). It should do something to correct the perspective we bring to bear on our own period.

I think there is a strong case to be made that we are now, in the strict sense of the word, in a transitional period between two stages in political consciousness: a transition marked not so much by the break-up of all the forces which constitute the basis of politics in British life, but rather by the break-up and fragmentation of one stage or epoch in consciousness and the formation of another. We need to understand the nature of this transition better than we do.

A good deal of work has been going on in the last decade which represents an effort to describe and to evaluate what has been happening to the society since the war. These changes concern the whole range of social and economic relationships in the society.

Much of this work is predicated upon the assumption that Britain has entered a 'post-capitalist' phase where – as a result of post-war affluence, the progressive separation of ownership from control in industry, the regulation of economic life by state intervention, the countervailing power of labour, and the redistribution of income via the welfare revolution – sharp disparities of power, wealth, and opportunity endemic in earlier stages in capitalist society have been markedly levelled. Secondly, the break-up of the old pattern of life and culture associated with working-class experience, and the shift in the occupational structure, are said to have brought about a decisive change in the political outlook and aspirations the mass of working people, and especially of the manual working class. Thirdly, the spread of middle-class patterns of life, the penetration of the mass media and the taking on of consumption values has led to a cultural dilution, which has seriously disturbed the values, the pattern of aspirations, and hence the basis of radical consciousness in society. Fourthly, that as a result of the large-scale organisation characteristic of this stage of economic development, patterns of conflict are becoming less those which can be attributed to conflicts of class interest, and increasingly are conflicts between individual and the bureaucratic machines. Economically, then, society is in its post-capitalist or at the very least its welfare capitalist stage: politically and culturally, it is entering its 'mass-society' phase.

It would take too long to resume this material here. In many cases, the controversial element in the argument has less to do with the facts than with what to make of them.[2] In fact the evidence we have does not support the notion of basic social and structural change in the society. On the other hand, the society seems to have changed sufficiently to present a significantly different image of itself those who live in it. J.H. Westergaard, speaking of what he calls 'the more sophisticated versions of the post-capitalist thesis', says: 'they point, not so much to a transformation of the economic structure of class as such, as to a transformation of the conditions relevant to the formation and direction of class consciousness: it is not the inequalities of class that have been reduced but their "transparency"' ('The Withering Away Of Class', p85 (see note 2). Mr Westergaard does not, however, seem to be convinced by this account. He argues correctly that, as heightened material aspirations and 'middle-class' expectations are assumed by a wider section of the working class, the level of political demand, so to speak, will be raised. And since, by definition, these levels of material achievement are beyond the reach of the bulk of the population, what we should expect is not a diminution in class consciousness, but instead a sharpening in political discontent. Thus he accepts that 'the nature of the class structure is certainly changing', but not that this is in the direction of a reduction in social conflict.

So far, I agree. But Mr Westergaard has not distinguished sharply enough between the potential for conflict and the actual state of political consciousness as we find it. True, the social and material achievements which people are led to expect as part of the inheritance of 'affluence' simply are not widely available. True, the tensions arising from the gap between expectation and achievement will be expressed in some way. It is also true that, though these tensions obviously exist, they have not – in Mr Westergaard's terms – been 'translated into political radicalism'. Why not? It must have something to do with how the issues are seen: that is to say, with their 'transparency'. And there must be factors at work in the formation of political consciousness which have so shaped the issues that they fail to take the configuration of a radical consciousness. What we have instead is the false consciousness of a transitional period, and the political conditions which have helped to make that consciousness so far prevail.

We can test the transitional nature of the period simply by taking paradoxical descriptions which can be made of it. For example, we could multiply the evidence to hand of the break-up of the older working-class communities and their supporting culture, and of the loosening of the hold, especially among younger people, of the traditional bonds of social class in the society. Yet one would have to put side by side with this the persistent fact that Britain remains a deeply entrenched class society. The strength of the establishment has become, if anything, more vivid: in part because of those elements in it which have survived, but also because of the new strengths which have been annexed to it. Its social composition may have altered, but its social distance from the rest of society has not diminished. If ownership and management are separate in function, they have come together at the pinnacle of the society to compose a new social elite, a complex and socially heterogeneous echelon of power, surrounded by its own intellectual, cultural, and symbolic supports. This phenomenon is sometimes taken to mean that the older aristocratic class enclosed the bourgeois industrial classes within its own orbit;[3] but, in fact, though many of the symbols of power in British life retain their feudal aura, the centre of British values represents the triumph of one distinctive kind of bourgeois culture – now so deeply inlaid in the society that it is felt only as a cultural presence, as a habit, an inflection of thought and feeling. (Marx called Britain 'the most bourgeois of bourgeois societies'.)

Thus Britain is neither a class society in the old sense, nor is it a classless society: paradoxically, it is closer to the truth to say that Britain is a society which, while remaining rigidly class-bound, gives the distinct impression that it is growing more classless. The Polish sociologist Ossowski calls this the phenomenon 'inegalitarian classlessness' (see endnote 1). The paradox of 'inegalitarian classlessness' remains closer to the heart of the truth because, in the absence of any political development which would serve to disclose – make transparent – the real movement and alignment of social classes in the society, it has at least the merit that it describes the movement of 'combined and uneven development' through which the society is passing.

These paradoxes of perception about our social situation could be extended over a very wide field. The period since the 1944 Education Act has seen a widening in educational opportunity; education has become one of the main mechanisms of social mobility in the society. Yet social class remains the strongest single factor in determining the pattern of educational chances. And even where the new system is able to promote (and in real terms, the extension of the educational franchise is a much more limited affair than is assumed), some conversion process is needed when the new elements in the system (brains, merit, awards) meet the old (blood, school, breeding, money, class) if the benefits of social mobility are truly to be cashed. In the same paradoxical way, the spread in the systems of communication has led to an increased sense of remoteness among the majority of people from the decisions which affect their lives – the false community of the media appears to atomise the audience in the very process of massing it for more effective penetration. The building of new communities, with their stress on the planned environment, has produced, if anything, a diminution in community involvement. And where the society is said to be changing most rapidly – in the occupational structure – it continues to yield a highly contradictory aspect. White collar occupations are growing: yet Britain is a pervasively working-class society. In the south-eastern conurbation one might get a sense of newer kinds of occupational groups and new patterns of life. North of the Midlands, one is struck by the stubborn perseverance, the unbroken continuity, of the old industrial civilisation of the past two centuries. Everywhere social experiences seem wildly discontinuous, incapable of being converted into generalisations which, allowing for the variety of local conditions, could be said to be broadly true both sides of the Humber.

A society in transition creates, epiphenomenally, a transitional consciousness of itself: provided the politics of the situation, or external stress, do not dissolve the paradoxes, and render the situation politically intelligible. Affluence, equality, classlessness may be myths and illusions. But we need to take account of the political conditions which have enabled the mystifications to flourish and thrive. It matters vastly what are the political conditions within which one kind of false consciousness comes to hold sway, because politics is the form in which the connexions are made between lived experience and the demands made upon the system. Certain kinds of politics will connect experience with demands in a meaningful relationship, will connect awareness of the nature of the system to aspiration, and aspiration for change to the agencies of change. But there are also false ways of connecting lived experience to the agency of change. And in the absence of the right kind of politics, the false connexions become the stabilising myths of the society.

One of the prime mechanisms of this false consciousness is the privatisation of politics. I mean something more than the home-centred stress which is supposed to be part of the progressive 'embourgeoisement' of the working class. I mean the experiencing of issues which are public in character as an unrelated series of private grouses. We can take a concrete example of how the manner and sequence in which 'issues' are 'experienced' can help to convert those issues, negatively, into private troubles. Take the health service. Legislated into being by a Labour government, and one of its most radical social measures, the health service was not only the opening of an era of welfare legislation, but the completion of an old agitation. It drew for its political support not on the existing social consciousness of 1945 alone, but on the accumulated experience of slump and depression and insecurity in the 1930s, and the sharing of limited resources during the war. But it was a bold stroke to bring that social agitation to political completion. At the beginning of the period of Tory rule, the concept of free medical provision for all had been so built in to the public consensus that it provided a common 'floor' to the expectations of the whole society. The Conservatives could only make the bid for power on the basis of a conversion to the welfare state. That was the purpose of the Butskell era in politics. Then the health service is subject to attack, both directly and indirectly. It is exposed to raiding and nibbling. It is hit directly by the general squeeze on the public sector and by stop-go economic policies. But it is also assailed, indirectly (and in a manner too subtle for Labour politicians to grasp), by the whole climate of 'affluence' which unwinds the welfare revolution in the direction of private provision and private consumption. Labour fights the battle defensively: not in terms of extending the inroads made, and of creating in the experience of public provision a counterweight to the experience of private 'affluence', but in terms of 'look what we did for you'. By the time we approach the end of the thirteen lean years of Tory rule, the health service is in need of a major general overhaul, impossible to achieve without a thorough modernisation of the service and an extension of its scope. But feeling and attitudes towards and about the service have crystallised in a period dominated by Tory individualism.

The 'demand' is thus shaped up, not in terms of a general expansion and development of community provision (in which the needs of patients, doctors, nurses and hospital staff proceed together), but in a series of structurally disconnected grouses. Among the public, the stories of inefficiency multiply. In the service, discontent with conditions of work increases. But the political opportunity to weld these two sets of pressure together in such a way as to create a mandate in the country for radical expansion is fatally missed. The Labour Party subordinates the creation of this social consciousness to the more limited aim of achieving the succession to power. False dichotomies are made between the two – as if, without a popular mandate carefully made, nurtured, and kept alive in the periods out of office, succession to power is anything more than a formal swing of the political pendulum. The moment passes. The confrontation does not take place. The issues fragment, disengage, dissipate. The general discontent becomes sectional discontents, and sectional discontents are by their nature conservative in temper, in that they seek to advance one section against another within the model of the scramble, the affluent free-for-all. What we have instead of an agitation for the expansion of the health service is a series of discontinuous and serialised interest groups: nurses – for more pay – against the public; public – for better health care – against the hospitals; doctors – for private sector salaries and conditions of work – against public, the service, government; indeed, given time, against the whole principle of free medical care. Thus we are brought to the paradoxical situation of a Labour Minister of Health facing the massed ranks of the doctors' lobby, with the public as detached spectators to the confrontation. In this way a major discontent is so shaped and distorted by the political situation that it provides the fuel, not for another instalment of social reform, but rather for the deeply reactionary notions of Mr Enoch Powell.

It matters profoundly what the political circumstances are in which the issues and conflicts arising from the society develop: whether they take on the political complexion of widening solid ties and shared burdens, or the complexion of competitive private provision, sectional interest groups and lop-sided individualism And this question is especially important now because, with the loosening of the older forms of social solidarity which were associated with working-class life and culture in previous stages of the industrial revolution, there is less of a 'natural' base in the life experience of working people for the first, rather than the second, alternative. I am not arguing that the break-up of the traditional solidarities is ipso facto a bad thing:

based as they were upon close communities, close affective ties, shared
deprivation, and traditions of resistance and deference, they provided
the support for working-class institutions such as the co-operatives
and the trade unions – but they also helped to circumscribe and
enclose. In their most important work in this field, the sociologists
Lockwood and Goldthorpe suggest that what is happening now is
a movement away from the old kind of collective culture – solidary,
based on instinctual social ties and shared traditional values – and
towards new kind of collectivism, 'based on rationalist calculation of
interest'.[4] Commenting on this thesis of 'instrumental collectivism',
Perry Anderson has recently written:

> Now clearly, this development can involve a loss of class conscious-
> ness and combativity, and its replacement by a narrower, sectional
> self-interest. But there is no reason why it must do so. On the
> contrary, 'solidary collectivism' is itself in many ways a narrow form
> of social consciousness ... The advent of 'instrumental collectivism'
> means for the first time the penetration of reason, of rationality, into
> this closed, affective universe. Of course, the form of this rationality
> may initially be that of the surrounding environment, the egoistic
> market rationality of neo-capitalism.[5]

Precisely. And the final sentence is the crucial one. The opening up
of the society to new patterns of life, new patterns of expectation, new
normative values and attitudes could *under certain political conditions*
represent a major access of strength to the cause of radicalism in the
society. But such have certainly not been the prevailing circumstances
of the past decade. It is the 'egoistic market rationality of neo-
capitalism' which has been the shaping 'spirit of the times'. Thus
social advance, in the context of thirteen years of Tory affluence, is
inevitably identified with what the sectional lobbies can squeeze for
their 'members' out of the society, rather than with what the society
as a whole can collectively make of its human and technical resources:
the period presents the aspect of a peculiarly one-eyed materialism, a
specially British kind of 'carnival' (see endnote 2). (This is one side to
it. The other side is the way in which, paradoxically, the society seems
to find its most potent imagery in the language of mental disorder,
disorientation and breakdown, in the metaphors of disturbed personal
relationships and neurosis. The two belong together. Bohemianism

is the hip, the off-beat bedfellow of suburban affluence, and though much of it is fashionable fellow-travelling, some of it is the most serious negative note sounded in the whole literary culture in recent years.)

Now the situation would have been serious enough had it been possible to identify the phase of 'the egoistic market rationality of neo-capitalism' with Conservative politics and culture. But the fact is that this is now the predominant ideology in the Labour Party as well, and that, under certain disguises, it appears to have its far-left supporters too. The most pervasive version is the 'doctrine of modernisation'.

Modernisation is the presiding theme of British politics today, the cause which unites all men of goodwill in the search for the future. Under its ambiguous shadow the most curious birds of passage now congregate. Mr Heath, of course, is a moderniser. So is the Chairman of ICI. Lord Snow is a moderniser. So is Mr Woodcock. Mr George Brown is the governor of modernising rhetoric. But the moderniser par excellence is Mr Wilson.

This is no freak development. It is important to understand that this slogan has deep roots in the society, in its problems. Even if the political circumstances did not press men into its fold, the long decline in Britain's economic fortunes, its inability to enter the period of automation and efficient competitive production with any confidence, the restrictive structure of British industry, its resistance to technical innovation, its outmoded and unreconstructed industrial capital – all these represent real problems for the society which cannot be overcome without structural change. Modernisation is one formula for drawing attention to this complex of issues. Further, the pressure for modernisation has some real basis in the structure of post-war society. The trend towards technocracy – by which I mean not technological education but technocratic attitudes – both in education and in the occupational structure, imposes, as a major element in the mosaic of attitudes in con-temporary Britain, the view that the only revolution now worth making is the technological one. Modernisation in this form has become a powerful idea in all advanced neo-capitalist societies. The view is that all that has happened in these societies so far can be summed up in the phrase 'traditional society'. And the only ideology capable of breaking up the social and cultural forms of traditional society, letting technology and its transforming power through, is the ideology of modernisation. It is, of course, an instrumental ideology – an ideology of means rather than ends. Its stresses fall upon technocratic innovation, bureaucratic structures and the criteria of efficiency. Its model of social relations is that of the 'experts' and the 'laymen', the 'elite' and the 'mass'. And so far as massing support for its programmes – programmes of 'the technical assistance' variety – is concerned, it seeks to mobilise men not according to their class, status or wealth, their interests, aspirations, goals, needs or ambitions, but simply according to whether or not they belong to the 'tradition of the new'.

Important as are the problems highlighted by this ideology, it is necessary to point out how much support for it means complicity with 'egoistic rationality' and the status quo.

First, the ideology of modernisation fatally short-circuits the formulation of goals, since the discussion about 'modernised' Britain is not about what sort of society it will be, qualitatively, but about the means to get to it – whatever 'it' is. All discussions about 'programme' and 'perspective' become discussions about instrumentalities. It was in this context that Mr Wilson, giving his most far-reaching statement about the scientific revolution to the party conference before the 1964 election, seriously suggested that there was no reason for the party to continue to tear itself to pieces in a fruitless discussion about socialism, since the scientific revolution would redefine socialism for the twentieth century. This is the apogee of technical determinism.

Secondly, the ideology of modernisation is a truncated ideology since it crudely foreshortens the historical development of the society. After all, though it is true that socialism was always, inter alia, about the 'modernisation of social life', it is about modernisation in some concrete social and historical setting. As Michael Walzer has pointed out, 'socialism was thought to involve significant transformations precisely of modern, that is, bourgeois life'.[6] And the transition from bourgeois to socialist society, though conceived in different ways in the different socialist traditions, involved the transformation of social relations, the reordering of priorities, the restructuring of power and privilege in the society. In other words modernisation was a means, or one part of the means, not the end. It had content. The current version foreshortens this whole perspective, so that the bourgeois phase – in which precisely industrial society was made and 'traditional' feudal society broken – becomes assimilated into 'traditional society', and all that follows is a matter of techniques rather than of structures, involving no transformations, no confrontations either of power or of values, no clash of interests. Thus Mr Wilson may modernise Britain.

But if he fails, Mr Heath might do it. Or Mr Grimond. Technology, so it is supposed, is beyond politics, beyond ideology. It is neutral. Apparently, *either* socialism *or* capitalism could 'electrify' the society.

Thirdly, the politics of modernisation is supposed to operate within the model of conflict-free bargaining. This evades or suppresses all the decisive moments politically when men might have to choose between competing and irreconcilable interests, between different versions of society and the social good. The politics of such an ideology is above all the manipulation of consensus – since it is assumed that all men of good will, modernisers to a man, combine together to defeat the traditionalists. It is according this model that old trade unionists and old entrepreneurs who take the highly old-fashioned view that capital and labour have conflicting interests in a free enterprise economy are both assimilated, rhetorically, into the same camp. They become the target of attack from the modernisers on both sides. They are outside the consensus. It was in this spirit of technical rationality that Mr Wilson made his bid for power in 1964, calling all men of the centre to his support. It is to maintain this consensus that trade unionists, businessmen, management, consumers and government – each with their own maintained and serialised positions of power – sign declarations of intent and aim their multi-pronged 'nickies' and 'neddies' at an incomes policy.[7] It is to this consensus that Mr Brown is continually speaking – belabouring the recalcitrant militants with one hand (the left) and the men of goodwill of the British Federation of Industries with the other. What dominates government activity, when it is not actually trying to master, without a popular mandate to do so, the structural problems of the system, is the manipulation of consensus and the politics of 'the bargain'. This three-cornered bargain is the basis of British politics today.

Of course, by seeking the support of men of goodwill everywhere, the Labour government ends up by having real political support nowhere: for since the society is pregnant with conflict but the model of politics the government is attempting to work is 'conflict-free', the whole geological structure of politics in the society is fragmented; and we move, inevitably, towards the politics of the floating vote, which is also the politics of psephology. It is simply not possible, given Britain's economic and social structure, and human and technical resources, to square, within one political programme, both unskilled manual workers and top management, both the defence of the pound sterling and the city, both industrial expansion and restraint, both the car manufacturers and the transport needs of the society, both the mark-up rate and the cost of living, both low-income housing and the land speculators, both Etonians and Scunthorpe Grammar, both the doctors' lobby and the health service, both private insurance and the old age pensioners. These conflicts, structural to the society, cannot all be absorbed and resolved in the drive for 'the new'. Particularly if the trajectory attempted is a 'radical' one, a transforming one. The conflict-free, modernising model of politics is a sure stabiliser of the status quo, since all roads lead to the kind of society we already have, social relations as they already exist, the share of the cake as it is at present divided: only 'modernised'. As Walzer comments, 'all processes arrive and are always arriving at the modern, but this is always a particular modern, determined by its history. Not even the spread of a single technology or the increasing inter-relatedness of the various divisions of mankind seems likely to produce in the near future a single history and a single modernity. We will continue to live in significantly different societies.' And so long as we do, politics – however masked – will remain the crucial choice between those differences.

It is now possible to speak directly of political commitment. The commitment of the socialist in this period is to the making of socialist consciousness, rather than the accession to political power. The weakness of the Labour government in office is a clear demonstration that the 'practical, pragmatic imperatives' which have dominated official party thinking and strategy, in both the Gaitskell and Wilson eras, were the wrong priorities. Not only have they led the party to the wrong tactic, they have also haltered and mystified loyal party workers and supporters. To take office in the name of structural change and reform without an accompanying consciousness and a popular mandate is to become the prisoner of the system (see endnote 3 on immigration). In the event the modernising flair of Mr Wilson, especially in his election campaigns, has proved a fatal gift, since it creates the illusion of radicalism and a radical response without the substance. Labour entered office in 1964 without a mandate to reconstruct social relations in British society, without a mandate to break the power of the vested interests which kept stop-go economic policies in being, without a mandate to reshape British foreign policy and commitments. It therefore finds itself having to play for reform within an unreconstructed social system, and to energise British industry and exports while placating the vested interests; while it is forced into a neo-imperialist stance in world affairs, and has become the initiator of one of the most formidable periods of 'stop' in the stop-go cycle. It is not expertise, technical sophistication, or the will to modernise that Labour lacks. It is politics.

The commitment to this kind of politics, is, of course, a complex matter, for consciousness – as we have been arguing – is not a matter of skilfully written party programmes but of a totalising political strategy, a strategy both of theory and praxis, both of programme and of organisation. It is a matter of setting out the tasks. The task begins with an understanding of the changing structure and culture of British society, and of the basic sub-structures – economic, social, technical, political, and cultural – which are typical to the society. It must take account of the environmental and economic resources which can be mobilised by a political strategy – for, as a comparison of Britain and the United States suggests, neo-capitalist societies can be either dynamic or atrophied, either resilient and aggressive or torpid and stagnant (just as socialist societies can be either rich or poor). The assessment of what we have to work with, and what structure of social relations we have to work within, is the basis for the dispersal of myths and illusions and the beginning of true political realism.

Then comes the unmasking of structural tensions and contradictions in the system, the demands which are likely to provide the dynamic for social transformation. These issues may be 'political' ones: but they may not. They may lie, first of all, in the points at which the system is encountered and confronted in the experience of men and women, the conflicts which, properly developed, may lead to a movement in which the whole system as a system is confronted on the political stage. We are dealing not with a set of abstract economic relations but with a whole social and cultural system. And the only political strategy which has the least hope of transforming such a system is that which makes a totalising confrontation with its every feature and part. But it is the inter-relatedness of the issues which is alone able to make the démarche from the existing society to any other a political possibility. To the building of this systematic confrontation with neo-capitalism as a social system, all men in all professions and all personal situations can contribute: for I have tried to show that the system has intellectual, cultural, technical and ideological 'sub-systems', as well as economic and social and organisational ones, and that it is the connexion of these parts, rather than the predominance of any determining one, which has displaced and emasculated progressive developments in the post-war period. This may seem highly theoretical, yet I believe that socialism in this decade has been crucially defeated in the realm of theory and ideology, and that the undertow to narrow pragmatism and technical criteria of efficiency, while seeming suitably tough-minded and realistic in the short run, is just what, in the long run, has led the politics of the left up the garden path to No 10 Downing Street.

But then, side by side with the development of a 'house of theory', and a strategy, is the question of organisation, the building of the movement. The most fashionable slogan among the modernising wing of the labour movement is that we are at the end of the 'building of the socialist movement': the task now is to take, keep, hold and wield political power. This too is part of the trap of pragmatism. Social change cannot come about without its human agencies: and the quality, character, structure, historical experience and organisation of the agencies of change is one of the determining factors in the 'real movement of history'. The experience and organisation of the trade union movement in Britain represents, at one and the same time, the conserving and stabilising strength of working-class politics, and a complex form of complicity with the ongoing system of society. It has placed its indelible stamp on the nature of the struggle for socialism in Britain. This is true of every movement of social revolution in every society. The form and circumstances of the Leninist party stamped the Russian revolution, as certainly as the Long March of the Chinese army of liberation and the character of the struggle in the Sierra Maestra marked the Chinese and the Cuban revolutions. Revolutions of different kinds transform and transpose – but they do not transform and transpose out of nothing: historical continuity is always preserved, and the means and methods of change which are adopted become in a sense the content of the transformation. The test of the movement to surpass neo-capitalism will be the ability of that movement, within its own organisation, to develop forms, structures, and relationships which represent real alternatives to those which belong, typically, to the dominant social system. A movement organised along bureaucratic lines, in which the 'experts/rank and file' or full-time politicians/ political consumers' dichotomies of the society are tragically mirrored, will never be the agent of a democratic, egalitarian revolution.

I have had some experience of two 'moments' in the past decade in which – partially, it is true, but significantly – a break has been made with the ongoing system. The first can be described as the 'moment of

1956', the year of Suez and Hungary, in which by a kind of double-reflex people were liberated mentally and politically from the 'fix' of Stalinism and Butskellism. Out of that liberation there emerged a period of political creativity in the widest sense – the involvement of young people in politics, the re-engagement of older people rendered inactive by the cramp of Stalinism abroad and by the 'apathy' of cold war politics at home, the first break in the ethos of east-west politics, the first demystification of the illusions of 'affluence' and the 'permanent welfare revolution'. The 'new left' – as a movement of ideas rather than as an organisation – was only a part of that break, but it was an important part: and within the ideas, the kinds of social criticism and of historical analysis which for a time moved in the orbit of the 'new left', there were to be found, I still believe, the elements for 'the house of theory'.

The other 'break' was in the anti-nuclear movement, a development related to the complex issues and feelings stirred to life in 1956, but which focused on the problems of war and peace, the nuclear threat, and Britain's relations with the world. However short this movement may have fallen of offering a fully developed ideology appropriate to the problems of nuclear war, it did more than any other to mark the period off politically from the earlier cold war consensus. And it threw up, in a maelstrom of conflicting ideas and policies, some crucial lessons for us in terms of the character of movements of dissent, especially in the area of democratic participation, and of the connexions between war, morality and social change in the modern world.

Both these 'moments' in the last decade touched the majority of people in the society in intangible ways, but fleetingly: and their impact may seem at the present time to have receded. But they represented, then and now, the few available styles of dissent from the post-war consensus, two related forms of political commitment. The only political commitments worth taking up in the next period are commitments which follow within their perspectives.

Endnotes

1. From Ossowski, *Class Structure in the Social Consciousness*, Land 1963, p97: 'Experience has shown that the term "classless society" has acquired another meaning than that involved in the Marxian ideal

type. The abolition of the class system can be understood as the wiping out only of those inequalities which result from class divisions. In this sense the abolition of social classes does not necessarily mean the abolition of the status hierarchy or of economic inequalities. The liquidation of levels in the social structure does not necessarily involve the destruction of the social ladder. The abolition of the system of class privileges does not entail the abolition of all the privileges whereby individuals differ from one another. The point is – which of these privileges are regarded as not being associated with the class system. The conception of the classless society, wherein classlessness by no means presupposes economic egalitarianism, appeared, it would seem, simultaneously with the triumph of the idea of modern democracy founded upon free competition, after the fall of the estate order and wiping out of estate privileges ... Today we meet this conception – the conception of a classless society which economically is not egalitarian on both sides of the line that divides the world into two camps.'

2. The term 'carnival' is used by Erikson in *Young Man Luther*, London, 1959, p71: 'Men, especially in periods of change, are swayed by alternating world moods which seem to be artificially created by the monopolists and manipulators of an era's opinions, and yet could not exist without the highly exploitable mood cycles inherent in man's psychological structure. The two most basic alternating moods are those of carnival and atonement. The first gives licence and leeway to sensual enjoyment, to relief and release at all costs; the second surrenders to the negative conscience which constricts, depresses and enjoins man for what he has left unsolved, uncared for, unatoned.' Raymond Williams points to this problem of alternatives between culture and affluence in class consciousness in an essay on Thomas Hardy in *The Critical Quarterly*, Winter 1964, pp343-4.

3. *Immigration*
The problem of immigration into Britain is a good illustration of the Labour Party's failure to recognise the need to create social consciousness before legislation. Despite liberal intentions they failed, in the ten years previous to office (the ten years of concentrated migration), either to confront the issue or to build in the country the kind of radical social platform which would permit them to legislate in a liberal manner. There were no Labour migration policies; no attempt to link social issues such as housing and land speculation with the problems of immigrant housing

in the twilight zones of the cities (the Rachman scandal over housing, which the Profumo crisis highlighted, was precisely such an opportunity); no attempt to confront creeping racialist attitudes within the party itself, particularly at local and constituency levels; no effort to create a mandate for giving coloured immigrants preferred treatment in the social services so as to level opportunities upwards. Then, at the general election of 1964, when race had been permitted to take its place in the centre of the political stage, shocked by electoral defeat at Smethwick and finding itself, in panic, constrained by racialist attitudes it had done nothing to combat, the Labour government 'had to' publish its illiberal white paper – a document which placed a ceiling on immigration at a figure (8500) arrived at in the most technically accomplished way (no doubt with a flurry of computers), but bearing no relation whatever to anything: simply plucked out of the air in an exercise of highly rational irrationalism. The notion that political action creates the conditions within which legislation takes place seemed, on this issue, as foreign to the new Labour ideology as it would have been to Burke or Bagehot.

Notes

1. E.P. Thompson, *The Making of The English Working Class*, Gollancz 1963.
2. Since this paper was first delivered, a very useful article has appeared which discusses these changes critically in much the way I would have wanted to do here. I am now able to make direct reference to it: see 'The Withering Away Of Class', by J.H. Westergaard, in Anderson and Blackburn (eds), *Towards Socialism*, Collins 1965.
3. See for example Perry Anderson's 'Origins Of The Present Crisis', in *Towards Socialism*: but also E.P. Thompson's reply, 'The Peculiarities of The English', in *Socialist Register*, No 3.
4. J.K. Goldthorpe, D. Lockwood, F. Bechofer, and J. Platt, *The Affluent Worker in the Class Structure*, Cambridge University Press 1969.
5. Perry Anderson, 'Problems of Socialist Strategy', in *Towards Socialism*, pp264-5.
6. Michael Walzer, *Dissent*, Autumn 1964.
7. The National Economic Development Council (NEDC) and the National Economic Development Office (NEDO) – both known as Neddy – and National Incomes Commission (NIC, Nicky) were set up towards the end of the Macmillan administration, and continued by the Wilson administration.

A world at one with itself

1970

THE ISSUE OF violence in the mass media has been posed in the familiar terms of the fantasy or fictional portrayal of violence there. But if the media are playing a role in the alleged escalation of social violence, it is almost certainly not *Z Cars*, *The Virginian*, *Callan* or *Codename* which are 'responsible'. What is at issue is not the fantasy role of fictional violence, but the alleged real effects of real violence. The area of broadcasting in question is that traditionally defined as 'news/current affairs/features/documentaries'. It is, for example, the only too real bodies of only too real Vietnamese, floating down an all too real Cambodian river, which some as yet unstated informal theory of cause and effect links in the minds of television's critics with the question of 'law and order'. Thus it is to the question of news that we must turn.

As it happens, news has just undergone an enormous expansion in the new radio schedules. In the philosophy of streamed radio which underpins the BBC's *Broadcasting in the Seventies*, news got a privileged place. Under the new dispensation, the avid listener is never more than half an hour away from the next news bulletin. But the really striking development is the growth of the news-magazine style of programme, on the *World At One* model.[1]

What constitutes the definition of news currently employed on radio programmes of this new type? I put the point in this way, and not in the more familiar terms of 'coverage' or 'bias/objectivity', because this constitutes the heart of the matter. Journalists throughout the media are notoriously slippery and defensive when thus confronted. 'The news', they assume, is clearly what it is: newsworthy people and events, happening 'out there' in the real world, at home and abroad.

The relevant questions are always technical ones: 'How adequately can we cover these events?', 'Is the coverage biased or objective?'. This view is legitimated by a body of journalistic folklore, with its ritual references to copy, deadlines and news angles. These sanction professional practice and keep non-professional busybodies at bay.

Of course, newsmen agree, the news can be either 'hard' or 'soft', graphically or neutrally presented (sensationalism/objectivity), a report from the front or a background analysis (actuality/depth). But these are matters of treatment – of form and 'flavour' – not of content or substance. It is worth observing that all these routine ways of setting up the problem are drawn from the press, reflecting both the common background of media newsmen in Fleet Street, and, more important, the powerful hold of models borrowed for radio or television from the press.

The notion that the news somehow discovers itself may be of service to the harassed newsgatherers and editors. Such professional 'common-sense constructs', such ad hoc routines, are employed in most large-scale organisations. They enable hard-pressed professionals to execute their tasks with the minimum of stress and role-conflict.

These idiomatic short-hands give the professional a map of the social system, just as the categories of classification in mental hospitals (see Erving Goffman), the clinical records of hospitals (see Harold Garfinkel), and the notebooks and case records of police and probation officers (see Aaron Cicourel), witness to the moral order and the system of meanings which other professionals use to give sense to their tasks.[2]

But, against this defensive strategy, it needs to be asserted that the news is a product, a human construction: a staple of that system of 'cultural production' (to use Theodor Adorno's phrase) we call the mass media. Journalists and editors select from the mass of potential news items the events which constitute 'news' for any day. In part, this is done by implicit reference to some unstated and unstatable criteria of the significant. News selection thus rests on inferred knowledge about the audience, inferred assumptions about society, and a professional code or ideology. The news is not a set of unrelated items: news stories are coded and classified, referred to their relevant contexts, assigned to different (and differently graded) spaces in the media, and ranked in terms presentation, status and meaning.

The process of news production has its own structure. News items which infringe social norms, break the pattern of expectations and contrast with our sense of the everyday, or are dramatic, or have 'numerous and intimate contacts with the life of the recipients', have greater news salience for journalists than others. As a highly reputable reporter observed to an irate group of student militants, who were questioning her as to why her paper reported every vote cast during the period of a university occupation, but nothing of the weekend teach-in: 'Votes represent decisions: decisions are news: discussion is not'.

The role of the news journalist is to mediate – or act as the 'gatekeeper' – between different publics – between institutions and the individual, between the spheres of the public and the private, between the new and the old. News production is often a self-fulfilling activity. Categories of news, consistently produced over time, create public spaces in the media which have to be filled. The presence of the media at the birth of new events can affect their course and outcome. The news is not only a cultural product: it is the product of a set of institutional definitions and meanings, which, in the professional shorthand, is commonly referred to as *news values*.

Statistics of crime represent not only the real movement of the crime rate, but the changing definition of what constitutes crime, how it is recognised, labelled and dealt with. To label as 'violent' every incident from skinhead attacks on Pakistanis, to Ulster, to protests against the South African tour, is to establish a certain way of seeing and understanding a complex set of public events.

Once the category of 'law and order' has come into existence as a legitimate news category, whole different orders of meaning and association can be made to cluster together. Terms of understanding – such as the criminal categories reserved for acts of collective social delinquency ('hooligans', say, or 'layabouts') – become transferred to new events like the clashes between citizens and the army in Ulster. It may be that there has been some objective increase in real-world violence; but the effect on news values is *even greater* than that would justify.

This shift is difficult to pinpoint in the brief radio or television news bulletin, though if we take a long enough stretch of time we can observe changes both in the profile and in the style of news reports. But in the format of the radio news magazine, which approximates more closely to the profile and treatment of a daily newspaper, the amplifying and interpretative function of the media comes into its own.

News magazines include studio interviews, reports from correspondents, replies to attacks, features and 'human interest' stories. This is where background classifying and interpretative schemes register most forcefully. In terms of direct bias, there seems less cause for concern. Within its limits, radio shows little direct evidence of intentional bias. It treats the spokesmen of the two major political parties with scrupulous fairness – more, in fact, than they deserve. But the troublesome question is the matter of unwitting bias: the institutional slanting, built in not by the devious inclination of editors to the political right or left, but by the steady and unexamined play of attitudes which, via the mediating structure of professionally defined news values, inclines all the media towards the status quo.

The operation of unwitting bias is difficult either to locate or prove. Its manifestations are always indirect. It comes through in terms of who is or who is not accorded the status of an accredited witness; in tones of voice; in the set-up of studio confrontations; in the assumptions which underlie the questions asked or not asked; in terms of the analytical concepts which serve informally to link events to causes in what passes for explanation.

Its incidence can be mapped by plotting the areas of *consensus* (where there is a mutual agreement about the terms in which a topic is to be treated), the areas of *toleration* (where the overlap is less great, and the terms have to be negotiated as between competing definitions) and the areas of *dissensus or conflict* (where competing definitions are in play).

Unwitting bias has nothing directly to do with the style of 'tough' interviewing, since, even in the areas of consensus issues, the professional ethic sanctions a quite aggressive, probing style (Hardcastle with Heath, Robin Day with Wilson) – though the probe does not penetrate to underlying assumptions.

Areas of *consensus* cover the central issues of politics and power, the fundamental sanctions of society and the sacred British values. To this area belong the accredited witnesses – politicians of both parties, local councillors, experts, institutional spokesmen.

Areas of *toleration* cover what might be called 'Home Office issues' – social questions, prisoners who can't get employment after discharge, little men or women against the bureaucrats, unmarried mothers, and so on. The more maverick witnesses who turn up in this group get, on the whole, an off-beat but sympathetic 'human interest' – even at lines a crusading – kind of treatment. Guidelines in this sector are less clear-cut. When such topics edge over into the 'permissive' category, they can arouse strong sectional disapproval. But here even the scrupulously objective news editor can presume (again, a matter of negotiation and judgment, not of objective fact) on a greater background of public sympathy, more room for manoeuvre.

Areas of *conflict* have their un-accredited cast of witnesses too: protesters of all varieties; shop stewards, especially if militant, more especially if on unethical strike; squatters; civil rights activists; hippies; students; hijackers; Stop the Seventy Tourers; and so on. In dealing with these issues and actors, interviewers are noticeably sharper, touchier, defending their flanks against any predisposition to softness.

One could plot the hidden constraints of this informal ideology in the media simply by noting the characteristic argument advanced against each of these groups. Unofficial strikers are always confronted with 'the national interest', squatters with 'the rights of private property', civil rights militants in Ulster with the need for Protestant and Catholic to 'work together', Stop the Seventy Tourers with the way their minority actions 'limit the right of the majority to enjoy themselves as they wish'.

I am not arguing here that these arguments should not be accorded some weight. I am remarking how, in the handling of certain issues, the assumptions which shape an interview item are coincident with official ideologies of the status quo. I recall numerous instances when Ulster civil rights militants were confronted with the consequences of violence. But I cannot recall a single instance when an Ulster magistrate or politician was confronted with the equally tenable view, succinctly expressed by Conor Cruise O'Brien, that since Ulster society has for long been based on the dominance of a minority over a majority, no fundamental change in that structure can be expected without its accompanying release of the 'frozen violence' inherent in the situation.

I know that Ulster is a particularly sensitive matter, that the BBC's impartiality came under direct fire during the events of September 1969, and that in this period a close executive watch was maintained over the news output. But then, my criticism is not of the wilful, intentional bias of editors and newscasters, but of the institutionalised ethos of the news media as a whole. The influence exerted by this ethos over actual broadcast programmes is precisely to be found on those occasions when men of quite varying temperaments and political views are systematically constrained in a certain direction.

I recall William Hardcastle's phrase, when reporting the American Anti-Vietnam demonstrations last year: 'the so-called Vietnam

Moratorium Committee'. William Hardcastle's objectivity is not in question. But I await, without much confidence, the day when *The World at One* will refer to 'the so-called Confederation of British Industries' or the 'so-called Trades Union Congress' or even the 'so-called Central Intelligence Agency'.

The sources for this hidden consensus must be located outside the broadcasting media proper, at the heart of the political culture itself. It is a view of politics based on the relative absence of violence in British political life, the relative degree of integration between the powerful corporate interest groups within the state. This negotiated consensus is both a historical fact and a source of ideological comfort. The sociologist Paul Hirst, in a recent paper on 'Some problems of explaining student militancy', gave a succinct sketch of this political style:

> What is the nature of this consensus? It is that parliamentary democracy is founded upon legitimate procedures of political action, and ... that parliament is the mode of pursuit and accommodating interests within the society. It provides legitimate means for the pursuance of interests without resort to open conflict ... British democracy raises the means of political action to the level of ends: the primary values of British political culture are specified by a body of existing institutions. These institutions and their maintenance have become the primary political goals.

We can only understand the limits and constraints within which 'objectivity' functions in the media when we have grasped the true sources of legitimation in the political culture itself.

We are now at the crunch. For the groups and events upon which, increasingly, the media are required to comment and report, are the groups in conflict with this consensual style of politics. But these are precisely the forms of political and civil action which the media, by virtue of their submission to the consensus, are consistently unable to deal with, comprehend or interpret. The nervousness one has observed in the treatment of these issues reflects the basic contradiction between the manifestations which the media are called on to explain and interpret, and the conceptual/evaluative/interpretative framework which they have available to them.

Whereas the core value of the political consensus is the adherence to 'legitimate means for the pursuance of interests without resort to open conflict', the highly heterogeneous groups I have mentioned are characterised either by political militancy, leading through extra-parliamentary politics to the varying types of 'confrontation', or by social disaffiliation, leading through collective and expressive acts of rebellion to the various types of civil disturbance. Civil righters, students, Black Power militants, political hijackers and kidnappers, shop stewards, fall into the political militancy category. Skinheads, hippies, squatters, soccer hooligans, psychedelic freak-outs, fall into the social disaffiliation category.

The collective label of 'violence' – and its twin metaphor 'law and order' – is at one and the same time both a staggering confusion of new and old meanings and a penetrating insight. As symbolic categories they only make sense when the issues they refer to are shifted from the explanatory context of media to the content of *politics*.

The effective question about the role of the media, then, is not Callaghan's –'Do the media *cause* violence?' – nor Wedgwood Benn's 'Is politics too important to be left to the broadcasters?' (with its obvious retort); but, rather, 'Do/can the media help us to understand these significant real events in the real world?' 'Do the media clarify them or mystify us about them?'

Actuality versus depth is not a simple technical choice. The distinction is already built into the structure of the national press. In the arena of news and foreign affairs, popular journalism does not permit systematic exploration in depth. In the 'quality' press, some measure of background interpretation and analysis is more regularly provided. Both these things are legitimated by the professional folk-wisdom. Thus, for the populars: 'The Great British Public is not interested in foreign news' – though how the regular reader of the *Mirror*, the *Express* or the *News of the World*, our circulation front-runners, could develop an intelligent interest in foreign affairs is a matter for speculation. And for the quality press there is 'the rigid separation of "hard" news from comment'.

Distinctions of format and depth of treatment flow, via the grooves of class and education, into the papers we get, and they are hardened and institutionalised in the social structure of the national press. But the relevance of this fragmented universe of press communication for a medium like radio at this time is highly questionable. The audience for news through the day is far less stratified by class and education than the readership of newspapers. Radio must operate as if its potential audience is *the whole nation*.

It follows that radio must find ways of making *both* the foreground event *and* the background context core aspects of its working definition of the news. Otherwise, the radio audience, whatever its range of interests, will be consigned effectively to getting a perpetual foreground.

This becomes a critical issue when the coverage is of groups and events which consistently challenge the built-in definitions and values enshrined in the political culture of broadcasters and audiences alike. This position redefines the concept of 'public service', in relation to radio, in a way which runs diametrically counter to the philosophy of rationalisation which infected *Broadcasting in the Seventies*. The press has little to contribute to the development of appropriate models.

Judged in these terms, the manifest tendencies in radio are not encouraging. A heady, breathless immediacy now infects all of the news-magazine programmes. In terms of their profile of items, these programmes progressively affiliate to the model of the daily newspaper. As events like political confrontation and civil disturbance escalate, so the coverage is doubled, quadrupled. As coverage expands, so we become even more alive to the actual 'violent' events and overwhelmed by their vivid sound and image. But as this coverage takes the characteristic form of *actuality without context*, it directly feeds our general sense of a meaningless explosion of meaningless and violent acts – 'out there' somewhere, in an unintelligible world where 'no legitimate means' have been devised 'for the pursuance of interests without resort to open conflict'.

'Out there', let us note, is a rapidly expanding area, covering most of the rest of the globe – IndoChina, Latin America, the Middle East, Africa, the Caribbean, Berkeley, Chicago, Tokyo – as well as some growing enclaves closer to home. Events of this order play straight into an *ideological gap* in the media – and in public consciousness. That gap is not filled by the media – or, rather, it is now being filled in a systematically distorted way.

Let me conclude with two examples. Take the spate of kidnappings of foreign diplomats in Latin America. These events were endlessly covered on radio and television, usually by reporters on the spot. There was some studio discussion; but the thrust was consistently towards actuality coverage; has he been shot? will the government pay the ransom? Will West Germany break off diplomatic relations? The model? Essentially: the front page of the *Daily Express*. What this coverage lacked was some framework which would make this bizarre series of events meaningful or intelligible.

I have been told that this kind of 'background piece' would be provided by the longer reports at the weekend by BBC foreign correspondents. But this is like telling a man whose regular and only newspaper is the *Mirror*, 'If you want to understand politics of Guatemala, read the *Sunday Times*.' The example is not fortuitous. For during the kidnapping the *Sunday Times* did print a fairly full background article on Guatemala – and a hair-raising, all too intelligible, story it turned out to be.

An even better example, and one where the press performed as badly as radio and television (with the exception of *24 Hours*) was the recent Black Power rioting in Trinidad. The most generally agreed judgment among intelligent West Indians about Trinidad and Jamaica is that the political situation there is highly explosive. Indeed, the real question is why either society has not, before now, gone down in a wave of riots by underprivileged blacks against the privileged coloured middle class. The answer is not unconnected with the presence both of Cuba and of the American fleet within easy striking distance of Kingston and Port of Spain.

The background to the foreground-problem of riots in Trinidad is the persistent grinding poverty of the mass of the people, intensified by basic conflicts of interest between the coloured middle class inheritors of the 'end of colonial rule' (one of the most conspicuous-consumption classes anywhere in the Third World) and the mass of peasants, workers and urban unemployed, who also happen to be black. Without this knowledge, the large-scale migration from the Caribbean to Britain, which has occupied so much 'foreground' space in recent months, is literally, unintelligible. It is another of those meaningless events, leading to the expected confrontations, and ultimately to 'violence'.

This gap between the urban and rural masses and a native bourgeoisie, grown flush in the hectic, post-colonial years of neo-imperialism, is *the* political fact about vast tracts of the Caribbean and Latin America. Yet radio discussions in studio uniformity expressed puzzlement at how Black Power could become an organising slogan in a country where the government is 'black'. The fact which needs clarification, of course, is that in the West Indies (unlike the United

States, where the permanent presence of a white power structure creates solidarity between all 'black brothers'), the emergent lines of social conflict are laid down precisely by the over-determined coalescence of class, power and gradations of colour.

Unfortunately, neither of the two accredited witnesses – Sir Learie Constantine, who regarded the riots as inexplicable, and Alva Clarke, who regarded them as 'a tragedy' – contributed to this process of conceptual clarification. When faced with this sudden eruption of yet another incidence of political violence, the explanatory concepts of 'neo-colonialism' and 'native bourgeoisie' were not available – nor anything else which could do duty for them – in the world of radio. Instead, the ingredients of the consensual view were quickly wheeled into place: 'The Prime Minister' ... 'resignations from the government' ... 'state of emergency' ... 'small groups of vandals roaming the streets' ... 'disaffection in the army' ... 'detachment of marines from nearby Puerto Rico' ... violence/law and order.

In one event after another, now, the same informal theories – supported by the same ideological commitments, and functioning as an 'objective' set of technical-professional routines – produce the same mysterious product with systematic regularity.

Notes

1 The *World at One* radio programme started broadcasting in 1965, and was seen as breaking new ground in news broadcasting. It was presented by journalists with Fleet Street experience and combined news and current affairs reporting. At the time this was regarded as controversial.
2. Erving Goffman, Harold Garfinkel and Aaron Cicourel were all writers who looked at meaning construction through social interaction, and at the ways in which rules and norms give meanings to actions in different social fields.

The 'first' New Left: life and times

1990*

THE 'FIRST' NEW LEFT was born in '1956', a conjuncture (not just a year) bounded on one side by the suppression of the Hungarian Revolution by Soviet tanks in November and on the other by the British and French invasion of the Suez Canal zone. These two events, whose dramatic impact was heightened by the fact that they occurred within days of each other, unmasked the underlying violence and aggression latent in the two systems which dominated political life at that time – Western imperialism and Stalinism – and sent a shock wave through the political world. In a deeper sense, they defined for people of my generation the boundaries and limits of the tolerable in politics. Socialists after 'Hungary', it seemed to us, must carry in their hearts the sense of tragedy which the degeneration of the Russian revolution into Stalinism represents for the left in the twentieth century. 'Hungary' brought to an end a certain kind of socialist 'innocence'. On the other hand, 'Suez' underlined the enormity of the error in believing that lowering the Union Jack in a few ex-colonies necessarily signalled the 'end of imperialism' or that the real gains of the welfare state and the widening of material affluence meant the end of inequality and exploitation.

'Hungary' and 'Suez' were thus boundary-marking experiences. They symbolised the break-up of the political Ice Age.

The New Left came into existence in the aftermath of these two events. It attempted to define a 'third' political space somewhere between these two metaphors. Its rise signified for people on the left in my generation the end of the tyranny, the imposed silences and political impasses, of the Cold War in politics, and the possibility of a breakthrough into a new socialist project.

The term 'New Left' is commonly associated these days with '1968', but to the '1956' New Left generation, '1968' was already a second, even perhaps a third, 'mutation'. We had borrowed the phrase in the 1950s from the movement known as the '*nouvelle gauche*', an independent tendency in French politics associated with the weekly newspaper *France Observateur* and its editor, Claude Bourdet. Bourdet, a leading figure in the French Resistance, personified the attempt, after the war, to open a 'third way' in European politics, independent of the two dominant left positions of Stalinism and social democracy, 'beyond' the military power blocs of NATO and the Warsaw Pact, and opposed to both the American and Soviet presences in Europe. This 'third position' paralleled the political aspirations of many of the people who came together to form the early British New Left.

The New Left represented the coming together of two related but different traditions – also of two political experiences or 'generations'. One was the tradition I would call, for want of a better term, communist humanism, symbolised by *The New Reasoner* and its founders, John Saville and Dorothy and Edward Thompson. The second is perhaps best described as an 'independent socialist' tradition. Many of the people in this second group were influenced by Marxism and some were, for a time, Communists. Nevertheless the majority were not, and its centre of gravity, in my reading, lay in that left student generation of the 1950s which maintained some distance from 'party' affiliations, and, in the disintegration of those orthodoxies in '1956', first produced *Universities and Left Review*. I belong to this second tradition.

It may help to understand that moment better if I speak personally. I was sympathetic to the left, had read Marx and been influenced by him while at school, but I would not, at the time, have called myself a Marxist in the European sense. In any event, I was troubled by the failure of orthodox Marxism to deal adequately with either 'Third World' issues of race and ethnicity or with the questions of racism or of literature and culture which preoccupied me intellectually as an undergraduate. Retrospectively, I would identify myself as one of those described by Raymond Williams in *Culture and Society* who, following, as a student of literature, the engagement between the Leavisites and the Marxist critics, was obliged to acknowledge that '*Scrutiny* won' – not because it was right, but because the alternative Marxist models were far too mechanical and reductive. (We did not yet have access to Lukacs, Benjamin, Gramsci or Adorno.) On the wider political front, I was strongly critical of everything I knew about Stalinism, either as a political system or as a form of politics. I opposed it as a model for a democratic socialism and could not fathom the reluctance of the few Communists I met to acknowledge the truth of what was by then common knowledge about its disastrous consequences for Soviet society and Eastern Europe.

Like the rest of the small number of 'Third World' students at Oxford, my principal political concerns were with 'colonial' questions. I became very involved in West Indian student politics. We debated and discussed, mainly, what was going on 'back home' in the expectation that before long we would all be there and involved in it; we argued about the West Indian Federation and the prospects for a new Caribbean economic order, the expulsion of the left from Manley's PNP Party in Jamaica under the pressures of the Cold War, the overthrow of the Jagan government in British Guiana with the suspension of the constitution and the moving in of British troops. There was no 'black politics' in Britain at that time; post-war migration had only just begun. Later, as I began to take a wider interest in British politics, I came more into contact with the 'Oxford left'. There was no 'mass' British political movement of the left or major popular political issue to which one could attach oneself. The choice seemed to be between a Labour Party which, at that moment, was deeply committed to an Atlanticist world-view, and the outer darkness of the 'far left'. The first time I ventured into a Communist Group discussion meeting was to debate with the CP the application of Marx's concept of class to contemporary capitalist society. At the time, I felt that this was an extremely bold move – such was the climate of fear and suspicion which prevailed.

After 1954, this climate began to change. There was a slow, hesitant revival of debate on the left, and a group began to emerge around these discussions. Many of us attended the 'Cole Group' (as G.D.H. Cole's seminar in politics was known), which, though formally an occasion for graduate students, doubled up as a wide-ranging discussion group of the broad left. Some of the earliest contacts and friendships that were later to be cemented by the formation of the New Left were first forged there. The student house where a number of us lived, in Richmond Road (in the old Jewish quarter, 'Jericho', behind Ruskin College), was another, more informal focal point of these discussions.

It is difficult, now, to conjure up the political climate of Oxford in the 1950s. Even for people like Alan Hall and myself, who debated political and theoretical questions with Communists but never had any intention of joining the party, the 'Cold War' dominated the political horizon, positioning everyone and polarising every topic by its remorseless binary logic. Its atmosphere was accurately caught in the first *ULR* editorial:

> The post-war decade was one in which declining political ortho-doxies held sway. Every political concept became a weapon in the cold war of ideas, every idea had its label, every person had his *[sic]* place in the political spectrum, every form of political action appeared – in someone's eyes – a polite treason. To recommend the admission of China to the UN was to invite the opprobrium of 'fellow-traveller'; to say that the character of contemporary capitalism had changed was to be ranked as a 'Keynesian liberal'. Between the high citadel of Stalinist Russia and the 'welfare state – no further' jungle of the mixed economy, there seemed nothing but an arid waste. [Caught between] these tightly compartmental-ised worlds ... British socialism suffered a moral and intellectual eclipse ... Nevertheless, the age of orthodoxies has once again been outstripped by historical events ... The thaw is on ...

This 'thaw' began as a slow, hesitant debate about a range of contem-porary issues: the future of Labour and the left in the wake of the Conservative revival; the nature of the welfare state and post-war capitalism; the impact of cultural change on British society in the early 'affluent' years of the decade. The pace of this debate was accel-erated by the Khrushchev revelations at the Twentieth Congress of the CPSU. The response to '1956' and the formation of a New Left could not have occurred without this prior period of 'preparation', in which a number of people slowly gained the confidence to engage in a dialogue which questioned the terms of the orthodox political argument and cut across existing organisational boundaries. Just as a way of characterising the range of this debate, Alan Hall and I spent the summer before Suez and Hungary trying to sketch out a book on the new contours of cultural change in 'Contemporary Capitalism' which would reflect this debate. We took away with us, among many other books, the following key texts: Crosland's *Future of Socialism*; Strachey's *End of Empire*; two chapters of what was to become Raymond Williams's *Culture and Society*; F.R. Leavis's *Culture and Environment*; Angus Maude's smug little book on *The English Middle Classes*; Osborne's *Look Back In Anger* and George Scott's 'angry young man's' autobiography, *Time And Place*.

Whether we knew it or not, we were struggling with a difficult act of description, trying to find a language in which to map an emergent 'new world' and its cultural transformations, which defied analysis within the conventional terms of the left while at the same time deeply undermining them. These reference points had all emerged in the discussion in the left circles we inhabited in the two years before Suez. The issue of the Oxford Labour Club magazine, *Clarion*, which our group edited in summer 1957, presented as its central political document a discussion of Richard Hoggart's *Uses of Literacy*. Noting that we had been criticised by both the orthodox Labourist wing and the student organiser of the CP for not having enough about politics and being too preoccupied with 'new and novel definitions', we replied that

> confusion and uncertainty are the perils of rethinking ... we may appear, for a time, to have left behind 'serious thoughts about the next Labour government'. But if it is true that 'the bottom has fallen out of politics' ... we must discover where it lies. You cannot construct a political programme over a vacuum.

These strands were dramatically condensed by the events of '1956'. Soviet tanks in Budapest terminated any hope that a more human and democratic brand of communism would evolve in Eastern Europe without prolonged trauma and social convulsion. Suez punctured the cosy illusion that (to adapt Tawney's phrase) 'you could skin the capitalist-imperialist tiger stripe by stripe'. The Trafalgar Square Suez demonstration was the first mass political rally of its kind in the 1950s, and the first time I encountered police horses face to face, or heard Hugh Gaitskell and Nye Bevan speak in public. Bevan's fierce denunciation of Eden, I remember, scattered the startled pigeons into flight ... One outcome of the ferment of '1956' was the publication of the two journals, *Universities and Left Review* and *The New Reasoner*, which, when they subsequently merged (in 1960), formed the 'first' *New Left Review*.

The Oxford left at that time was very diverse. There was a small number of CP members, who were somewhat embattled because of their association with an unpopular and, in Cold War terms, 'subversive' organisation, although actually they knew and were known and liked by 'everybody' in Oxford at the time. Next, there was the great body of 'Labour Club' supporters, the majority firmly attached to Fabian, Labourist and reformist positions, and a few with their eyes fixed unswervingly on their coming parliamentary careers. Then there were a small number of 'independents', including some serious Labour people, intellectually aligned with neither of these two camps, who shuttled somewhat uneasily between them. The latter group attracted more than its fair share of exiles and migrants, which reinforced its cosmopolitanism. 'Chuck' Taylor was a French-Canadian Rhodes scholar; Dodd Alleyne was Trinidadian; I was Jamaican; Sadiq al Mahdi was later to play a significant role in the Sudan; Clovis Maksoud was a founder member of the Syrian Ba'ath Party.

As it became clear that similar debates were developing in other universities we thought there ought to be some common platform for this emerging student 'left'. This explains the word 'Universities' in the title of the journal we eventually produced. 1956, however, destroyed the student-bound confines of this debate and catapulted us into the maelstrom of national and international left politics.

The Oxford part is, of course, only half the story. The New Left had equally important, though very different, roots in another tradition, represented by *The New Reasoner*. This tendency had a quite different formation in Communist and Popular Front politics in Britain. The revelations of the Twentieth Congress stimulated inside the party a painful reassessment of the whole Stalinist experience, and *The Reasoner* first appeared, in this context, as an internal opposition bulletin insisting on an open and public 'calling to accounts'. It was only after they lost their struggle for the right to express what were officially defined as 'factional' opinions, and the disciplines of democratic centralism were mobilised against them, that the majority of the 'Reasoners' either left the Party or were expelled and *The New Reasoner* appeared as an independent journal of the left. The final issue of *The Reasoner* was planned and produced before Suez and Hungary but, for it, these events were 'epochal'. In the aftermath of Hungary large numbers of people left the Communist Party, and *The New Reasoner* and subsequently the New Left provided some of them with a political rallying point without which many would doubtless have abandoned politics for good.

The New Left therefore represented the coming together of two different political traditions. How did this occur, and how well did it work? The organisational details of the amalgamation between the two journals can be quickly summarised. They continued to publish in tandem for a while, advertising and promoting each other. After a time the two editorial boards began to meet regularly around a broader political agenda, to appoint editorial board members in common and to recruit new ones, like John Rex, Peter Worsley, Alasdair MacIntyre, Norman Birnbaum, Michael Barratt Brown, Ralph Miliband, Paddy Whannel and Raymond Williams, who did not originally belong to either.

Both boards were increasingly preoccupied with the struggle to sustain the financial and commercial viability of two journals. Even more pressing was the cost in human capital. For many of us, normal life had more or less been suspended in 1956. Some had not stopped running round in circles since – to borrow Lady Eden's graphic phrase – 'the Suez Canal flowed through the drawing room', and were by then in a state of extreme political exhaustion. There were also, more positively, the opportunities we were missing to create a much wider, united political platform for our position. While we were aware of our differences, our perspectives had come closer together in the months of collaboration. Out of this variety of factors came the decision to merge and, with more suitable candidates like E.P. Thompson and others being unwilling to serve, I rashly agreed to become the first editor of *New Left Review*, with John Saville acting as chairman of the editorial board.

New Left Review in this form lasted two years. It was never, I think, as successful or distinctive a journal as either of its predecessors – a failure which clearly reflected my own editorial inexperience. The bimonthly rhythm and the pressures to connect with immediate political issues pushed us into becoming more of a left 'magazine' than a 'journal'. This required a shift of journalistic and editorial style which did not square with the original political intention and for which the board was unprepared. There were differences of emphasis and style of work between the board, which carried the main political weight and authority of the movement, and the small working editorial group that began to assemble around Carlisle Street.

The 'New Reasoners' belonged to a political generation formed by the politics of the Popular Front and the anti-fascist movements of the 1930s, the European Resistance movements during the war, the 'Second Front' campaigns for 'friendship with the Soviet Union' and the popular turn to the left reflected in the 1945 Labour victory. Although some younger Communists in the *ULR* tendency also belonged to this tradition, their relation to it was always different. In its overwhelming majority, the *ULR* generation's centre of gravity was irrevocably 'postwar'. This was a difference not of age but of formation – a question of *political generations*, within which the war constituted the symbolic dividing line. These differences did produce subtle tensions which surfaced around the new journal. Although these differences never threatened our underlying solidarities and sense of common purpose, they made close working collaboration difficult at times.

These differences of formation and political style of work were magnified by the location of the two tendencies in two quite distinct social and cultural milieux. *The New Reasoner*'s base was in Yorkshire and the industrial North. Although it had many readers elsewhere, it was organically rooted in a provincial political culture – not just that of the labour movement but also of organisations like the Yorkshire Peace Committee – and was intensely suspicious of 'London'. *ULR* also attracted support from many parts of the country; but it very much belonged to what the 'Reasoners' thought of as the 'cosmopolitan' or 'Oxford/London' axis. Although we did not consciously understand it at the time, the 'ULR-ers' were 'Modernists', if not actually 'rootless cosmopolitans'. As a colonial, I certainly felt instinctively more at home in the more socially anonymous metropolitan culture, though I regretted *ULR*'s lack of organic connections to non-metropolitan working-class life.

It should by now be clear that even within the editorial boards of the original journals, the New Left was far from politically monolithic and certainly never became culturally or politically homogeneous. The tensions were, for the most part, humanely and generously handled. But any careful reader of the different journals will quickly be able to identify real points of difference and, on occasion, fiercely contended debates surfacing in their pages. It would therefore be quite wrong to attempt to reconstruct, retrospectively, some essential 'New Left', and to impose on it a political unity it never possessed. Nevertheless, although no two members would offer the same list, there was a set of linked themes – a 'thematics', if you like – which commanded wide enough assent to make it distinctive as a political formation.

In my reading, this centred on the argument that any prospect for the renewal of the left had to begin with a new conception of socialism and a radically new analysis of the social relations, dynamics and culture of post-war capitalism. Far from constituting a modest updating exercise, this was a far-reaching, ambitious and multifaceted intellectual project. So far as socialism was concerned, it meant coming to terms with the depressing experiences of both 'actual existing socialism' and 'actual existing social democracy' and transforming, in the light of those experiences, the very conception of 'the political'. So far as the latter was concerned, what we called modern 'corporate capitalism' had very different economic, organisational, social and cultural forms. It functioned according to a different 'logic' from that of entrepreneurial capitalism, described in Marx's classic theses or embedded in the language and theory of the left and inscribed in its agendas, its institutions and its revolutionary scenarios. For many of us (though not for everyone) this struggle to ground socialism in a new analysis of 'our times' was primary and originating – where the whole New Left project began. This was both a theoretical and a political question, since from the mid-1950s onwards, Labour – having lost the 1951 and 1955, and shortly thereafter the 1959, elections – started to tear itself apart in the first post-war 'revisionist' debate which had these questions at its centre.

The dominant account offered was that we were entering a 'post-capitalist' society in which the principal problems of social distribution had been solved by the post-war boom coupled to the expansion of the welfare state, Keynesian macroeconomic regulation and the 'human face' of the managerial revolution. All these were elements of what later came to be known as 'corporatism' – big capital, big state – or, from another point of view, the 'post-war consensus'. They had led to an erosion of traditional class cultures and the 'embourgeoisement' of the working class.

Opposed to this scenario was the 'Old Left' argument that, since the system was still patently capitalist, nothing of any significance had changed. The classes and the class struggle were exactly what and where they had always been, and to question this was to betray the revolutionary cause. The majority of the New Left, however, refused this binary logic, arguing that post-war capitalism *had* changed. The new forms of property, corporate organisation and the dynamics of modern accumulation and consumption required a new analysis. These processes had had effects on social structure and political consciousness. More broadly, the spread of consumerism had disarticulated many traditional cultural attitudes and social hierarchies, and this had consequences for politics, the constituencies for change and the institutions and agendas of the left, with which socialism must come to terms. Lacking much indigenous material to go on, the American analysts – Riesman, Galbraith, Wright Mills – who were at the cutting edge of these developments provided us with our main purchase on these arguments.

Closely linked to this was the argument about the contradictory and politically indeterminate 'drift' of social and cultural change. These changes fell short of a transformation of society, yet clearly but ambiguously dismantled many of the old relations and formations on which the whole edifice of the left and the project of socialism had historically been constructed. Again, there were at least two competing versions of this. One was that, since the fundamental class structure of British society remained intact, 'change' could be only of the most superficial 'sociological' kind. It picked up incidental and mainly stylistic differences in such marginal areas as new attitudes and life-styles amongst young people, new patterns of urban life, the movement out of the inner cities, the growing importance of consumption in everyday life, the 'weakening' of older social identities, and so on, which did not touch 'the fundamentals'. This fundamentalist account was matched, on the other side, by a relentless celebration of change for its own sake in which the new mass media had acquired a massive investment. With the expansion of the new journalism, the spread of mass culture and the rise of commercial television, society seemed bewitched by images of itself in motion, reflecting off its shiny consumer surfaces. Life was increasingly described here in the mindlessly trendy imagery of the absolute divide between 'then' – that is, 'before the war' – and 'now', after free orange juice, school meals, the Labour government and *Rock Around the Clock* …

Again, the New Left insisted on occupying neither of these simple alternatives, choosing instead a more complex 'third' description. We were not necessarily at one in terms of how we understood these shifts (the debate between Edward Thompson, Raphael Samuel and myself on my speculative piece 'A Sense of Classlessness' (see Chapter 2 in this book), in the pages of *ULR* is one *locus classicus* of this debate), but we were agreed about their significance. In my view, much that was creative, albeit chaotic and impressionistic, about the 'picture of the world' which came from the pages of New Left writing owed its freshness and vitality (as well as its utopianism) to the effort to sketch the meanings of these rapidly shifting contours of change. That is indeed one place where the New Left investment in the debate about culture first arose. First, because it was in the cultural and ideological domain that social change appeared to be making itself most dramatically visible. Second, because the cultural dimension seemed to us not a secondary, but a constitutive dimension of society. (This reflects part of the New Left's long-standing quarrel with the reductionism and economism of the base-superstructure metaphor.) Third, because the discourse of culture seemed to us fundamentally necessary to any language in which socialism could be redescribed. The New Left therefore took the first faltering steps of putting questions of cultural analysis and cultural politics at the centre of its politics.

In these different ways, the New Left launched an assault on the narrow definition of 'politics' and tried to project in its place an 'expanded conception of the political'. If it did not move so far as the feminist principle that 'the personal is political', it certainly opened itself up to the critical dialectic between 'private troubles' and 'public issues', which blew the conventional conception of politics apart. The logic implied by our position was that these 'hidden dimensions' had to be represented within the discourses of 'the political' and that ordinary people could and should organise where they were, around issues of immediate experience, begin to articulate their dissatisfactions in an existential language and build an agitation from that point. (This was the source of our much-debated 'socialist humanism'.) The expanded definition of the political also entailed a recognition of the proliferation of the potential sites of social conflict and the constituencies for change. Although we were in favour of a strong trade unionism, we contested the idea that *only* those at the 'point of production' could make the revolution.

In our report in *NLR 1* on the London Club's work in Notting Hill, for example, we spoke of racial oppression, housing, property deterioration and short-sighted urban planning alongside the more traditional themes of poverty and unemployment; we spoke of young Blacks on the street while youth clubs were closed, working mothers without crèches and children without playgrounds, as equally central to any modern conception of the 'degradations' of modern capitalism – though we remained blind to the ways in which even this expanded conception of politics was still inscribed in gendered categories. Doubtless this over-expanded definition traced the connections between different domains very weakly and blurred the cutting edge of our strategy, but it was the inevitable outcome of a powerful belief that the language of socialism *must* address the question of 'how we live now and how we ought to live'.

The critique of reformism and its singularly British representative, 'Labourism', was entailed in this enlarged discourse of 'the political'. In the light of Stalinism and the Cold War, reformism appeared the obvious, rational alternative for anyone who wished to redistribute wealth more evenly and have a more socially just society, but who was also committed to the 'civilised values' of the Western world. Edward Thompson described this Hobson's choice, in his article in *Out of Apathy*, as an Orwellian dilemma. We looked for a more radical and structural transformation of society: partly because we were committed to many of the fundamental perspectives of the classical socialist programme; partly because we saw in modern capitalism a greater, not a lesser, concentration of social power, and could trace the impact of 'commodification' in areas of life far removed from the immediate sites of wage-labour exploitation – but above all because of the much broader critique we had of 'capitalist civilisation and culture'. Questions of alienation, the breakdown of community, the weakness of democracy in civil society and what the early American New Left, in its Port Huron statement, called 'quality of life' issues, constituted for us as significant an indictment of the present regime of capital as any other – an indictment we thought irremediable within an unreformed and untransformed society and culture. No one expressed the fundamental and constitutive character of this argument for and within the New Left more profoundly than Raymond Williams.

It was in this sense that we remained 'revolutionaries', though few retained any faith in a vanguardist seizure of state power by a small minority unaccompanied by any broader democratic and cultural 'long revolution', or a shift in the 'mode of production' achieved by bureaucratic state control. Both seemed implausible scenarios under conditions of modern class democracies, and unlikely to produce those automatic transformations which the traditional left anticipated. The opposition between 'reform' and 'revolution' seemed to many of us outdated: more a way of swearing at and anathematising others than having any real analytic-historical value in its own right. We sought, in different ways, to bypass it.

In these and other significant ways, the dominant tendency of the New Left was 'revisionist' (then not such a dirty word as now) with respect both to Labourism and to Marxism. We had come into existence and now lived in the age of 'many Marxisms'. We confronted the 'freezing' of Marxism in Eastern Europe into a sterile state dogma. We watched 'Marxist' tanks overthrowing the 'Marxist' provisional government of Imre Nagy and Georg Lukacs in Hungary. The 'Reasoners' occupied this revisionist space in one way – as Communist dissidents. The 'ULR-ers' occupied it in another way, for most of our generation had entered politics *through* the debate with orthodox and doctrinal versions of Marxism. Few, if any, of us could have been described, after 1956, as 'orthodox' – principally because, though we held different positions about how much of Marxism could be transposed without 'revision' to the second half of the twentieth century, all of us refused to regard it as a fixed and finished doctrine or sacred text. For example, of considerable importance to some of us was the rediscovery, through Chuck Taylor, of Marx's early *Economic and Philosophical Manuscripts*, with its themes of alienation, species being and 'new needs', which he brought over from Paris in 1958 in French, and which only shortly thereafter became available to us in an English translation.

There were many other 'themes' which any comprehensive account would be obliged to discuss: for example, the debate around 'socialist humanism', the analyses of the Third World and, in connection with CND, 'neutralism', NATO and disarmament; the debates about popular culture and the media. However, since the New Left is so often 'tagged' as mainly an intellectual formation, it may be more appropriate to remind readers that the 'first' New Left, however mistakenly, thought of itself as a 'movement' rather than simply a 'journal', and that only with the passage to the 'second' generation in the early 1960s was this project abandoned.

Shortly after the publication of the first issue, *ULR* called its first 'readers' meeting' on an inauspicious Sunday afternoon, which was followed by the foundation of the London *ULR* Club. For its first meetings, the four editors invited the distinguished contributors to the first issue to address their readers. The first speaker was Isaac Deutscher, whose title, 'The Red Sixties', proved not quite as prophetic as it sounds, since Deutscher predicted, not '1968', but the dramatic changes in the Soviet Union which he was convinced would quickly follow the Khrushchev revelations. This was a huge, exciting occasion, and large beyond all expectations. The four editors rearranged the room in the Royal Hotel in what Raphael Samuel assured us was the intimate manner of the Berlin political cafés of the 1930s and went off to have a meal. When we returned, there were seven hundred people waiting outside the building, and one or two (including Suzy Benghiat, later to be a leading figure in the London New Left Club) had drafted themselves to set an entrance price and take the money.

In the early years the *ULR* Club (later the London New Left Club) attracted to its weekly meetings audiences of three and four hundred drawn from across the whole spectrum of the left. For a time it provided an extremely important, lively, often contentious focal point for people with no other formal political commitment. It differed from the typical 'left' organisation or sect in that its purpose was *not* to recruit members but to engage with the political culture of the left on a very broad front through argument, debate, discussion and education. It became an important independent centre for left politics in London, particularly after it found a permanent home, through another of Raphael Samuel's nerve-rackingly risky but brilliantly innovative ventures, in the Partisan coffee bar in Carlisle Street. This was the first left 'coffee bar' in London, with a club house and library on the floors above, which had been lovingly redesigned by Ernest Rodker, a fine carpenter and one of the most active and committed club members. On the fourth floor it housed the offices of *ULR* with its one full-time employee: Janet Hase, the Australian business manager. After the merger, they became the offices of *NLR*. However, weekly club meetings continued to take place in larger venues around central London, since the Partisan was too small to house them. Following the merger, a number of 'New Left clubs' sprang up around the country. (The last issue of *NLR* which I edited, no. 12, listed thirty-nine in various stages of political health.)

A brief description of the activities of the London Left Club will give some indication of what this 'movement' around New Left ideas was like. There were well-publicised and large weekly public meetings with a very wide range of speakers. Gaitskell, Crosland, Crossman and others from the Labour leadership came to debate with us. A range of smaller discussion groups flourished around the Club, including an Education, a Literature, a Teachers' and a Schools group. The cultural debates and activities were considered as important as the more 'political' ones. Arnold Wesker and John Arden connected us to the 'new drama' and its home at the Royal Court; Lindsay Anderson, Karel Reisz and Alex Jacobs to Free Cinema, the British Film Institute and the National Film Theatre; Paddy Whannel and others to the London jazz scene; Roger Mayne to new movements in documentary photography; Germano Facetti and Robin Fior to new ideas in design and typography. There were visits to and discussions at new venues like the Whitechapel Gallery.

The position of the Club in central London, the fact that many of us were secondary-modern teachers – coupled with pressures from 'friends' of the Club, like Colin MacInnes, about the failure of the left to put down roots in this emerging post-war culture or to recruit 'modern' young people to its cause – gave the New Left Club an uncertain 'stake' in the emerging youth culture of the period. (Under the influence of MacInnes, I wrote about this aspect of the New Left in 'Absolute Beginnings' in the final issue of *ULR*.) Inevitably the London Club became part of the wider metropolitan culture and the Partisan was, for a time, a key point in the subterranean culture of Soho life. Other clubs reflected, in programme and composition, the cultural and political character of their localities: the Manchester and Hull Left Clubs were close to the local labour movement; the Fife Socialist League was linked, through Lawrence Daly, to an independent socialist movement amongst Fife miners in Scotland, the Croydon and Hemel Hempstead Clubs had a more 'cross-class' or even '*déclassé-new-town*' feel to them.

Very early on, the London New Left Club pioneered in central London the propaganda and leafleting for the first CND Aldermaston March, which the club membership supported *en masse*. This was the beginning of close links between the New Left, the modern peace movement in Britain and the birth of CND as a mass political organisation. The clubs also mounted a sustained propaganda campaign in relation to the policy debates in the Labour Party about the 'revision of Clause 4'. Gaitskell himself had inserted the cultural question into this political agenda when he argued after the 1959 defeat that Labour's social base had been permanently eroded by 'the telly, the fridge and the second-hand motorcar'. Pessimists might like to know that we spoke quite openly at the time of 'Fifteen years of Tory rule? Mr Selwyn Lloyd's finger on the trigger? Mr Lennox Boyd's rifles over Africa? Mr Macmillan's face on TV? *Again?*'. The Club engaged with the full range of these themes. We published replies to Labour Party discussion documents, debated the Crosland theses on which they were based, set up exhibitions on cultural issues at Labour Party conferences. We mounted, for example, the first – and only? – exhibition at an annual Labour Party Conference offering a political critique of commercial advertising. We also produced a free, cyclostyled daily broadsheet for delegates, *This Week*. I am proud to say that it was in its pages that I first described Harold Wilson as 'Mr Facing-Both-Ways'.

Among its other activities, the New Left Club in London became deeply involved in 1958 with the race riots in Notting Hill and with the anti-racist struggles of the period around North Kensington. We participated in the efforts to establish tenants' associations in the area, helped to protect black people who, at the height of the 'troubles', were molested and harassed by white crowds in an ugly mood between Notting Hill station and their homes, and picketed the Mosley and National Front meetings. George Clark, who later pioneered an early form of 'community politics' in North Kensington, first cut his teeth on this experience. Michael de Freitas – later to have another career as 'Michael X' – was one of the 'street hustlers' who, as a result of this intervention, came over to the side of the tenants he had been hired to hassle. In the course of this work we first stumbled across the powerful traces of racism inside the local Labour Party itself, and Rachel Powell, an active club member, unearthed the scandal of 'Rachmanism' and white landlord exploitation in Notting Hill, but failed to persuade the media to take it seriously until it later surfaced as a side-show to the Profumo Affair.

Peter Sedgwick once acutely observed that the New Left was less a movement than a 'milieu'. He was noting the lack of tight organisational structure, the loose conception of leadership, the flat hierarchies, the absence of membership, rules, regulations, party programme or 'line' which characterised the New Left, in sharp contrast with other political tendencies and sects on the far left. These organisational features were the product of our critique of Leninist and democratic centralist forms of organisation and the emphasis on self-organisation and participatory politics, which we can now see retrospectively as 'prefigurative' of so much that was to come afterwards. He may also have been obliquely commenting on the low level of working-class participation – or, to be more accurate, the 'cross-class composition' of many, though by no means all, of the New Left clubs. This could be seen as – and indeed was – a serious weakness, but oddly enough, it also had some compensations. Where the clubs were particularly strong was in those social strata emerging within and across the rapidly shifting, recomposing-decomposing class landscapes of post-war Britain. This separated us, not from ordinary working people, for we had many of those as active supporters, but from the political cultures of the traditional labour movement and the revolutionary cadres of the sects. Nevertheless, it gave the New Left a privileged access to the grinding, grating processes of contradictory social change.

With all their weaknesses, the clubs signified the project of the New Left to be a new kind of socialist entity: not a party but a 'movement of ideas'. We aimed to constitute an intervention in British political life and to develop a self-organising and participatory political practice which would be prefigurative of socialism itself – and an effective critique of the political practices typical of either the major parties or the left sects. It was said that by 1962-63 many Left clubs were in decline – and so they were. But that is not the point. The clubs and other 'movement' aspects of the 'first' New Left were not only symptomatic of our politics but a sign that, for us and for the left, the *question of agency* had become deeply problematic. The 'second' New Left – which began, after a brief, brilliant interlude of 'troika' rule, with Perry Anderson's accession to the editorship, the restructuring of the editorial board and the exodus of many of the 'old' New Left members – was a much more rigorous theoretical project, committed to a more orthodox, less 'revisionist', reading of Marxism, and was pursued with remarkable flair and single-mindedness. But it was *not* a project which constituted the question of political agency as in any way problematic, either theoretically or strategically.

These questions of political organisation, strategy and style are best exemplified in relation to certain concrete political questions of the time, though they may be thought to have wider implications. CND and the Labour Party are perhaps the most useful examples. Peggy Duff, General Secretary of CND and the outstanding organiser of the antinuclear movement in that period, subsequently wrote, in her book *Left, Left, Left*, that in the end, CND swallowed up the New Left. I do not agree with this judgement, but I understand what lay behind it. Once involved, the New Left gave CND its sustained and unqualified support. Their fates became closely intertwined, and, indeed, both experienced a related decline in the mid-1960s. Nevertheless, the New

Left also had a project in relation to CND: to broaden its politics; to 'educate', in Gramsci's sense, the moral impulses which brought most people to the peace movement into a wider politics of the left; and to make explicit the connections between 'the bomb', capitalism, NATO, Stalinism, the Warsaw Pact. But we pursued that project through an 'open' rather than a sectarian strategy. We were committed to working alongside CND, rather than operating parasitically on it.

This was in sharp contrast to the 'hard' left and Trotskyist sects, who by and large adopted a cynical but classically sectarian practice towards CND. They treated the peace movement as a 'soft' recruiting ground: to them, it was a movement dominated by misguided moral and religious enthusiasts, a few of whom could, however, be picked off for a more 'serious' enterprise and parachuted into the nitty-gritty of 'real politics' somewhere else. In this conception, 'real politics' is so often not where everybody else is, but always 'somewhere else'. The Trotskyists were to do exactly the same thing again with young people and students in 1968, picking off recruits from the student movement for a few heady months of selling 'the paper' outside the factory gates before, brutalised by this entirely gestural mimicry of revolutionary politics, the young recruits made good their escape, once and for all, from left politics of any kind.

We adopted this approach partly out of conviction, partly because we thought the movement of ordinary people *into* politics – breaking with the crust of conventional opinions and orthodox alignments in their own lives, on a concrete issue, and beginning to 'take action for themselves' – was more politically significant than the most correct of 'correct lines'. Those foxed by such references to 'correctness' may like to recall that one had to debate as a serious issue the question of whether or not the Soviet bomb was a 'Workers' Bomb' and therefore more worth keeping than the capitalist one. Another reason was that we saw in embryo in CND a new kind of political mobilisation – beyond, so to speak, the big party battalions – which reflected certain emergent social forces and aspirations characteristic of their time, in relation to which it was necessary for the left to develop a new political practice.

CND was one of the first of this type of 'social movement' to appear in post-war British politics – a popular movement with a clear radical thrust and an implicit 'anti-capitalist' content, formed through self-activity in civil society around a concrete issue, but lacking a clear class composition and appealing to people across the clear-cut lines

THE 'FIRST' NEW LEFT

of traditional class identity or organisational loyalties. It was already possible to recognise in these new movements features of modern society, and points of social antagonism which – like the civil-rights movement at the time, and feminist and sexual questions, ecological and environmental issues, community politics, welfare rights and anti-racist struggles in the 1970s and 1980s – have proved difficult to construct within the organisational agendas of the traditional left. Without these social movements, however, no contemporary mass political mobilisation or movement for radical change in modern times is now conceivable.

Moreover, the New Left itself belonged to the same conjuncture as CND. It was the product of the same decay in the 'relations of representation' between the people, the classes and the parties which has become so much more pronounced in the 1970s and 1980s and mobilised similar social forces. As we wrote in the last issue of *ULR*:

> Here is a movement of people drawn from very different backgrounds, tired of the two-way shuffle of the political party bureaucracies, fed up with the Cold War slogans of 'massive retaliation' and the 'Two Camps' cast of mind, terrified by what C. Wright Mills calls 'the drift and thrust' to World War III. We cannot claim credit for the vigour and success of this movement, but we have been proud to contribute to it, and, through the journals and the clubs, to develop some of its socialist implications. Similarly with the movements of protest against the Hola Camp atrocities and the Nyasaland 'crisis'. Such groups of people find a common cause with us, not merely because of the individual issues but because, by doing so, they are helping to establish the only basis upon which socialism can be built: the principle that, whatever kind of world we want, we are going to have to make it for ourselves and the sooner we stand up, say what it is, and fight for it, the quicker it will be in coming. If the *New Left Review* has any political roots, they will be *there*. Without CND supporters, Anti-Ugly protesters [a protest movement against the banality and conformism of post-war British architecture], African demonstrators, Free Cinema and the Society for the Abolition of The Death Penalty, we would be nowhere.

Ultimately, what CND posed for the New Left – as new social movements always do – was the problem of how to articulate these new impulses and social forces with the more traditional class politics of the left; and how, through this articulation, the project of the left could be transformed. The fact that we had no greater success than the left has had since in trying to construct a 'historical bloc' out of such hetero-geneous social interests, political movements and agendas, in building a hegemonic political practice out of, and with, these differences, does not negate the urgency of the task. What we can 'learn' from the 'first' New Left here is what questions to ask, not which answers work. (Two decades later feminism found itself log-jammed in the same place, caught between the 'Vanguards' and the 'Fragments'.) On the other hand, the failure to resolve it had – and has – consequences. There is no question that the 'first' New Left was weakened by its failure to find a strategic way through this dilemma and remained somewhat disaggre-gated between its very different constituencies.

Many people in and around the New Left were members of the Labour Party. Many were not. As a movement, our attitude to the Labour Party was quite clear. Our independence from organisational links, controls, party routines and discipline was essential for our political project. The majority vote for unilateralism at the Labour Party Conference, for which many of us campaigned, was a clear example to us of 'defeat-in-victory', as a result of mistaking a platform victory for the winning of new popular political positions. Inside the machine, CND withered and shrivelled into a talisman, a fetish of party conference resolutions, plaything of the manoeuvres of the block vote, without touching ground in the political consciousness or activity of many actual people. It is still being defended by the left in this fetishised form.

At the same time we recognised that the fate of socialism in Britain was inextricably bound up with the fate and fortunes of Labour. We recognised Labour as, for good or ill, the party which had hegemonised the vast majority of the organised working class with a reformist politics. We honoured its historic links to the trade union movement. We acknowledged it as the engine of the 'welfare state' revolution of 1945, which we never underestimated because it represented a reform, rather than an overthrow, of the system. We remained deeply critical of the Fabian and Labourist cultures of the Labour Party, of its 'statism', its lack of popular roots in the political and cultural life of ordinary people, its bureaucratic suspicion of any independent action or 'movement' outside its limits, and its profound anti-intellectualism. We opposed the deeply undemocratic procedures of the block vote and the party's empty 'constitutionalism'. Yet we knew that the Labour Party represented, whether we liked it or not, the strategic stake in British politics, which no one could ignore.

We therefore developed an open and polemical politics in relation to the Gaitskell leadership, on the one hand, and the 'nothing-has-changed-reaffirm-Clause-4' perspective of the traditional left on the other; taking up – here as elsewhere – a third position, opening a 'third front'. In the revisionist debates of the 1950s and 1960s we opposed the post-capitalist 'human face of corporate capitalism' theses proposed in Crosland's *The Future of Socialism*, while recognising him as a formidable and intelligent opponent. In relation to the left, we insisted against the doctrinal immobilism of much of the Labour and trade-union left – on the necessity of grounding the perspectives of the left in a new analysis of the novel conditions of post-war capitalism and social change. Some people would continue to work for this inside the Labour Party; others worked outside. We did not see how there could be a 'correct' line on this issue when there was so little relationship between what people wanted politically and the vehicle for achieving it. Our strategy was therefore to sidestep it and instead to involve people, whatever their affiliations, in independent political activity and debate. As we wrote in *ULR* 6, 'for the first time since the war, there is, particularly among young people, a left movement which is not the prisoner of any sect, and yet which is not to be automatically won to the Labour Party, even as an opposition within it.'

This 'parallel' strategy required, as its necessary condition, the maintenance of journals and clubs, a network of contacts, forms of demonstration, argument and propaganda which articulated this 'third position', which were not subject to the routines of Transport House but were nevertheless designed to break back into and have an effect on the internal politics of the Labour Party and the labour movement. We called this strategy (subsequently treated with scathing irony by some *enragés* of the New Left Mark 2 during the High Noon of 1968, but in hindsight not so simple or foolish a 'war of position' as they made it appear) the strategy of 'one foot in, one foot out'.

What type of organisational leadership did these strategies pre-suppose? The metaphor to which we constantly returned was that of 'socialist propaganda'. As Edward Thompson put it in the final issue of *The New Reasoner*:

The New Left does not propose itself as an alternative organisation to those already in the field; rather, it offers two things to those within and without the existing organisations – a specific propaganda of ideas, and certain practical services (journals, clubs, schools, etc).

The notion of a 'socialist propaganda of ideas' was, of course, borrowed directly and explicitly from William Morris and the relationships forged in the Socialist League between intellectuals, struggling to make themselves what Gramsci called 'organic', and the working class. We had all read and been inspired by the 'Making Socialists' chapter of Edward Thompson's *William Morris: Romantic to Revolutionary.* Indeed, the first editorial of *NLR* was framed at either end by a quote from Morris's *Commonweal* article of July 1885: 'The Labour Movement is not in its insurrectionary phase'. I added: 'we are in our missionary phase'.

Although it was not, as they say these days, 'fully theorised', this conception of leadership was based on certain clear presuppositions. The first was the necessity of challenging the conventional anti-intellectualism of the British labour movement and overcoming the traditional division between intellectuals and the working class. The second was the repudiation of three alternative models: 'vanguardist' and 'democratic centralist' conceptions of revolutionary leadership; Fabian notions of the middle-class 'experts' giving socialism from within the state machine to the working classes; and the traditional Labour left faith in constitutional mechanisms, conference resolutions, winning the block votes and 'electoral contests with slightly more "left" candidates'. Third, our view was that changes in British society had brought a large number of the new, post-war social strata within reach of socialist education and propaganda. Fourth, we had a deep conviction that, against the 'economism' of the Stalinist, Trotskyist and Labourist left alike, socialism was a *conscious* democratic movement and socialists were *made*, not born or 'given' by the inevitable laws of history or the objective processes of the mode of production alone.

We also challenged the prevailing view that social change as such, even the so-called 'affluent society', would objectively and of itself erode the appeal of socialist propaganda and that socialism could arise only out of immiseration and degradation. Our emphasis on people taking action for themselves, 'building socialism from below' and 'in the here and now', not waiting for some abstract Revolution to transform everything in the twinkling of an eye, proved, in the light of the re-emergence of these themes after 1968, strikingly prefigurative (despite all the other differences between the New Lefts of '1956' and '1968').

> We have to go into towns and cities, universities and technical colleges, youth clubs and Trade Union branches and – as Morris said – *make socialists* there. We have come through 200 years of capitalism and 100 years of imperialism. Why should people – naturally – turn to socialism? There is no law which says that the Labour Movement, like a great inhuman engine, is going to throb its way into socialism or that we can, any longer … rely upon poverty and exploitation to drive people, like blind animals, towards socialism. Socialism is, and will remain, an active faith in a new society, to which we turn as conscious, thinking human beings. People have to be confronted with experience, called to the 'society of equals', not because they have never had it so bad, but because the 'society of equals' is better than the best soft-selling consumer capitalist society, and life is something *lived,* not something one passes through like tea through a strainer.

This position may seem naive and has certainly been dubbed 'utopian' and 'populist' since. But it was populist in the 'Narodnik' sense of 'going to the people' and in terms of what they/we might become, rather than in the Thatcherite sense of massaging popular consent by cynical appeals to what the people are said by their betters to want. We had an instinctive, if not well formulated, notion that the socialist project had to be rooted in the 'here and now' and connect with lived experience: with what we have since learned to call 'the national-popular'. 'The people' is, of course, always a discursive construction and the blurring of a precise social referent in the populism of the early New Left was certainly significant. But there is more than one kind of 'populism' and it can, despite all its problems, be articulated either to the right or the left, and serve either to short-circuit or to develop popular antagonisms. The 'populism' of the early New Left was certainly of the latter sort, as Edward Thompson, its main architect, put it in *The New Reasoner:*

> What will distinguish the New Left will be its rupture with the tradition of inner party factionalism, and its renewal of the tradition of open association, socialist education, and activity, directed towards

the people as a whole ... It will insist that the Labour Movement
is not a thing but an association of men and women; that working
people are not the passive recipients of economic and cultural condi-
tioning, but are intellectual and moral beings ... it will appeal to
people by rational argument and moral challenge. It will counter the
philistine materialism and anti-intellectualism of the Old Left by
appealing to the totality of human interests and potentialities, and
by constructing new channels of communication between industrial
workers and experts in the sciences and arts. It will cease to postpone the satisfactions of Socialism to an hypothetic period 'after the
Revolution', but will seek to promote in the present and in particular
in great centres of working-class life, a richer sense of community.

Needless to say, the tensions and contradictions implicit in this
'populism' were never wholly resolved. The rapid shifts in social structure of the post-war period, which we constantly tried to characterise
without pinning them down precisely, cut unevenly into the New
Left and we failed to build these differences into a new 'historical
bloc', though that was our implicit aim. The tensions already alluded
to between the provincial 'North' and cosmopolitan 'London', like
later versions of the 'North/South' divide, were much more complex
than this simple opposition suggests. Nevertheless, they shadowed
some critical differences in the pace and character of class recomposition and social decomposition in post-war British society and came to
stand metonymically for the diversifying ground of politics, without
providing any principle of articulation. The tensions between 'intellectuals' and 'activists' were a continuing, if largely unspoken, problem
connected to the much wider issue of the uncertain status of intellectuals in English cultural life generally and the disabling philistinism
of the left. Cutting across all these tensions from another direction was
the almost totally hidden question of gender – the fact that the great
majority of the editorial-board leadership were men and that many
of those on whom the actual 'labour' of keeping the whole enterprise
going fell were women: the usual sexual division of labour, reproduced
so often in the left. About this last question the New Left preserved –
as did the rest of the left – a profound unconsciousness.

We hoped that the clubs would develop their own independent
organisation, leadership and channels of communication (perhaps
their own newssheet or bulletin), leaving the journal free to develop

its own project. But we lacked the resources to bring this about, which exacerbated in the clubs feelings that they had no control over the journal, and in the editorial board the fear that a journal of ideas could not be effectively run by committees. It was, in effect, this last issue and the cross-pressures associated with it which finally precipitated my own resignation from the editorship of *New Left Review* in 1961.

It is not for me to attempt any overall assessment of the 'first' New Left, which I see as only a first stage in the constitution of a new kind of left politics. It seems absurd to attempt to defend its record in detail or to impose, retrospectively, a consistency it did not possess. Its strengths and weaknesses, errors and mistakes, remain and are unanswerable – to be learned from rather than repudiated. Nevertheless I would make the sharpest distinction between what we did and how we did it, and the wider project. I remain as committed to the latter, thirty years later, as I was then. The 'third space' which the 'first' New Left defined and tried to prise open still seems to me the only hope for the renewal of the democratic and socialist project in our new and bewildering times.

PART 2: THATCHERISM

Racism and reaction

1978

IN HIS BOOK *Black and White*, which is a study of the negro in English society 1555 to 1945 – a book worth reading – James Walvin recounts how in the last decade of the sixteenth century, England was troubled by an expanding population and a shortage of food: 'as hunger swept the land, England was faced by a problem which taxed the resources of government to the limits'.[1] He adds that immigrants were seen as adding to the problem, since 'no group was so immediately visible as the blacks' – which, it may surprise you to know, by then had been distributed already in their thousands in English cities as a result of the growing involvement of England in the slave trade. Queen Elizabeth I accordingly wrote to the Lord Mayors of the country's major cities: 'there are of late divers blackamores brought into the realm, of which kind of people there are alreadie here to manie, consideryng howe God hath blessed this land with a great increase of people'. She recommended that 'those kind of people be sent forth of the land'. And indeed, in January 1601, she repeated her advice in the rather more official form of a Royal Proclamation allowing a Lubeck merchant to take 'such Negroes and blackamores which are carried into this realm, to the great annoyance of her own liege people'.

Walvin doesn't record whether this is the first British 'moral panic' about race. But the incident does give us a little bit of historical perspective on the theme of this lecture, which is about the English reaction to race in the postwar period. It also suggests something about the mechanism involved: that it isn't quite of such recent origin as we might suppose. I mean, specifically, the mechanism by which problems which are internal to British society, not ones which are visited on it from the outside, come to be projected on to, or exported into, an excessive preoccupation with the problem of 'race'. This decade is not the first time that the English official mind, when forced to contemplate a 'crisis', has turned the conversation in the direction of 'the blacks'.

This is, in a way, the first and perhaps the most important point that I want to make. Let me put it rather more generally. There is, it seems to me, an overwhelming tendency to abstract questions of race from what one might call their *internal* social and political basis and contexts in British society – that is to say, to deal with 'race' as if it has nothing intrinsically to do with the present 'condition of England'. It's viewed rather as an 'external' problem, which has been foisted to some extent on English society from the outside: it's been visited on us, as it were, from the skies. To hear problems of race discussed in England today, you would sometimes believe that relations between British people and the peoples of the Caribbean or the Indian sub-continent began with the wave of black immigrants in the late 1940s and 1950s. 'The English and race' is frequently debated as if it is a brief and indeed temporary interlude, which will shortly be brought to an end. These poor, benighted people, for reasons which the British sometimes find it hard to bring to mind, picked themselves up out of their villages and plantations and, quite uninvited, made this long, strange and apparently unpredictable journey to the doors of British industry – which, as you know, out of the goodness of their hearts, gave them jobs. Now the 'good times' are over, the kissing has to stop. The national patience is exhausted. The fund of goodwill has been used up. It's time the problem 'went back where it came from'. The British people, I am told, require to be assured that the problem of race will have a definite and conclusive end.

It seems to me that the tendency to pull race out from the internal dynamic of British society, and to repress its history, is not, as might be supposed, confined to the political 'right' of the spectrum. It is also, in my opinion, to be found on the liberal 'left'. For the 'right', immigration and race has become a problem of the control of an external flow, or, as the popular press is fond of saying, 'a tidal wave': cut off the flow and racism will subside. The liberal 'left', on the other hand, have long treated race and immigration as a problem in the exercise of 'good conscience': be kind to 'our friends from overseas' – then racism will disappear. Neither side can nowadays bring themselves to refer to Britain's imperial and colonial past, even as a contributory factor to the present situation. The slate has been wiped clean. Racism is not endemic to the British social formation. It has nothing intrinsically to do with the dynamic of British politics, or with the economic crisis. It is not part of the English culture, which now has to be indeed protected against pollution – it does not belong to the 'English ideology'. It's an external virus somehow injected into the body politic and it's a matter of *policy* whether we can deal with it or not – it's not a matter of *politics*.

I hope to persuade you that this view cannot be true. It is not true of the historical past. And it is certainly not true of the decades since the 1950s, the 'high tide' of post-war black migration to Britain. We can't account for the emergence of a specifically *indigenous* British racism in this way. This last phase, the 1950s, 1960s and 1970s, is of course the main subject I want to come on to in a moment. But something first must be said about the historical aspects. Britain's relations with the peoples of the Caribbean and the Indian sub-continent do not, of course, belong to and begin in the 1940s. British attitudes to the ex-colonial subject peoples of a former time cannot be accurately charted from the appearance of a black proletariat in Birmingham or Bradford in the 1950s. These relations have been central features in the formation of Britain's material prosperity and dominance, as they are now central themes in English culture and in popular and official ideologies. That story should not indeed require to be rehearsed. Britain's rise to mercantile dominance, and the process of generating the surpluses of wealth which set economic development in motion, were founded on the slave trade and the plantation system in the Americas in the seventeenth century. India provided the basis for the foundation of Britain's Asian empire in the eighteenth; the penetration by trade of Latin America and of the Far East was the centre-piece of Britain's industrial and imperial hegemony in the nineteenth. In each of these phases, an economic and cultural chain – in short, to be brutal, the imperialist chain – has bound the fate of millions of workers and peasants in the colonial hinterlands to the destiny of rich and poor in the heartland of English society. The wealth – drawn off through conquest, colonisation and trade – has slightly enriched one English class after another. It has supported the foundation of one flourishing urban culture after another. It has led to one phase of economic development after another. It is, in a sense, geography and distance which has rendered this long historical connection invisible. It's only in the very last phase of British imperialism that the labouring classes of the satellite countries and the labouring classes of the metropolis have had to confront one another directly 'on native ground' in large numbers. But that is not the same thing as saying that their fates have not long been indissolubly connected.

I want to make the proposition that the very definition in the 1970s of what it is to be English has been articulated around this. If the blood of the colonial workers has not mingled extensively with the English, then their labour-power has long entered the economic blood-stream of British society. It is in the sugar you stir; it is in the sinews of the famous British 'sweet tooth'; it is in the tea-leaves at the bottom of the next 'British' cuppa.

I want to turn on that point and argue that the development of an indigenous British racism in the post-war period *begins* with the profound historical forgetfulness – what I want to call the loss of historical memory, a kind of historical amnesia, a decisive mental repression – which has overtaken the British people about race and empire since the 1950s. Paradoxically, it seems to me, the native, home-grown variety of racism begins with this attempt to wipe out and efface every trace of the colonial and imperial past. Clearly, that is one effect of the traumatic adjustment to the very process of bringing Empire to an end. But, undoubtedly, it has left an enormous reservoir of guilt and a deep, historical, resentment. It's not possible to operate surgically so directly on popular memory without leaving scars and traces. And, undoubtedly, this reservoir of resentment and guilt, which does not find easy expression any longer in, for instance, the forms of popular imperialism in which it did at the end of the nineteenth century, but which is nevertheless there, has undoubtedly nourished and provides something of a reservoir for the indigenous racism of the 1950s and 1960s. Its lingering legacy may in fact account for something of racism's popular appeal in the last twenty years. Thus, that history has to be reckoned with, by one way or another. But it cannot alone explain the growth of a home-grown racism in Britain in the last twenty years.

To do this, we have to turn to the factors which are more internal to British society, factors which have made racism a growing and dynamic political force in Britain since the 1950s. And here perhaps I should say that it's not helpful to define racism as a 'natural' and permanent feature – either of all societies or indeed of a sort of universal 'human nature'. It's not a permanent human or social deposit which is simply waiting there to be triggered off when the circumstances are right. It has no natural and universal law of development. It does not always assume the same shape. There have been many significantly different *racisms* – each historically specific and articulated in a different way with the societies in which they appear. Racism is always historically specific in this way, whatever common features it may appear to share with other similar social phenomena. Though it may draw on the cultural and ideological traces which are deposited in a society by previous historical phases, it always assumes specific forms which arise out of *present* – not past – conditions and organisation of society. It may matter less that Britain has, over four centuries, been involved in modes of economic exploitation and political dominance, on a world scale, which frequently operated through the mechanism of race. This only signals the potential – perhaps, the propensity – of the society to travel that route again. But the indigenous racism of the 1960s and 1970s is significantly different, in form and effect, from the racism of the 'high' colonial period. It is a racism 'at home', not abroad; it is the racism, not of a dominant but of a declining social formation. It is to the construction of this home grown variety that I want now to turn.

First, it's necessary to establish some kind of rough periodisation. But in doing this, I ask you to hold two different perspectives in mind at the same time. I think we must look, what I call *sequentially*, at the way in which racism has been constructed and developed through the three decades; at its development as a process; at its forms and its deepening impact from one stage to another. Here we are interested in what the turning points have been. But at the same time, I think it's important to look *laterally* at what are the other things with which this developing racism has been connected.

We start at the period of the late 1940s and 1950s, the period of initial settlement. Here, we find the build up of black workers in the labour-hungry centres of British production. It's a period when industry is, of course, swinging over from war-time to peace-time production. It leads in to the great productive 'boom' of the mid-1950s. The main outlines of the pattern of black settlement are established in this phase: the inner-city black concentrations, multiple-occupancy, the density of black labour in certain specific occupational sectors. In this period, accommodation and adjustment between blacks and whites is on the agenda. The black population, on the whole, maintain what I would call a 'low profile'. They draw their curtains both against the cold and against the 'outsider'. They efface themselves as an intrusive presence. They are tiptoeing through the tulips. It's a period of muted optimism about the hope and dream of long-term black and white assimilation.

The real environment where this proposition is to be tested is, of course, in the jobs and localities where black and white workers meet and live. There are, indeed, even in this early phase, problems of adjustment between blacks and whites. What is not present are the strictly defined lines of informal segregation between blacks and whites which has come to be the prevailing social pattern in such areas. The whole period is one which Sivanandan has called the 'laissez-faire' period in British immigration politics. It's the period of the 'open door'. Remember that it's lubricated by the economic boom. The need in British industry to draw heavily on this new reserve army of labour weakens both any official resistance to the introduction of a black proletariat and the sense of competition for jobs between blacks and whites. The segmentation of blacks and Asian workers in particular occupational sectors helps in this shielding process. But above all, rising living standards in this period provide just that economic space, just that room for economic manoeuvre, especially in the urban areas, which gives people from different ethnic backgrounds a little room to settle and move in, to put it crudely. The modest 'optimism' about race in this period is closely dependent on a general climate of economic optimism and the one is an expression of the other.

The real history of that early phase remains to be written. But the first signs of an open and emergent racism of a specifically indigenous type appears, of course, in the race riots of Notting Hill and Nottingham in 1958. These riots cannot be directly attributed to the early warning signs of a developing economic crisis, though those are undoubtedly on stage. Notting Hill is a classic scenario for the appearance of indigenous racism: it's one of those 'traditional urban zones' where, for the first time, the incipient 'colony' life of blacks begins for the first time to flourish and expand at the very heart of the British city.

In the race riots of 1958, there are three constituent elements. The first is the appearance, for the first time in real terms since the 1940s, of an active fascist political element: the Unionist movement and the dissident League of Empire Loyalists. They saw, quite correctly, that the uneven development of culture in an area like this, with its incipient but growing urban problems, provided a more favourable terrain for the construction of a native racism than, for example, the more traditional structures of an older area of settlement, like Brixton. They introduced the syntax of racism into street-corner politics for the first time openly in the post-war period. But, in effect, they were at that stage more symptom than cause.

The second element, however, is more important. It is the structured antagonism between 'colony' blacks and sections of the indigenous white working class and petty-bourgeoisie of this decaying 'royal' suburb. It is against this fulcrum – which marks the interconnection between the politics of race and the politics of the inner city – that the wheel of British racism first begins to turn.

The third, and active element – that which attracted the publicity and the talk – was white teenagers. Here, looking laterally, it is worthwhile reminding you that Notting Hill race riots have two histories, not one. It has a history in the development and the emergence of British racism and also in the panics about youth and affluence and permissiveness in the 1950s. It is part of that double structure. If the presence of blacks within the area touched sources of public anxiety about competition over scarce resources and coming competition over jobs and so on, the spectacle of black and white youths, locked in confrontation around the tube station and the back streets of North Kensington, fed directly into a deep and troubled anxiety about the whole process of post-war social change – a process, incidentally, for which the term 'Youth' had by then become a vivid social metaphor. In its famous editorial 'Hooliganism is Hooliganism', *The Times* mapped the Notting Hill events directly, not into the problem of race or of urban poverty, but into the problem of hooliganism, teenage violence, lawlessness, anarchy, together with the football spectator – an ancient ring that term has – and the railway carriage breaker – an even more ancient formulation. 'All', *The Times* said, 'are manifestations of a strand of our social behaviour that an adult society can do without'. As the economic downturn begins and youth culture surges forward, Britain introduces, in 1962, the first Commonwealth Immigration Act, which imposes controls on the 'flow of black people into the society'.

The second turning point is 1964. For, by now, the economic boom has tapered off, and the classes which have to be addressed about the growing material problems – which in the 1950s you will remember were defined as never to appear again – are no longer composed of runaway Teddy Boys or football hooligans, but adult white workers, and their families. The location of the new turning point in the emergence of post-war racism therefore takes place not in the decaying transitional zone of Notting Hill but in the very heartland of traditional and conservative Britain: Smethwick, the Midlands. Peter Griffiths's successful campaign which centred on black immigration in the 1964 election marks the first moment when racism is appropriated into the official policy and programme of a major political party and legitimated as the basis of an electoral appeal, specifically addressed to the popular white classes. Here is the beginning of racism as an element in the official politics of British populism – racism in a structured and 'legitimate' form. The defeat of a Labour minister on the issues proved the penetration of this ideology into the organised working class and to the labour institutions themselves. It revealed the degree to which, as a consequence, of everything that had happened to the labour movement in the 1950s and 1960s, sectors of the working class were by now clearly exposed and vulnerable to the construction of a popular racism. The Smethwick victory is a turning point in the history of British racism. It is followed by the 1965 White Paper on Immigration from the Commonwealth, which, as Robert Moore has recently observed, 'laid the ideological basis for subsequent policy in this area and as a result, the argument that the numbers of immigrants was the essence of the problem'.

Between 1964 and 1968, the date of our third 'turning point', it seems that the world itself, not just Smethwick, turned. It turned, of course, specifically about race. The dream of assimilation of black people to white culture is laid low and interned in the mid-1960s. The black population draws back into its defensive enclaves and, much affected in the 1960s by the rise of black struggles, especially in the United States, begins to develop a different, distinct and more actively engaged political ideology. But 1968 is also, of course, a cataclysmic year, not only in Britain but elsewhere: in the US, France, Italy, Germany, Japan and Czechoslovakia. It is the period of growing protests against the Vietnam War. It's the year of the student revolutions, of black power and black separatism, of the cultural underground; of 'hot' summers followed by 'hot' autumns. It inaugurates, in Britain and elsewhere, a period of profound social, cultural and political polarisation. It is when the great consensus of the 1950s and early 1960s comes apart, when the 'politics of the centre' dissolves and reveals the contradictions and social antagonisms which are gathering beneath. It is, more specifically, a period in which the state and the dominant classes perceive, not simply what had tended to transfix them in the 1950s, that is to say the plague of 'permissiveness', the loss of traditional standards and landmarks, but something much worse than that – something close to an organised and active conspiracy against the social order itself. It is the year in which President Nixon wins an infamous victory by summoning up the 'silent majority' in the service of 'law and order'.

'Powellism' is formed in this moment, in this crucible. By 'Powellism' I mean something larger and more significant than the enunciation of a specifically defiant policy about race and the black population by a single person. I mean the formation of an 'official' racist policy at the heart of British political culture. Mr Powell's personal pronouncements on race in 1968 and 1969 have since become justly famous. It is not so frequently remarked that 'Powellism', though it undoubtedly derived its cutting edge from the resonance of its racial themes, was indeed directed more widely at the general crisis of the social order itself; at the conspiracy of radical and alien forces threatening the society, at what Mr Powell himself called the 'Enemy Within'. Nor can the articulation of this talk of 'conspiracy' and 'threats to the social order' be laid exclusively at his door. A range of politicians and public spokesmen in the press and the media in this period are mesmerised by the spectacle of a society which is careering into a social crisis.

A crisis of authority

It is this whole crisis, not race alone, which is the subject and object of the law and order campaigns of the period and the increasingly vigorous appeal to 'tough measures'. But, undoubtedly, as far as what one might call the 'crisis' talk in British society is concerned, it is largely thematised through race. Race is the prism through which the British people are called upon to live through, then to under-stand, and then to deal with, the growing crisis. The 'Enemy' is 'within the gates'. 'He' is nameless: 'he' is protean: 'he' is every-where. He may even, we're told at the one point, be inside the Foreign Office, cooking the immigration figures. But someone will name him. He is 'the Other', he is the stranger in the midst, he is the cuckoo in the nest, he is the excrement in the letterbox. 'He' is – the blacks. This ideology, which is formed in response to a crisis, must of course, to become a real and historical political force, connect with the lived experiences of the 'silent majorities'. It must be given a concrete purchase on the lives of citizens, on their everyday going and comings, on their conditions of existence, if they are to feel that the 'threat to society' is palpable and real. When the 'silent' and beleaguered majorities – the great underclasses, the great, silent 'British public' – are made to 'speak' through the ventriloquism of its public articulators, it is not surprising that it 'speaks' with the unmistakeable accent of a thoroughly home-grown racism. In this period 'Powellism' may be kept out of political power. But in this period it dominated and defined the ideological terrain. Both the Act of 1968 with its explicit use of racial categories, and the 1971 Act, which succeeded in bearing down on dependents and families of black and Asian workers, are tributes to its profound and long term success, that is to say, its popular, mobilising appeal.

It is on the back of that moment that the great backlash of the 1970s comes to be constructed. It moves on each of the fronts at once: political, industrial, economic, racial, ideological. As the true depths of the British economic recession begin to be revealed and as the state girds up its loins to confront directly what is called the hidden materialism of the working class, we witness the construction of what I have come to call a 'soft law and order' society. The law itself becomes, in this period, in part the engine of this social regression.

On the industrial front, it is indeed the law which is recruited directly into the confrontation with the working class. On the political front, it is the law which is mobilised against radicals and demonstrators and 'extremists'. It is in this period that the syntax was formed of extremists versus moderates, without which at one stage it seemed impossible for the media to comment on politics at all. The legal harassment of the black colony populations, the overt racist homilies against the whole black population by judges in courts, the imposition of tough policing and arrest on suspicion in the colony areas, the rising hysteria about black crime and the identification of black crime with 'mugging', must all be seen the context of what, in the early 1970s, is a decisive turn in the whole society into a form of popular authoritarianism. Here what we had defined earlier as a set of discrete panics about race can no longer be identified in that way. It is impossible to separate them out. The lulls between them now are only temporary: the running warfare between unemployed black youth and the police; the swamping tactics of the Special Patrol Groups in the colony areas; the arrests of black political activists 'on suspicion'; the scare, fanned by sections of the press, against Ugandan and then Malawi Asians – the great, prophesied 'tidal wave' at last. Here are the 'scandalous' stories of Asian families 'living in luxury off the Council' – which is only the black counterpart of that general assault on the welfare state which has produced its white counterpart in stories of welfare scroungers drawing their dole on the Costa Brava. There are the beginnings of attacks on black centres and black book shops, the murder of Asian youths, the confrontations in Brockwell Park and other scenes of set warfare, the fining and focussing down of the problem of race into its concrete conditions in the inner-city. In these areas, the programmes of urban aid have failed to stem the tide of poverty and decay. The cycles of unemployment and the fears of recession are beginning to bite. Young blacks are increasingly unemployed – drifting, as every unemployed section of the working class historically has, into petty crime and pilfering. The colony areas are the incipient basis for an increasingly restless and alienated population. This is where the crisis bites. Practically, these areas have to be *policed* with increasing strictness. But, also, the crisis has to be explained. Ideologically it has to be dealt with, contained and managed. Blacks become the bearers, the signifiers, of the crisis of British society in the 1970s: racism is its 'final solution'. The class which is called upon to bear the brunt of a deepening economic crisis is divided and segmented – along racial lines. If racism had not existed as a plausible way in which the underclasses of society could have 'lived through' the crisis of the British social formation in the 1970s, it would surely have had to be invented then.

This is not a crisis of race. But race punctuates and periodises the crisis. Race is the lens through which people come to perceive that a crisis is developing. It is the framework through which the crisis is experienced. It is the means by which the crisis is to be resolved – 'send it away'. It is the means through which the movement, at the level of politics and the state, is 'pioneered' towards what we must now regard as a quite exceptional movement and form: a movement which comes to rely much less than it had in the previous two decades on the construction of consensus, and much more on the law and on coercion. Race is the sound in the working of the society, or a social order, which is girding itself up to iron times, preparing to take tough measures for tough circumstances. It is, above all, the language of racism which has the effect of connecting the 'crisis of the state' *above* with the state of the streets, and little old ladies hustled off pavements in the depths down *below*. That is to say, it makes the 'crisis' real for ordinary people. It's like hanging, it 'wonderfully concentrates the popular mind'.

In his famous speech at Northfield during the 1970 election, Mr Powell had warned of what he called the 'invisible enemy within' – students 'destroying' universities and 'terrorising' cities, 'bringing down' governments; of the power of the form of the modern mob – the demonstration – making 'governments tremble'; the success of disorder, 'deliberately fomented for its own sake', the near-destruction of civil government in Northern Ireland; and the accumulation of what he called 'further combustible material' of 'another kind'. The problem, however, he asserted, has been 'miscalled race'. Race is being used, he suggested, to mystify and confuse the people. The real target is not race. It is the great liberal conspiracy, inside government and the media, which has held ordinary people up to ransom, making them fearful to speak the truth for the fear of being called 'racialist' and 'literally made to say that black is white'. It is race – but now as the pivot of this 'process of brainwashing by repetition of manifest absurdities'; it is race as a 'secret weapon', 'depriving them of their wits and convincing them that what they thought right was wrong'; in short, it's race as the conspiracy of silence against the silent and long suffering majorities – the white majorities. This is the language of an authentic, regressive, national populism. It is articulated, of course, through the potent metaphors of race. Its echo, of course, lives on, expanded and amplified in the panic climate of 1978 – even if the terms are different, the rhetoric less compelling, and the accent more 'refined'. Populist racism is no longer the preserve and prerogative of a minority which is prophesying in the wilderness. It has become 'naturalised' – the normal currency of exchange at the heart of the political culture about this question, and it can be read, any day, on the front page of the *Daily Mail*.

I have said that the emergence of an ideology of indigenous racism has often assumed what I called the form of a 'moral panic'. I want now to say a word about what a moral panic is and how I think it operates. Moral panics have been defined as follows, in a quotation from Stan Cohen's book *Folk Devils and Moral Panics*, which is a study of mods and rockers in the 1960s:

> Societies appear every now and then to be subject to periods of moral panic. A condition, an episode, person or group of persons emerges to become defined as a threat to societal values and interests; its nature is presented in a stylized and stereotypical fashion by the mass media; the moral barricades are manned by editors and bishops and politicians and other right-thinking people; socially accredited experts pronounce their diagnoses and solutions; ways of coping are evolved, or more often resorted to; the condition then disappears or submerges or deteriorates and becomes more visible. Sometimes the panic is passed over and forgotten, but at other times it has more serious and long-term repercussions and it might produce changes in legal and social policy or even in the way in which the societies conceive themselves.[2]

That definition, which is about youth and the way in which society has reacted to the problems of youth in the 1950s and 1960s, could, I think, with very little alteration, be extended to the emergence in Britain of an indigenous racism. The important features of the 'moral panic' as an ideological process are these: it represents a way of dealing with what are diffuse and often unorganised social fears and anxieties. It deals with those fears and anxieties, not by addressing the real problems and conditions which underlie them, but by projecting and displacing them on to the identified social group. That is to say, the moral panic crystallises popular fears and anxieties which have a real basis, and, by providing them with a simple, concrete, identifiable, simple, social object, seeks to resolve them. Around these stigmatised groups or events, a powerful and popular groundswell of opinion can often be mustered. It is a groundswell which calls, in popular accents, on the 'authorities' to take controlling action. 'Moral panics', therefore, frequently serve as ways of pioneering practices by the state which, in the end, increase effective social control, but with this difference: it is the movement towards a closing of a society which has the popular legitimacy, which has been able to win popular consent. That is to say, the moral panic is one of the forms in which a largely voiceless and essentially powerless section of the community can draw attention and give expression to their concrete problems and call for remedies and solutions. Thus, the language of moral panics, whether they're about race or youth, provide a set of simple explanatory terms. They provide a popular vocabulary of discontent and are the way in which the people address themselves to their problems and address those problems to those in power. They consequently also provide vocabularies and motive and action through which the people themselves can be addressed. And in formal democracies, where policies, especially when they are tough and constraining, have to be given popular legitimacy and consent, 'moral panics' can also sometimes provide the basis by which a kind of authoritarianism can be *constructed*.

We have, undoubtedly, in the late 1960s and 1970s, seen both parts of this process in operation. We have seen a distinctive movement towards a movement of closure and of control in the state, and the complementary construction of popular authoritarian ideologies, of which racism is, in my view, only one. Both have operated, of course, in the condition of a deepening economic recession. Though they are not reducible to the economic level, they are quite specific ideological processes. They need to be understood as such. Indeed, whichever political party has been in power and in control of the management of the crisis, the ideological terrain has undoubtedly been defined and colonised through this shift into authoritarianism.

So we can find it in the general assault on the concept of welfare, the militant advocacy of the virtues of social competition and of what are now called 'social market values'. We find it in the assault on 'progressive' and 'comprehensive' trends in education, in the call for a 'return' to standards and to the traditional curriculum, and to discipline and authority in the classroom and, if necessary, to corporal punishment and the cane. We can find it in the aggressive defence of traditional moral standards and values and the traditional family, and the opposition to every tentative movement of liberalisation in the moral and sexual area and, above all, in the position of women. We find it in the 'moral backlash' itself, in the summons to worship at the traditional shrines and pieties.

Race is only one of the elements in this wider ideological crusade to 'clean up' Britain, to roll up the map of progressive liberalism and to turn the clock of history back to the times when the world was 'safe for ordinary Englishmen'. And parties in power, of whatever political complexion, which fondly imagine that they are in command of the forces and tendencies which are moving and shaping popular consciousness, and do not remotely appear to understand the degree to which they are not riding, but *ridden*, well, they too are driven and directed by this wave. The historical stage, the political agenda, has been set, quite often, in the 1970s, in the ideological terrain specifically, and the political and economic forces have followed in the channels which they have opened up.

I want to insist that race is *one* element of this crisis which belongs to the British social formation as a whole, and that it has been a leading, indeed a key, element in the process. It is grounded in natural, obvious, visible, biological facts. It is a way of drawing distinctions and of making differences in practices which are perfectly 'natural', which are given, which are universal, which we are told all of us house a trace of. It has, for instance, become an acceptable explanation of some features of racism in the British police, in their interactions with the black population, that, after all, they are only a cross-section of the 'great British public'. That is to say, there is bound 'naturally' to be a due proportion of 'racists' among them. Race provides precisely the set of simplifications which makes it possible to deal with and explain troubling developments of that kind. After all, who now wants to begin to explore and unravel the complex tissue of political and economic forces which have created and sustained the poverty of inner-urban working-class districts? Who has time for that complicated exercise, especially if it requires us to trace and make connections between things which it is better to keep apart? Above all, if there is a simple, obvious and more natural explanation at hand? Of course they are 'poor' because the *blacks* are *here*. That is not a logical proposition, but ideologies do not function by logic – they have logic of their own. Race has provided, in periods of crisis and upheaval, precisely such a self-justifying circle of explanations.

I want to end by insisting on that. I want to insist that racism is not a set of false pleas which swim around in the head. They're not a set of mistaken perceptions. They have their basis in real material conditions of existence. They arise because of the concrete problems of different classes and groups in the society. Racism represents the attempt ideologically to construct those conditions, contradictions and problems in such a way that they can be dealt with and deflected in the same moment. That instead of confronting the conditions and problems which indeed do face white and black in the urban areas, in an economy in recession, they can be projected away through race.

Until the specificity of a British racism which has those real authentic material conditions at its roots, which does indeed address the real problems of the people, which is not a set of phoney conspiracies generated in the heads of the ruling class, which has a real life at the base of the society – until we can confront a racism which is specific in that sense, we haven't a hope, in my view, of turning the tide.

Notes

1. James Walvin, *Black and White: Negro and English Society, 1555-1945*, Allen Lane 1973.
2. Stan Cohen, *Folk Devils and Moral Panics: Creation of Mods and Rockers*, MacGibbon and Kee 1972.

1970: Birth of the law and order society

1978

As soon as the dominant social group has exhausted its function, the ideological bloc tends to crumble away; then 'spontaneity' may be replaced by 'constraint' in even less disguised and indirect forms, culminating in outright police measures and *coups d'etat.*

Gramsci[1]

The crisis is permanent. The Government is provisional.

Marx[2]

O N THE 4 January 1970, the *Sunday Times* noted: 'Among the incipient ghettos in Britain today, Handsworth, Birmingham displays the classic symptoms: poor housing, a strained education system, households struggling to make ends meet, and few social amenities. It also has the usual hustlers, prostitutes and ponces. Second generation blacks are beginning to show a resistance to all authority.' This prophetic sketch was based on Gus John's report to the Runnymede Trust, subsequently to form the basis of his book, *Because They're Black,* written with Derek Humphry.[3] The article was headed – making the by-now required link – 'Must Harlem Come to Birmingham?' Within a fortnight, Mr Powell had taken it upon himself to reply, as it were, to the question. In a challenge to the Tory Party leadership to bring the race question out 'into the open ... without prevarication or excuse', Mr Powell warned that, 'through its own past sins of omission', Britain was 'menaced by a problem which at the present rate will by the end of the century be similar in magnitude to that of the United States'. Except as part of a vigorous repatriation campaign, Mr Powell added, measures of special aid to high immigrant areas were 'positively harmful in their net effect'. He referred to his prophecy, twenty months earlier, of racial bloodshed to

come. He made no new predictions. Instead, he quoted a Leeds solic-
itor, an Under-Secretary at the Home Office and the Newsletter of the
Manchester Community Relations Council to show that other responsible spokesmen shared his view that 'racial violence could flare up
anywhere in Britain'.[4] A week or so earlier the Spring offensive against
the South African Springboks tour opened. The Liberal MP David
Steel, who had helped to organise a peaceful demonstration, was suddenly confronted by 'a small, chanting, banner-waving band of about
40 souls', who 'took up positions opposite the turnstiles … and proceeded to hurl abuse of a fairly virulent kind at both intending
spectators and the four-deep line of stationary policemen'. When he
asked one of the group who was in charge, he received the reply,
'Nobody in charge of us'. 'Irrational processes', Mr Steel observed,
'will produce irrational reactions'.[5]

In this sharpening climate, the Tory Shadow Cabinet met in secret
conclave at Selsdon Park. There was no mistaking the mood and spirit
in which this preparation for power took place, nor the vigorous, pre-
election crusading themes which emerged from their deliberations.
The *Sunday Times* correspondent, Ronald Butt, entitled the emerging
platform, 'A Soft Sell on Law and Order'.[6] Here, the American
comparisons – this time with the Nixon-Agnew campaign – were
no longer indirect and implicit. The law-and-order theme 'enables
the Party to reassure the silent majority of the public that it shares
their concern'. The keynote was widely deployed. It referred to 'interference with the liberty of people going about their ordinary business
by demonstrating minorities'. Threatening noises – soon to become a
scandalous and widespread real practice – were made about the use
of the conspiracy charge, a toughening of the law of trespass and the
power of the magistracy. The demonstration theme was connected
directly, by Butt, with 'vandalism and the rise of organized crime'.
Selsdon Man, however, had another, equally important face. This was
the side turned in the direction of industrial and economic policy,
where abrasive measures, tied to the strict discipline of the market
mechanism, were proposed for the shake-up and shake-out of British
industry – coupled, of course, with a promise of tough action to curb
the power of the unions and to bring the unofficial strike to a dead
halt. Buoyed up on a wave of popular and populist enthusiasms, the
Shadow Cabinet turned to the electorate, and took to the towns and
cities of Britain in its pre-election barnstorm.

The impact of the law-and-order theme was immediate. True, as the *Guardian* remarked, Mr Heath's 'law and order' was not quite President Nixon's – 'the right of the citizens to walk their own streets, free of the fear of mugging, robbery or rape'. True, the Selsdon version was pointed at a nebulous package of popular fears and stereotypes – what the *Guardian* called 'a gallimaufry of subjects – student unrest, political demonstrations, the Permissive Society, long hair, short hair and perhaps in time medium-length hair as well'.[7] True, 'to introduce conspiracy charges for demonstrators, as some have suggested, would be a shameful abuse of the law … Tolerance is a two-way traffic'. But the law-and-order themes orchestrated together in the dim, moral twilight of Selsdon Park were not intended for the comfort of the *Guardian*'s undoubtedly liberal, undoubtedly minority, readers. There was no silent majority to be won there. The *Sunday Express*, on the other hand, thought the theme powerful enough to give it the front-page headline on the Sunday following the Selsdon Park conclave: 'DEMO CLAMP-DOWN IF TORIES GET BACK'.[8] The crusade in the country was gaining momentum. Lord Hailsham, whom Selsdon Park had released into a renewed burst of moral energy, linked the interruption of High Court proceedings by 'a group of young hooligans', the beating to death of Michael de Gruchy by 'a group of youths', the rise in the proportion of offences in which firearms were used, and the fact that 'an increasing part of the life of every policeman consists of incidents of abuse, insults and provocation nightly hurled … by street-corner hooligans' with the law-and-order theme. This colourful scenario was entitled 'The Menace Of The Wild Ones'. These fears, he reassured his audience, were not limited to 'imaginary women in flowered hats and prominent teeth'. Organised crime and violence, he suggested, 'cannot be separated from private dishonesty or public demonstration in defiance of law'. Geoff Hammond, sentenced to life for 'queer-bashing', Peter Hain, who endorsed the digging up of cricket pitches, 'the Welsh Language Society and all those who are willing to put their own opinions … above the law … undermine the whole fabric of society by challenging the system of law itself on which all of us in the end depend'.[9] The construction of nightmares had commenced in earnest. Within a week, the future Lord Chancellor made a savage attack on Labour for 'presiding complacently' over the biggest crime wave of the century. He invited the Home Secretary to declare that 'he would not parole deliberate killers or assailants of police, warders, innocent witnesses and bystanders'. 'The permissive and lawless society', he added for good measure, effecting yet another startling convergence, 'is a by-product of Socialism'.[10] 'These questions of law and order', Mr Heath told his *Panorama* audience, 'are of immense concern to ... almost every man and woman in this country'.[11] Or soon would be, with a little help from their friends. Lord Hailsham added: 'The theme is the safety of the citizen as he lives in his own home with his wife and children, as he goes about the streets, as he attends his places of amusement ... as he tries to accumulate property for his family and his old age free from fraud, as he works, plays and votes'.[12]

In this atmosphere, which the most measured commentators could only describe as one of mounting, often carefully organised, public hysteria, the students at Warwick University occupied the administration buildings and began to consult the personal and political files which this 'community of scholars' had been keeping on them; and a group of Cambridge students noisily interrupted a private dinner being held to celebrate the success of the Greek colonels at the Garden House Hotel. This renewal of student protest moved Mr Heath to contribute another brick or two to the construction of the populist crusade. He traversed in his speech the whole terrain of authority (unions, universities, government) versus disorder (strikes, sit-ins) in a powerful coupling of the two great thematics of Selsdon Man: 'Great factories, railways, airports are brought to a standstill by strike action ... Great seats of learning ... are disrupted by rebellious students'. Both, however, descanted towards a political, indeed, an electoral conclusion: 'We [i.e. the Conservatives] are not going to become a nation of pushovers'.[13] It was a threat he intended to honour.

Earlier in the year Mr Powell had re-emerged as another of the key signifiers of the crisis. In April he called the teachers, on strike for higher pay, 'Highwaymen' who 'threatened the fabric of law and order'.[14] A week before the election, at Northfield in Birmingham, he warned of 'the invisible enemy within' – students 'destroying' universities and 'terrorising' cities, 'bringing down' governments; of the power of the 'modern form' of the mob – the demonstration – in making governments 'tremble'; the success of 'disorder, deliberately fomented for its own sake' in the near-destruction of civil government in Northern Ireland; and the accumulation of 'combustible material' of 'another kind' (i.e. race) in this country, 'not without deliberate intention in some quarters'. The government's capitulation to the anti-apartheid movement's campaign against the South African cricket tour was pinpointed: 'It may have been a happy chance that this particular triumph of organised disorder and anarchist brain-washing coincided with the commencement of the General Election campaign. For many people it lifted the veil; for the first time, they caught a glimpse of the enemy and his power'.[15] Earlier that week, in Wolverhampton, he had implied that the immigration figures had been so consistently underestimated that 'one begins to wonder if the Foreign Office was the only department of state into which enemies of this country were infiltrated'. There is little need to reiterate here how discordant themes are being plotted together, how the motifs of organised disorder and an 'enemy within', with its ambiguous hint of subversion and treason, are serving to raise the nemesis of anarchy to the level of the state itself. It is important, however, to observe how the *race* question had been thematised at a higher level in Mr Powell's new scenario. The problem, he asserted at Northfield, had been deliberately 'miscalled race'. Race was being used to mystify and confuse the people. The real target was the great liberal conspiracy, inside government and the media, which held ordinary people to ransom, making them fearful to speak the truth for fear of being called 'racialist', and 'literally made to say black is white'. It was race – but now as the pivot of 'this process of brain-washing by repetition of manifest absurdities', race as a secret weapon 'depriving them of their wits and convincing them that what they thought was right is wrong': in short, race as part of the conspiracy of silence and blackmail against the silent majority. The intense populism of this line of attack fell on eager ears, especially in Mr Powell's stamping-ground in the West Midlands.

It was 'the enemy and his power' – The Enemy, and his accomplice, the 'conspiracy of Liberal Causes'; the hard conspiratorial centre and its soft, woolly-headed, deluded periphery – around which Mr Powell's penetrating rhetoric in these two speeches circled. It was useless to enquire precisely the shape of this 'enemy'. The point precisely was his protean quality: everywhere and, seemingly, nowhere. The nation's existence was threatened, the country 'under attack by forces which aim at the actual destruction of our nation and society', as surely as when Imperial Germany was building dreadnoughts; but the nation continued, mistakenly, to 'visualise him in the shape of armoured divisions, or squadrons of aircraft'. They failed to see his common presence, now 'in his student manifestation', now in 'disorder, deliberately fomented for its own sake as an instrument of power' in the province of Ulster, perhaps in the very heart of government itself.[16] In dispersing the 'enemy' to every corner and aspect of national life, and simultaneously concentrating and crystallising his protean appearances in the single spectre of 'the conspiracy within', Mr Powell, in his usual extraordinary way, distilled the essence of that movement by which the generalised panic of a nation and the organised crusade of the populists issue at one crucial moment of time, into the ideological figure of a 'law-and-order crusade'. It is quite critical, however, to bear in mind that, though few other speakers in the first half of 1970 achieved so all-inclusive a range and power of reference as Mr Powell did on these occasions, he was only bringing to a conclusion a process to which many, in and outside the Conservative Shadow leadership, had contributed, articulating what many rank-and-file members of the 'silent majority' were thinking, feeling and calling for in those terrifying months. It would be altogether mistaken to attribute the birth of a 'law-and-order' society to Mr Powell. Its midwives were more numerous and varied. Mr Powell simply saluted its appearance with an astonishing display of rhetorical fireworks, sealed its existence with fire and brimstone.

It was the weekend before the Election; and Mr Wilson, whose unflappability on these occasions knows no bounds, still harboured the illusion that Labour could win …

The June election in 1970 marks the official tip of the pendulum, the passage of positions, the formal appearance on the stage of the 'theatre of politics', of a profound shift in the relations of force between the contending classes, and thus in the balance between consent and coercion in the state, which had been initiated at a deeper level in the previous years. This shift in the character of 'hegemonic domination', or, better, the deepening in the crisis of hegemony, which assumes a qualitatively new shape after 1970, must not be missed, nor its specific features misread or oversimplified.

Labour had preserved the parliamentary illusion that, governing with the consent of the trade union movement in its pocket, it could carry off discipline 'by voluntary consent' where the Tories could not. The Tories knew better, partly because this option was not open to them. But this important difference in political perspective and in the composition of the social alliances favoured by each party should not conceal the fact that, from about 1967 onwards, the state – whichever political colouration it assumed, and in either a soft-sell or hard-sell disguise – was, *structurally* on a collision path with the labour movement and the working class.

This brings us to what may seem a paradoxical feature of the passage which the June election marks. Almost to the edge of the election itself, the pace of the Tory return to power was set by the law-and-order campaign. In the days immediately before, however, the traditional issues of British electoral politics, inflation, prices, the economy, wages, etc – come roaring back into prominence; and the election itself *seems* to be decided, after all, on more sensible, calm, rational and reasonable criteria. It is not the first, and by no means the last time that a 'scare' pre-election mood suddenly gives way to more stable electoral issues and, once the poll is over, the 'panic' seems to have been inconsequential. Was the whole law-and-order build-up, then, merely 'sound and fury, signifying nothing'? It is true, as Hugo Young in the *Sunday Times* noted, that though the Tory manifesto offered 'a general deliverance' from all manner of threat, it also marked 'a clear retreat from the trumpetings out of Selsdon Park'.[17] Such discrepancies between the reality of the danger posed, the generality of the way it is perceived and the remedies proposed are a feature of moral panic, which, precisely feeds on such gaps in credibility. However, it is true that no swift and sweeping 'law-and-order' measures were taken by the returning government. As righteous indignants like Mr Heath assumed the mantle of First Minister, apostles of fundamentalism like Mr Powell retired to the back benches, and moral re-armers like Lord Hailsham donned wig and robe and approached the Woolsack, it was easy to imagine that the whole hairy episode had been nothing more than a Spring *divertissement* to keep the Party supporters in good heart.

This may be deceptive. First, we must remember a 'peculiarity' of the English route: the English tendency to do softly softly, pragmatically and piece-meal, what other countries do in one fell, dramatic swoop; just as Britain rather sidled up to its '1968', so it edged, bit by bit, towards a law-and-order mood, now advancing, now retreating, moving in a crab-like way, sideways into Armageddon. Second, the *tempo* of reaction *does not* slacken; it quickens – more significantly, it changes direction and character. In this second period there begins the regular, immediate escalation of *every* conflictful issue up the hierarchy of control to the level of the state machine – each issue is instantly appropriated by the apparatuses of politics, government, the courts, the police or the law. What, before January, was a spiralling-upwards movement – local crusading pushing the authorities towards increased repression – becomes, after the mid-1970 tip-over, an automatic and immediate pincer movement: popular moral pressure from below and the thrust of restraint and control from above *happen together*. The state itself has become mobilised, sensitised to the emergence of the 'enemy' in any of his manifold disguises; the repressive response is at the ready, quick to move in, moving formally, through the law, the police, administrative regulation, public censure, and at a developing speed. This is what we mean by the slow 'shift to control', the move towards a kind of *closure* in the apparatuses of state control and repression. The decisive mechanisms in the management of hegemonic control in the period after June 1970 are regularly and routinely based in the apparatuses of constraint. This qualitative *shift* in the balance and relations of force is a deep change, which all the token signs of moderation and retreat, responsibility and reasonableness, in the councils of government should not, for a moment, obscure.

Above all (and besides facilitating the routinisation of repression), the law-and-order campaign of 1970 had the overwhelming single consequence of legitimating the recourse to the law, to constraint and statutory power, as the *main*, indeed the only, effective means left of defending hegemony in conditions of severe crisis. It toned up and groomed the society for the extensive exercise of the repressive side of state power. It made this routinisation of control normal, natural, and thus right and inevitable. It legitimated the duty of the state itself, in the crucial areas of conflict, to 'go campaigning'. The first target was Mr Powell's forces of 'organised disorder and anarchist brainwashing'. In the ensuing months the full force of the repressive side of the state is openly and systematically turned against *this* anarchist disorderly flank. But, less obviously, the licensing of the state to campaign had a pay-off in areas which at first sight seemed distant from the enemy of anarchist disorder: namely, in the attempt, now gathering steam, to discipline, restrain and coerce, to bring also within the framework of law and order, not only demonstrators, criminals, squatters and dope addicts, but the solid ranks of the working class itself. This recalcitrant class – or at least its disorderly minorities – had also to be harnessed to 'order'. If what concerns us here is not a simple unmasking of a temporary 'conspiracy of the state' but its deeper and more structural movements, then it is of critical importance to understand just precisely what it is which *connects*, behind all the appearances, the opening of an official law-and-order campaign in January 1970, and the publication of the Industrial Relations Bill in the closing weeks of December.

What had really united the Conservative Party in the pre-election period was less the rhetoric of disorder, but rather a more traditionally phrased emphasis on 'the need to stand firm', not to give in, to restore *authority* to government. This theme of national unity and authority provided the all-important positive face to the more negative themes of 'law and order'. Shortly before the election, Mr Heath had approached the electorate with the affirmation that 'The Conservative Party is the party of one nation ... the next Conservative Government will ... safeguard the unity of the nation through honest government and sound policies.' The aim was to reaffirm the Nation as unified around a common – and moderate – set of goals, which the Heath government best embodied and expressed. All those who stood outside this 'trade union of the nation' were stigmatised as 'extremists'. The minority activities of squatters and demonstrators most vividly embodied this tendency. But the growing 'extremism' of working-class militancy – strikingly borne in upon the new government by a succession of new wage demands from dockers, miners, local authority manual workers, electricity-supply workers and dustmen – was undoubtedly the larger and more deep-seated trend. It directly threatened the new Heath economic strategy. It posed a direct challenge to the authority of government; and – with the spectre of May 1968 not yet banished from the collective Cabinet mind – it awakened fears of the possibility of the deadly 'student-worker' alliance. It was against this flank that, in the event, the government turned its 'law-and-order' campaign. Within six weeks of taking office, the new Minister for Employment, Mr Carr, told the CBI that the government would support employers who faced strike action over wage demands. The Chancellor, Mr Barber, told the TUC in no uncertain terms that 'there has got to be a steady and progressive cooling down. From now on employers have got to stand firm'.[18] Then Mr Carr sketched out the elements of the Industrial Relations Bill, with soothing thoughts that, after all the trade unions were responsible institutions, would not willingly act against the law of the land, that legal sanctions were envisaged as being used only in rare cases, and that personal liability would only arise where individuals acted outside their union's control and authority.

This application to the class struggle of the thin edge of the legal wedge was overwhelmingly supported by the media – for example (to take the two papers we watched most closely) by both the *Sunday Express* and the *Sunday Times*: the former in its hysterical and instinctive way, the latter in its more sober and rational voice. Both accepted the government's paradigm 'explanation' for industrial unrest: while the *Sunday Express* hysterically saw red militants at the bottom of every strike – in the docks, at Pilkingtons, at the pitheads – and the arrival of the 'suitcase militant', the *Sunday Times*, following the publication of the Industrial Relations Bill, quietly, but decisively, put its editorial weight behind the legislation, and in a manner wholly in line with the conspiratorial version fast becoming received political doctrine: 'The identification of militants as both prime movers of inflation and the prime targets of the Bill has now been clearly spelled out'.[19]

It is difficult, in the calculus of coercion, to measure precisely the combined effect of the 'law-and-order' lead from on high, the sharpening of the legal engine against the working class from within the heart of the Cabinet itself, the steady percolation of a conspiratorial reading of Britain's 'troubles' through the media, and the slow but sure escalation of control against potentially disorderly targets on the ground. There is no evidence of a concerted campaign; but the over-all trajectory is unmistakable.

In July, Mr Justice Melford Stevenson handed down jail terms of nine to eighteen months on six, and borstal sentences on two, of the Cambridge students accused in the Garden House demonstration in Cambridge against the Greek colonels. This was the first post-election occasion in which the full force of the law was seen in operation against political demonstrations, one of the focal points of the 'law-and-order' campaign. The indications it gave were not propitious. Of the 400 participating, sixty were identified (with the help of the proctors), but only a representative, exemplary fifteen were charged. The charges against them were made, progressively, more serious in the period before trial. And though the jury only convicted those against whom some specific unlawful act could be proven, the convicted first offenders were, smartly and summarily, put away.[20] Stephen Sedley, one of the defence lawyers, wrote, after the failure of the appeal:

The police and the DPP have been encouraged by this trend to strike increasingly hard through the court at those they believe to represent a threat to law and order – demonstrators, Black Power activists, squatters, students. This trend towards politically motivated prosecutions has shown a distinct upswing. 1970 has seen the high point so far, but there is probably worse to come.[21]

Sedley's reference to 'Black Power activists' and the law was no casual aside. Black-power militancy was no doubt advanced in Britain by the steady punctuation of news from the United States. But the rising temperature of race did not require any transfusions of energy from across the water, and it was no process of simple imitation which brought the serious erosion of black-white relations thundering back into the headlines in the second half of 1970. This deterioration was nothing new, as we have seen; what *was* new was the fact that the general race-relations crisis now assumed, almost without exception, the particular form of a confrontation between the black community and the police. John Lambert's judicious survey of this declining situation was published in 1970.[22] It was followed by Derek Humphry's careful but well-documented and damning account, *Police Power and Black People*, which clearly demonstrated the sudden, sharp rise to confrontation which came to a head in the summer of 1970, and extended, on an ever-rising curve into 1971 and 1972.[23] The Liverpool Community Relations Council, established in June 1970, was almost immediately overwhelmed by black complaints of harassment by the police. An hour-long programme on this topic by Radio Merseyside, which referred to the fact that 'in certain police stations, particularly in the city centre, brutality and drug planting and the harassing of minority groups takes place regularly' passed without considered defence by the local police.[24] There were clashes between blacks and the police, in August, in Leeds, in Maida Vale, and at the Caledonian Road station, among others. Notting Hill became the scene of a running battle. The police made raid after raid on the Mangrove Restaurant, which – one constable told the court – 'as far as I am concerned' was the headquarters of 'the Black Power Movement'. (Asked in court if he knew what black power was, he replied: 'I know roughly what black power is – it is a movement planned to be very militant in this country.' That seemed to be enough.)

In October, the British Black Panthers called a conference to complain of what they believed to be a conscious campaign to '"pick off" Black militants' and to 'intimidate, harass and imprison black people prepared to go out on the streets and demonstrate'. The charge was repudiated by Scotland Yard; but, as Humphry remarks, 'the commendable high-mindedness of the Yard's Press Bureau does not accord with the reality of the situation'.[25] There was no let up of the pressure.

Equally ominous moves were afoot in the areas of legislation and the courts. The Tory concern with civil disturbance had led the Shadow Cabinet to invite Sir Peter Rawlinson, the Shadow Attorney General, to frame new 'trespass' legislation 'to combat the excesses of demonstrators'.[26] Few lawyers envied him his task; but some at least – had they been able to foresee the outcome of his failure – might have wished him better luck. For the failure to improve on the law of trespass, clearly, in this case, intended as a legal deterrent against such exploits as the activities of Peter Hain and his anti-South African demonstrators, and the rapid spread of the squatting campaign to Southwark and other parts of south-east London – did not in the least deter the government's resolve.[27] Instead, it strengthened and widened it. The subsequent reactivation of the ancient law of conspiracy, the principal form in which legal coercion came finally to be impressed upon the protest movements and industrial militancy in the following two or three years, was the direct consequence of the relative failure of this first stage in the moulding of an alternative legal 'engine of government'. During 1970, it was the giving of a new lease of life to the ancient common law charges of 'unlawful and riotous assembly' which provided the 'law-and-order' campaign with its first political scapegoats – the Cambridge students gaoled at the Garden House trial.

Yet, if the 'Garden House' was, from this point of view, the most ominous trial of the year, 'law and order' also had another, less political, meaning in the courtroom, as the following report demonstrates:

'A DETERRENT sentence is not meant to fit the offender, it is meant to fit the offence,' said Mr. Justice Ashworth in the Appeal Court on Monday. 'When meting out a deterrent sentence it is idle to go into the background of each individual', echoed the Lord Chief Justice, Lord Parker. With these words their Lordships confirmed uniform sentences of three years on eighteen Birmingham youths who had been involved in gang fights. There was no regard for the fact that three of them had no previous conviction, that none of them had been found with an offensive weapon and that the police had admitted they had failed to round-up the ringleaders. Most important, perhaps, one of the youths had been receiving psychiatric treatment for a month before the fight.[28]

If everything in 1970 moves up to the threshold of 'law', some commentators were already pointing forward to the threshold which was increasingly to dominate the 1970s: the threshold of violence. Asking 'who is safe in this world of violence?', Angus Maude listed examples from right around the world to demonstrate his thesis that we now inhabited a 'new world of violence': the throwing of two CS gas canisters in the House of Commons; the 'cutting loose' with a tommy gun by Puerto Ricans in the US Congress; the Garden House riot; Bernadette Devlin in Ulster; the banning of the South African cricket tour; and 'the series of airline outrages and kidnappings of Western Ambassadors in South America'.[29] Violence, he added, was a self-perpetuating mindless disease, used 'only too often' by 'weak minorities' to 'blackmail the majorities'. In 1970, in the name of the majority – still unfortunately too silent – the state organised itself to strike back.

Notes

1. Gramsci, 'Notes on Italian History' in *Selections from the Prison Notebooks*, Lawrence & Wishart 1971, p61.
2. Marx, 'The Crisis in England and the British Constitution', in *Marx and Engels On Britain*, Progress 1953, p424.
3. D. Humphry and G. John, *Because They're Black*, Penguin 1971.
4. Manchester CRC letter in the *Sunday Times*, 18 January 1970.
5. *Guardian*, 7 February 1970.
6. *Sunday Times*, 8 February 1970.
7. *Guardian*, 7 February 1970.
8. *Sunday Express*, 1 February 1970.
9. *Sunday Express*, 8 February 1970.
10. *Sunday Express*, 22 February 1970.
11. Quoted in *Sunday Times*, 8 February 1970.
12. Lord Hailsham, quoted in *Guardian*, 12 February 1970.
13. *Sunday Express*, 8 March 1970.

14. *Sunday Times*, 5 April 1970.
15. *Sunday Times*, 14 June 1970.
16. Ibid.
17. *Sunday Times*, 7 June 1970.
18. *Sunday Times*, 11 August 1970.
19. *Sunday Times*, 6 December 1970.
20. See *Sunday Times*, 12 July 1970.
21. *The Listener*, 8 October 1970.
22. John Lambert, *Crime, Police and Race Relations: A study in Birmingham*, Oxford University Press 1970.
23. D. Humphry, *Police Power and Black People*, Panther 1972.
24. Ibid.
25. Quotes from ibid.
26. *Sunday Times*, 1 February 1970.
27. See R. Bailey, *The Squatter*, Penguin 1973.
28. *Sunday Times*, 18 October 1970.
29. *Sunday Express*, 26 July 1970.

The great moving right show

1979

No one seriously concerned with political strategies in the current situation can now afford to ignore the 'swing to the right'. We may not yet understand its extent and its limits, its specific character, its causes and effects. We have so far – with one or two notable exceptions – failed to find strategies capable of mobilising social forces strong enough in depth to turn its flank. But the tendency is hard to deny. It no longer looks like a temporary swing in the political fortunes, a short-term shift in the balance of forces. It has been well installed – a going concern – since the latter part of the 1960s. And, though it has developed through a series of different stages, its dynamic and momentum appears to be sustained. We need to discuss its parameters more fully and openly on the left, without inhibition or built-in guarantees.

Certain aspects have won attention from the left: the present government's tough industrial and economic strategy in face of the recession and crisis in capital accumulation; the emergence of 'Thatcherism' and the anti-left campaigns; the rise of the National Front as an open political force. But the full dimensions of the precipitation to the right continues to evade a proper analysis. This may be because the crisis continues to be 'read' by the left from within certain well-entrenched and respectable 'common sense' positions. Many of these no longer provide an adequate analytic or theoretical framework: the politics which flows from them thus continues to fall far short of its aim.

Thus there are some who would still argue that 'worse means better' – i.e. a sharpening of the contradictions. Such a position is often based on a belief in the inevitable rising tempo of class struggle and the guaranteed victory of 'progressive forces everywhere'. Those who hold it have short political memories. They forget how frequently in recent history a sharpening of the contradictions has led to 'settlements' and solutions which favoured capital and the right, rather than the reverse. The commonest response on the left is probably to interpret the 'swing to the right' as a simple expression of the economic crisis. Thus 'Thatcherism' is – give or take one or two elements – the corresponding political bedfellow of a period of capitalist recession: the significant differences between this and other variants of Tory 'philosophy' being conceived as without any specific pertinent political or ideological effects. And the National Front is the long-anticipated irrational face of capitalism – the class enemy in familiar fascist disguise.

Specific features

This position neglects everything particular and specific to *this* historical conjuncture. It views history as a series of repeats. It is predicated on a notion of a social formation as a simple structure in which economic factors will be immediately and transparently translated to the political and ideological levels. It falls under the sign of all 'economisms' in supposing that, if you operate on the 'determining level' – the economic front – all the other pieces of the puzzle will fall neatly into place. It thus prevents itself, theoretically and politically, from working on those related but distinct contradictions, moving according to very different tempos, whose condensation, in any particular historical moment, is what defines a conjuncture. It neglects Lenin's reminder of 'an extremely unique historical situation' in which 'absolutely dissimilar currents, absolutely heterogeneous class interests, absolutely contrary political and social strivings have merged … in a strikingly "harmonious" manner …'.[1] It takes for granted what needs to be explained: how a capitalist economic recession is presided over by a social democratic party in power (politically) with mass working-class support and organised depth in the trade unions, but 'lived', for increasing numbers of people, through the themes and representations (ideologically) of a virulent, emergent 'petty-bourgeois' ideology. These features of the current situation are not so much expressions of the economic crisis (its political and ideological reflection) as they are factors which *have effects* – including effects on the economic crisis itself and its possible solutions.

One also encounters in this discussion variants of 'revolutionary optimism' and 'revolutionary pessimism'. The pessimists argue that we mustn't rock the boat, or demoralise the already dispersed forces of the left. To them one can only reply with Gramsci's injunction: to address ourselves 'violently' towards the present as it is, if we are serious about transforming it. The optimists cast doubt on the doubters: look for the points of resistance – the class struggle continues. Of course, in one sense, they are right. We must look behind the surface phenomena, we must find the points of intervention, we mustn't underestimate the capacity for resistance and struggle. But, if we are correct about the depth of the rightward turn, then our interventions need to be pertinent, decisive and effective. Whistling in the dark is an occupational hazard not altogether unknown to the British left. 'Pessimism of the intelligence: optimism of the will'.

Fascism

Finally, there is 'fascism'. There is a sense in which the appearance of organised fascism on the political stage seems to solve everything for the left. It confirms our best-worst suspicions, awakening familiar ghosts and spectres. Fascism and economic recession together seem to render transparent those connections which most of the time are opaque, hidden and displaced. Away with all those time-wasting theoretical speculations! The Marxist guarantees are all in place after all, standing to attention. Let us take to the streets. This is *not* an argument against taking to the streets. Indeed, the direct interventions against the rising fortunes of the National Front – local campaigns, anti-fascist work in the unions, trades councils, women's groups, the mobilisation behind the Anti-Nazi League, the counter-demonstrations, above all Rock Against Racism (one of the timeliest and best constructed of cultural interventions, repaying serious and extended analysis) – constitute one of the few success stories of the conjuncture. But it *is* an argument against the satisfactions which sometimes flow from applying simplifying analytic schemes to complex events. What we have to explain is a move towards 'authoritarian populism' – an exceptional form of the capitalist state – which, unlike classical fascism, has retained most (though not all) of the formal representative institutions in place, and which at the same time has been able to construct around itself an active popular consent. This undoubtedly represents a decisive shift in the balance of hegemony, and the National Front has played a 'walk-on' part in this drama. It has entailed a striking weakening of democratic forms and initiatives, but not their suspension. We may miss precisely what is specific to this exceptional form of the crisis of the capitalist state by mere name-calling.

The swing to the right is part of what Gramsci called an 'organic' phenomenon:

> A crisis occurs, sometimes lasting for decades. This exceptional duration means that uncurable structural contradictions have revealed themselves ... and that, despite this, the political forces which are struggling to conserve and defend the existing structure itself are making efforts to cure them within certain limits, and to overcome them. These incessant and persistent efforts ... form the terrain of the conjunctural and it is upon this terrain that the forces of opposition organise.[2]

Gramsci insisted that we get the 'organic' and 'conjunctural' aspects of the crisis into a proper relationship. What defines the 'conjunctural' – the immediate terrains of struggle – is not simply the given economic conditions, but precisely the 'incessant and persistent' efforts which are being made to defend and conserve the position. If the crisis is deep – 'organic' – these efforts cannot be merely defensive. They will be formative: a new balance of forces; the emergence of new elements; the attempt to put together a new 'historical bloc'; new political configurations and 'philosophies'; a profound restructuring of the state and the ideological discourses which construct the crisis and represent it as it is 'lived' as a practical reality; new programmes and policies, pointing to a new result, a new sort of 'settlement' – 'within certain limits'. These do not 'emerge': they have to be constructed. Political and ideological work is required to disarticulate old formations, and to rework their elements into new configurations. The 'swing to the right' is not a reflection of the crisis: it is itself a response to the crisis. I want to examine certain features of this response, concentrating on some neglected political-ideological aspects.

Economic crisis

We must examine first the precipitating conditions. This is a matter of a set of discontinuous but related histories, rather than neat, corresponding movements. In economic terms, Britain's structural industrial and economic weakness emerges in the immediate aftermath of the post-war boom. The 1960s are marked by the oscillations between recession and recovery, with a steady underlying deterioration. These effectively destroy the last remnants of the 'radical programme' on the basis of which Wilson won power in 1964, and to which he tried to harness a new social bloc. By the end of the 1960s, the economy has dipped into full-scale recession – slumpflation – which sustains the exceptional 'Heath course' of 1971-4, with its head-on collisions with organised labour. By the mid-1970s, the economic parameters are dictated by a synchronisation between capitalist recession on a global scale, and the crisis of capital accumulation specific to Britain – the weak link in the chain. Domestic politics has thus been dominated by crisis-management and containment strategies: dove-tailed through an increasingly interventionist state, intervening to secure the conditions of both capitalist production and reproduction. The strategy has a distinctively corporatist character – incorporating sections of the working class and unions into the bargain between state, capital and labour, the three 'interests'. Crisis management has drawn successively on the different variants of the same basic repertoire: incomes policy, first by consent, then by imposition; wage restraint; social contracting. The 'natural' governor of this crisis has been the party of social democracy in power. This last factor has had profound effects in disorganising and fragmenting working-class responses to the crisis itself.

At the ideological level, however, things have moved at a rather different tempo, and in certain respects predate the economic aspects. Many of the key themes of the radical right – law and order, the need for social discipline and authority in the face of a conspiracy by the enemies of the state, the onset of social anarchy, the 'enemy within', the dilution of British stock by alien black elements – are well articulated before the full dimensions of the recession are revealed. They emerge in relation to the radical movements and political polarisations of the 1960s, for which '1968' must stand as a convenient, though inadequate, notation. Some of these themes get progressively translated to other fronts as the confrontation within organised labour, and the militant resistance it meets, develops during the Heath interregnum. For the constitution of the principal thematics of the radical right, this must be seen as a formative moment.[3]

The radical right

The radical right does not appear out of thin air. It has to be understood in direct relation to alternative political formations attempting to occupy and command the same space. It is engaged in a struggle for hegemony, within the dominant bloc, against both social democracy and the moderate wing of its own party. Not only is it operating in the same space: it is working directly on the contradictions within these competing positions. The strength of its intervention lies partly in the radicalism of its commitment to break the mould, not simply to rework the elements of the prevailing 'philosophies'. In doing so, it nevertheless takes the elements which are already constructed into place, dismantles them, reconstitutes them into a new logic, and articulates the space in a new way, polarising it to the right.

This can be seen with respect to both positions. The Heath position was destroyed in the confrontation with organised labour. But it was also undermined by its internal contradictions. It failed to win the showdown with labour; it could not enlist popular support for this decisive encounter; in defeat, it returned to its 'natural' position in the political spectrum, engaging in its own version of bargaining. 'Thatcherism' succeeds in this space by directly engaging the 'creeping socialism' and apologetic 'state collectivism' of the Heath wing. It thus centres on the very nerve of consensus politics, which dominated and stabilised the political scene for over a decade. To sustain its possible credibility as a party of government in a crisis of capital, 'Thatcherism' retains some lingering and ambivalent connections to this centre territory: Mr Prior is its voice – but sotto voce. On other grounds, it has won considerable space by the active destruction of consensus politics from the right. Of course, it aims for a construction of a national consensus of its own. What it destroys is that form of consensus in which social democracy was the principal tendency. This evacuation of centrist territory has unleased political forces on the right kept in reign for most of the post-war period.

The contradiction within social democracy

But the contradiction within social democracy is the principal key to the whole rightward shift of the political spectrum. For if the destruction of the Heath 'party' secures hegemony for 'Thatcherism' over the right, it is the contradictory form of social democracy which has effectively disorganised the left and the working-class response to the crisis.

This contradiction can be put in stark and simple terms; and considerable strategic conclusions flow from it. As follows: To win electoral power social democracy must maximise its claims as *the* political representative of the interests of the working class and organised labour. It is the party capable of (a) mastering the crisis, while (b) defending – within the constraints imposed by recession – working-class interests. It is important here to remember that social democracy is not a homogeneous political entity but a complex political formation. It is not *the* expression of *the* working class 'in government', but the principal means of representation of the class. Representation here has to be understood as an active and formative relationship. It organises the class, constituting it as a political force – a social democratic political force – in the same moment as it is constituted. Everything depends on the ways, the apparatuses and the 'philosophies' – the means – by which the often dispersed and contradictory interests of a class are welded together into a coherent position which can be articulated and represented in the political and ideological theatres of struggle.

The expression of this representative relationship of class-to-party, in the present period, has depended decisively on the extensive set of bargains negotiated between Labour and the trade union representatives of the class. This 'indissoluble link' is the practical basis for the claim to be the natural governing party of the crisis. This is the contract it delivers. But, once in government, social democracy is committed to finding solutions to the crisis which are capable of winning support from key sections of capital, since its solutions are framed within those limits. But this requires that the indissoluble link be used, not to advance but to discipline the class and organisations it represents. This is only possible if the link – class-to-party – is dismantled and if there can be substituted for it an alternative articulation: government-to-people. The rhetoric of 'national interest', which is the principal ideological form in which a succession of defeats have been imposed on the working class by social democracy in power, are exactly the sites where this contradiction shows through – and is being constantly reworked. But government-to-people dissects the field of struggle differently from class-to-party. It sets Labour, at key moments of struggle – from the strikes of 1966 right through to the present 5 per cent norm – by definition 'on the side of the nation' against 'sectional interests', 'irresponsible trade union power', etc.

This is the terrain on which Mr Heath played such destructive games in the lead-through to the Industrial Relations Act and its aftermath, with his invocation of 'the great trade union of the nation', and the spectre of 'holding the nation up to ransom'. 'Thatcherism', deploying the discourses of 'nation' and 'people' against 'class' and 'unions' with far greater vigour and popular appeal, has homed in on the same objective contradiction. Within this space is being constructed an assault, not on this or that piece of 'irresponsible bargaining' by a particular union, but on the very foundation and *raison d'être* of organised labour. Considerable numbers of people – including many trade unionists – find themselves reflected and set in place through this interpellation of 'nation' and 'people' at the centre of this mounting attack on the defensive organisations of the working class.

Anti-collectivism

A closely related strand in the new philosophy of the radical right is the theme of anti-collectivism and anti-statism. 'Thatcherism' has given this traditional arena of conservative 'philosophy' expansive play. At the level of organising theoretical ideologies, anti-statism has been refurbished by the advance of monetarism as the most fashionable economic credo. Keynesianism was the lynch-pin of the theoretical ideologies of state intervention throughout the post-war period, assuming almost the status of a sacred orthodoxy or *doxa*. To have replaced it in some of the most powerful and influential apparatuses of government, research and the universities, and restored in its place Friedman and Hayek, is, in itself, a remarkable reversal. Neither Keynesianism nor monetarism win votes in the electoral marketplace. But in the doctrines and discourses of 'social market values' – the restoration of competition and personal responsibility for effort and reward, the image of the over-taxed individual, enervated by welfare coddling, his initiative sapped by handouts by the state – 'Thatcherism' has found a powerful means of popularising the principles of a monetarist philosophy: and, in the image of the welfare 'scavenger', a well-designed folk-devil. The elaboration of this populist doctrine – to which Sir Keith Joseph and Mr Boyson, leader writers in the *Telegraph*, the *Economist* and the *Spectator*, opinion leaders in the *Mail* and *Express* and many others have given their undivided attention – represents the critical ideological work of constructing for 'Thatcherism' a populist common sense. It is a particularly rich mix because of the resonant traditional themes – nation, family, duty, authority, standards, self-reliance – which have been effectively condensed into it. Here elements from many traditional ideologies – some already secured at earlier times to the grand themes of popular Conservatism, many others with a wider popular connotation – have been inserted into and woven together to make a set of discourses which are then harnessed to the practices of the radical right and the class forces they now aspire to represent.

Aspects of the repertoire

Two aspects of this rich repertoire of anti-collectivism only should be remarked on here. The first is the way these discourses operate directly on popular elements in the traditional philosophies and practical ideologies of the dominated classes. These elements – as Laclau among others has recently argued – always express a contradiction between popular interests and the power bloc. But, since they have no intrinsic, necessary and historically fixed class meaning, but can be effectively composed as elements within very different discourses, themselves articulated to and by different class positions and practices, it marks the neutralisation of that contradiction to have successfully colonised them, for the right.

The second point is a related one. For what is represented here (again, in an active sense) is indeed the materiality of the contradiction between 'the people', popular needs, feelings and aspirations on the one hand, and the imposed structures of an interventionist capitalist state – the state of the monopoly phase of capitalist development – on the other. In the absence of any fuller mobilisation of democratic initiatives, the state is increasingly encountered and experienced by ordinary working people as, indeed, not a beneficiary but a powerful, bureaucratic imposition. And this 'experience' is not misguided since, in its effective operations with respect to the popular classes, the state is less and less present as a welfare institution and more and more present as the state of 'state monopoly capital'. Social democracy cannot, of course, exploit any of this terrain to its advantage. First, it holds to a neutral and benevolent interpretation of the role of the state as incarnator of the national interest above the class struggle. Second, in the representations of social democracy (and not only there, but also on the left) the expansion of the state is understood as, in itself, and without reference to the mobilisation of effective democratic power at the popular level, virtually synonymous with 'socialism'. Third, the enlarged interventionist state is the principal instrument through which the party of social democracy attempts to manage the capitalist crisis on behalf of capital. Fourth, in this phase, the state is inscribed through every feature and aspect of social life. Social democracy has no alternative viable strategy, especially for 'big' capital (and 'big' capital has no viable alternative strategy for itself), which does not involve massive state support. Thus in any polarisation along this fissure, Labour is undividedly 'with' the state and the power bloc – and Mrs Thatcher is, undividedly, out there 'with the people'. It can now be seen that the anti-statist elements in the discourses of the radical right are key supports for the new populism. It is no rhetorical flourish. To add that it then does some service in making respectable the radical right assault on the whole structure of welfare and social benefits is only to say that the work of ideological excavation, if well done, delivers considerable political and economic effects.

Education

We might turn to another area of successful colonisation by the radical right: the sphere of education. Until very recently, the social democratic goals of 'equality of opportunity' and 'remedying educational advantage' were dominant throughout the world of secondary education. The struggle over comprehensivisation was its political signature. Contestation in this area has only gradually developed, through a series of strategic interventions. The 'Black Paper' group – at first no more than a rump – has moved from very modest beginnings to the point where it could justly be claimed (and was) that their preoccupations set the agenda for the 'Great Debate' which the Labour government initiated last year. In the 1960s 'progressive' and 'community' education made considerable advances within state schools. Today, 'progressivism' is thoroughly discredited: the bodies of a whole series of well-publicised schools – William Tyndale and after, so to speak – lie strewn in its path. The panic over falling standards and working-class illiteracy, the fears concerning politically-motivated teachers in the classroom, the scare stories about the 'violent' urban school, about the adulteration of standards through the immigrant intake, and so on, have successfully turned the tide in the education sphere towards themes and goals being established for it by the forces of the right. The press – especially those three popular ventriloquist voices of the radical right, the *Mail*, the *Sun* and the *Express* – have played here a quite pivotal role. They have publicised the 'examples' in a highly sensational form – and they have drawn the connections.

These connections and couplings are the key mechanisms of the process by which education as a field of struggle has been articulated to the right. There are long, deep-seated resistances within the philosophy of state education to any attempt to measure schooling directly in terms of the needs and requirements of industry. That these were resistances often shot through with ambiguity is not so important for our purposes. However it arose, this reluctance to cash the school in terms of its immediate value to capital was one on which campaigns could be based with some hope of professional and administrative support. These defences have now been dismantled. Clear evidence is supposed to exist that standards are falling: the principal witnesses to this alarming trend are employers who complain about the quality of job applicants: this, in turn, must be having an effect on the efficiency and productivity of the nation – at a time when recession puts a premium on improving both. Once the often ill-founded elements can be stitched together into this chain of 'logic', policies can begin to be changed by leading educationists of the political right, indirectly, even before they take charge.

And why? First, because the terrain on which the debate is being conducted has been so thoroughly reconstructed around this new 'logic' that the groundswell for change is proving hard to resist. Second, because Labour itself has always been caught between competing goals in schooling: to improve the chances of working-class children and the worse-off in education, and to harness education to the economic and efficiency needs of the productive system. We can see now that this contradiction, even within the social democratic educational programme, is a reworking of what earlier we called the principal contradiction of social democracy in this period. The educational experts and spokesmen, the educational press, sections of the profession, the media, many educational interest groups and organisations, have been operating exactly on the site of this dilemma and – in conditions of recession – have convinced the government. It in turn has now taken up the lead in promoting debates and policies designed to make this equation – success in education=requirements of industry – come true.

The 'Great Debate'

Thus the agenda for the 'Great Debate' was indeed set for social democracy by the social forces of the right; and the government, which initiated it, is almost certainly convinced that this is a largely 'non-political debate' – 'like debates about education ought to be'. Yet, in order to bring this about, a major restructuring of the state apparatuses themselves has had to be executed. The DES has been set aside, and new state apparatuses, capable of realising the equation in more immediate and practical forms, have moved into a central position in the field – the Manpower Services Commission, the new TSA re-training programmes in further and technical education, and its ancillary supports, etc. Here, training and retraining programmes directly geared into the demands and movements of industry and the silent de-skilling and reskilling of the unemployed can proceed.

Again, this is no merely imposed or rhetorical strategy. The recomposition of the educational state apparatuses and the redirection of resources and programmes is the site of a very real and profound construction of a field of the state, from above. But many aspects of the strategy also seem to win consent and support from parents. Perhaps because, in a period of scarce jobs, working-class parents are glad to see their children undergoing the process of being skilled – even if it is for particular places in routine manual labour or, in many instances, for places which are unlikely to exist at all when and if industrial production revives. Perhaps it is because, if comprehensivisation, in the form in which it was implemented, and other radical education programmes, are not going after all to deliver the goods for working-class children, then they may have to be content to be 'skilled' and 'classed' in a way that seems appropriate.

The shift in educational strategy thus says, in effect, to such parents: you are in the educational subordinate class; the way out is by moving up, through increased educational competition; what counts in this competition is a standard training, acceptable social skills, respect for authority and traditional values and discipline. In the face of the massive failures of social democratic policies on schooling to turn the tide of educational disadvantage, the positive aspirations of working people for the education of their children can be redirected towards the support for a traditional education, programmes of discipline and 'relevance to industrial experience'. In the 1960s, parental involvement belonged to 'de-schooling' and Ivan Illich: in the 1970s, it is one of the strongest cards in the educational pack being shuffled by Mr St John Stevas, shadow spokesman for education.

Law and order

If education is an area where the right has won territory without having to win power, two other areas in the repertoire of the radical right – race and law and order – are ones where the right has traditionally assumed a leading role. We can be brief about them since they have gained considerable attention on the left in recent months. They are chosen as examples here only to make a general point. On law and order, the theme – more policing, tougher sentencing, better family discipline, the rising crime rate as an index of social disintegration, the threat to 'ordinary people going about their private business' from thieves, muggers, etc, the wave of lawlessness and the loss of law-abidingness – are perennials of Conservative Party Conferences, and the sources of many a popular campaign by moral entrepreneur groups and quoting editors. But if the work of the right in some areas has won support over into its camp, the law and order issues have scared people over. In some versions of the discourse of the radical right, moral interpellations play an important role. But the language of law and order is sustained by moralisms. It is where the great syntax of 'good' versus 'evil', of civilised and uncivilised standards, of the choice between anarchy and order, constantly divides the world up and classifies into its appointed stations. The play on 'values' and on moral issues in this area is what gives to the law and order crusade much of its grasp on popular morality and common sense conscience. Yet despite this, it touches concretely the experiences of crime and theft, of loss of scarce property and fears of unexpected attack in working-class areas and neighbourhoods; and, since it promulgates no other remedies for their underlying causes, it welds people to that 'need for authority' which has been so significant for the right in the construction of consent to its authoritarian programme.

Race constitutes another variant, since in recent months questions of race, racism and relations between the races, as well as immigration, have been dominated by the dialectic between the radical-respectable and the radical-rough forces of the right. It was said about the 1960s and early 1970s that, after all, Mr Powell lost. This is true only if the shape of a whole conjuncture is to be measured by the career of a single individual. In another sense, there is an argument that 'Powellism' won: not only because his official eclipse was followed by legislating into effect much of what he proposed, but because of the magical connections and short-circuits which Powellism was able to establish between the themes of race and immigration control and the images of the nation, the British people and the destruction of 'our culture, our way of life'. I would be happier about the temporary decline in the fortunes of the National Front if so many of their themes had not been so swiftly reworked into a more respectable discourse on race by Conservative politicians in the first months of this year.

I have looked exclusively at some political-ideological dimensions of the emergence of the radical right, not to evoke wonder at its extent, but to try to identify some things which are specific to it, which mark its difference from other variants which have flourished since the war. The first is the complex but interlocked relationship of the right to the fortunes and fate of social democracy when the latter takes power in a period of economic recession, and tries to provide a solution 'within certain limits'. It is always the case that the right is what it is partly because of what the left is: here we are dealing with the effects of a lengthy period of social democratic leadership. The second is its popular success in neutralising the contradiction between people and the state/power bloc and winning popular interpellations so decisively for the right. In short, the nature of its *populism*. But now it must be added that this is no rhetorical device or trick, for this populism is operating on genuine contradictions, and it has a rational and material core. Its success and effectivity does not lie in its capacity to dupe unsuspecting folk but in the way it addresses real problems, real and lived experiences, real contradictions – and yet is able to represent them within a logic of discourse which pulls them systematically into line with policies and class strategies of the right. Finally – and this is not limited to this analysis, though it seems especially relevant – there is the evidence of just how ideological transformations and political restructuring of this order is actually accomplished. It works on the ground of already constituted social practices and lived ideologies. It wins space there by constantly drawing on these elements which have secured over time a traditional resonance and left their traces in popular inventories. At the same time, it changes the field of struggle by changing the place, the position, the relative weight, of the condensations within any one discourse and constructing them according to an alternative logic. What shifts them is not 'thoughts' but a particular practice of class struggle: ideological and political class struggle. What makes these representations popular is that they have a purchase on practice, they shape it, they are written into its materiality. What constitutes them as a danger is that they change the nature of the terrain itself on which struggles of different kinds are taking place; and they have pertinent effects on these struggles. Currently, they are gaining ground in defining the 'conjunctural'. That is exactly the terrain on which the forces of opposition must organise, if we are to transform it.

Notes

1. V.I. Lenin, 'Letters from Afar' in Lenin, *Collected Works, Vol. 23*, Progress Publishers 1964, p306.
2. Gramsci, *Selections from the Prison Notebooks*, Lawrence and Wishart, London 1971, p179.
3. We have attempted a fuller analysis of this moment elsewhere, in the chapters on the 'Exhaustion of Consent' and 'Towards the Exceptional State' in Hall, Clarke, Critcher, Jefferson and Roberts, *Policing The Crisis*, Macmillan 1978. [A section of 'Towards the Exceptional State' is reproduced in this book, as '1970: Birth of the law and order society'.]

The 'Little Caesars' of social democracy

1981

THE LEFT IS clearly in some difficulty as to how to explain or respond to the new Social Democratic/Liberal regrouping in the 'centre'. The formation of the Council for Social Democracy (CSD) and of a Social-Democratic bloc in parliament, is, at one level, such a media-inspired and stimulated phenomenon that it is hard to know how to make a realistic assessment of its electoral and political prospects. Its pragmatism, soul-searching 'good sense', the eminent 'reasonableness' of its leading figures, the agony of their hesitations, the renunciation of 'doctrinaire extremes', the rhetoric of 'novelty', are all calculated to project just that illusion of a viable centre, free of monetarist and Marxist 'dogma', dear to the centrist instincts of many sections of the press.

Commentators like Peter Jenkins of the *Guardian* have been hoping and praying so long for this deliverance from the burden of socialism that it is impossible to know any longer whether columns like his represent sober political analyses or just more self-fulfilling prophecies. Pollsters and political analysts have been predicting the 'swing to moderation' for so long that they might well have simply created Social Democracy themselves, if Dr Owen and Mr Rodgers had hesitated much longer. Rarely in recent memory has a political grouping looked forward with such confidence to becoming the decisive element in a hung Parliament on the basis of so sketchy and gestural a programme. The argument is that there is a vacuum in the centre which has to be filled. The CSD has so far responded to this challenge by being as vacuous as they could possibly be.

Journals like the *Economist*, which abhors a vacuum, have rushed in to provide the CSD with a programme which they so conspicuously lacked.[1] The economic part of the programme included, inter alia, a commitment to 'the pursuit of equality' (a 'fundamental ambition of social democracy') and a wealth tax. Clearly too extreme for Dr Owen, whose own recent writings have avoided the theme of equality like the plague. The polls had to construct a hypothetical set of policies to provide their interviewees with some credible basis for responding to the question 'Would you vote for a Social Democratic party – and, if so, why?' The results have simply compounded the confusion. One *Sunday Times* poll suggested that the Social Democrats would attract support for (among others) the following reasons: they supported (a) more public spending on welfare, and (b) wider worker participation in industry. Neither immediately distinguishes them from their Labour and Liberal rivals. Is Social Democracy, then, just a nine day's wonder, which is not worth discussing seriously? Not necessarily. Though this doesn't mean, either, that we should take it at its own, highly-inflated self-evaluation.

A deeper process of realignment?

For one thing, it now represents a significant re-grouping of parliamentary forces. Post-war parliamentary politics have been marked by many contradictory cross-currents. But the big parliamentary formations, and the two-party system, have, despite several flutters, remained remarkably stable and durable. There have been few significant regroupings. Open splits and group defections from the Labour Party are even rarer, despite prolonged internecine warfare. It is fifty years since the last one. The left has more often looked like splitting off than the right, which, until recently, has maintained its dominance. Moreover, the departure of the doctrinaire right (for the CSD is nothing if not militant in its 'moderation') marks the isolating out of certain political elements which, up to now, have co-existed with other currents in the unholy mix of 'Labour Socialism'. For years Mr Crosland was the spiritual leader of the group which has now formed the CSD. But Croslandism retained links with more traditional Labour themes (e.g. the strong commitment to equality of opportunity), even though he regarded them as old-fashioned. Mr Hattersley is the last representative of this current. The rest have given up on the labour movement. This represents the breaking of certain historic ties. Their appearance as an independent force thus signals a crisis and break in the system of parliamentary representation. And though such breaks do not always mark significant movements (the 'Lib-Lab' pact was more or less pure parliamentary opportunism, marking only the deep degeneration of the Callaghan government in the squalid evening of its rule), they sometimes do – as the break-up of Liberalism at the turn of the century undoubtedly did. It is hard to know, sometimes, just which conjuncture one is in. But, as Gramsci once reminded us, 'crises of representation', when 'social classes become detached from their traditional parties', and organisational forms and leaderships 'who constitute, represent and lead them are no longer recognised ... as their expression' can form part of a more general crisis of ruling-class hegemony. The question, then, is whether Social Democracy is simply a new allocation of seating arrangements in the House of Commons, or part of a deeper process of the realignment of political forces. This possibility should not be dismissed as easily as it has been by the left in recent months.

Thatcherism in difficulties

Gramsci offered two reasons why such crises of authority might arise, the most relevant being that 'the ruling class has failed in some major political undertaking for which it has requested or forcibly extracted the consent of the broad masses'. In those terms, the 'objective conditions' look remarkably favourable. For such a historic failure – to wit, the task of stemming the precipitate decline of British capitalism – is precisely what is now before us. Both the major variants within the governing political repertoire are in various stages of collapse. The social-democratic version, Mark I – the management of capitalist crisis by neo-Keynesian demand management, corporatist politics and the disciplining of working-class demands through incomes policy – is deeply discredited. Its viability seeped away through two long, disheartening Labour regimes. And now the 'radical alternative' – the restoration of capitalist imperatives through the application of unmodified social market principles – is also coming apart at the seams. The monetarist, free-enterprise credentials, economic strategies and capitalist revivalism of the Thatcher government are in deep disarray. The Great Reversal, on which everything was staked, has failed to appear. The government is losing its struggle with public spending and money supply at approximately the same rate as it is losing its most powerful allies. The CBI is as close to open revolt as so weak-kneed and suppliant a body can ever come. The Treasury Select Committee, led by one of the most powerful independents in the Tory Party, Mr Du Cann (maker and destroyer of leaders before now), has delivered the new doctrines a near-mortal blow. The apostle of anti-statism, Sir Keith Joseph, has given away more public money to prop up failing or near-bankrupt state industries than the last three or four Chancellors put together. Faced with the long awaited showdown with the unions, the government looked into the face of the NUM, and withdrew. Mrs Thatcher's bellicose adventurism on the world scene – exceedingly dangerous as it is in its own terms – cannot be relied on to divert attention forever from the harsh economic realities at home.

'Thatcherism' has certainly already succeeded in shifting the balance of social forces in the country decisively to the right. But it has failed in the second task of the great populist adventure – to flush out the social democratic vestiges within the power bloc and then reconstruct it, so as thereby to restructure society and the economy.

'Thatcherism' may have *already* fulfilled its 'historic mission'. But neither of the major electoral machines now offer themselves as a credible occupant of power at another turn of the electoral wheel. Not only is Thatcher clearly in difficulties but the Tory Party is very divided. Labour is no longer what it was: but what it is, and, even more, what it will become as a result of the internal crisis which Thatcherism has provoked within its ranks, is not yet clear. Its political character is highly indeterminate. The signs are therefore well set for the 'recovery' of more centrist ground. If the Social Democrats were prepared, selectively, to reflate; to restore some version of incomes policy; and to mastermind a modest revival by ditching the struggle against inflation and ruthlessly backing private industry against the state sector, they still might not attract popular support; and there is no evidence that they would succeed in the 'historic task' any better than their rivals. But they could look like another – the last? – viable political alternative. And they could secure powerful support 'from above', amongst all those forces currently detaching themselves from the Thatcher path to the brink. They are British capitalism's last political ditch.

Growing volatility

This makes Social Democracy a powerful pole of attraction of a cross-party coalitionist type – the 'exceptional' alternative towards which, since the Lloyd George coalition, the British political system has tended to veer in moments of severe crisis (remember Macdonald, and Mr Heath's 'Grand National Coalition'?). This does not guarantee it popular support. But here there may be other trends which strengthen its case. There is what political scientists have been calling the 'growing electoral volatility' of the British voters. Between 1945 and 1970, each of the two major parties polled over 40 per cent of the votes at general elections. Their electoral base seemed reasonably secure. But in the 1970s, their share of the vote has fallen significantly. Party identifica-tion has weakened, votes have become more fluid. No administration has gone its full term and then succeeded in being re-elected. The old rotation of parties in power has continued: but on an increas-ingly weak base. This now finds supporting evidence in the findings of the polls that a hypothetical Social Democratic-Liberal alliance would attract a significant proportion of 'floating' and fed-up voters in about equal numbers from both Labour and the Conservatives. The scenario then goes that they would form the decisive bloc in a divided Parliament. Electoral reform would become the principal political bargaining point. Proportional representation would then destroy the hegemony of the two-party system forever, and secure a permanent majority for 'the Centre'.

The trends are certainly clear, even if the scenario is less convincing. Mrs Thatcher may make Royal Progresses; but the two-party political system is in deep disrepute. Her popularity may well reflect the fact that she appears to transcend it, with her appeal to Nation and People above 'party', and is prepared to destroy it in order to reconstruct it. But people do sense that we are at or near the limit of the present political arrangements and dispositions. Yet the meaning of this phenomenon is hard to interpret. The political scientists explain it in one way. Here, at last, appears the 'true' voter: less traditional in political alignments, unattached to dogma and doctrine, rationally calculating political choices on a purely pragmatic, non-ideological, non-class basis: 'Economic Man' in the polling booth – the great pluralist dream. It confirms the wished-for break-up of the class structure of British political culture. And it is said to 'prove' that the true heart of the political system and of the 'British voter' lies in the Centre. Rationality and Moderation have fallen into each other's arms.

A gravitation to the right – not the centre

This is more sell-fulfilling prophecy than hard political analysis. The interpretation of a natural gravitation of British politics to 'the Centre', eschewing all extremes, would make more sense if the parties had represented over the decades the spectacle of alternating extremes. But, until recently, judged in terms of real strategies rather than ideological polemics and stage-managed caricatures, both parties have long struggled precisely to occupy this mythical 'middle ground', provided by a capital-led mixed economy, incomes policy, neo-Keynesianism and corporatism. The social-democratic consensus has been the baseline from which both sides have attempted to govern, and to which, in the end, even adventurists like Mr Heath (in his 'Selsdon Man' period) were ultimately driven back. It is the failure, precisely, of the Centre, old-style, and the steady erosion of its repertoire of crisis-management, which has provoked successive movements in recent years towards more extreme alternatives. It is the collapse and bankruptcy of 'the Centre' which generated increasing pressure towards these extremes. And if the revival of the left within the Labour Party is one way of inheriting this collapse, it has been much more evident on and towards the right. First, the populist undercurrents of 'Powellism'; then Mr Heath's boom-or-bust excursion, before the miners and the U-turn; then the formation of the Keith Joseph 'Adam Smith' kitchen cabinet; finally – as it became clear that the doctrines of Hayek and Friedman would need to connect with the reactionary instincts of the Tory backwoods – the formation, radical offensive and electoral success of the 'Thatcher party'. This progressive abandonment of 'the Centre' has taken place for the best of all possible reasons: it failed. Things got worse, not better, under its increasingly weak and nerveless leadership. This suggests that the increasing volatility of the electorate is best explained, not in terms of the natural and inevitable gravitation of British politics to the 'middle ground', but because of the manifest inability of the two variants of consensus politics to stem the tide of British economic disintegration and progressive deindustrialisation.

What's more, the evidence from the movement of public opinion suggests, not the permanence and stability of 'centrist' ideas, but a steady gravitation towards the extreme right. A recent paper has shown that, among voters strongly identifying with Labour, support for more nationalisation, more spending on social services, retaining

Labour's links with the trade unions and sympathy with strikers all fell between the 1960s and the 1970s.[2] Support among the same sections for the sale of council houses, keeping the grammar schools, cutting government spending, cutting profits tax, and strengthening law and order and immigration controls have all swung significantly in Mrs Thatcher's direction. Manual workers who are also Labour supporters and trade unionists showed markedly higher shifts of opinion – again in this direction – than other groups, long before the very significant swing to the right in 1979 which brought the most radical-right government of the post-war period to office. This is particularly strong in the area of the Thatcherite populist issues – anti-unions, anti-statism, anti-welfare. When these are placed alongside the cluster of issues which Crewe and others have called 'Populist Authoritarian' – the so-called 'moral' issues of race, law and order, private initiative and self-reliance, where even Labour supporters, strongly pro-Labour on other issues, suddenly become explicitly 'Thatcherite' – the evidence of a natural gravitation to centrist politics is thin. The underlying movement is undoubtedly rightwards. Lack of faith in the two major parties may, therefore, draw people in desperation towards a middle-ground alternative. But not because this is where the natural fulcrum of the British voter permanently and inevitably comes to rest. Social Democracy must occupy 'the Centre' because it is there. Besides, that is where they are. But their strongest card will not be the promise to 'restore the Centre', but the vaguer threat to 'break the political mould'. In so doing, they inherit, not the mantle of Attlee, but the legacy of Mrs Thatcher – for, though they may deflect it in a different direction, that is what she promised too. Whether it is possible to 'break the mould' and 'return to the Centre' at the same time is the particular card trick or sleight-of-hand on which the fortunes of Dr Owen, Mr Rodgers, Mrs Williams and Mr Jenkins (a 'breaker of moulds'?) now depend.

The real character of Social Democracy

What, then, is its real political character and content? The break with 'Labour Socialism', however muted in some instances, is real and deep. It is a final break with the historic Labour-trade union connection. This is mounted as firmly on the back of the 'trade-unions-are-too-powerful' crusade as anything in Mrs Thatcher's vocabulary, though it is less virulently put. It is also a break with even a residual connection to working-class politics – even the rudimentary form in which this is still acknowledged by the traditional Labour right – 'Labour as the party of the working class in government'. At this level, Social Democracy is thoroughly managerialist in its political style. It will have no organised political base – only the 'detached voter', combined with a power base in parliamentary rule. It is 'for' democracy – in so far as this highlights the undemocratic nature of British trade unionism; and especially in so far as it means (or meant) 'one-man-one-vote' for the Labour leadership, and the total independence of the parliamentary party from democratic accountability. This is nothing positively new, since for both the press and for Mrs Thatcher, 'democracy' only works when it allows the 'silent majority' to out-vote the left. In earlier days, the Social Democrats were the group within the Gaitskell orbit most prepared to put its democratic conscience into permanent cold storage so long as the trade union block vote delivered the right result to the right. It is deeply and passionately hostile to every manifestation of the left. The media have signally failed to bring out that the single most important factor which precipitated the final break was the very thought that non-Labour trade unionists might somehow be able to exert an indirect influence over the leadership election – and I don't think it was the Federation of Conservative Trade Unionists they had most in mind!

On the economic front, it is the party of 'incomes policy' in the classic sense: i.e. as an instrument with which to discipline the demands of labour and restore them to their rightful position – led by the overriding imperatives of capitalist profitability and competitiveness. Neo-Keynesian in their sympathy for reflation, the Social Democrats are nevertheless as committed as Mrs Thatcher and Sir Keith are to the leadership of big industrial capital and the play of market forces. That is what they mean by a 'mixed economy'. They emerge as the only, true EEC 'party' – not even in the robust sense of Mr Heath, blowing the cold wind of European competition through the cobwebbed boardrooms of British industry: more as an article of faith. The unity through competition of free-market capitalisms is what they mean by 'Internationalism'. 'A socialist who works constructively within the framework of a mixed economy' is the image to which Dr Owen recently aspired. His reference points – Sweden, Austria,

West Germany and Holland. His memorable dates – the assimilation
of the German SPD to reformism at the Bad Godesberg meeting in
1959, and the overturning of the 1960 Labour Conference decision for
unilateralism. Which 'moulds' are likely to be broken by these ancient
instruments is something of a mystery. It is the restoration of the old
through the appearance of constructing something new

A traditional recipe

Despite its cavilling at the cost of Trident, Social Democracy is fervent
in its support for NATO and the Western shield. Indeed, in being
less committed to the British independent deterrent, it is likely to be
more suppliant to Washington's grand Alliance strategy than even
its Labour predecessors. The Social Democrats, in the week of the
Thatcher-Reagan resumption of the role of world policemen, and
amidst the talk of NATO Retaliatory Forces and offensive Cold War
postures, did not allow themselves to blink an eye at what precisely
this loyal subordination to NATO strategy promises to become under
the Reagan-Haig-Thatcher hegemony. Instead, they chose to open
their parliamentary career by taking Labour to the cleaners about its
wobbling indecisiveness over unilateralism.

This may look, when pieced together, like a very ancient and
familiar concoction. The novelty appears to lie in the terminology
with which their politics of the Centre is verbally glossed. Despite
their commitment to 'the new', the Social Democrats have failed to
identify a single new political constituency around a single new issue.
Feminism is a good case in point, where a strong, vigorous and radical
movement has developed, to which the traditional political cultures
of both the established left and the right are deeply inhospitable. If
any organised force were in a position to disconnect the feminist
movement and women from the left, and to articulate a limited
version of feminist demands to a 'new' kind of political programme,
Social Democracy ought to be. One or two public figures have indeed
given this as their principal reason for evacuating the left for centre
ground with embarrassing speed. But it must be said that this is more
in the eye of the beholders than it is anywhere evident in the political
complexion of the new Centre. Apart from offering the person of Mrs
Williams to fortune, Social Democracy has not made a single gesture

towards attracting this new social force. It gives every appearance of not knowing it exists and of not knowing how or where to identify and address it, if it did. Indeed, despite the promise of nationwide campaigns and local groups, Social Democracy is at present totally devoid of any single vestige of popular politics or popular mobilisation. It is exclusively and doctrinally attached to the prospects of 'politics from above'.

The only single gesture in this direction is in the fulsome talk about 'participatory democracy'. This is Social Democracy's way of attempting to colonise the growth of anti-corporatism/anti-statism, which has been one of the principal forms of popular alienation from Labour. Here, like Thatcherism before it, Social Democracy is indeed working on a real contradiction. Labour-in-power became the means, not for generating a decisive shift of wealth and power towards the popular classes, but a mode of representing the popular classes 'in government' – which, in conditions of recession, rapidly became a means of disciplining popular demands from above. The corporatist triangle is now, and rightly, seen as a directive style of political management – directed against the people, while at the same time incorporating them through their representatives. This has consolidated the Big State over the people – an identity which Mrs Thatcher was quick to exploit. This is a contradiction within the very heart of Labourism, with its deep parliamentary constitutionalism, its conception of the state as a neutral instrument of reform, its inexplicable belief that Labour governments can both 'represent working class interests' and manage capitalism without something giving, and, above all, its fear and suspicion of popular democratic politics in any form. Mrs Thatcher exploited this identity between Labour and the state to considerable advantage. By 1979, Labour seemed much the same as Big Brother, much involved in pushing people around to no visible effect; while Mrs Thatcher was the populist champion of 'the people' against the power bloc: a pretty remarkable reversal.

Participation without democracy

Social Democracy is gunning for the same space. But whereas Thatcherism sought to master the antagonism between 'people' and 'power bloc', transforming it, at a critical point, into a populist movement for National Unity around the new social market programme – bearing Mrs Thatcher, at the same time, into the power bloc – Social Democracy hopes to exacerbate the contradiction and transform it through the programme of 'participatory democracy', and 'decentralisation'. Dr Owen and Co are doctrinaire 'decentralisers'. This new doctrine circles around the same themes: 'the bureaucratic centralisers, the corporatists who now dominate British socialism, the mood of authoritarianism … the state … seen as the main instrument of reform'.[3] It operates on the same dichotomies: liberty versus equality. Like Mrs Thatcher, and against the long socialist tradition, it privileges liberty over equality. In this sense, it belongs firmly within a much longer process – that of bending and articulating liberalism (and liberal political economy) to the conservative rather than the radical pole. Authoritarianism and the state as an instrument of reform, Dr Owen argues, has not been 'counterbalanced' by a 'libertarian streak'. But whereas Thatcherism, detaching 'liberty' and 'equality', connects it with *authority* ('Free Market' – liberty; Strong State – authority), Social Democracy deflects it towards a third pole, in its struggle to win space from the left. Not authority but – fraternity: 'the sense of fellowship, co-operation, neighbourliness, community and citizenship'. The authentic centrist, cross-class, coalitionist code words. Participation gives people a feeling of belonging. Decentralisation gives them the illusion of real power. 'Small is beautiful' is a popular slogan in the era of state capitalism. There is no question but that, somewhere in this space, socialism has long since ceased to operate – to its profound cost. It has deeply lost its popular, anti-power block, democratic vision. There is space, after all, here – as the enemies of socialism in both the right and the centre know well.

But 'participation' without democracy, without democratic mobilisation, is a fake solution. 'Decentralisation' which creates no authentic, alternative sources of real popular power, which mobilises no one, and which entails no break-up of the existing power centres and no real shift in the balance of power, is an illusion. It is a transformist solution. It conflates the unthinkable with the improbable – all the while giving the strong illusion of 'moving forwards'. Transformism is the authentic programme of the moderate left in a period of progressive political polarisation along class lines. Its function is to dismantle the beginnings of popular democratic struggle, to neutralise a popular rupture, and to absorb these elements passively, into a compromise programme. Its true novelty is that it conflates the historic programmes of the classic, fundamental parties of the left and the right. It is the restoration of the old through the appearance of constructing something new: 'revolution' without a revolution. Passive revolution 'from above' (i.e. Parliament). Gramsci noted two aspects of the programme of 'transformism' which are apposite to our case. The moment when 'individual political figures formed by the democratic opposition parties are incorporated individually into the conservative-moderate political class': and the moment when 'entire groups of leftists pass over into the moderate camp'. We are entering the second.

A 'Caesarist' solution

Since the break-up of the great Liberal formation in the early years of this century, the British political system has shown an increasing tendency, in periods of crisis, to turn to Caesarist solutions. 'Caesarism' is a type of compromise political solution, generated from above, in conditions where the fundamental forces in conflict so nearly balance one another that neither seems able to defeat the other, or to rule and establish a durable hegemony. Gramsci reminds us that 'Caesarist solutions' can exist without 'any great "heroic" and repre-sentative personality' – though in the earlier period there were indeed contenders for this role 'above party and class'. But, he adds:

> The parliamentary system has also provided a mechanism for such compromise solutions. The 'Labour' governments of Macdonald were to a certain degree solutions of this kind ... Every coalition government is a first stage of Caesarism ...

In a period when the discipline of unemployment is sending a shiver of realism through the labour movement, it may seem over-optimistic to argue that we now confront a situation of stalemate between the fundamental classes. Yet this does once more seem to be the case. Thatcherism lacks the economic space or the political clout to impose a terminal defeat on the labour movement. The working class and its allies are so deep in corporate defensive strength that they continue to provide the limit to Thatcherism despite their current state of disor-ganisation. Irresistible force meets the immovable object. On the other hand, the labour movement lacks the organisation, strategy, programme or political will to rule. So far it has failed to act as the magnet for new social forces, thereby itself embracing new fronts of struggle and aspiration. It still shows no major sign of reversing its own long decline. Such stalemates are ready-made for the appearance of grand compromise.

Whether this is a solution which can more than temporarily stem the tide remains to be seen. Sometimes 'Caesarism' is only a temporary staving off of deeper currents. Sometimes it can lead, through successive variations, to the formation of a new type of state. More often, it is 'an evolution of the same type along unbroken lines'. This is certainly not to say that it cannot temporarily succeed; or that, having succeeded in winning electoral support, it will not (as Thatcherism has done before it) have real effects in preventing that reshaping of the left and of socialism which alone can provide a real alternative – permitting, instead, Labour in a parallel way, only to recompose itself along familiar lines. A Labour government, succeeding to its third rotation in power, under such conditions, would certainly neutralise socialism for a very long time to come. That, after all, may be what Social Democracy is *really* about.

Notes

1. 'A Policy for Pinks', *Economist*, 14 February 1981.
2. Tony Fitzgerald in an unpublished paper on movements in public opinion.
3. David Owen, 'Power To The People', *Sunday Times*, 25 January 1981.

The empire strikes back

1982

EMPIRES COME AND go. But the imagery of the British Empire seems destined to go on forever. The imperial flag has been hauled down in a hundred different corners of the globe. But it is still flying in the collective unconscious.

As the country drifts deeper into recession, we seem to possess no other viable vocabulary in which to cast our sense of who the British people are and where they are going, except one drawn from the inventory of a lost imperial greatness. And now the country is going to war. Going to war for a scatter of islands eight thousand miles away, so integral a part of the British Imperium, so fixed in our hearts, that we have not managed to build a decent road across the place or to provide it with a continuous supply of power.

But this all-too-familiar story – the real history – from our imperial annals has been displaced by a more potent myth. *Civis Britannicus Sum.* We have set sail in defence of a high principle – and now, as if by magic, the powers we thought had departed from us have returned. In a dangerous, difficult and complex world, it is still possible to let a few of the old truths shine forth. 'Our boys' are 'out there' again; and, despite 'the tragic loss of life', Britain can show the 'Johnny-Argies' a thing or two, yet. No tin-pot, banana-republic, jumped-up dictator can tweak this lion's tail. Pull it – and the Empire still strikes back!

Rumour and speculation to the contrary, Mrs Thatcher did not invent the Falklands crisis. But she certainly now regrets that it was General Galtieri, not she, who thought of it first; for it is doing her government and its historic mission a power of good. What else is Mr Cecil Parkinson – Tory Party chairman, but with no high ministerial responsibilities and not, so far as is known, a notable naval strategist – doing in the War Cabinet, if he's not there for the purpose of exploiting the crisis to the political hilt in the best and continuing interests of the Conservative Party?

It has already delivered tangible rewards. Three million people and more are unemployed; the whole social infrastructure is being savaged by cuts; the economy continues to bump along the seabed. Our Hunter Killer subs seem able to surface, but the economy stubbornly refuses to do so. Yet, even before the Falklands crisis, these facts had failed to convert themselves into a popular revulsion against the government due to the absence of a credible alternative. (Oh, economic determinism – three million unemployed equals a 100 per cent swing to Labour – where art thou now?)

The programme of the radical right is still very much in business, with no U-turn in sight. It is, clearly, still the dominant political force. And now, powered by an imperial adventure that would have seemed out of date in 1882, the government is riding high in the opinion polls, some fifteen or twenty points ahead of its nearest rivals – at the mid-term, when most other post-war governments have been clutching at straws.

It has come, unscathed, through the local elections. Were Mr Parkin-son to stoop his unyielding back so low as to give the Prime Minister the opportunist advice to call a snap election tomorrow, the latest poll suggests that 52 per cent of manual workers, a lead of 9 per cent among trade unionists, as well as more men than women, would be prepared to vote Conservative: a historic reversal, were it to be realised.

The opposition has been effectively disorganised. Labour is split. The leadership and the parliamentary majority, hoisted aloft by the windy gases exhaled in frontbench speeches – sound and fury, signifying a total loss of grip on the political reality – is firmly attached to the tail of a patriotic war. As if Labour's cause has anything to gain from dabbling in patriotic jingoism except more Tory votes.

The left, opposed to the war in a principled stand, is nevertheless isolated, silenced by the usual media blackout. And – speaking of the media – SDP support is crumbling, as the South Atlantic steals the headlines: except, of course, for Dr Owen, man of the future, reliving each intense moment from past heroic engagements when he was at the Falklands helm, as if from the bridge or operations room of some imaginary aircraft carrier. Worst of all is the spectacle of a Conservative government leading the nation towards the sunrise, into what is indisputably a popular war. The naval imperialism – 'mistress of the waves' – on which past British greatness was built paid off a few better than it did the majority. But it has been a popular cause before and – with so much else that is nasty, brutish and unpromising to think about – has become so again.

'Public opinion is fickle. Wait until the casualty lists start rolling in.' They will have to be British names, for Argentinian dead don't rank. For the moment, the most solid hope of halting the fighting is the sombre calculation of how the country would take the despatch of some ship of the size of the *HMS Invincible* to the icy depths of the South Atlantic, courtesy of a French, South African, Israeli or international arms trade Exocet missile. Empire has struck.

Its antiquated character remains one of the most striking features of the Falklands crisis. The early inaction of the left was no doubt attributable to sheer disbelief at this return of the repressed in the middle of the nuclear missile age. The task force is a great armada – though the last one was blown out of the water, breaking up in the outer Hebrides. The fleet can no longer fire a broadside or get an Exocet missile off its trail or keep the skies free of 'Argies'.

Yet the language of the Battle of Jutland and the Battle of Britain survives. Those great vessels, named after historic cities, with their expensive equipment and their precious human cargo, would be so many sitting ducks – of the bathroom variety – if only the 'Argies' had learned the lesson of the stockpile. Others will. That the common humanity and emotion of families waving their relatives off at the quayside should be recruited into this quest for past glories is an obscenity – a piece of political recidivism. But it would be wrong to assume that the charge of anachronism would make Mrs Thatcher stumble or hesitate for a moment.

After all, the return to the traditionalist reference points of the past has been one of the main lynch-pins of Thatcherism's ideological project. It is at the heart of its populism. 'Mrs Thatcher called yesterday for a return to traditional values', the *Guardian* reported in 1978. She has been advancing steadily towards the past ever since. 'Together', she assured her audience about her visit to President Reagan in 1981, 'we have discovered old verities'. Again and again, the simple, tried and trusted virtues and ideals which stood our fathers and mothers in such good stead have been identified with the definition of what is 'great' about 'Great Britain'.

'I think it's astonishing how true many of the deep, fundamental values have remained, in spite of everything. Things may have changed on the surface, but there is still tremendous admiration for true values', she assured the readers of *Woman's Realm* in 1980. The return of Britain to greatness has been identified with the fixed reference points of good old British common sense. In search of the populist connection, Mrs Thatcher and her allies in the press and elsewhere have unashamedly gone for the great simplifications.

The economy can be managed on the same principles as the family budget: you can't spend what you haven't got. Mrs T is simply our most-beloved Good Housekeeper. Children should be brought up as our parents brought us up. Mothers should stay at home. Tin-pot dictators must be stood up to. These are the grand truths which history and experience teach: what she called, at the Conservative Women's Conference on the eve of her election victory, the 'tried and trusted values of common sense'. Better than 'trendy theories' – and all that thinking.

Her approach is instinctual. 'If you can't trust the deeper instincts of our people, we shouldn't be in politics at all.' And essentialist: these are the essential human qualities of the British people, inscribed in their destiny. The assumption of the radical right to power has been safely located within Tory traditions, by a highly selective form of historical reconstruction. 'I know you will understand the humility I feel at following in the footsteps of great men like our leader in that year, Winston Churchill, a man called by destiny to raise the name of Britain to supreme heights in the history of the free world.'

What event, what image, is more calculated to draw these different strands together and condense them into a compelling symbol in popular consciousness than one more great imperial adventure on the high seas, especially when gut patriotism is laced with gut moralism. 'Nothing so thrills the British people as going to war for a just cause.'

The Falklands crisis may have been unpredicted, but the way it has been constructed into a populist cause is not. It is the apogee of the whole arc of Thatcherite populism. By 'populism' I mean something more than the ability to secure electoral support for a political programme, a quality all politicians in formal democracies must possess. I mean the project, central to the politics of Thatcherism, to ground neoliberal policies directly in an appeal to 'the people'; to root them in the essentialist categories of common-sense experience and practical moralism – and thus to construct, not simply awaken, classes, groups and interests into a particular definition of 'the people'.

At different stages of the populist project, different themes have been drawn into service in this attempt to capture common sense for traditionalism and the right: race ('people of an alien culture'); nationality (the new Act, under which, incidentally, the Falklanders ceased to be citizens of any special kind); foreign policy (the Iron Lady episode); and law and order; have helped to give 'what the nation is' and 'who the people are' its particular traditionalist inflection.

This is a high-risk strategy for the right. It entails mobilising the people in a populist arousal, sufficient to cut across and displace other, more compelling definitions, interests and contradictions and to supplant alternative images and meanings. The 'people' must be mobilised if they are to join the party in the crusade to drive from the temples of the state all the creeping collectivists, trendy Keynesians, moral permissives and soft appeasers who have occupied it in the era of the social-democratic consensus. Yet in order to prevent a populist mobilisation from developing into a genuinely popular campaign, the arousal of populist sentiment must be cut off at just the correct moment, and subsumed or transformed into the identification with authority, the values of traditionalism and the smack of firm leadership. It is an authoritarian populism.

It is also a delicate and contradictory ideological exercise. It has been required, for example, to square the circle consisting of the free market, competitive individualist tenets of neoliberalism, as well as the organic metaphors of flag, patriotism and nation. This work of populist transformation and synthesis can be seen in the very person of the great populist herself: the steely manner; the lugubrious approach; the accent, revealing the expropriation of provincial Grantham into suburban Finchley; the scrupulously tailored image – just now, draped in black, as if half anticipating sorrowful news from abroad about 'our boys' doing so well 'out there' against 'them'; the smack of firm leadership; the oceanic reserves of class patronage and – from the heights of this assumption of authority – the popular touch.

It is the success with which all the chords of populist sentiment, feeling and memory have been struck at once, which testifies to the sureness of touch with which the Falklands crisis has been handled ideologically. The most powerful popular memory of all – the war, when we came to the rescue of oppressed people 'under the heel of the dictator'; 1940, when 'we stood alone' against enormous odds; and

'1945' – Churchill's triumph, not the founding of the welfare state – has been totally colonised by the right.

We have been invited to relive our last great moments of national greatness through the Falklands war. In the process, the legitimacy, the popularity and the justice of the one is transferred to the other. In this way, and to the astonishment of the left, Thatcherism has literally stolen the slogans of national self-determination and anti-fascism out of mouths. The sovereignty of people, the right of self-determination, the wickedness of dictators, the evil of military juntas, the torch of liberty, the rule of international law and the anti-fascist crusade: in a hideous but convenient ventriloquism, they have been run up the flagpole of the right.

As the 'war cabinet' drapes itself in the ensign of the Royal Navy, and the *Mail* remembers its past, who cares that the long-standing, well-documented obscenities of the Argentine regime against its people did not disturb Mrs Thatcher's sleep until the day before yesterday? Who minds that Argentina has so speedily become the only offending fascist military junta in Latin America, and that neighbouring Chile, where the roll-call of 'the disappeared' is almost as long, is a friend of democracy?

Until a few weeks ago, the Argentinian generals were slipping in and out of quiet briefing rooms in Western military establishments and training schools around the globe. Until yesterday, Mrs Thatcher's only concern about the international arms trade was how Britain could – to coin a phrase – 'make a killing' in that lucrative market.

Tomorrow, once the junta has been taught a lesson, and the national spirit revived by a little blood-letting, things will no doubt slowly return to 'business as usual'; a much-relieved General Haig will send his advisers back to Buenos Aeyer-es, where they naturally belong. When flags unfurl, there is no time – fortunately – for awkward contradictions. The British can take heart. The navy, with a little effort, sails. Flags fly. Things are simple, after all.

We are up against the wall of a rampant and virulent gut patriotism. Once unleashed, it is an apparently unstoppable, populist mobiliser – in part, because it feeds off the disappointed hopes of the present and the deep and unrequited traces of the past, imperial splendour penetrated into the bone and marrow of the national culture. Its traces are to be found in many places and at many levels. An imperial metropolis cannot pretend its history has not occurred. Those traces, though buried and repressed, infect and stain many strands of thinking and action, often from well below the threshold of conscious awareness. The terrifying images of the past weigh 'like a nightmare, on the brains of the living'.

The traces of ancient, stone-age ideas cannot be expunged. But neither is their influence and infection permanent and immutable. The culture of an old empire is an imperialist culture; but that is not all it is, and these are not necessarily the only ideas in which to invent a future for British people. Imperialism lives on – but it is not printed in an English gene. In the struggle for ideas, the battle for hearts and minds which the right has been conducting with such considerable effect, bad ideas can only be displaced by better, more appropriate ones.

Ancient thoughts will only cease to give us a compelling motive for action if more modern thoughts can grip the popular imagination, bite into the real experience of the people, and make a different kind of sense. To do this would require a recognition of the critical importance of the ideological terrain of struggle – and the construction of the instruments by which such struggles are conducted. Yet the Labour Party, the labour movement and the left have no national paper: all we can do is read the *Guardian* and pray! No powerful journal of opinion, no political education, no organic intellectual base from which to engage popular consciousness, no alternative reading of popular history to offer, no grip on the symbolism of popular democratic struggle.

The left thinks it is 'materialist' to believe that because ideas do not generate themselves out of thin air, they do not matter. The right of the labour movement, to be honest, has no ideas of any compelling quality, except the instinct for short-term political survival. It would not know an ideological struggle if it stumbled across one in the dark. The only 'struggle' it engages in with any trace of conviction is the one against the left.

More scandalous than the sight of Mrs Thatcher's best hopes going out with the navy has been the demeaning spectacle of the Labour front-bench leadership rowing its dinghy as rapidly as it can in hot pursuit. Only, of course – here, the voice of moderation – 'not so far! Slow down! Not so fast!'

The crisis of Labourism

1984[*]

THERE ARE WORRYING signs that the labour movement is simply not willing to grasp, or is incapable of grasping, the seriousness of the position into which it has fallen. Crises are not reversed simply by thinking about them. But to recognise that they exist – and to try to analyse why they are occurring – is the first, essential requirement for overcoming them. Simply to deny their existence is to exhibit the political nous of the ostrich.

In place of the radical reappraisal which this seems to require, however, what one hears is the troubling noise of a great deal of whistling in the dark: the solid affirmation, against all the evidence, that 'we can still win', 'things will turn our way', 'unemployment will deliver the vote to us in the end' or, at best, 'we are going through a difficult patch, but Labour is going to form the next government'. As Gramsci once observed, you must turn your face violently towards things as they really are. The reality for Labour is that it is only just holding its own in popularity with the electorate, in circumstances which ought to be favourable. More seriously, it does not seem capable of forming a credible alternative or making a decisive political impact on the electorate. And without a major revival, there can be no realistic possibility of another Labour government this decade, let alone of socialism this century.

'Things' are not automatically turning Labour's way. The short-term electoral indicators point the other way – in a situation of extreme political volatility. The two-party electoral mould has been shaken by the 'unthinkable' Labour/SDP split; and the party's morale has clearly been deeply affected by it. These short-term reversals only compound the long-term political and ideological trends which have now been moving steadily against Labour for some years, as shown in the erosion of its popular base and solid class character, especially since the mid-1970s.

Many people will say this is gross exaggeration, founded on an inexcusable pessimism. With scandals and banana skins liberally strewn everywhere, surely the Tory magic is at last dispersing? The authoritarian face of Mrs Thatcher, now more or less permanently on view, lacks a great deal of its former immediate populist appeal. Postponing elections, taking away basic civil rights, demolishing councils because you do not like their political complexion is not the most obvious route to sustained popularity in a democracy. For a time Mrs Thatcher and her government seemed virtually error-proof, swimming with every tide. If the tides have not turned, have they not, at least, manifestly ebbed?

On the Labour side, there has been a partial upturn in the opinion polls. Some of the splits and divisions have been healed. The left in the constituency parties is both more vigorous and in much better heart. The Benn victory at Chesterfield was a welcome bonus. There is a new, younger, more vigorous leadership, with a young, vigorous, boyish, freckle-faced leader, who has an infectious grin, a passion for rugby and a fondness of the too well sculptured question at *Question Time.*

Do these and other advances mean that the crisis is now over? Perhaps it never existed. Is Labour poised for political revival? Is it ready to run the country? Is it once more *the* alternative party of government? Does it show evidence of once more becoming a popular political force?

These are dubious propositions. First, despite the revival, Labour is still a very long way behind. To win a majority it would have to capture every seat where it lay second in the 1983 election: a formidable challenge. The SDP may not be the threat it was, but the split in the anti-Thatcher forces is exceedingly damaging structurally and wears a look of permanence. It is a situation designed to provide a structural bloc against movement to the left – which is why Dr Owen (who has gravitated so far rightward he has virtually disappeared over the western horizon altogether) takes such fiendish delight in it. Meanwhile the Thatcherites, by their sheer bloody-minded determination to press on, will continue to set the terms, define the parameters, establish the benchmark of 'political reality'.

The new Kinnock-Hattersley leadership shows little sign as yet of becoming a popular political force, as opposed to a (not very successful) electoral machine. Apart from the issue of the health service, it has shown little understanding of the need to confront the real basis of Thatcher populism in the country at large. Its perspective is still narrowly confined to the terrain of the labour movement and the daily accommodations of policy which its contradictory structure requires. More significantly, it still lacks a really sound grasp of the parameters of Labour's crisis or the ascendancy of Thatcherism, which should be rooted in a searching analysis of Labour's own record over the past two decades. Neil Kinnock is solidly in touch with the well-springs of Labourist culture – and that is important. But he has no feel for the language and concerns of the new social movements, and that is dangerous. He has embraced Eric Hobsbawm's analysis, give or take the ambiguities about alliances with the Alliance.[1] But he does not understand the politics of putting together a new historical bloc of forces, which is very different from an electoral marriage of convenience with the Alliance (in my view, a much more questionable proposition).

I make no prejudgements, but I offer a benchmark: no one who thinks feminism and the women's movement is a bit of a joke will lead Labour towards socialism in this century. Everybody loves a Welshman. But the Labour vote in Wales is down to 37 per cent – a country in which, as Hobsbawm pointed out, 'everything combined to create a Labour and socialist stronghold'.

What the ranks are closing against is precisely the kind of searching and agonising analysis which is necessary before anyone can chart a new course. There is a manifest hardening of Labour hearts against 'the pessimists'. Resentment is growing like rising damp against those inside and outside the ranks 'telling us what to do'. Only those insulated from the grassroots, it is said, could be so disloyal as to believe that the crisis is *inside* the labour movement as well as out there in the real world.

These aspects constitute important enough problems of strategy and development for Labour. But, essentially, the problem has not gone away because it did not in the first place consist of a temporary loss of electoral popularity. That was symptom, not cause. What is at issue is the disintegration of the historic social democratic programme of Labour, pursued in and out of government since the war. What has 'turned' is that underlying consensus in the political culture around the historic compromise struck in the post-war years, which has underpinned British politics and which gave Labour its legitimate claims of office as the alternative party of government. Gone are the conditions which enabled Labour governments in office to convince the electorate that they could keep the capitalist economy alive *and* pay off their social and industrial constituencies: Labour's historic compromise with labour. It cannot be done in times of economic recession. What 'went' was the solidity of the political formations around that compromise – Labourism as a particular constellation of social forces. We may or may not agree on how far that social basis for Labourist politics has eroded, or what new constituencies there are for radical political change. But there cannot be serious argument about the scale of the problem. It is not simply attributable to the misplaced pessimism of a few free-floating intellectuals.

The complacent view of Labour's crisis is held in place by the consoling illusion that it all happened with the Falklands and, therefore, that 1983 was the backwash of a brief but passing phase. This view is historically incorrect and hence politically misleading. Strategically, the election of 1979 was a more significant turning point than 1983, though the scale of the disaster was less manifest. 1979, in turn, was the product of a major reversal culminating in the middle of the Callaghan government – the 1975-9 period. *Those* were the years when the basis of post-war reformism was destroyed. There, the first turn into monetarism occurred – led by Labour, not by the Tories. It was then that the oil hike exposed the vulnerability of the British economy. By that time trade-union unpopularity was far advanced – and nowhere was it so unpopular as inside the Labour cabinet. That was where the savaging of public expenditure began. Those were the conditions in which the re-education of the Labour leadership in the 'new realism' of managing a capitalist crisis was completed.

They were also the circumstances in which Mrs Thatcher emerged to capitalise on the crisis, put her finger on the experiences of the people and disperse Labour's exhausted programme to the four corners of the political wilderness. Against that backcloth, she engineered the fatal coupling of the anti-Labourist, anti-statist, anti-equality, anti-welfare spirit with the revitalised gospel of the free market. Thus the qualitatively new and unstable combination of 'Thatcherism' – organic national patriotism, religion of the free market, competitive individualism in economic matters, authoritarian state in social and political affairs, began to cohere as an alternative social philosophy. It was then that the seepage of Labour's popular support quickened into a torrent. In its wider sense the crisis is not of Mrs Thatcher's making alone. Historically, Labour is deeply implicated in it.

Take the question of politics and class. The left is convinced that too much 'analysis' will lead to the growth of a post-class politics in which Labour abandons its historic mission to represent the working class. But no one can pretend that the British class structure still mirrors the portrait drawn by Engels in 1844, or that, then and now, the relationships between class, party and political representation have ever been simple or one-way. The relevance of the class issue to British politics does not require us to say that class formations do not change, since palpably they do. And when they do, the strategies and dynamics of class politics will also shift, leaving to one side those organisations transfixed in earlier structures, like beached whales. After all, such shifts have occurred before within the history of British capitalism. Labour, 'Labourism' as we know it, and modern trade unionism are all the product precisely of one such shift in the 1880-1920 period. We may again be at a similar watershed.

No one, looking around Britain today, would deny the pertinence of class relations. No one seriously concerned to analyse the nature of present class formations could fail to recognise the changing class composition of our society: the decline of certain traditional sectors and the growth of new sectors; the shift in patterns of skill; radical recomposition as a result of the new gender and ethnic character of labour; the *new* divisions of labour resulting from changing technologies, and so on.

Likewise, no one would deny the enormous variety of class circumstances and experiences, the internal divisions and sectionalisms and the differential cultures which contemporary British society exhibits; with the emergence of new social forces leading to what Marx once called 'the production of new needs'. But nor can we afford to ignore the many pressures and forces emerging from contradictions in social life, which are, like everything in Britain, inscribed within class but do not have a simple class vs class origin.

Political issues often touch us as social consumers rather than as producers; are more pertinent to domestic life, the neighbourhood or locality than the 'point of production'; are democratic questions, which affect us as citizens rather than class subjects; are issues of personal and sexual politics which influence the structures of our everyday life: these now constitute the social politics of our era. They are backed by strong constituencies and movements, in which, of course, working people have a stake, but which do not necessarily move according to the tempo of the industrial class struggle. The articulation of these arenas of struggle with the changing rhythm of traditional class politics is the political challenge confronting Labour and the labour movement today. What an increasing majority of people feel is not that all these lines converge naturally in and around Labour but – quite the reverse – that there is now the most massive disjuncture between where the real movements, issues and subjects of politics are and the ways in which they are traditionally represented in the political marketplace.

There is not – and never has been – *the* given unity of *the* working class in Britain, which Labour could simply 'reflect' in its programmes. There have always been the divisions and fracturings we would expect under an advanced capitalist division of labour. Underlying these are certain shared conditions of exploitation and of social and community life which provide the contradictory raw materials from which the complex unity of a class could possibly be constructed; and out of which a socialist politics *could* be forged, but of which there was never any guarantee. How else are we to unite the very different needs, demands and ideas within the class and constitute those necessary bridges and alliances with other sectors which are currently essential to any popular political ascendancy? Where, for example, would a socialist strategy be without having at its centre the needs and demands of the many disadvantaged groups and communities at the receiving end of the Thatcher recession? Yet Labour can neither win elections nor lead the country into the next decade as the party of disadvantaged minorities alone. They have to become part of a wider popular strategy.

Now, what is the common political programme which resonates with both these experiences and outlines a political strategy capable of uniting them within a programme for socialism? Could we develop such a programme on the basis of the current division between waged and unwaged? Or without addressing the contradiction between the defence of the working conditions of the employed and the need of the unemployed for jobs? Could we retain the leapfrogging between high- and low-paid workers on which the whole economistic trade union strategy of the 1960s and 1970s depended, or attempt to construct a political alliance between the two extremes without disturbing the divisions between black and white or men and women?

People sometimes speak as if all we have to do to construct a new social alliance is to add up incrementally the demands of everybody who happens to be in the room at the time. The fact is that, because of the variety of social experiences and the uneven consequences of capitalist development, these different needs and demands are often genuinely contradictory. They have to be subsumed and 'reconciled' within some larger programme, which only a party aiming to become a popular political force is capable of putting together. They also have to retain their integrity, their autonomy and their difference within that programme if the alliance is to be anything more serious than a marriage of electoral convenience. This is a totally different conception of how to form a 'historical bloc', which recognises its difference from an electoral marriage of convenience. These are the strategic political questions which lie behind Labour's so-called 'recovery'. They require a strategy of renewal, a fundamental and permanent recasting which is certainly not yet on the labour movement's agenda.

Take the debate on council housing. Suppose that, instead of adopting instantly fixed positions 'for' or 'against' the existing form of public housing provision, we proceeded in the following way: first, define what it is the private market in housing *cannot do*. Besides identifying the variety of needs it cannot actually meet, this approach will develop the broader socialist critique of the distortions produced by pursuit of the private property ethic. It will look at the inadequacy of 'the market' as the measure of human need – and thereby question the very roots of Thatcherism.

Next, proceed to the massive changes which have actually taken place in the patterns of residential and family life, the new needs that have arisen, the variety of demands – whether from working-class families who cannot afford to buy; young homeless blacks adrift in the city; single-parent families; unmarried working women or gay men living on their own with the need for decent and secure places to live, and so on. In short, expose the socialist principle behind the provision of housing as a social need for a diverse society and *then* try to design a housing policy which reflects both the venerable tradition of public housing and the real world of the 1980s and 1990s. The conclusion of such a discussion may well be to reaffirm the present thrust of Labour's housing policies. But it would be a programme which had withstood the pressure of 'socialism in our time'.

Unemployment is another key issue. The problem here is that very few people put much faith in Labour's capacity to reverse the trend. On this, as on so many other questions, Mrs Thatcher so far continues to win the battle for hearts and minds; and those who command the definitions command the credibility. A deep fatalism has, therefore, settled over the country in this respect, which is part of the fashionable collapse before the Thatcherite world view that goes under the name of the 'new realism'. The new realism is really a capitulation to the belief that, after all, market forces *are* economic reality and there is no point arguing with or seeking to modify or influence market forces. Unemployment is, therefore, the responsibility of world trends, outside our capacity to influence. The problem is that this ideologically motivated 'explanation' contains a tiny, rational core. Some part of unemployment is indeed the consequence of a deep, capitalist world recession. Some of it is also structural; located in the endemic structural weakness of the British economy and in the restructuring of our economic base which is progressing – unevenly, as it always does under capitalism – at a very rapid rate under conditions of recession.

Of course, something can be done to reverse the trend of mass unemployment and deindustrialisation. But, to be convincing, the short-term measures have to be credible and concrete, and the long-term strategy has frankly to acknowledge and address the structural problems. Labour has so far done neither convincingly. 'Jobs' and 'more welfare' are the pious hopes to which the so-called 'Alternative Economic Strategy' was reduced before it altogether disappeared – a paper tiger. In the long term – while microchips eat people's jobs, word processors themselves show secretaries the way to the local dole office and miners are forced to base their claims to a decent life on the strategy of mining pits until the sea begins to seep through the pit floor – Labour has nothing strategic to say about the strategy for economic revival.

This was clearly evident in the terrible strategic defeat which the miners suffered in March.[2] To invite people in the tightest of economic squeezes to come out on strike when coal stocks are at record levels is to act, frankly, with the political nous of the leaders of the Charge of the Light Brigade. To imagine that people will sacrifice their livelihoods on the unevidenced assurances of their leadership, and without an opportunity to argue through and express their commitment in a democratic form, is to misread the relationship between leaders and troops and to misunderstand the rationality of working-class action.

To expect that the defensive position is enough on which to build a long-term alternative economic strategy is profoundly to misread the current mood of the working class. Of course, Thatcherism's clear intention was indeed to savage and butcher the pits and destroy the mining communities. Of course, politically, the government meant to break the organised strength of the unions. Of course, the miners clearly perceived what was at issue. But to mistake the moment of 1983 for 1972 or 1974 was an unforgiveable error. Saltley Gates was a heroic moment: but there is no automatic button marked 'Destruct Mrs Thatcher'. To believe this is not to build on an understanding of, but to be transfixed by, the past. The miners were offered three reasons for supporting the strike: in memory of those who had built the union; for their families; and 'as men', who have a duty to stand tip and fight. Glowing sentiments. And yet, in their backward trajectory, their familial and masculinist assumptions, those words fall on my ears as archaic. The cause is correct. The language is a dying one.

In an article which provoked much controversy on the left, Michael Ignatieff argued that the miners' strike represented the end of class politics as we have known it. Raphael Samuel in reply argued, inter alia, that the defence of a class community was the essence of the issue. Both views seemed to me to be incorrect or, rather, each expressed only half the truth. The miners' strike certainly contained a powerful 'class' dimension. But politically it was not, as Arthur Scargill represented it, a 'class-versus-class' showdown, because, far from 'the class' being united, it was deeply divided. The political task was not to fight a united heroic battle but to unify the miners, in order to unify the class, in order to unify a wider social bloc around the issues. The internal divisions within the miners' union had real, material and ideological conditions of existence, and were not simply attributable to the lack of some pre-existing and unproblematic class unity or solidarity. Seen in the light of the failure to address this critical and difficult political task, the absence of a ballot and the contempt which many showed for the very idea of the 'bourgeois' deviation of a vote, when a 1917 'Winter Palace' scenario was unfolding before their eyes, was a gigantic tactical error, as well as a major error of principle. One result was that the strike was dominated, and ultimately defeated, precisely by the splits and divisions which our ritualistic commitment to the formulae of 'class politics' prevented us from understanding or addressing. There followed the police protecting the 'right' of one section of 'the class' to go to work against the interests of another section of 'the class', the media construction of the strike as 'about' law and order and violence, and the failure of one of the most strategic encounters of Mrs Thatcher's three terms.

The rational core in Ignatieff's argument is that, though in a sense the very issue of class politics was at issue in the strike, it could not ultimately be won in the coalfields and mining communities alone, but only by generalising the strike into a wider social struggle, projecting it on to the stage of national politics, in which various sectors of society far removed from any pit-head felt, not only (as millions clearly did) sympathy at a distance for the miners and their families, but understood that there was something directly at stake for them too. Around what issue could this building of a broad popular alliance have been developed? In part, around the question of the future of energy. But, much more crucially, what the miners' strike posed was whether, in making the painful transition from one stage of industrial development to another (as sooner or later Britain must), the 'cost' in human and social terms is going, as it was in previous transitions, to be borne by the sectors of the society who are most vulnerable to technological change, who are then simply thrown on the scrapheap of history, their communities and cultures offered up on the altar of efficiency and 'modernisation': or whether, this time round, it is to be a social cost on all of us, on the society as a whole. We know what Thatcherism's answer is on this question. What is the left's?

The failure to see that an answer to this question was required, let alone to address it, was (notwithstanding the crucial strategic mistakes committed, despite his great courage, by Arthur Scargill) ultimately a political one, and must be laid at the door of the Labour leadership. If Labour has no other function, its role is surely to generalise the issues of the class it claims to represent on the stage of national politics and debate. Instead, its main aim seemed to be damage limitation. It wanted to be rid of the miners' strike (as, later, it wished to be rid of the GLC) instead of seeking to transform that struggle.

The strike was thus doomed to be fought and lost as an old rather than as a new form of politics. To those of us who felt this from very early on, it was doubly unbearable because – in the solidarity it displayed, the gigantic levels of support it engendered, the unparalleled involvement of the women in the mining communities, the feminist presence in the strike, the breaking down of barriers between different social interests which it presaged – the miners' strike was in fact instinctually with the politics of the new; it was a major engagement with Thatcherism which should have marked the transition to the politics of the present and future, but which was fought and lost imprisoned in the categories and strategies of the past.

In this climate of fatalism, a trace of the old recividism appears: 'what we need are more jobs but those can only be provided if industry becomes more competitive and more profitable. Therefore, do not rock the boat.' Of course, as long as capitalist imperatives prevail, there is a sort of logic in saying that more jobs will depend on the revival of capitalist industry. That is the logic in which reformism is always caught. In fact, of course, there is no historical evidence either for the belief that recession produces an automatic turn to the left. Fascism has emerged as often out of such circumstances as socialism. Neither is inevitable. The outcome depends ultimately on how the struggle is conducted.

The problem about expecting unemployment to serve as an electoral conveyor belt is that Labour's alternatives run headlong into the brick wall of an ideological campaign which Thatcherism has already largely won. This has successfully imprisoned common sense thinking about the economy on the horns of the following dilemma: the only way to reduce unemployment is to increase public spending, but this will inevitably lead to inflation. We are trapped between the millstones of dislike of unemployment and fear of inflation. Thatcherism has effectively encapsulated all the economic alternatives within the terms of this brutal 'either/or'. It is part of a wider strategy, which it has also conducted with masterly effect. It has two prongs.

The first point in the 'new realism' consists of convincing people that the nation has been living beyond its means, paying itself too much, expecting perks and benefits it can't afford, and indulging in all that consumption, permissiveness and pleasure. Very unBritish! Realities must be faced! Expectations are out of control and must be lowered. In that campaign, British masochism is a powerful ally. When the economy is not being represented in terms of the household budget ('you can't buy more at the shops this week than you have in the kitty'), then it is likened to the British weather. One good summer has to be paid for, in psychic currency, by at least five winters of discontent.

The second prong of the strategy is to disconnect, in the popular mind, the word 'public' from its association with anything that is good or positive, and to harness it instead to a chain of negative associations which automatically connect it with everything that is nasty, brutish, squalid and bureaucratic – and to exalt, in its place, the private market as the sole criterion of the Good Life.

This has been the strategic ideological project of the new right. It consists, first, of the struggle to disorganise the left; to interrupt the social-democratic consensus which has dominated and defined the political settlement between left and right since the war. Second, it aims to command popular conceptions of what is 'good for the country'. And third, it seeks to reverse every sign and signal pointing towards leftish or social-democratic solutions and move them in the opposite direction.

In 1945, it seemed that the only way to get less well-off people decent health care was to break the circuit of money and market in health and establish a public form of provision. In 1983, the aim is to make it seem inevitable that the only decent health service people can get is that which they pay for privately. This is much more than eroding the welfare state – a thing not wholly unknown to Labour governments. It is also, as the Social Affairs think tank put it, 'breaking the spell of the welfare state' – dismantling it ideologically as a constant reference point, an inevitable fact of the political scene that is taken for granted.[3] The historical project of Thatcherism is to reconstruct and redefine the political terrain, to alter the balance of political forces and to create a new kind of popular common sense, in which the market, the private, possessive, competitive 'man' (sic) are the only ways to measure the future.

'Hard-headed' Labour politicians dismiss all this as ideological window-dressing (and ideology is not serious politics), or as mere manipulation ('the Tories don't really believe it'). But the light that shines in Mr Tebbit's eye or the one that has gone askew in Sir Keith's – is the light of the salvationist, the 'born again'. They regard the catechism of capitalism, so tarnished and discredited among the young in the 1960s and 1970s, as the Sermon on the Mount. It is a creed to live by, to bring up children by; a faith which will move capitalist mountains; the salvation of the civilised world – the 'free west'. For such things, Mr Heseltine is willing to commit nuclear suicide. Mrs Thatcher clearly commands the gift of translating this version into the homespun idioms of daily life. She has the populist touch. But the stake in the struggle remains the popular will. Why is Labour, then, politically illiterate about it?

THE CRISIS OF LABOURISM

One explanation is that Labour understands perfectly well, but is incapable of organising a popular political and ideological struggle of this kind. It can mobilise the vote, provided it remains habitually solid. But it shows less and less capacity to connect with popular feelings and sentiments, let alone transform them or articulate them to the left. It gives the distinct impression of a political party living on the capital of past connections and imageries, but increasingly out of touch with what is going on in everyday life around it.

A second reason is that it has always been deeply suspicious of the self-activation of the working class. It is often the actual base for, but not the organising centre of, local or national campaigns. It has become an electoral rather than a political machine. Extra parliamentary activity politics and campaigning in any political space other than that directed to the House of Commons or within the confines of the formal electoral system produces in its leadership the deepest traumas and the most sycophantic poems of praise for parliamentarism. Yet it is precisely the confinement within the parliamentary mould and Labour's containment within a formal definition of the 'political' which has been its undoing.

A further explanation is that it does not possess the material means with which to wage this kind of popular political/ideological struggle. Of course, it has to operate in the public terrain where the media are either entirely colonised by the populist right – like the popular press – or so solidly grounded in right-wing, neoliberal assumptions that to start a conversation on radio or an interview on television from any other baseline is literally unthinkable these days.

But, even within the media as they currently exist, Labour commands no intellectual presence. It has never acquired a proper legitimacy. And that is partly because – apart from the handful of experts who advise its committees on policy matters – it has not organised a core of 'organic intellectuals'. Labour, then, still looks like a party which has never heard of the strategy of a 'war of position' – that is, struggling for leadership and mastery over a whole number of different fronts in the course of making itself the focal point of popular aspirations, the leading popular political force.

An even more worrying possibility is that Labour does not believe such a struggle to be necessary because it does not take mass political-ideological struggle seriously. Anti-Marxist as it is in its political culture, Labourism is profoundly 'economistic' in outlook and ideology. It really does suppose that economic facts transmit themselves directly into working-class heads, without passing through the real world. Working-class consciousness is as automatic as self-programming underground trains: once Labour, always Labour. And yet the clear signs are that political automatism is certainly at an end – if ever it existed.

Automatism was grounded on the assumption that Labour's political support is rooted in the material circumstances of the class Labour claims to represent: 'the culture of the working class is the culture of Labour'. But is it, in that obvious, immediate sense? The consequences of uneven economic restructuring, long-term economic change and short-term deindustrialisation are bearing down directly on these traditional Labour communities, whether occupational ones like mining, or ecological ones like Bermondsey. The heartland of the Labour vote, the backbone of its traditional support, the traditionalist roots of its loyalists, have been profoundly disaggregated. The traditional vanguard sectors are also increasingly a dwindling proportion of the modern working class, though not for that reason insignificant or less important. The pattern of support in urban areas, where Labour has traditionally amassed giant majorities, is changing both in scale and political character. Unemployment is savaging the given structure of skills; technical developments are fragmenting occupational communities. The age, gender and ethnic structure of Labour's potential social support in the country is changing rapidly and profoundly and, so far we can see, permanently.

Changes of these kinds fragment the class culture of the party as a political formation. They give rise to new constituencies, new demands. They generate new tensions and demand new forms of organisation, changing the social infrastructure of Labour politics. One has only to think of the profound shift in the character of industrial conflict from the private to the public sector, and add to that the social composition and character of social strata which, from this point of view, have represented the vanguard of the class in action against Thatcherism, to catch a glimpse of how out of date is the typical Labour view of the connections between party and class.

Far from guaranteeing Labour's inevitable return to popular ascendancy, the inevitability of Labourism – its automatism – is now Labour's most serious blockage to establishing a hegemony in these conditions.

What is at stake is no more and no less than 'the people': the popular will. Stuck at the end of the strategy of 'social democracy from above' for so long, 'the people' are taking a terrible revenge on Labour. Decades of block votes, things sewn up in backrooms, deals done in compositing meetings, localities where Labour mafias have ruled the roost like small-time Borgias, a view of politics which depends on mobilising the respectability rather than the radicalism of the working class (and, in the actual contradictory nature of class consciousness, both do exist, to be mobilised by different political forces), the engineering or hydraulic view of electoral politics – these have become deeply ingrained in the culture of Labourism. But the times are changing.

As a consequence, some Labour voters, especially in the more prosperous south-east, are nodding at the canvassers when the knock on the door comes – but slipping, sliding, eroding, drifting into uncharted paths as soon as they go away, and they meet and talk in the pub, on the job, in families, with mates, hanging out the washing, calculating the pennies and the kids' chances in a microchip world of permanent unemployment. Are they really recidivist Tories at heart? No. Are they Labour's automatic electoral fodder? It would be unwise for Labour to bank on it.

Can they be won to a vision, not simply a programme, of the future? Here there is something to learn from Thatcherism, after all. Paradoxically, she does raise hearts and minds an inch or two because, vile, corrupt, awful as her vision of the future is, we know what it is. We can imagine what life according to the gospel of free enterprise, patriarchal respectability and authoritarian order would be like. We know how we would be expected to bring up our children, make them manage their pocket money; how women should live; who should have babies and under what circumstances; who should, and should not, go to bed with whom; how teachers in our classrooms should dress and what lessons are to be read in the religious education hour – as well as what the Public Sector Borrowing Requirement should be. It is an 'alternative future'. It is a philosophy of life.

The one thing nobody knows is what Labour conceives to be an 'alternative way of life'. It currently possesses no image of modernity. It provides no picture of life under socialism. It has failed so far to construct an alternative 'philosophy' of socialism for modern times. In its profound empiricism, it has mistaken adaptation to the present as progress towards the future. In fact, realistically, Labour can never adapt enough to become the 'natural inheritor' of capitalism. It has no alternative but to renew itself and its vision or to go out of business. Whether it is capable of that renewal or not remains an open question now, which is why the 'crisis of labourism' is not quite so exaggerated as it may at first have appeared.

Notes

1. Eric Hobsbawm, 'Labour's Lost Millions', *Marxism Today,* October 1983.
2. This essay was first published in 1984, but revised in 1988. Hence Hall writes from knowledge that the miners' strike of 1984-5 finally conceded defeat in March 1985.
3. Digby Anderson, June Lait, David Marsland, *Breaking the Spell of the Welfare State*, Social Affairs Unit, Centre for Policy Studies, London 1981.

The state: socialism's old caretaker

1984

WHERE DOES THE left stand on the state? Straightforward ... or is it? Not any longer. Ten years ago, the left was broadly for state intervention and state agencies – of the appropriate kind. But postwar experience, and Thatcherism, are forcing a major rethink.

My aim here is to explore an issue which is central to the strategy for the renewal of the socialist project, about which, however, I detect considerable confusion among socialists. This is the issue of the state. Now a great deal has been said about the role of the capitalist state by the left, especially in recent times. It has almost acquired the status of a fashionable political topic. My purpose is not to review this already complex literature, but to come at the problem from a slightly different angle. I believe that the status of the state in current thinking on the left is very problematic. Many socialists now stand in a very different place, on the question of the state, than they would have taken up ten or twenty years ago. And yet, I believe that we have not fully confronted or explained to ourselves why we have changed our minds or how this new thinking about the state is likely to influence strategies for the left.

I am well aware that this kind of exploration is a dangerous exercise. One of our present dilemmas on the left is the habit of thinking that we already know what the content and future of socialism is. We talk of socialism as if it were an already completed agenda: the script of a play which is already written and only waiting for someone to put it on stage. Of course, there is a tradition of socialist thought and struggle to draw on. But tradition is a tricky concept, especially for the left; a two-edged sword, more diverse and contradictory in reality than we make it appear when we construct it retrospectively. Our thinking about socialism must also reflect the history and experience of socialism as it actually exists – with all its vicissitudes. It must also ground itself in current realities, take the pressure of our time, reflect the world around us in order to transcend it. Paradoxically, socialism will perish unless it is able to grow out of the very soil of modern capitalism, which despite everything, is still expanding, still revolutionising the world in contradictory ways.

I do not, therefore, believe that what 'we have always thought about the state' on the left will necessarily *do* for the next ten decades; or that posing ourselves difficult questions is necessarily a sign of the weakening of faith. We should leave Faith to the Believers. Indeed, that other way – socialism as an already finished project – is one of the most powerful sources of, and an excuse for, that profound sectarianism which has always had a strong presence on the left and which I detect rising like the smog once again, as those who dare to put a question mark over our received wisdoms are instantly accused of treason, labelled as the enemy, or dismissed as 'pink professors misleading the left' (in Tariq Ali's recent, immortal phrase) and despatched into outer darkness.

So why the problem?

Braving the terrors of excommunication from the newly appointed guardians of orthodoxy, let us pose once more the question of where we stand on the question of the state. It is not difficult to see why the state has become problematic in recent years. This must reflect, on the one hand, our response to the whole experience of 'actual existing socialism', where, instead of progressively withering away, the state has become a gigantic, swollen, bureaucratic force, swallowing up almost the whole of civil society, and imposing itself (sometimes with tanks), in the name of the People, on the backs of the people. Who, now, can swallow without a gigantic gulp the so-called temporary, passing nature of the 'dictatorship of the proletariat'? On the other hand, the very same period, since the end of World War II, has witnessed a parallel, gigantic expansion of the state complex within modern capitalism, especially in Western Europe, with the state playing an increasingly interventionist or regulative role in more and more areas of social life. It has become far and away the largest single employer of labour, and acquired a dominant presence in every sector of daily existence. What are we to make of *that* unexpected development, never adequately predicted in the classical Marxist literature?

Even more difficult to work out is, what is our attitude towards this development? On the one hand, we not only defend the welfare side of the state, we believe it should be massively expanded. And yet, on the other hand, we feel there is something deeply anti-socialist about how this welfare state functions. We know, indeed, that it is experienced by masses of ordinary people, in the very moment that they are benefiting from it, as an intrusive managerial, bureaucratic force in their lives. However, if we go too far down *that* particular road, whom do we discover keeping us company along the road but – of course – the Thatcherites, the new right, the free market 'hot gospellers', who *seem* (whisper it not too loud) to be saying rather similar things about the state. Only they are busy making capital against us on this very point, treating widespread popular dissatisfactions with the modes in which the beneficiary parts of the state function as fuel for an anti-left, 'roll back the state' crusade. And where, to be honest, do we stand on the issue? Are we for 'rolling back the state' – including the welfare state? Are we for or against the management of the whole of society by the state? Not for the first time, Thatcherism here catches the left on the hop – hopping from one uncertain position to the next, unsure of our ground.

Perhaps it might help if we knew how we got into this dilemma. How *did* we get here? This is a vast topic in its own right, and I propose to look at only four aspects here. First, how did the British left become so wedded to a particular conception of socialism through state management, the essence of what I want to call 'statism' or a 'statist' conception of socialism? Secondly, I want to sketch some of the reasons why the very expansion of the state, for which so many on the left worked so hard, turned out in practice to be a very contradictory experience. Third, I want to confront head on the confusion caused on the left by the 'libertarianism' of the right – the way Thatcherism has exploited the experience of welfare statism and turned it to the advantage of the new right. Finally, I want to consider some aspects of the changing social and economic relationships today which have influenced spontaneous attitudes on the left – what I call the growth of a left libertarianism. In conclusion, I can only roughly indicate some directions in which our thinking needs to be developed.

The history

First, how did the British left get so deeply embedded in a statist conception of socialism? After all, it was not – as many people imagine – always like that. The state did not have that central, all-pervasive role

in early socialist thinking. Marx and Engels understood the role of the
capitalist state in developing a whole social and political order around
a particular mode of exploitation, and spoke briefly but vividly about
the need to destroy it in its existing form. But their thinking about
the *future* role of the state in the transition to socialism was extremely
sketchy. Other radical currents of thought in British socialism were,
if anything, more anti-state than pro-state in their general tendency.
Even in the key period, between the revival of socialism in the 1880s
right through to the 1920s and the emergence of the Labour Party in its
modern constitutionalist form as the majority party politically representing the working classes, a statist-oriented brand of socialism within
Labourism and the labour movement had to contend with many other
currents, including of course the strong syndicalist currents before
and after World War I, and later the ILP's ethical Marxism, with their
deep antipathy to Labour's top-downwards, statist orientation. One of
the many tricks which the retrospective construction of tradition on
the left has performed is to make the triumph of Labourism over these
other socialist currents – the result of a massive political struggle, in
which the ruling classes played a key role – appear as an act of natural
and inevitable succession.

And yet, it was precisely in this critical period – between the
1880s and the 1920s, when the parameters of British politics for the
following fifty years were set for the first time – that statism took root
in British political culture. In those days, what we now call 'statism'
went under the title of 'collectivism'. What is crucial for our analysis is
the fact that there were many collectivisms. 'Collectivism' was a highly
contradictory formation, composed of different strands, supported in
different ways by the right, the centre and the left – if, for convenience,
we can use those somewhat anachronistic labels. Collectivism was
regarded by many sections on the right, and by some influential sectors
of the leading classes, as the answer to Britain's declining fortunes.
The country – the new collectivists believed – required a programme
of 'national regeneration'. This could only be undertaken if the old
shibboleths of laissez-faire were finally abandoned and the state came
to assume a far greater role of organic leadership in society. A 'populist'
bloc of support, they believed, could be won amongst the dominated
classes for such a project, provided the latter were 'squared' by state
pensions and other Bismarck-type benefits. This was the programme
of both the 'social imperialist' and the 'national efficiency' schools,

and of the highly authoritarian populist politics associated with them. And though they did not carry their programme in detail, they were extremely influential in pioneering the shift in the allegiance of British capital from its former commitment to laissez-faire, to its newer link with a certain type of capitalist state interventionism.

Statism equals socialism

There is no space to deal with the links between collectivism and the 'centre', but it is a critical link in the story to remember that it was also on this very question of 'the state' that the 'old' Liberalism transmuted itself into the 'new' Liberalism: the new Liberalism was, in its own time, the pioneer of the thinking which lay behind the early instalment of the welfare state (in the 1906-11 Liberal administration), and, in our time, it is really the political force which created that space in British politics which we would now call 'social democracy'.

But the key factor for our purposes was the progress which collectivism made, under essentially Fabian inspiration, inside the labour movement and in the Labour Party. In this period Fabianism established its ascendancy as the philosophy of socialism for Labour. Collectivism became, to be blunt, what the Webbs and their many followers meant by socialism. That is, progressive legislation, social welfare, a measure of redistributive justice, pioneered through the state by a political elite legislating on behalf of the working classes (who were required to elect 'their government' to office but who were, of course, too inexpert to rule on their own behalf); resulting in a gigantic state complex, administering more and more of society in the interest of social efficiency, where the experts and the bureaucrats would exercise a 'benevolent dictatorship' through the state, servicing society's many and complex needs. It was in this formative period that the statist conception of socialism became riveted in place, as the dominant current within Labourism and the British left.

We have no space to sketch the long, torturous route which led from the emergence of this statist conception of socialism in the 1920s to the much-transformed reality of the modern state and state interventionism as we know it after 1945. Suffice it to say that the path from one to the other was by no means straightforward. Nevertheless, the welfare state was constructed after 1945 on those earlier

foundations, and is rightly regarded as the crowning achievement of
the post-war Labour government, the high tide of the spirit of popular
'war radicalism', and the most advanced achievement of the reformist
tradition of British social democracy.

The logic behind this development in the second half of the
twentieth century is not difficult to understand, even though we
may not subscribe wholeheartedly to it nowadays. The argument
ran as follows: capitalism has a thrust, a logic of its own – the logic
of private property, capital accumulation, possessive individualism
and the free market. This logic 'worked', in the sense that it created
the modern capitalist world – with, of course, its necessary 'costs':
exploitation, poverty, insecurity for the masses, class inequality, the
many inevitable victims of its 'successes'. The left, it seemed, had only
one alternative: to break the 'logic of the market' and construct society
around an alternative logic – a socialist one. But to do this, it needed
an alternative centre of power, an opposing rallying-point, to that of
capital and the market. This opposing force was *the state*. Either the
state could be used to make inroads into the 'logic of the market',
to modify its excesses, abate its extremes, graft alternative goals (e.g.
needs not profits) on to the system, impose a redistributive logic on
the unequal ways in which capitalism 'naturally' distributes its goods
and resources – the reformist alternative. Or, the power of capital and
the market, installed behind the capitalist state, had to be actively
broken ('smashed'), and the major social processes 'socialised' or made
public by being progressively absorbed and taken over into the state –
the revolutionary road. Both, it is clear, involved, to different degrees,
massive inroads into the 'logic' of the market by expanding the role
of the state.

The two great blocs

I believe this crudely drawn political landscape, blocked out into
its two, great, opposed 'continents' – the domain of capital and
the market versus the domain of the logic of social needs, imposed
through the state – is how the vast majority of us first entered into
basic political thinking. It is only a slight exaggeration to say that
these remain the two fundamental formations in British political
culture – more inclusive, in a way, than the traditional division into

left and right. They have helped to set the parameters within which British politics have fluctuated since the turn of the century. An essential part of the 'historic compromise' between the classes struck in the interwar period was the new balance established between 'state' and 'civil society'. On this basic 'settling of the boundaries' much of the stability of Britain as a capitalist democracy has depended. It was the shifting of these boundaries, in some sectors, away from the free play of market forces, and closer to the reform-through-the-state pole, which constituted the 'revolution' of the Keynesian welfare state and the post-1945 settlement. This new consensus, basically, lasted up to the advent of Thatcherism in the mid-1970s. It is this 'settling of boundaries' which the new right challenged. Restoring the free market principle to its former ascendancy is once again the fulcrum of politics, the key dividing line between right and left. That is why the question of the left's attitude to the state now matters so profoundly.

All this makes it sound as if the balance of forces on this question has been steadily moving in the reformist direction. Why, then, has this development of the state been so problematic for the left? One reason is that the state has gone on expanding and developing powered, so to speak, by both the right and the left. We still speak of the 'capitalist state'. But, in fact, we no longer behave as if it had a single, monolithic class character. The left, despite its rhetoric, has its part of the state too: the welfare state, which distributes benefits to the needy; serves society's needs; redistributes resources to the less well-off; provides amenities – and all on a universalistic basis, rather than on the market terms of 'ability to pay'. The NHS is the classic example. Despite its dependence on the private sector and the inroads into it made by private medicine, the NHS is still generally regarded and experienced as having broken the logic which connected health and medical care to wealth and the private ability to pay, and installed in its place the idea of medical need served by a universal provision. The history of Nye Bevan's struggles to install the NHS demonstrates not only how bitterly the market forces resisted this inroad into their territory, but how impossible it would have been without an alternative centre, capable of organising a materially different system of provision – the state.

How could anyone who understood the material difference which this has made in the lives of countless ordinary people regard this development as contrary to the logic of socialism? We – rightly – want to see more of this, not less: more aspects of life organised on a similar principle. The recent Centre for Policy Studies pamphlet proposed cutting back on welfare not simply on pragmatic grounds of cost, but, as its title proclaims, as a way of *Breaking the Spell of the Welfare State*. And those boys – Sir Keith Joseph's shock troops masquerading as an independent research unit – know what they are doing. This centrality of the state to the left is not confined to the area of welfare and benefits. We have tended to think that the nationalisation measures of the 1940s and 1950s, and the Keynesian interventions in economic life, which increased rapidly in the 1960s and 1970s, failed, not because they went too far, but because they did not go far enough. The left is still basically wedded to a *positive* view of the state's role in socialist construction.

The two-edged state

Matters are not quite so simple. Few areas of the welfare state are as clear cut in their positive image as the NHS. And the welfare and benefit side is not the only form in which the state has expanded in post-war society. We have seen the parallel expansion of the *warfare* state, too. And of the repressive, 'policing' aspects of the state: the state as coercive agent, defending the social order, punishing the deviant, extending its surveillance into civil society, disciplining the citizenry on to the straight and narrow, its operations increasingly shrouded in secrecy, beyond all normal forms of accountability. The 'Orwellian' state is alive and well, not only in Eastern European socialist democracies, but in Western European class democracies, alongside the welfare state. The state which gives out benefits also snoops on its recipients. Then there is the size and scale of the administrative side of the state, coupled with its bureaucratic mode of operation. People, when they are being 'done good to' by the state, increasingly experience it, in reality, as being 'put in their place' by it: by 'experts' who always know better, or state servants who seem oblivious to the variety of actual needs on the other side of the counter. The feeling is very deep that the way the welfare state works makes people into passive, greedy, dependent *clients* much of the time, rather than people claiming rights from a state which is supposed to be their state, representing them against the logic of the market.

Then there is the awareness that welfare states have become general throughout capitalist systems, with levels of benefit in many other countries that have long since outstripped ours, and performing functions not only imposed on capital by the working class but necessary to the survival of capital. Free secondary education is, after all, *both* a long standing radical demand and a reform imposed on the idea of an educational market place *and* the degree of training and skilling a modern capitalist system requires. The welfare-reformist and the reproductive aspects of the state are increasingly difficult to distinguish. As state functions multiply, so more of us are working in state-related jobs. The changing composition of the working class and the changing pattern of industrial conflict have moved increasingly to these contested sites within the state. Even there we are aware of the *double-sided* character of our work. The slogan which most accurately expresses our dilemma and captures this contradictory reality is 'In And Against The State'. Increasing numbers of us are, regularly, *both*.

New right libertarianism

This brings us to the 'libertarianism' of the new right. Because it is exactly this contradictory experience of the state on which Thatcherism capitalised. It rooted itself in these dissatisfactions, and inflected them into a whole broadside against the very principle of welfare *as such*. The new right harnessed these popular discontents to its cause, converted a dislike of the bureaucratic features of statism into a full-scale assault on the 'creeping tide of socialism' and the 'nanny state'. On these negative foundations it built the new positive gospel of the market as the universal provider of goods and of The Good; launched the savaging of public expenditure as a testament to Virtue; initiated the privatisation 'roll back'; and raised the war-cry of Freedom and its identity with the free market. The new right presented itself as the only party committed to oppose the exponential growth of the state, its penetration into every corner of life. This was one of the key ways in which Thatcherism cut into the territory of the traditional left, disorganised its base and made itself 'popular'.

The problem for the left is that the dissatisfactions with the state are real and authentic enough – even if Thatcherism then mis-describes and mis-explains them. Thatcherism did not invent them – even if its remedies for the problem are fictitious. Further, it exposed a weakness of the existing system which the left had made too little of: the deeply *undemocratic* character of state-administered socialism. Most disconcerting of all, this revealed that the left and the new right share, on this question, some of the same ground!

This was particularly disconcerting because the left believes that ideology marches in exclusive blocks of ideas, each block attached to its appropriate class or political position. It is therefore extremely odd to find the left sharing with 'the class enemy' a critique of statism – even if, when the conclusions from that critique are drawn, the two sides radically part company. Of course, the problem here lies in the fact that ideology does *not* function in blocks. The idea of liberty, on which the whole anti-state philosophy was predicated, does not belong exclusively to the right. They appropriated a certain version of it, linked it with other reactionary ideas to make a whole 'philosophy' and connected it into the programme and the forces of the right. They made the idea of Freedom equivalent to and dependent on the freedom *of the market* – and thus necessarily opposed to the idea of Equality. But freedom or liberty – in the wider sense of social emancipation – has always been a key element in the philosophy of the left. Within this chain of ideas, emancipation *depends on* equality of condition. It is the equation with the market and possessive individualism which limits it. So what the left urgently needs is to re-appropriate the concept of freedom and give it its real expression within the context of a deepening of democratic life as a whole. The problem is that *this* socialist conception of Freedom is not compatible with – is in fact deeply undermined by – the idea of a state which takes over everything, which absorbs all social life, all popular energies, all democratic initiatives, and which – however benevolently – governs society *in place of* the people.

Choice

Perhaps we can all agree about 'emancipation'. It has a resonant feel to it, and touches very deep chords – as the new right correctly understood. But what about another, trickier aspect of Freedom: the question of *choice?* I am not sure the idea of 'choice' has so far played a very central role in thinking on the left. And yet the most widespread and basically correct 'image' of actual existing socialism among ordinary working people is the drab lack of diversity, the omnipresence of planned sameness, the absence of choice and variety. Our concept of socialism has been dominated by images of scarcity. The trouble is that on the question of choice, capitalism and the free market seem so far to have the best tunes. But *is* the idea of choice, which is intrinsic to the whole critique of statism, an *essentially* reactionary, right-wing capitalist idea?

I suspect this is partly a generational matter. Socially, culturally, in everyday economic life, younger people set enormous store by choice and diversity. And they see as the principal enemies of diversity *both* big, corporate capital *and* the big state. They know what Thatcherite economists do not seem to know – that the maximisation of popular choice does *not* flourish in the storehouse of corporate capital, with its carefully calculated marketing and financing strategies. And they do not naturally associate it with the equally corporatist 'bureaucratic' modes of operation of the state. But, unfortunately for the left, they *have* found a measure of choice in what we can only call the interstices of the market. At the small end of the market, where the big battalions and competition to the death do not entirely dominate, small initiatives sometimes have a chance, and a degree of entrepreneurship can create openings, or recognise a new need, even a new *social* need, and experiment to a degree with satisfying it. I certainly don't mean to paint a rosy picture of the degree of openness which exists here: *all* markets are constrained above all by inequality. But most of the innovatory trends in everyday life with which younger people spontaneously identify – in music, clothes, styles, the things they read and listen to, the environments they feel comfortable in – operate on what one can only call an 'artisan capitalism' basis. These things are in constant danger of being regulated out of existence by the state or ripped off by the big commercial providers.

Left libertarianism

Nevertheless, inevitably, the actual daily cultural experience of diversity has come to be identified with a certain conception, or rather, a certain experience of *the market*. And this is by no means confined to non-political people. Culturally, where would the left be today without initiatives like *City Limits* or a thousand other small, 'independent' publications; or Gay Sweatshop and hundreds of other little theatre groups; or Virago and History Workshop and Readers and Writers Cooperative and Compendium and Centreprise and Comedia and – you name it? Young people on the left or right do not expect to hear the new sounds which speak to them of their time on either BBC or ITV, though they might catch them from the 'independents' clustered around Channel Four, from Radio Laser or even, God help us, the dreaded, arch-commercial, 'pirate' Radio Caroline. Many of these initiatives operate precariously in the margins of the capitalist market. But even when you move from the margins of the market, the positive sentiments of younger people on the left, post-1968, instinctively gravitate to those local or 'grass roots' initiatives, where people, by their direct self-activity, can be persuaded to supplement or develop new struggles around the existing bureaucratic forms of provision of the state. The libertarianism of the right has been matched, I believe, by a steady and unstoppable, slow but strong current of 'libertarianism' on the left – mirroring, in its own way, many of the broader social and economic trends at work in society, transforming daily life and everyday attitudes, including those of the younger generations on the left.

Does all this then add up to a covert invitation to give up another set of 'old' socialist ideas, lie back and learn to love the free market? Not at all. But it *is* an invitation to open our minds and fertilise our imaginations a little by direct infusions from the contradictory reality of what Marx, in his simple way, used to call 'real history'. For one thing, we know that, wherever in Eastern Europe, under actual-existing socialism, the system of rigid economic planning of life, from steel factories to hat pins, has been relaxed a little, the first – though not necessarily the final – form which this has assumed is a return, within the framework of socialist planning, of some 'free market mechanisms'. And this is not a problem to be left to left economists and experts on Eastern Europe, since the image and reality of actual-existing socialism is a problem for *all* socialists and has been such a trump card in the right's struggle against the very appeal of socialism in the West. The second lesson we might draw is linked with this re-evaluation of a whole historical experience, though not in a directly organisational way. It is simply the re-examination of the new impetus towards choice, the new spirit of pluralism and diversity, which has become such a driving force of the masses under advanced capitalism, and which will have to be more centrally reflected in our thinking about socialism if we are ever to convince large numbers of people that socialism is a superior 'way of life' to that which, with all its ups and downs, they already know. Why else should the toiling masses under capitalism ever commit themselves to an alternative which offers them *less* than they can currently get?

No room for naivety

I don't think we can afford to be *naive* about the state. Negatively, though the state is a contradictory force, it does have a systematic tendency to draw together the many lines of force and power in society and convert them into a particular 'system of rule'. In that sense, the state *does* continue to organise and orchestrate the space of capital accumulation in its broad societal aspects, and hold a partic-ular, exploitative social order in place. This is *not* a neutral function – though it is not the state's only function, either. But insofar as it is its role, the state has to be dismantled, and another conception of the state put in its place. The lesson I think we can draw here is that we have as yet a wholly inadequate conception of how a socialist state would operate in ways which are radically different from that of the present version.

We can't afford to be naive about the market either. It *is* the principal exploitative mechanism of a capitalist social order when set to work in the context of private property and capitalist economic forms. I am not sufficient of an economic expert to know whether some aspects of the market can be combined with socialist economic forms, but I am sure we need to ponder the idea more deeply. Certainly, I feel sure that socialism cannot exist without a conception of *the public*. We are right to regard the 'public sector', however little it represents a transfer of power to the powerless, as an arena constructed against the logic of capital. The concept of 'public health' *is* different from the idea of private medicine because it deals with the whole environment of health, which is more than the sum of individual healthy bodies – a *social* conception of health as a need, a right.

'Public transport' is not simply a practical alternative to private transport because it embodies conceptions of equal access to the means of mobility – to movement around one's environment as a publicy validated right. The idea of 'public space' signifies a construction of space *not* bounded by the rights of private property, a space for activities in common, the holding of space in trust as a social good. In each case the adjective *public* represents an advance in conception on the limits of possessive individualism, of liberal thought itself. In this conception of the public and the social, socialism is *still ahead*. And the public can only be carved out of market space, capital's space, by the engine of state action.

The state and society

On the other hand, 'the public' cannot be identical with the state. Once the logic of capital, property and the market are broken, it is the diversity of social forms, the taking of popular initiatives, the recovery of popular control, the passage of power from the state *into* society, which marks out the advance towards socialism. We can envisage a 'partnership' between state and society, so long as the initiative is always passing to society, so long as the monopoly over the management of social life does not come to a dead halt with the state elite, so long as the state itself is rooted in, constantly draws energy from, and is pushed actively, by popular forces. One of the reasons why some of the things which have developed around the GLC are so exciting, so pre-figurative for the left, is precisely that one begins to see here and there a glimmer of a local state transforming the ways in which it 'represents' society politically; being more dependent on the passage of power, through the state, *to* the constituencies than it is on monopolising power; and thus one also sees a glimpse of how a new principle, centralised through the instrumentality of the state, can then yield space to a wide variety of different forms, social movements and initiatives in civil society. What is no longer tenable or tolerable is the state-management of society in the name of socialism. Pluralism, in *this* sense, is not a temporary visitor to the socialist scene. It has come to stay.

We could put all this another way by reminding ourselves that what Marx spoke of when he referred to socialism was the *social* revolution. The democratisation of society is as important as dismantling the bureaucracies of the state. Indeed, perhaps the most important lesson of all is the absolute centrality to all socialist thinking today of the deepening of democracy. Democracy is not, of course, a formal matter of electoral politics or constitutionalism. It is the real passage of power to the powerless, the *empowerment* of the excluded. The state cannot do this for the powerless, though it can enable it to happen. They have to do it for themselves, by finding the forms in which they can take on the control over an increasingly complex society. Certainly, it does not happen all at once, through *one* centre – by simply 'smashing the state', as the sort of socialist thinking which is fixated on the state would have it. It has to happen across a multiplicity of sites in social life, on many different fronts, including, of course, the state itself, whose tendency to concentrate power is precisely what constitutes it as a barrier to socialism. Gramsci advanced the profound idea that hegemony is not constituted only by the state, but in the multiple centres of civil society. It follows that an alternative conception of socialism must embrace this struggle to democratise power across all the centres of social activity – in private as well as public life, in personal associations as well as in compulsory obligations, in the family and the neighbourhood and the nursery and the shopping centre as well as in the public office or at the point of production. If the struggle for socialism in modern societies is a war of position, then our conception of socialism must be of a society of *positions* – different places from which we can all begin the reconstruction of society for which the state is only the anachronistic caretaker.

Blue election, election blues

1987

THATCHERISM'S THIRD TERM was not unexpected, but the reality of it is devastating and will take some time to think through properly. It is all the more depressing because, in the event, Labour had such a good campaign. For three weeks it looked like a party that could actually win and hold power. Kinnock's self-confidence, though overplayed, proved infectious. Organisationally, the party looked for once as if it belonged to the twentieth century. The manifesto was muddled; but, once the campaign got off the ground, it found an image and acquired political definition. Labour managed to 'stage' a broad political choice for the nation between the party of greed, privilege and self-interest and the party of caring, collective provision and the underprivileged. This was the only chance Labour had, and it went for it with surprising energy.

However, though Labour's 'good' campaign put heart into party activists and the committed left, it did not in the end shift the overall disposition of the vote. Some voters may have changed their minds but the swings cancelled one another out. There was no massive change of heart in the final three weeks. Few voters, for instance, seem to have been swayed by the famous party election television broadcasts, which caused such excitement amongst media pundits and so much heart-searching amongst the Labour faithful. The election, in short, was won (i.e. lost) in those terrible months and years since 1983. Thatcherism's victory was rooted not in any temporary fluctuations of support, but in the deep movements and tendencies which have been reshaping the British political map. The problem the left now faces is structural and organic.

One clue to this may lie in a persistent trend over the past five years. Asked what *policies* they supported, significant majorities consistently preferred Labour on unemployment, health, housing, education – the welfare issues. During the campaign, these remained the most important issues for the majority of voters polled.

In fact, Labour actually had some success in pushing them up the political agenda. However, both before and during the election, if asked about *image* – who was 'doing a good job', 'giving the country a lead', making people 'feel good to be British again' – a majority consistently said 'Maggie'. The same thing has been going on in America, where no majorities could be found for specific policies like winding up welfare programmes, yet, when it came to 'making you feel good to be American', people said Ronnie was their baby.

One way of interpreting this trend is that, increasingly, the electorate is thinking politically, not in terms of *policies* but of *images*. This doesn't mean that policies don't matter. It does mean that policies don't capture people's political imaginations unless constructed into an *image* with which they can identify. Far from this being a sign of voter irrationality, there are a number of quite 'rational' reasons why there should be a trend in this direction in the advanced 'class democracies' like Britain and the US.

First, we live in a world where decisions are both complex and remote, and the big bureaucracies of state and market control a great deal of social life. So people are quite 'rational' to believe that they can't intervene with much hope of success, *in detail*, into policy matters, nor can they affect the fine-tuning of economic or policy machines.

Second, the electorate is now mercilessly exposed to ceaseless massaging by the media and to 'disinformation' from the politicians. It isn't surprising that politics, too, is being absorbed into this game of impression-management.

Third, voters know perfectly well that, these days, a five-year mandate will be interpreted any way the party in power likes. The abolition of the GLC was never 'popular', but that didn't stop Mrs Thatcher from doing what was politically expedient. Democracy, even in the narrow sense of 'government by popular consent', didn't once sully the lips of a single Tory spokesperson, and is a concept altogether foreign to Thatcherism's universe. 'Choice' was counterposed to 'democracy' precisely because, whereas the latter is public and social, the former can be defined in wholly private and individual (i.e. 'family') terms.

In all these circumstances, people aren't wrong to imagine that what is required of them as citizens is simply to express a broad, undefined 'preference' for one scenario or another, this image or that. Some people regard this as a trivialisation of politics. But images are not trivial things. In and through images, fundamental political questions are being posed and argued through. We need to take them more seriously than we do. Mrs Thatcher claimed she was excited to be not just fighting for power, but helping to 'set the agenda for the twenty-first century'. But, how else can you discuss what Britain and the British people are to become, except in terms of broad images? The future has to be imagined – 'imaged', to coin a word.

The question of political imagery is not a matter of presentation, but of ideology, which is a different and altogether more serious matter. One reason why Labour did better than most of us expected is that, this time, it did engage in ideological struggle. One reason why the campaign failed to shift minds, hearts and votes was that it lost that struggle, despite its efforts. And part of the reason why Labour lost it is that, while it has only just begun to take these questions seriously, Thatcherism has been intervening ideologically with consummate skill *ever since 1979*.

Why has it taken Labour and the left more generally so long to appreciate the strategic importance of the ideological arena? In part, the answer lies in the way the left normally thinks about 'politics'. Electoral politics – in fact, every kind of politics – depends on political identities and identifications. People make identifications symbolically: through social imagery, in their political imaginations. They 'see themselves' as one sort of person or another. They 'imagine their future' within this scenario or that. They don't just think about voting in terms of how much they have, their so-called 'material interests'. Material interests matter profoundly. But they are always *ideologically defined*. Contrary to a certain version of marxism, which has as strong a hold over the Labour 'centre' as it does on the so-called 'hard left', material interests, on their own, have no necessary class belongingness. They influence us. But they are not escalators which automatically deliver people to their appointed destinations, 'in place', within the political-ideological spectrum.

One reason why they don't is because people have *conflicting* social interests, sometimes reflecting conflicting identities. As a worker a person might put 'wages' first: in a period of high unemployment, 'job security' may come higher; a woman might prioritise 'child-care'. But what does a 'working woman' put first? Which of her identities is the one that determines her political choices? Take another example. I am a socialist and therefore passionately in favour of state education but

I have a daughter who is taking O-levels in a hard-pressed LEA. Do I stick by my political principles or squeeze her into a 'better' school?

In fact, the harder things get in Thatcher's Britain and the more competitive they become, the more divided society is. And the more divided it is, the more these ideological conflicts bear down on people's actual lives, cutting their 'natural' social and political identifications in two. Appealing to the 'real experience' of poverty or unemployment or underprivilege won't do the trick. Even poverty and unemployment have to be ideologically defined. A young unemployed person *may* interpret this experience to mean that you should work and vote to change the system. But it could equally be defined as a sign that you should throw your fortune in with the winners, climb on the bandwagon, earn a fast buck and look after 'number one'. Material interests did not, on their own, guarantee an automatic majority for Labour in the working class this time, and it won't necessarily do so in the future, *because it never has*.

This does not mean that ideology determines everything. If nobody was prospering under Thatcherism, ideology alone could not parachute such an 'illusion' into the heads of the majority. However, if *some* people are doing well – as they are, especially, in personal terms, in the 'South' – and the ideological climate is right, and the alternative ways of measuring how 'well' you are doing are effectively silenced or stigmatised, then the small number who define themselves as 'doing well' will be swelled by a much larger number who identify with this way of 'getting on'. Elections are won or lost not just on so-called 'real' majorities, but on (equally real) symbolic majorities: a 'symbolic majority' includes all who identify ideologically with the enterprise culture as the way of the future, who see themselves in their political imagination as likely to be lucky in the next round. They form an 'imaginary community' around Thatcherism's political project.

The whole point of Thatcherism as a form of politics has been to construct a new social bloc, and in this project ideology is critical. A social bloc is, by definition, *not* homogeneous. It does not consist of one whole class or even part of one class. It has to be constructed out of groups which are very different in terms of their material interests and social positions. The question is, can these differences of position and interest be constructed into a 'unity'? (It never is a unity, in the strict sense.) Can these diverse identities be welded together into a 'collective will'?

In the second term, Thatcherism did not make a single move which was not also carefully calculated in terms of this hegemonic strategy. It stepped up the pace of privatisation. But it took care, at every step, to harness new social constituencies to it, to 'construct' an image of the new, share-owning working class, and to expand the bloc, symbolically, around the image of 'choice'. It has not only attacked state education and the health service. It has created, side by side and in competition with them, among the majority of users and right in the heart of the working class, an alternative image: quicker service via private health and a better chance for kids in a deregulated education system – the 'fast-lane' schools and inner-city technology colleges.

Don't for a moment underestimate the resonance which a slogan like 'power to the people' carries in our over-bureaucratised, over-managed, under-resourced society. Of course, only a few can actually *choose* to be better off in these ways. But, for the time being, a lot of people think this is the only way open to them to advance in a society where competition and selectivity have become the name of the game. If that's the only game in town, some of them will play it!

Building a new social bloc means not only 'symbolically' including as many different groups as you can in your project, but also symbolically excluding the enemy. The 'loony left' image was one powerful example. Once the one-liner was launched, the deep symbiosis between Thatcherism and the press guaranteed it an uninterrupted flight. It locked together in a single image high rates and political extremism with those powerful subliminal themes of race and sex. The discourse of the 'loony left' was a code. In London it made it possible to expunge the legacy of the GLC, and to bring into the election, race (the anti-anti-racism backlash) and sex (the anti-feminism, anti-gay, anti-permissive, post-Aids backlash – Thatcherism's hidden 'moral agenda') without a word having to be explicitly spoken. So successful was it that the Labour leadership, the party machine, much of the traditional 'hard left', slick *New States-men* and all, could also make a heavy investment in it without having to reveal their hand about race, feminism or sexual politics. Instead of engaging with the 'loony left' image, Labour in effect colluded with it. In the weeks before the election, the leadership cast its vote unflinchingly for the 'traditional' image, in search of the 'traditional Labour voter'. Again, everybody understood that this, too, was a code. It is a code for 'back to the respectable, moderate, trade unionist, male-dominated working class'. Mr Kinnock appeared as a manly, 'likely lad' who owed everything to the welfare state. His 'familial' image carried not a single echo or trace of feminist struggles over two decades. The investment in 'strong leadership' and in 'ordinariness' carried its own message. It signalled the distancing of Labour from all those 'fringe issues' and a commitment to rooting Labour political loyalties exclusively through an identification with the traditional culture of the left.

This was the image with which Labour chose to engage, ideologically, with Thatcherism. The key question is, can Labour win with it? Can it harness the fragmented experiences of living in Great Britain Limited to a new, radical, political will? Can it construct around Labour a new social bloc?

Of course, millions of people desperately need the welfare state. And identification with parts of it remains strong. So, in some areas, the traditionalist appeal did lend conviction to Labour's programme. It also contained an element of forward projection – in the form of the question 'what sort of society would you prefer to live in?'

On the other hand, it was also fatally narrow and backward-looking. It did not have roots in the things which are transforming social and economic life and it lacked a convincing strategy for, or image of, modernisation. Labour may have carried conviction on the 'fair shares', redistribution, front; but it lacked credibility on the 'wealth-creating' front. It could not construct a picture of what a wealthy *society* might be like or how it could be created. And since many identifications were made, not in terms of social wealth but in 'family fortunes', it had no image to set against Thatcherism's image of personalised and privatised 'prosperity'.

The sober truth is that Labour probably did as well with this traditionalist image as it was possible to do. It does not and cannot carry majority support. It appeals to some sectors of, but cannot unify, the working class. And it certainly is not hegemonic enough to construct out of our increasingly fragmented and divided society a new social bloc or collective political will for the future.

In the aftermath of the election, many people have been seeking consolation in the belief that the appeal to the 'traditional Labour voter' could, at least, carry half the country – the 'North'. The 'North' has become a sort of geographical metaphor for where the traditional Labour voter now resides. If only things were so neatly divided, Labour's traditionalist appeal would make more sense. But, unfortunately, that story is deceptively neat. The 'North' is not just a geographical entity: it is also a state of mind. Looked at in this way, the picture becomes a good deal bleaker.

First, the 'North' is not as solid as it looks. There are plenty of 'South-minded' working-class people living in the 'North'.

Second, the disaster which Labour suffered in London and the South East suggests that many people there who may be 'North' in their living standards, conditions and even origins have, nevertheless, become 'Southerners' in their heads. The 'new' working class in the geographical 'South' now identify and vote in a majority for Thatcherism. They no longer identify themselves with Labour's traditional working-class Labour voter. What is more, many people in the underclasses – the unskilled, part-timers, young unemployed, women living alone, black people, the homeless, inner-city casualities – don't see themselves or identify with this traditionalist image either. Looked at not so much in terms of economic class but as ideological identification,

Labour could not and cannot for the foreseeable future make any inroads into the social landscape of the 'South' on the narrow basis of the image they chose.

Third, the 'North' is not impervious to Thatcherite inroads as we shall see in the coming months. The inner-cities strategy will not bring about long-term sustained growth in the 'North', but it is going to erode Labour's political base in the great industrial urban areas. Thatcherism in the 'South' has already had considerable success in targeting the big-spending Labour councils, the comprehensive schools and council housing – three major pillars of Labour's political base. In the next months we are going to witness a similar assault, economically and ideologically, on Labour's base in the 'North', with blistering effects.

There will be a flood of small businesses, pump-primed by industrialists who know on which side their political bread is buttered. The press will trumpet its immediate 'success' and Lord Young will be 'economical' with more statistics. Labour authorities will be side-lined by 'alternative' private channels of growth, and isolated for attack (some version of the London 'loony left' ideological missile is at this very moment cruising up the M1). Thatcherism can't 'restore' Britain's old industrial base – but that is not the project. It may not be able to positively win over everybody – but that is not necessary either. It has never had an overwhelming social majority on anything. But it can mobilise the crucial two-thirds, which is enough. Not all of them are, as yet, Tory voters, but many who still vote Labour or Alliance have begun to benefit from Thatcherism, or are making pragmatic adjustments to it.

What's more, not all the two-thirds needs to be in any real sense 'prosperous'. All Thatcherism has to do to erode Labour's 'Northern' bastions is to lay a base for *just enough* people to put their feet, tentatively, on the new Thatcherite ladders of success. Firstly, it has to convince them that, concretely, this is a more likely way to a better, more prosperous life than any other alternative on offer. Secondly, it has to convince others who have not yet begun to do well to cast their lot in with the free-market society. Once this threshold has been crossed, a much larger number – a strategic majority, the necessary two-thirds – move in their heads. The balance shifts. The 'North' has begun its symbolic journey 'Southwards' …

What, then, about the possibility of constructing the different social constituencies into a new social bloc around Labour's traditionalist appeal? Clearly, few modernising industrialists can be harnessed to Labour's current strategy. Big business is now pro-Thatcher, not simply in pragmatic but in ideological terms. They 'believe'. They understand that Thatcherism is not just a strategy which favours capital; it must also be a strategy for the whole society, 'for capital'. The middle classes are interestingly split. The self-made middle classes – numerically, the overwhelming majority – who inhabit the culture of the private sector, are Mrs Thatcher's ideological vanguard. They have talked their way into an impregnable philosophy of 'number one'. The 'public sector' middle classes in education, local government or the social services are not so directly in touch with the new prosperity and are more inclined to seek rewards from socially useful and personally rewarding forms of work which have been brutally savaged by the new criteria of 'value-for-money' and 'efficiency'. They are more detached from Thatcherism. But this does not help Labour as much as it might, since the Alliance now soaks up their disenchantment with Thatcherism – it's a 'nicer' option.

In the aftermath of the election, many people on the left are arguing that Labour's only hope lies in the working class. However, Thatcherism's electoral hegemony continues to rest precisely on certain parts of the working-class vote. Where Labour commands a majority, that majority is overwhelmingly working-class. But the working class is not overwhelmingly Labour. Indeed, there is no such thing as 'the' working-class vote any more. Divisions, not solidarities, of class identification are the rule. There are large and significant sectors of the 'working class' as it really is today – the unemployed, semi-skilled and unskilled, part-time workers, male and female, the low-paid, black people, the 'underclasses' of Thatcherite Britain – who no longer see themselves in a traditional Labour way. In Greater London and the South East, Labour failed to connect with the forces that are remaking the working class. Skilled workers in the new industries, and the expanding clerical and office workforce, are, in their majority, voters for Thatcherism. There are more of them in the South East than in the North, but the balance is changing and will continue, unevenly, to do so. The sectors of this vote who are home owners or new shareholders are even more committed.

What then of the new social constituencies which, in any case, have less of a clear-cut class identity? Women, whether in or out of full-time work, did *not* vote overwhelmingly for Thatcherism and have not done so since 1979. But Labour made absolutely no direct, strategic or distinctive investment in what, from any point of view, is a historic shift of political identification. Presumably, on the analogy with 'black sections', to do so would be 'sexist'! By the same token, the 'ethnic' vote is less and less a Labour possession – and after the disastrous handling of the black sections issue, who can blame them? More owners of Asian small businesses are beginning to vote by class rather than by race. A proportion of Afro-Caribbean people will not be far behind.

None of this augurs well for the future. Politics does not reflect majorities, it constructs them. And there is no evidence that Labour's commitment to traditionalism can construct such a majority. Certainly, the consequences of Thatcherite restructuring are horrendous. But larger and larger numbers of people no longer experience all this as 'traditional Labour voters'. Even less can they articulate their aspirations through the traditional Labour image. The question of Labour becoming in a deep sense the majority party of society is therefore not about whether it can rally and mobilise its past, but whether it has a convincing alternative scenario to Thatcherism for the future. It cannot build such an alternative by, however honourably, replaying '1945' in 1987. It can only honour its past by aiming to move forwards. But to do so it needs a strategy for modernisation and an image of modernity. What the election suggests is that Labour, far from opening the hard road to renewal, largely turned its back on it. It is therefore not surprising that – despite the good feelings and high morale – its historic decline continues.

The meaning of new times

1988

HOW NEW ARE these 'new times'? Are they the dawn of a New Age or only the whisper of an old one? What is 'new' about them? How do we assess their contradictory tendencies – are they progressive or regressive? These are some of the questions which the ambiguous discourse of 'new times' poses. They are worth asking, not because 'new times' represents a definitive set of answers to them or even a clear way of resolving the ambiguities inherent in the idea, but because they stimulate the left to open a debate about how society is changing and to offer new descriptions and analyses of the social conditions it seeks to transcend and transform. If it succeeds in this but accomplishes nothing else, the metaphor of 'new times' will have done its work.

As the questions suggest, there is considerable ambiguity as to what the phrase 'new times' really means. It seems to be connected with the ascendancy of the new right in Britain, the USA and some parts of Europe over the past decade. But what precisely is the connection? For example, are 'new times' a product of 'the Thatcher Revolution'? Was Thatcherism really so decisive and fundamental? And, if so, does that mean that the left has no alternative but to adapt to the changed terrain and agenda of politics, post-Thatcherism, if it is to survive? This is a very negative interpretation of 'new times': and it is easy to see why those who read 'new times' in this way regard the whole thing as a smokescreen for some seismic shift of gravity by the left towards the right.

There is, however, a different reading. This suggests that Thatcherism itself was, in part, produced by 'new times'. On this interpretation, 'new times' refers to social, economic, political and cultural changes of a deeper kind now taking place in western capitalist societies. These changes, it is suggested, form the necessary shaping context, the material and cultural conditions of existence, for *any* political strategy, whether of the right or the left. From this position, Thatcherism represents, in fact, in its own way, an attempt (only partially successful) to harness and bend to its political project circumstances which were not of its making, which have a much longer history and trajectory, and which do not necessarily have a 'new right' political agenda inscribed in them. Much turns on which version of 'new times' one subscribes to.

If we take the 'new times' idea apart, we find that it is an attempt to capture, within the confines of a single metaphor, a number of different facets of social change, none of which has any necessary connection with the other. In the current debates, a variety of different terms jostle with one another for pride of place, in the attempt to describe these different dimensions of change. They include 'post-industrial', 'post-Fordist', 'revolution of the subject', 'postmodernism'. None of these is wholly satisfactory. Each expresses a clearer sense of what we are leaving behind ('post' everything?) than of where we are heading. Each, however, signifies something important about the 'new times' debate.

'Post-industrial' writers, like Alain Touraine and André Gorz, start from shifts in the technical organisation of industrial capitalist production, with its 'classic' economies of scale, integrated labour processes, advanced division of labour and industrial class conflicts. They foresee an increasing shift to new productive regimes – with inevitable consequences for social structure and politics. Thus Touraine has written of the replacement of older forms of class struggle by the new social movements; and Gorz's most provocative title is *Farewell To The Working Class*.[1] In these forms, 'new times' touches debates which have already seriously divided the left. There is certainly an important point about the shifting social and technical landscapes of modern industrial production regimes being made in some of these arguments, though they are open to the criticism that they fall for a sort of technological determinism.

'Post-Fordism' is a broader term, suggesting a whole new epoch distinct from the era of mass production, with its standardised products, concentrations of capital and its 'Taylorist' forms of work organisation and discipline. The debate still rages as to whether 'post-Fordism' actually exists, and if it does, what exactly it is and how extensive it is, either within any single economy or across the advanced industrial economies of the West as a whole. Nevertheless, most commentators would agree that the term covers at least some of the following characteristics of change. A shift is taking place to new 'information technologies' from the chemical and electronic-based technologies which drove the 'second' industrial revolution from the turn of the century onwards – the one which signalled the advance of the American, German and Japanese economics to a leading position, and the relative 'backwardness' and incipient decline of the British economy. Secondly, there is a shift towards a more flexible specialised and decentralised form of labour process and work organisation, and, as a consequence, a decline of the old manufacturing base (and the regions and cultures associated with it) and the growth of the 'sunrise', computer-based, hi-tech industries and their regions. Thirdly, there is the hiving-off or contracting-out of functions and services hitherto provided 'in house' on a corporate basis. Fourthly, there is a leading role for consumption, reflected in such things as greater emphasis on choice and product differentiation, on marketing, packaging and design, on the 'targeting' of consumers by lifestyle, taste and culture rather than by the Registrar General's categories of social class.

Fifthly, there has been a decline in the proportion of the skilled, male, manual working class and the corresponding rise of the service and white collar classes. In the domain of paid work itself, there is more flexi-time and part-time working, coupled with the 'feminisation' and 'ethnicisation' of the workforce. Seventhly, there is an economy dominated by the multinationals, with their new international division of labour and their greater autonomy of nation state control. Eighthly, there is the 'globalisation' of the new financial markets. Finally, there is the emergence of new patterns of social divisions – especially those between 'public' and 'private' sectors and between the two-thirds who have rising expectations and the 'new poor' and underclasses of the one-third that is left behind on every significant dimension of social opportunity.

It is clear that 'post-Fordism', though having a significant reference to questions of economic organisation and structure, has a much broader social and cultural significance. Thus, for example, it also signals greater social fragmentation and pluralism, the weakening of older collective solidarities and block identities and the emergence of new identities, as well as the maximisation of individual choices through personal consumption, as equally significant dimensions of the shift towards 'post-Fordism'.

Some critics have suggested that 'post-Fordism' as a concept marks a return to the old, discredited base-superstructure or economic-determinist model, according to which the economy determines everything and all other aspects can be 'read off' as simply reflecting that 'base'. However, the metaphor of 'post-Fordism' does not necessarily carry any such implication. Indeed, it is modelled on Gramsci's earlier use of the term, 'Fordism', at the turn of the century to connote a whole shift in capitalist civilisation (which Gramsci certainly did not reduce to a mere phenomenon of the economic base). 'Post-Fordism' should also be read in a much broader way. Indeed, it could just as easily be taken in the opposite way – as signalling the *constitutive* role which social and cultural relations play in relation to any economic system. Post-Fordism as I understand it is not committed to any prior determining position for the economy. But it does insist – as all but the most extreme discourse theorists and culturalists must recognise – that shifts of this order in economic life must be taken seriously in any analysis of our present circumstances.

A recent writer on the subject of contemporary cultural change, Marshall Berman, notes that 'modern environments and experiences cut across all boundaries of geography and ethnicity, of class and nationality, of religion and ideology' – not destroying them entirely, but weakening and subverting them, eroding the lines of continuity which hitherto stabilised our social identities.[2]

The return of the subject

One boundary which 'new times' has certainly displaced is that between the objective' and subjective dimensions of change. This is the so-called 'revolution of the subject' aspect. The individual subject has become more important, as collective social subjects – like that of class or nation or ethnic group – become more segmented and 'pluralised'. As social theorists have become more concerned with how ideologies actually function, and how political mobilisation really takes place in complex societies, so they have been obliged to take the *subject* of these processes more seriously. As Gramsci remarked about ideologies, 'To the extent that ideologies are historically necessary they have a validity which is "psychological"'.[3] At the same time, our models of 'the subject' have altered. We can no longer conceive of 'the individual' in terms of a whole, centred, stable and completed Ego or autonomous, rational 'self'. The 'self' is conceptualised as more fragmented and incomplete, composed of multiple 'selves' or identities in relation to the different social worlds we inhabit, something with a history, 'produced', in process. The 'subject' is differently placed or *positioned* by different discourses and practices.

This is novel conceptual or theoretical terrain. But these vicissitudes of 'the subject' also have their own histories, which are key episodes in the passage to 'new times'. They include the cultural revolution of the 1960s; '1968' itself, with its strong sense of politics as 'theatre' and its talk of 'will' and 'consciousness'; feminism, with its insistence that 'the personal is political'; the renewed interest in psychoanalysis, with its rediscovery of the unconscious roots of subjectivity; the theoretical revolution of the 1960s and 1970s – semiotics, structuralism, 'post-structuralism' – with their concern for language, discourse and representation.

This 'return of the subjective' aspect suggests that we cannot settle for a language in which to describe 'new times' which respects the old distinction between the objective and subjective dimensions of change. 'New times' are both 'out there', changing our conditions of life, and 'in here', working on us. In part, it is us who are being 'remade'. But such a conceptual shift presents particular problems for the left. The conventional culture and discourses of the left, with its stress on 'objective contradictions', 'impersonal structures' and processes that work 'behind men's (sic) backs', have disabled us from confronting the subjective dimension in politics in any very coherent way.

In part, the difficulty lies in the very words and concepts we use. For a long time, being a socialist was synonymous with the ability to translate everything into the language of 'structures'. But it is not only a question of language. In part, the difficulty lies in the fact that men so often provide the categories within which everybody experiences things, even on the left. Men have always found the spectacle of the 'return' of the subjective dimension deeply unnerving. The problem is also theoretical. Classical marxism depended on an assumed correspondence between 'the economic' and 'the political': one could read off political attitudes and objective social interests and motivations from economic class position. For a long time, these correspondences held the theoretical analyses and perspectives of the left in place. However, any simple correspondence between the 'political' and 'economic' is exactly what has now disintegrated – practically and theoretically. This has had the effect of throwing the language of politics more over to the cultural side of the equation.

'Post-modernism' is the preferred term which signals this more *cultural* character of 'new times'. 'Modernism', it argues, which dominated the art and architecture, the cultural imagination, of the early decades of the twentieth century, and came to represent the look and experience of 'modernity' itself, is at an end. It has declined into the International Style characteristics of the freeway, the wall-of-glass skyscraper and international airports. Modernism's revolutionary impulse – which could be seen in surrealism, Dada, constructivism, the move to an abstract and non-figurative visual culture – has been tamed and contained by the museum. It has become the preserve of an avant-garde elite, betraying its revolutionary and 'populist' impulses.

'Post-modernism', by contrast, celebrates the penetration of aesthetics into everyday life and the ascendancy of popular culture over the High Arts. Theorists like Fredric Jameson and Jean-François Lyotard agree on many of the characteristics of 'the postmodern condition'. They remark on the dominance of image, appearance, surface-effect over depth (was Ronald Reagan a president or just a B-movie actor, real or cardboard cut-out, alive or *Spitting Image*?). They point to the blurring of image and reality in our media-saturated world (is the Contra war real or only happening on TV?). They note the preference for parody, nostalgia, kitsch and pastiche – the continual reworking and quotation of past styles – over more positive modes of artistic representation, like realism or naturalism. They note, also, a preference for the popular and the decorative over the brutalist or the functional in architecture and design. 'Post-modernism' also has a more philosophical aspect. Lyotard, Baudrillard and Derrida cite the erasure of a strong sense of history, the slippage of hitherto stable meanings, the proliferation of difference, and the end of what Lyotard calls the 'grand narratives' of progress, development, Enlightenment, Rationality, and Truth, which, until recently, were the foundations of Western philosophy and politics.[4]

Jameson, however, argues very persuasively that post-modernism is also 'the new cultural logic of capital' – 'the purest form of capital yet to have emerged, a prodigious expansion into hitherto uncommodified areas'.[5] His formulations remind us that the changing cultural dynamic we are trying to characterise is clearly connected with the revolutionary energy of modern capital – capital *after* what we used to call its 'highest stages' (Imperialism, Organised or Corporate capitalism) – even *later* than 'late capitalism'.

'Post-industrialism', 'post-Fordism', 'post-modernism' are all different ways of trying to characterise or explain this dramatic, even brutal, resumption of the link between modernity and capitalism. Some theorists argue that, though Marx may have been wrong in his predictions about class as the motor of revolution, he was right – with a vengeance – about capital. Its 'global' expansion continues, with renewed energy in the 1980s, to transform everything in its wake, subordinating every society and social relationship to the law of commodification and exchange value. Others argue that, with the failures of the stalinist and social-democratic alternatives, and the transformations and upheavals now taking place throughout the communist world, capital has acquired a new lease of life.

Some economists argue that we are simply in the early, up-beat half of the new Kondratiev 'long wave' of capitalist expansion (after which the inevitable downturn or recession will follow). The American social critic whom we quoted earlier, Marshall Berman, relates 'new times' to 'the ever-expanding drastically fluctuating capitalist world markets' (*All That is Solid*, p16). Others, with their eye more firmly fixed on the limits and uneven development of capital on a global scale, emphasise more the ceaseless rhythm of the international division of labour, redistributing poverty and wealth, dependency and over-development in new ways across the face of the earth. One casualty of this process is the old idea of some homogeneous 'Third World'. Nowadays, Formosa and Taiwan are integrated into the advanced capitalist economies, as Hong Kong is with the new financial markets. Ethiopia or the Sudan or Bangladesh, on the other hand, belong to a different 'world' altogether. It is the new forms and dynamic of capital as a global force which is marking out these new divisions across the globe.

However, it seems to be the case that, whichever explanation we finally settle for, the really startling fact is that *these* new times clearly belong to a time-zone marked by the march of capital simultaneously across the globe and through the Maginot Lines of our subjectivities.

The title of Berman's book, *All That is Solid Melts Into Air* (a quotation from *The Communist Manifesto*), reminds us that Marx was one of the earliest people to grasp the revolutionary connection between capitalism and modernity. In the *Manifesto* he spoke of the 'constant revolutionising of production, uninterrupted disturbance of all social relations, everlasting uncertainty and agitation' which distinguished 'the bourgeois epoch from all earlier times'. 'All fixed, fast-frozen relationships, with their train of venerable ideas and opinions, are swept away, all new-formed ones become obsolete before they can ossify. All That is Solid Melts Into Air.'

Indeed, as Berman points out, Marx considered the revolution of modern industry and production the necessary precondition for that Promethean or Romantic conception of the social individual which towers over his early writings, with its prospect of the many-sided development of human capacities. In this context, it was not the commodities which the bourgeoisie created which impressed Marx, so much as 'the processes, the powers, the expressions of human life and energy; men (sic) working, moving, cultivating, communicating, organising and reorganising nature and themselves' (*All That is Solid*, p93). Of course, Marx also understood the one-sided and distorted character of the modernity and type of modern individual produced by this development – how the forms of bourgeois appropriation destroyed the human possibilities it created. But he did not, on this count, refuse it. What he argued was that *only socialism* could complete the revolution of modernity which capitalism had initiated. As Berman puts it, he hoped 'to heal the wounds of modernity through a fuller and deeper modernity'.

Now here exactly is the rub about 'new times' for the left. The 'promise' of modernity has become, at the end of the twentieth century, considerably more ambiguous, its links with socialism and the left much more tenuous. We have become more aware of the double-edged and problematic character of modernity: what Theodor Adorno called the 'negative dialectic' of enlightenment. Of course, to be 'modern' has *always* meant 'to live a life of paradox and contradiction … alive to new possibilities for experience and adventure, frightened by the nihilistic depths to which so many modem adventures lead (e.g. the line from Nietzsche and Wagner to the death camps), longing to create and hold onto something real even as everything melts'.

Some theorists argue – the German philosopher, Jurgen Habermas is one – that this is too pessimistic a reading of 'Enlightenment' and that the project of modernity is not yet completed. But it is difficult to deny that, at the end of the twentieth century, the paradoxes of modernity seem even more extreme. 'Modernity' has acquired a relentlessly uneven and contradictory character: material abundance here, producing poverty and immiseration there; greater diversity and choice – but often at the cost of commodification, fragmentation and isolation. More opportunities for participation – but only at the expense of subordinating oneself to the laws of the market. Novelty and innovation – but driven by what often appear to be false needs. The rich 'West' – and the famine stricken South. Forms of 'development' which destroy faster than they create. The city – priviled scenario of the modern experience for Baudelaire or Walter Benjamin – transformed into the anonymous city, the sprawling city, the inner city, the abadoned city …

These stark paradoxes project uncertainty into any secure judgement or assessment of the trends and tendencies of new times, especially on the left. Are new times to be welcomed for the new possibilities they open? Or rejected for the threat of horrendous disasters (the ecological ones are uppermost in our minds just now) and final closures which they bring in their wake? Terry Eagleton has recently posed the dilemma in comparable terms, when discussing the 'true aporia, impasse or undecidability of a transitional epoch, struggling out as it is from beneath an increasingly clapped out, discreditable, historically superannuated ideology of Autonomous Man (first cousin to Socialist Man) with no very clear sense as yet of which path from this pile of ruins is likely to lead us towards an enriched human life and which to the unthinkable terminus of some fashionable new irrationalist barbarism'.[6] We seem, especially on the left, permanently impaled on the horns of these extreme and irreconcilable alternatives.

It is imperative for the left to get past this impossible impasse, these irreconcilable either/ors. For this there are few better (though many more fashionable) places to begin than with Gramsci's 'Americanism and Fordism' essay, which is of seminal importance for this debate, even if it is also a strangely broken and 'unfinished' text. 'Americanism and Fordism' represented a very similar effort, much earlier in the century, to describe and assess the dangers and possibilities for the left of the birth of that epoch – 'Fordism' – which we are just supposed to be leaving. Gramsci was conducting this exercise in very similar political circumstances for the left – retreat and retrenchment of the working-class movement, ascendancy of fascism, a new surge of capital 'with its intensified economic exploitation and authoritarian cultural expression'.

If we take our bearings from 'Americanism and Fordism' we are obliged to note that Gramsci's 'catalogue of ... most important or interesting problems' relevant to deciding 'whether Americanism can constitute a new historical epoch' begins with 'a new mechanism of accumulation and distribution of finance capital based directly on industrial production'. But his characterisation of 'Fordism' also includes a range of other social and cultural phenomena which are discussed in the essay: the rationalisation of the demographic composition of Europe; the balance between endogamous and exogamous change; the phenomenon of mass consumption and 'high wages'; 'psychoanalysis and its enormous diffusion since the war'; the increased 'moral coercion' exercised by the state; artistic and intellectual movements associated with 'Modernism'; what Gramsci calls the contrast between 'super-city' and 'super-country'; feminism, masculinism and 'the question of sex'. Who on the left now has the confidence to address the problems and promise of new times with a matching comprehensiveness and range? The sad fact is that a list of 'new questions' like that are most likely to engender a response of derision and sectarian back-biting at most meetings of the organised political left today – coupled with the usual cries of 'sell-out'!

This lack of intellectual boldness on the left is certainly, in part, attributable to the fact that the contradictory forces associated with new times are just now, and have been for some time, firmly in the keeping and under the tutelage of the right. The right has imprinted them with the apparent inevitability of its own political project. However, as we argued earlier, this may have obscured the fact that what is going on is not the unrolling of a singular, unilinear logic in which the ascendancy of capital, the hegemony of the new right and the march of commodification are indissolubly locked together. These may be *different* processes, with different time-scales, which the dominance of the right in the 1980s has somehow rendered natural and inevitable.

One of the lessons of new times is that history does not consist of what Benedict Anderson calls 'empty, homogeneous time', but of processes with different time-scales and trajectories. They may be convened in the same conjuncture. But historic conjunctures of this kind remain complex, not simple: not in any simple sense 'determined' but *over-determined* (that is, the result of a fusion or merging of different processes and contradictions which nevertheless retain their own effectivity, 'the specific modalities of their actions').[7] That is really what a 'new conjuncture' means, as Gramsci clearly showed. The histories and time-scale of Thatcherism and of new times have certainly overlapped. Nevertheless, they may belong to different temporalities. Political time, the time of regimes and elections, is short: 'a week is a long time in politics'. Economic time, sociological time, so to speak, has a longer *durée*. Cultural time is even slower, more glacial. This does not detract from the significance of Thatcherism and the scale of its political intervention, about which we have been writing. There is nothing slow, glacial or 'passive' about the Thatcherite revolution, which seems by contrast brutally abrupt, concise and condensed.

Nevertheless, from the perspective of the longer *durée* of new times, Thatcherism's project can be understood as operating on the ground of longer, deeper, more profound movements of change which *appear* to be going its way, but of which, in reality, it has been only occasionally, and fleetingly, in command over the past decade. We can see Thatcherism as, in fact, an attempt to hegemonise these deeper tendencies within its project of 'regressive modernisation', to appropriate them to a reactionary political agenda and to harness to them the interests and fortunes of specific and limited social interests. Once we have opened up this gap, analytically, between Thatcherism and new times, it may become possible to resume or re-stage the broken dialogue between socialism and modernity.

Consider another question with which people on the left perpetually tease and puzzle one another: what kind of 'transition' are we talking about and how total or how complete is it? This way of posing the question implies an all-or-nothing answer. Either it *is* a New Epoch, or nothing at all has changed. But that is not the only alternative. We are certainly not debating an *epochal* shift, of the order of the famous transition from feudalism to capitalism. But we have had other transitions from one regime of accumulation to another, within capitalism, whose impact has been extraordinarily wide-ranging. Think, for example, of the transition which Marx writes about between absolute and relative surplus value; or from machine-facture to 'modern industry'; or the one which preoccupied Lenin and others at the turn of the century and about which Gramsci was writing in 'Americanism and Fordism'. The transition which new times references is of the latter order of things.

As to how complete it is: this stand-and-deliver way of assessing things may itself be the product of an earlier type of totalising logic which is beginning to be superseded. In a permanently Transitional Age we must *expect* unevenness, contradictory outcomes, disjunctures, delays, contingencies, uncompleted projects overlapping emergent ones. We know that Marx's *Capital* stands at the beginning, not the completion, of the expansion of the capitalist 'world market'; and that earlier transitions (such as that from household to factory production) all turned out, on inspection, to be more protracted and incomplete than the theory suggested.

We have to make assessments, not from the completed base, but from the 'leading edge' of change. The food industry, which has just arrived at the point where it can guarantee worldwide the standardisation of the size, shape and composition of every hamburger and every potato (sic) chip in a Macdonald's Big Mac from Tokyo to Harare, is clearly just entering its 'Fordist' apogee. However, its labour force and highly mobile, 'flexible' and deskilled work patterns approximate more to some post-Fordist patterns. The motor industry, from which the Age of Fordism derived its name, with its multiple variations on every model and market specialisation (like the fashion and software industries), is, in some areas at least, on the move towards a more post-Fordist form. The question should always be, where is the 'leading edge' and in what direction is it pointing.

The cultural dimension

Another major requirement for trying to think through the complexities and ambiguities of new times is simply to open our minds to the deeply *cultural* character of the revolution of our times. If 'post-Fordism' exists, then it is as much a description of cultural as of economic change. Indeed, that distinction is now quite useless. Culture has ceased (if ever it was – which I doubt) to be a decorative addendum to the 'hard world' of production and things, the icing on the cake of the material world. The word is now as 'material' as the world. Through design, technology and styling, 'aesthetics' has already penetrated the world of modern production. Through marketing, layout and style, the 'image' provides the mode of representation and fictional narrativisation of the body on which so much of modern consumption depends.

Modern culture is relentlessly material in its practices and modes of production. And the material world of commodities and technologies is profoundly cultural. Young people, black and white, who can't even spell 'postmodernism' but have grown up in the age of computer technology, rock-video and electronic music, already inhabit such a universe in their heads.

Is this merely the culture of commodified consumption? Are these necessarily Trivial Pursuits? (Or, to bring it right home, a trendy 'designer addiction' to the detritus of capitalism which serious left magazines like *Marxism Today* should renounce – or even better denounce – forever?) Yes, much – perhaps, even most – of the time. But underlying that, have we missed the opening up of the individual to the transforming rhythms and forces of modern *material* life? Have we become bewitched by the question of who it is, in the short run, that reaps the profit from these transactions (there are vast amounts of it being made), and so missed the democratisation of culture which is *also* potentially part of their hidden agenda? Can a socialism of the twenty-first century revive, or even survive, which is wholly cut off from the landscapes of popular pleasures, however contradictory and 'commodified' a terrain they represent? Are we thinking dialectically enough?

One strategy for getting at the more cultural and subjective dimensions of new times would be to start from the objective characteristics of post-Fordism and simply turn them inside out. Take the new technologies. They not only introduce new skills and practices. They also require new ways of thinking. Technology, which used to be 'hard-nosed' is now 'soft'. And it no longer operates along one, singular line or path of development. Modern technology, far from having a fixed path, is open to constant renegotiation and re-articulation. 'Planning', in this new technological environment, has less to do with absolute predictability and everything to do with instituting a 'regime' out of which a plurality of outcomes will emerge. One, so to speak, plans for contingency. This mode of thinking signals the end of a certain kind of deterministic rationality.

Or consider the proliferation of models and styles, the increased product differentiation, which characterises 'post-Fordist' production. We can see mirrored there wider processes of cultural diversity and differentiation, related to the multiplication of social worlds and social 'logics' typical of modern life in the West.

There has been an enormous expansion of 'civil society', related to the diversification of social worlds in which men and women now operate. At present, most people only relate to these worlds through the medium of consumption. But, increasingly, we are coming to understand that to maintain these worlds at an advanced level requires forms of collective consumption far beyond the restricted logic of the market. Furthermore, each of these worlds also has its own codes of behaviour, its 'scenes' and 'economies', and (don't knock it) its pleasures. These already allow those individuals who have some access to them some space in which to reassert a measure of choice and control over everyday life, and to 'play' with its more expressive dimensions. This 'pluralisation' of social life expands the positionalities and identities available to ordinary people (at least in the industrialised world) in their everyday working, social, familial and sexual lives. Such opportunities need to be more, not less, widely available across the globe, and in ways not limited by private appropriation.

This shift of time and activity towards 'civil society' has implications for our thinking about the individual's rights and responsibilities, about new forms of citizenship and about ways of ordering and regulating society other than through the all-encompassing state. They imply a socialism committed to, rather than scared of, diversity and difference.

Of course, 'civil society' is no ideal realm of pure freedom. Its micro-worlds include the multiplication of points of power and conflict, and thus exploitation, oppression and marginalisation. More and more of our everyday lives are caught up in these forms of power, and their lines of intersection. Far from there being no resistance to the system, there has been a proliferation of new points of antagonism, new social movements of resistance organised around them; and, consequently, a generalisation of 'politics' to spheres which hitherto the left assumed to be apolitical: a politics of the family, of health, of food, of sexuality, of the body. What we lack is any overall map of how these power relations connect and of their resistances. Perhaps there isn't, in that sense, one 'power game' at all, more a network of strategies and powers and their articulations – and thus a politics which is always positional ...

One of these critical 'new' sites of politics is the arena of social reproduction. On the left, we know about the reproduction of labour power. But what do we really know – outside of feminism – about ideological, cultural, sexual reproduction? One of the characteristics of this area of 'reproduction' is that it is both material and symbolic, since we are reproducing not only the cells of the body but also the categories of the culture. Even consumption, in some ways the privileged terrain of reproduction, is no less symbolic for being material. We need not go so far – with Baudrillard – as to say 'the object is nothing' to be able to recognise that, in the modem world, objects are also signs, and we relate to the world of things in both an instrumental and a symbolic mode.[8] In a world tyrannised by scarcity, men and women nevertheless express in their practical lives not only what they need for material existence but some sense of their symbolic place in the world, of who they are, their identities. One should not miss this drive to take part or 'come on' in the theatre of the social – even if, as things stand, the only stage provided is within what the Situationists, in 1968, used to call the 'fetishised spectacle of the commodity'.

Of course, the preoccupation with consumption and style may appear trivial – though more so to men, who tend to have themselves 'reproduced', so to say, at arms-length from the grubby processes of shopping and buying and getting and spending, and therefore take it less seriously than women, for whom it was destiny, life's 'work'. But the fact is that greater and greater numbers of people (men *and* women) – with however little money – play the game of using things to signify who they are. Everybody, including people in very poor societies whom we in the West frequently speak about as if they inhabit a world *outside* of culture, knows that today's 'goods' double up as social signs and produce meanings as well as energy. There is no clear evidence that, in an alternative socialist economy, our propensity to 'code' things according to systems of meaning, which is an essential feature of our sociality, would *necessarily* cease – or, indeed, should.

A socialism built on any simple notion of a 'return to Nature' is finished. We are all irrevocably in the 'secondary universes' where Culture predominates over Nature. And culture, increasingly, distances us from invoking the simple, transparent ground of 'material interests' as a way of settling any argument. The environmental crisis, which is a result of the profound imbalance between Nature and Culture induced by the relentless drive to subordinate everything to the drive for profitability and capital accumulation, cannot be resolved by any simple 'return' to Nature. It can only be resolved by a more human – that is, socially responsible and communally responsive – way of *cultivating* the natural world of finite resources on which we all now depend. The notion that 'the market' can resolve such questions is patently – in the light of present experience – absurd and untenable.

This recognition of the expanded cultural and subjective ground on which any socialism of the twenty-first century must stand relates, in a significant way, to feminism, or better still, what we might call 'the feminisation of the social'. We should distinguish this from the simplistic version of 'the future is female', espoused by some tendencies within the women's movement, but recently subject to Lynne Segal's persuasive critique.[9] It arises from the remarkable – and irreversible – transformation in the position of women in modern life as a consequence not only of shifts in conceptions of work and exploitation, the gendered recomposition of the workforce and the greater control over fertility and reproduction, but also the rebirth of modern feminism itself.

Feminism and the social movements around sexual politics have thus had an unsettling effect on everything once thought of as 'settled' in the theoretical universe of the left. And nowhere more dramatically than in their power to decentre the characteristic conversations of the left by bringing on to the political agenda the question of sexuality. This is more than simply the question of men on the left being 'nice' to women or lesbians or gay men, or beginning to address their forms of oppression and exclusion: it has to do with the revolution in thinking which follows in the wake of the recognition that *all* social practices and forms of domination – including the politics of the left – are always inscribed in and to some extent secured by sexual identity and positioning. If we don't attend to the ways in which gendered identities are formed and transformed, and how they are deployed politically, we simply do not have a language of sufficient explanatory power at our command with which to understand the institutionalisation of power in our society and the secret sources of our resistances to change. After another of those meetings of the left where the question of sexuality has cut through like an electric current which nobody knows how to plug into, one is tempted to say *especially* the resistances to change on the left.

Thatcherism was certainly fully aware of this implication of gender and identity in politics. It has powerfully organised itself around particular forms of patriarchy and cultural or national identity. Its defence of 'Englishness', of that way of 'being British', or of the English feeling 'great again', is a key to some of the unexpected sources of Thatcherism's popularity. Cultural racism has been one of its most powerful, enduring, effective – and least remarked – sources of strength. For that very reason, 'Englishness', as a privileged and restrictive cultural identity, is becoming a site of contestation for those many marginalised ethnic and racial groups in the society who feel excluded by it and who hold to a different form of racial and ethnic identification and insist on cultural diversity as a goal of society: in new times.

The left should not be afraid of this surprising return of ethnicity. Though ethnicity continues to be, in many places, a surprisingly resilient and powerfully reactionary force, the *new* forms of ethnicity are articulated, politically, in a different direction. By 'ethnicity' we mean the astonishing return to the political agenda of all those points of attachment which give the individual some sense of 'place' and position in the world, whether these be in relation to particular communities, localities, territories, languages, religions or cultures. These days, black writers and film-makers refuse to be restricted to only addressing black subjects. But they insist that others recognise that what they have to say comes out of particular histories and cultures and that everyone speaks from positions within the global distribution of power. Because these positions change and alter, there is always an engagement with politics as a 'war of position'.

This insistence on 'positioning' provides people with co-ordinates, which are especially important in face of the enormous globalisation and transnational character of many of the processes which now shape their lives. The new times seem to have gone 'global' and 'local' at the same moment. And the question of ethnicity reminds us that everybody comes from some place – even if it is only an 'imagined community' – and needs some sense of identification and belonging. A politics which neglects that moment of identity and identification – without, of course, thinking of it as something permanent, fixed or essential – is not likely to be able to command the new times.

Could there be new times without new subjects? Could the world be transformed while its subjects stay exactly the same? Have the forces remaking the modern world left the subjects of that process untouched? Is change possible while we remain untransformed? It was always unlikely and is certainly an untenable proposition now. This is another one of those many 'fixed and fast-frozen relationships, venerable ideas and opinions' which, as Marx accurately predicted, new times are quietly melting into thin air.

Notes

1. André Gorz, *Farewell to the Working Class*, Pluto 1982.
2. Marshall Berman, *All That is Solid Melts Into Air,* Simon and Schuster 1983.
3. Antonio Gramsci, *Selections from the Prison Notebooks*, Lawrence and Wishart 1971, p377.
4. Jean-François Lyotard, *The Post-Modem Condition: A Report of Knowledge,* Manchester University Press 1984.
5. Fredric Jameson, 'The Cultural Logic of Capital', *New Left Review* 146, July/August 1984.
6. Terry Eagleton, 'Identity', ICA 6, 1987, p47.
7. Louis Althusser, 'Contradiction and Over-determination', in *For Marx*, Penguin 1969.
8. Jean Baudrillard, *The Mirror of Production*, Telos 1979, p62.
9. Lynne Segal, *Is the future female?: troubled thoughts on contemporary feminism*, Virago 1987.

And not a shot fired

1991

THE TEMPTATION TO pay our last respects to Mrs Thatcher on the occasion of the final issue of MT is too strong to resist. How would she feel if the journal which gave her so much respectful attention during her long political reign – even going so far as to name a whole political philosophy after her – were to neglect to do the honourable thing in its closing pages? Some readers may think that, as Julian Critchley recently remarked, her remains having been shown to the Tory Party conference, she should now be permitted a decent interment. After all, everyone (even *Marxism Today*) seems convinced that Major's smiling face presages a return to business as usual. There is even a hint of a new phenomenon unfolding before us – 'Majorism', with its rising public expenditure, more interventionist role for the DTI (and, it is to be hoped, the Rottweiler kennels for Michael Howard), a citizens' charter for consumers, civilised briefings on gay rights from Sir Ian McKellen, and a crafty, crab-like approach (avoiding Tebbit traps and Ridley-like potholes on route) towards the Maastricht summit. Where is the savage excess, the brutalism, of the Thatcher years now? Can there be anything more worth saying about them?

The centre of political gravity has certainly shifted. The whole political atmosphere is different. But 'Thatcher-ism' was never designed to refer primarily to this level of the political game. What of its deeper objectives, underlying strategies and long-term directions? My argument is that, while every effort is being undertaken to make the memory of the Thatcher government disappear, Thatcherism is still working its way through the system. Success does not mean that everybody was converted to Thatcherism, or that it triumphed completely, or even that Thatcher will have a political after-life. Addicted to the euphonious cadences of her lovely voice as I became, even I never believed in her political immortality. But that was never what we argued, hard as our critics struggled so to construct it. Thatcherism's 'success' means that we are still living in the aftermath of its social revolution: in particular, of that new *social regime* which Thatcherism installed, in civil society and public and institutional life.

Whereas most postwar governments attempted mainly to 'manage things', Thatcherism had a project – a set of long-term, strategic objectives, a model which it used as a template of reconstruction and a strategy for putting this into effect. In short, it was engaged in a 'hegemonic form of politics'. This way of looking at Thatcherism was Gramscian in inspiration, a way of defining the distinctiveness of its politics: this was not a zero-sum, all-or-nothing, game, but more like Gramsci's 'incessant efforts' to shift decisively the balance of forces. We called it a 'project' – the project of 'regressive modernisation' – as a way of insisting on its strategic and historic character. The analysis also took on some of the overtones of the so-called 'regulationist school' (writers like Aglietta, Lipietz and others) who were influenced by Gramsci's 'Americanism and Fordism' essay. They argued that the key periodisations within capitalism were the shifts from one 'regime of regulation' to another; and these always entailed both a new 'regime of accumulation' and a new 'mode of social and political regulation'. Lipietz defined the latter as 'a body of interiorised rules and social processes ... norms, habits, laws, regulating networks ... that ensure the unity of the process'. (It was around these themes that the critique of Thatcherism and the 'New Times' analysis converged in these pages.)

Alas! 'Hegemony' is one of those foreign words which stick in the gullet of pragmatic Englishmen, refusing to be absorbed into the lower stomach. The left translated it as outright victory in a 'war of manoeuvre', not – as it really was – the objective of a 'war of position'; and, finding no simple triumphs, breathed deeply again. The idea that Thatcherism had a 'project' proved equally unacceptable to that tribe of political pundits who grub around in the shallow earth of parliamentary life, vainly hoping to glimpse something of historic importance flitting by in the corridors of power. They consoled themselves with the thought that Thatcherism was solely preoccupied with the pragmatics of 'staying in power' – an observation of stunning banality which passed for sophisticated wisdom in the serious press. We might as well have tried spitting in the wind.

What was Thatcherism's 'project'? One way of understanding this is in terms of that catchphrase of the Thatcher era – 'market forces'.

'Market forces' represents more than a rational preference for markets over centralised planning as the more effective form of modern economic organisation. It makes 'the market' into an organising principle of social life – a law as general, for born-again Thatcherites, as 'the class struggle' ever was to marxists.

It is the *only* valid language of moral and social calculation, because it obeys an objective logic, driven by the 'hidden hand' of impersonal forces, and is not interest-laden, context-bound or morally constrained. The 'social good' can only be calculated by reducing it to individual needs, aggregated on the basis of a formal (and empty) 'equality': it means imposing the collective will of a mythical majority on the unruly but sovereign interests of individuals and is therefore, by definition, the beginning of tyranny. Thus, 'There is no such thing as "society", there is only individuals and their families'.

The left never took this seriously as a 'philosophy', that is, ideas which organise and regulate practice. It preferred to explain Thatcherism in moralistic terms – as the usual wickedness of 'the old gang'. Thus it constantly underestimated the depth of the 'culture of individualism', the cogency of classic liberal political economy and the historical embeddedness – alongside other philosophies, to be sure – with which its discourses and practices are rooted in the everyday life of the first 'market society' on earth. To put it briefly, the left lacked a conception of the kind of social revolution which brings a new regime into place.

The Thatcherites, however, not only espoused the market as a social gospel, but, like latter-day saints, did not shrink from its necessary corollaries: the use of state power to drive the model through; the 'deregulation' of all institutional arrangements; the massive accumulation of economic, social and cultural power in the hands of the classes who own, manage and run things – an inevitable consequence of all market systems; the 'privatisation' of social problems; the restoration of the divine 'right to manage'; and – that unintended but inevitable consequence of the gap between the religious zeal of the Mission and the pragmatics of its implementation – the Ministerial Lie.

The private sector, which was already disciplined in a general way by 'market forces', but may have applied them in the past in less rigorous ways, has been disciplined with remarkable single-mindedness. But the main thrust of reform is most vivid and penetrating in the public sector. There is not a school, hospital, social service department, polytechnic or college in the country which has not been so remodelled. The practices of daily life, the professional ethics, the language which is spoken in meetings, the way documents are prepared, work routines designed and priorities defined and fixed – all have been totally reframed. The restructuring drive is remorseless, all the more so given the social conservatism, institutional inertia and bureaucratic deformation of our public institutions, as well as the absence of any alternative strategy for their reform, which makes them sitting ducks. Take the case of the NHS. The details have been too well rehearsed to repeat here. In any case, important as they are, it is possible to get bogged down in a pragmatic discussion (which the media are only too happy to conduct) about whether this aspect is preferable to that (of the order of, 'would you prefer to be just hanged, or drawn and quartered as well?'), while losing sight of the process. It is clear that from the outset Thatcher was determined to reshape the NHS; not because she is a wicked ogre who wants sick people to suffer, but because its principles of organisation – universality of provision on an equal basis, funded through public taxation, and the decommodification of health and illness – ran counter to every shibboleth of her new model 'philosophy'. Of course, if you ask ministers, who have to calibrate the pragmatics of support and the timing of legislation, they will deny this. But the Thatcherite 'think tanks', whose task it was to pioneer ideas in their pure form and let ministers worry about the timing, wouldn't. They know that it was unthinkable for a government committed to reconstructing social life on the principle of 'market forces' to leave intact the NHS and all it stood for.

Such a dismantling was set in train by the PM herself before the 1983 election, and only abandoned when it became clear that, as *MT* argued at the time, in the NHS Thatcherism finally met the limit of how far the British people were willing to go along with the destruction of the post-war settlement. Tactically, she backed off: 'The NHS is safe in our hands'. But she did not back off strategically. After the 1987 election, 'dizzy with success', to quote Stalin, she returned to the attack. Robin Cook is absolutely correct to describe the reform process which Kenneth Clarke then set in motion as 'privatisation', if by that word we understand, not the selling-off of hospitals and GP practices, but the gradual and relentless disciplining of the NHS according to the market model. The media's attempt to stage-manage a rebuttal on the tendentious ground that, after all, the NHS is not being auctioned off like British Gas, was an exercise in collusive bad faith.

The conception of 'choice' which underpins the NHS reforms has two major and decisive weaknesses. First, it assumes, as classic liberalism always has, that the means of exercising choice – money – is evenly distributed. But the very market model on which it is based ensures that this cannot and never will be so. The granting of an equal right which can only be exercised unequally is a form of 'negative freedom'; and this critique applies as much to Hayek and Thatcher as it did to Locke and Adam Smith. The second problem is that modernity is more individuated but it is also more complex and thus more interdependent. Health, like transport, education, public amenities and a host of other things, cannot be reduced in the modern world to an individual calculus.

This point is well illustrated by what is happening in education. Market choice needs information and, in the attempt to get schools to 'mimic' the market, the equivalent of 'price' (the point of equilibrium between demand and supply) is now the league tables of schools. These are not worth the paper they are printed on, in terms of the historic failure to educate all children to a standard which modern life requires, since the tables cannot measure the main factor which underpins this failure – the massive discrepancies between the different backgrounds from which schools draw their pupils and the relative measures of success of different pedagogies with variable intakes. No matter. League tables are what we will be given, since they are how parents are going to 'choose', and how parental 'demand' is going to be funnelled from one school to another (and how, accordingly, weak schools will become weaker, and academically good schools more academic, and the structure of educational opportunities more deeply unequal).

Higher education, meanwhile, is being submitted to market disciplines in a more direct manner. The long-delayed expansion is being driven through by tying the funding of polytechnics and colleges to their capacity to compete in 'the educational marketplace'. This means that numbers must rise, unit costs must fall and no new expenditure must be undertaken. The consequences, as everyone who teaches knows, are that staff numbers have fallen drastically (some polytechnics have lost a third of their academic staff over the last decade), staff-student ratios and teaching contact hours have risen dramatically, and inevitably the quality of teaching is suffering – at the very time when less well-prepared students from educationally-disadvantaged groups are coming into higher education for the first time. The one thing which will not lead to staff increases or get teachers more money, time to think or research, or promotion, is – teaching. That is because, though the market is not yet fully installed, it has already ensured that polytechnics and colleges are conceived, managed, funded and measured as business machines. Teaching is simply one of those unmeasurable 'goods' – a by-product of the management, accountancy and computer systems experts, which are the only categories of staff to have actually increased.

What we are outlining here, then, is a philosophy, a model, a strategy – the elements of a new social regime. If expressed in cookbook terms, the recipe would go something like this (*Mrs Thatcher's Cookbook*, price £200 from *Marxism Today*'s Cookery Department): First, take your institution by the scruff of the neck and 'cap' it. Secondly, detach or float off as many operations as possible. If necessary, break the power and authority of any representative arrangement still attached to the carcass. Then, using market mechanisms, induce or squeeze people and services out of the public into the private system, which you should have ready at hand. Season and eat. That is the Model.

Then comes the Strategy. Send in the Thatcherite shock troops, in three waves. The first is the new echelon of managers who, whatever their private political inclinations (they are all, of course, honourable people, kind to their families and dumb animals), function as the New Model Army. Their task is to restore managerial prerogative, break the power of the professionals and their ethic, and restructure the institutions along market lines. They operate at the coal face of the system, and are responsible for the day-to-day implantation of the new habits, routines, disciplines, the language of calculation, the fine tactical decisions, which gradually *institutionalise* the new 'regime'. These hired technicians of the Thatcher Revolution now operate in every sector, and they speak that metallic discourse of 'managerialism' which is the main product of the business schools which have mushroomed in every educational institution.

The second wave consists of businesspeople, who must be recruited into the governing strata. Their task is to tutor and educate public institutions into the mysteries of market calculation. It needs to be added that, since the British business class is the most ill-educated, the least intellectually formed and the most deeply philistine governing class in the Western world, this move – fulfilling an old dream of that wily reprobate Lloyd George – is the equivalent of recruiting a whole generation of Benthamite simplifiers into positions of strategic power and influence. There they now sit, in their pinstripe shirts and detachable white collars, in the few minutes they can spare from lunching and launching their own market-driven enterprises, guardians of the entrepreneurial re-education of schools, colleges, polytechnics, universities, hospitals, arts councils, public services and amenities. They are shortly to inspect schools – a task given them by that renowned expert in classroom pedagogy, Mr Clarke, no doubt as a reward for the breadth of their intellectual achievements. They may not know much but at least they know what they like …

The 'third wave' consists of the 'independent consultants', called in to advise on implementing 'efficiency' measures. Though invited to conduct objective reviews, they are not only deeply imbued with the managerialist ethic, but are usually well-apprised before they start of the 'improvements' which the institution which invited them in desires to make. Surprise, surprise – that is exactly what they discover these institutions 'need' – a beautifully logical and self-fulfilling exercise. They have the advantage of giving 'cuts' a spuriously impersonal air and thus lend the imposition of 'market forces' a veneer of legitimacy.

These 'independent consultants' sometimes seem to have become an 'official' arm of the implantation of a market regime in every institution in the country. Anyone who does not recognise the main outlines and consistency of the 'model' and the 'strategy' just outlined either does not work in a large public institution, or is not in touch with the strategies which now govern them or with how they are being reshaped. Most people spend their waking hours learning the new language of incentives, cost-effectiveness, quality audits, performance indicators and the rest of the managerial newspeak, in which the crude calculus of market forces is covered over by the thin fig leaf of systems analysis mumbo-jumbo and quack psychology. Ways of thinking, formulating strategies and defining objectives which reflect the actual practices they are engaged in have become 'lost languages', and a whole new form of institutional non-speak has been born.

One institution of higher education recently, discussing the lack of adequate planning for new courses, expressed this problem as a failure 'to think with any clarity about the nature and delivery of our product portfolio'. It is just over a decade since these were referred to as 'courses' and the customers for whom they are being designed 'students' and the activity 'education'. And not a shot has yet been fired ...

It is this utterly transformed landscape over which Labour is preparing to 'take power', hoping to graft a few humane considerations onto a world which has been fundamentally remodelled. It is hoping to find the humane heart of a welfare society beating still beneath the Thatcherite veneer. And so it may be.

But our public institutions are not simply underfunded. They lack a strategic place in the scheme of things. And they now operate according to a completely different logic. The plain fact is that the left has nothing remotely like a 'social philosophy' which it can state in anything remotely resembling the pithy, memorable and succinct form of Thatcher's which we quoted earlier.

And the fact that Major lacks one too is no consolation. He has been driven back by the horrendous social calamities which face every modern society which tries to sustain modernity by 'market forces' alone. But, though he has tried out a few alternatives (the classless society, the citizen's charter), they lack conviction, because, unlike Thatcherism, they are not harnessed to any deep institutional logic or strategy. So Majorism is an un-hegemonic project, as much pulled along in the slipstream of the Thatcher revolution, which is still unrolling, as the left.

An alternative is not, of course, easy to dream up or snap into place. The left, for example, cannot simply *reverse* Thatcher's 'There is no such thing as society', since it cannot any longer subscribe to the proposition that 'there is no such thing as the individual, there is only society'. For this would be to return to exactly the simplifying, essentialising collectivism which such very diverse forces as Thatcherism, 'actual existing socialism' and the diversity and differentiation of modern life, between them, have dismantled.

One of the problems about the current NHS debate, for example, is that, faced with the imposition of the market model and its manifest inequalities, we are tempted to pretend that all was well with it before. But we know that this was not the case. It is not simply that the old styles of state ownership and management of the public sector are politically out of favour for the time being: they have failed to provide the scale and range of services, the models of control and accountability, the flexibility and sensitivity to consumer needs in a diversifying society, or the innovations, that would have allowed them to keep in touch with modern developments. Nor is this simply because they were bureaucratic and inefficient as well as unwieldy, defensive and undemocratic to their 'clients': as we have seen with the collapse of the communist experiment, the flaws of the state-managed economy and society are profound and extensive, and any left alternative cannot now avoid confronting that historic failure.

The problem is that, having faced up to that unpalatable fact, many people fell back on an uncritical acceptance of 'markets'. But their anti-social side effects have not simply withered away. We have not squared up to or pushed beyond this impasse. In fact, all markets operate on the basis of prior, non-market conditions of existence. They always need to be subject to real, wide-ranging and effective regulation. Above all, they need to be harnessed and framed by a much wider *social strategy*, one that can be materialised in terms of an actual institutional regime.

Since at least the emergence of mass democracy and perhaps before then, *the* critical issue of modern politics is and remains the balance between public and private forms (and spheres) of regulation. Feminist debate has demonstrated both how complex this line is in modern societies and how deceptive is the notion of a clear-cut, mutually exclusive boundary between them. The lesson now needs to be applied to our thinking about 'the public sphere'. Without this, many of the excellent and innovative ideas about how to redesign particular sectors of public life (such as those in *MT*'s excellent issue on the subject) lack any unifying principle or overarching strategy.

We have not yet conducted any deep or searching discussion on where the line between the private and the public is to be redrawn: which areas are to be principally regulated by which principle and how the 'private' is to be overdetermined by some wider social logic. We do not know what forms of regulation are capable of submitting the laws of the market to this more general strategic social conception; or – more important, from the point of view of the argument advanced here – what an alternative public 'regime of regulation' would look like and the institutional models by which it is to be instituted.

We know 'the social' exists. But we do not know, in post-state socialist modern societies, how to calculate it. This is now the most important agenda item for the left.

Our mongrel selves

1992

THE GREAT DISCOURSES of modernity – in this respect marxism no less than liberalism, both, in their different ways, Enlightenment 'grand narratives' – led us to expect, not the revival but the gradual disappearance of the nationalist passion. Attachments to nation, like those to tribe, region, place, religion, were thought to be archaic particularisms, which capitalist modernity would, gradually or violently, dissolve or supersede. Globalisation, drawing more and more of the globe into the net of the capitalist market, is, of course, no recent phenomenon. It has been going on since the Spanish and the Portuguese initiated the West's 'encounter' with the Rest at the end of the fifteenth century. The recent integration of financial systems, the internationalisation of production and consumption, the spread of global communications networks, is only the latest – albeit distinctive – phase in a long, historical process.

However, this has not necessarily resulted in the destruction of those specific structures and particularistic attachments and identifications that go with the more localised communities that a homogenising modernity was supposed to replace. Of course, the forces of capitalist modernity, in their combined and uneven development, have radically dislocated the societies into which they penetrated. But the so-called 'logic of capital' has operated as much through difference – preserving and transforming difference (including sexual difference) – as by undermining it.

The engine of this expansionist history was the European nation state, with its well-defined territorial boundaries, national economies and increasingly national cultures. Of course, side by side with this were the flows – of capital, goods, labour – between and across national frontiers. As Immanuel Wallerstein has observed, 'At the very moment that one has been creating national cultures, each distinct from the other, these flows have been breaking down national distinctions'.

This tension between the tendency of capitalism to develop the nation state and national cultures and its transnational imperatives is a contradiction at the heart of modernity that has given nationalism and its particularisms a peculiar significance and force at the centre of the so-called new transnational global order. Negotiating this contradiction was one of the key conjuring tricks of Thatcherism; and it was the failure to resolve it – the illusion that Britain could snatch the goodies of a 'single market' without sacrificing an inch of national sovereignty, or 'Englishness' as a cultural identity, to the European idea – that finally dethroned Mrs Thatcher and has brought her successor to the brink of the post-Maastricht abyss.

Paradoxically, globalisation seems to have led to a strengthening of 'local' allegiances and identities. One result has been a slow, if uneven, erosion of the 'centred' nationalisms of the west European nation state and the strengthening of both transnational relations and local identities. Two features of this very uneven process have been the re-valorisation of smaller, subordinate nationalisms and movements for national and regional autonomy by precisely those groups whose identities were subsumed under what Ernest Gellner calls the 'political roof' of the big nation states; and the parallel growth of a defensive reaction by those national cultures that see themselves threatened culturally from their peripheries. At the same time as this has been going on in western Europe, we have seen the break-up of the Soviet Union and eastern Europe, and the revival of ethnic nationalisms among peoples submerged for decades within the super-nationalism of the Soviet sphere of influence. This seems to reflect a complicated double-movement – the attempt by these emerging peoples to reconstitute themselves as nations representing both a reaction against the Soviet and state-socialist past, and a hope, which may turn out to be illusory, that 'nationhood' is the only passport or entry-ticket they have to the new west European prosperity.

Hence the confusing spectacle of what we may call ascending and descending nationalisms, locked in a sort of combined-and-uneven double helix. It seems clear that, despite the often over-rationalist expectations favoured by the internationalist perspectives of the left, nationalism is not only not a spent force; it isn't necessarily either a reactionary or a progressive force, politically. To quote Ernesto Laclau, nationalism 'has no necessary political belongingness'. It is capable of being inflected to very different political positions, at different historical moments, and its character depends very much on the other traditions, discourses and forces with which it is articulated. The nationalisms of 'small nations', which are produced as the counter-discourses to exploitation and cultural colonisation and linked with critical cultures and political traditions, have a very different political meaning and trajectory from those that have been generated as the historical reaction against imposed state socialism, but have reappeared in political cultures with strong ethnic or religious absolutist traditions. There is no question that the decline of the centralised nation states, with their incorporating cultures and national identities, implanted and secured by strong cultural institutions, which tend to subsume all differences and diversity into themselves, presents an unprecedented opportunity for smaller nationalisms to realise their aspirations for autonomy in new, more effectively self-governing arrangements. Nevertheless, it is important to acknowledge that the drive to nationhood in many of the 'ascending' small nationalisms can often take the form of trying to construct ethnically (or culturally, religiously or racially) closed or 'pure' formations, in the place of the older nation states or imperial formations to which they belonged; or, in Gellner's terms, of trying to realise the aspiration, which they see as the secret of success of the great nation states of western modernity, of gathering one people, one ethnicity, under one political roof.

But the history of the nation states of the west has never been of this ethnically pure kind. Without exception, as Daffyd Elis Thomas pointed out again recently, they are without exception ethnically hybrid — the product of conquests, absorptions of one people by another. It has been the main function of national cultures, which are systems of representation, to represent what is in fact the ethnic hotch-potch of modern nationality as the primordial unity of 'one people'; while that of their invented traditions has been to project the ruptures and conquests, which are their real history, backwards in an apparently seamless and unbroken continuity towards pure, mythic time. What's more, this hybridity of the modern nation state is, in the present phase of globalisation, being compounded by one of the largest forced and unforced mass migrations of recent times. So that, one after another, western nation states, already 'diaspora-ised' beyond repair, are becoming inextricably multicultural — mixed ethnically, religiously, culturally and linguistically. Yet many of the new nationalisms are busy trying, often on the basis of extremely dubious myths of origin and other spurious claims, to produce a purified 'folk' and to play the highly dangerous game of 'ethnic cleansing'. Here, the real dislocated histories and hybridised ethnicities of Europe, which have been made and remade across the tortured and violent history of Europe's march to modernity, are subsumed by some essentialist conception of national identity, by a surreptitious return to 'tradition' – often of the 'invented' kind, as Hobsbawm and Ranger define it – that recasts cultural identity as an unfolding essence, moving, apparently without change, from past to future.

Lest we think that this kind of ethnic absolutism is restricted to the Balkans, which west Europeans have always thought unfit to govern themselves, we must remember that versions of it are alive and well in the old 'modern' nation states. In the face of the proliferation of cultural difference, and the multi-ethnic character of the new Britain, and threatened on the other side by the encroaching trauma of an emerging European identity, we have seen over the past decade a particularly defensive, closed and exclusive definition of 'Englishness' being advanced as a way of warding off or refusing to live with difference – a retreat from modernity that no exercise in managerial newspeak or the 'new entrepreneurialism' can disguise or deflect. Confronted by an openly racist far right in France or Germany, the British are apt to be smoothly superior and complacent. Nevertheless, the particular forms of cultural racism that have grown up under Thatcherism's shadow condense into a single discourse questions of race and ethnicity and questions of nation, and national and cultural belonging. The so-called 'Tebbit test' indicates the way in which 'cultural belongingness' (an exclusive form of ethnicity) has replaced genetic purity and functions as the coded language for colour.

As Paul Gilroy observed in *There Ain't No Black in the Union Jack*:

> A form of cultural racism which has taken a necessary distance from crude ideas of biological inferiority now seeks to present an imaginary definition of the nation as a unified cultural community. It constructs and defends an image of national culture, homogeneous in its whiteness, yet precarious and perpetually vulnerable to attack from enemies within and without.

Something of the same fear of difference can be seen, in different forms, everywhere in the 'new Europe', as the most heterogeneous

peoples hastily cobble together some unitary European cultural identity as a shield, not only against neighbours with whom they have
lived peacefully for centuries, but also against north Africans, Turks
and others drawn to Europe from the peripheries. These tendencies have their respectable allies and supporters here, and their not
so respectable shock-troops elsewhere in Europe, as those displaced
by the destruction of indigenous economies, the pricing out of crops
and the crippling weight of debt, as well as by poverty, drought and
warfare, buy a one-way ticket and head across borders to a new life in
the west.

Raymond Williams repeatedly affirmed what he called the 'rooted
settlements' – 'lived, worked and placeable social identities' – to set
off against the 'abstractions' of modern national cultural identities.
With unerring accuracy, his writings place who or what is responsible
for these dislocations, against which national identity is summoned as
a reliable defence: 'It is, in the modern epoch, capitalism which has
disrupted and over-ridden natural communities and imposed artificial
orders. It is, then, a savage irony that capitalist states have again and
again succeeded in mobilising patriotic feelings in their own forms
and interests.'

The persistent emphasis in Williams on 'actual lives' in 'knowable
communities' is salutary in the current post-Maastricht confusion. For,
much as one may support the shift from a narrow little-Englandism
to a broader European perspective, one has also to acknowledge that
the idea that, overnight, something called a 'European identity' could
be willed into being at the behest of a single market represents a
conception of culture and an understanding of the mechanisms of
social identification so shallow that it deserves the come-uppance
the Danes so tellingly delivered in their referendum. The more one
'believes in Europe' – or, to put it more accurately, the more the
question of Europe appears to be a contested concept worth struggling
over and around – the more important are the questions of Which
Europe? What is European culture? Whose European identity? – and,
indeed, of how and whether it might be possible to be 'black and
European'. Williams saw the dangers of constructing a spuriously
unified cultural identity and falsely continuous national history when
the real history is one of ruptures and discontinuities – 'industrial
conflict within rapid economic development and agrarian conflict
within impoverishment, depopulation and marginalisation'. National

cultural revival, he insisted, requires 'the working through of a history among now radically dislocated and subordinated people, rather than the fortunate resurgence of a subdued essence'. Nevertheless, his emphasis on 'actual and sustained social relationships' as the principal basis of identification and cultural 'belongingness' presents many difficulties, which take us back to that original stress, in Williams's work, on culture and community as 'whole ways of life'. Whose way? Whose life? One way or several? Isn't it the case that, in the modern world, the more we examine 'whole ways of life', the more diverse, and cut through by complex patterns of similarity and difference, they appear to be?

Modern people of all sorts and conditions, it seems to me, have had, as a condition of survival, to be members, simultaneously, of several, overlapping, 'imagined communities'; and the negotiations between and across these complex borderlines are characteristic of modern identity itself. Lest one view this capacity to live in and negotiate several 'worlds' at once as a sign of the modern alienated condition, a burden laid on the post-modern, western nomadic subject alone, it is worth recalling that the burden of 'double consciousness' that W.E.B. Du Bois identified was the burden of consciousness of the slave, and his/her descendants, who, as C.L.R. James observed, are obliged to be 'in western civilization, who have grown up in it, yet are not completely a part of it'.

In *Towards 2000*, Williams discusses the response of the white working-class man to what he calls – too euphemistically by half – 'the most recent immigrations of more visibly different peoples', and the angry confusions and prejudices that are triggered when, as he puts it, the blacks (for it is them – us – who are the 'visibly different peoples') 'intersect with the most selective forms of identity'. He acknowledges that the reaction to the presence of foreigners easily slides into specifying this 'otherness' as black. But he objects to this always being labelled 'racism', and especially to what he calls the 'standard liberal reply' – 'But they are as British as you are' – which, he argues, is to employ 'a merely legal definition of what it is to be British':

> It is a serious misunderstanding when full social relations are in question to suppose that the problems of social identity are resolved by formal definitions. For ... an effective awareness of social identity depends on actual and sustained social relationships. To reduce

social identity to formal definitions at the level of the state is to collude with the alienated superficialities of 'the nation' ... which are the limited functional terms of the modern ruling class.

This passage seems to me to contain a series of powerful truncations and ellipses, and it is therefore no surprise that, in a now famous exchange in *There Ain't No Black in the Union Jack*, Paul Gilroy, quite correctly, fastened on it as representing in its implications a racially exclusive form of social identity, and a sign of the degree to which Williams's work, like so much other thinking on the left, remains both blind to questions of race and framed by certain unexamined 'national' cultural assumptions. As Gilroy asked, how 'full' must 'full social relations' be? How 'actual' are the social relationships between blacks and whites in many inner-city communities and how 'sustained' do they have to be to include equality of respect?

It is true that social identity cannot be reduced to formal legal definitions. But if you are a black woman trying to secure rights of citizenship from the local DSS office or an Asian family running the gauntlet of the immigration authorities at Heathrow, 'formal legal definitions' matter profoundly. They cannot be made conditional on cultural assimilation. Since cultural diversity is, increasingly, the fate of the modern world, and ethnic absolutism a regressive feature of late-modernity, the greatest danger now arises from forms of national and cultural identity – new or old – that attempt to secure their identity by adopting closed versions of culture or community, and by the refusal to engage with the difficult problems that arise from trying to live with difference. The capacity to live with difference is, in my view, the coming question of the twenty-first century. New national movements that, in their struggle against old closures, reach for too closed, unitary, homogeneous and essentialist a reading of 'culture' and 'community', will have succeeded in overcoming one terrible historical hurdle only to fall at the second.

I feel compelled to close, as it were, from another place – that of the millions of displaced cultures and fractured communities of the south, who have been moved from their 'settled communities', their 'placeable feelings', their 'whole ways of life'. They are the products of the new diasporas, obliged to inhabit at least two identities, to speak at least two languages, to negotiate and translate between them.

In this way, though they are struggling in one sense at the margins of modernity, they are at the leading edge of what is destined to become the truly 'late-modern' experience. They are the products of the cultures of hybridity. They bear the traces of particular cultures, traditions, languages, systems of belief, texts and histories that have shaped them. But they are also obliged to come to terms with and make something new of the cultures they inhabit, without simply assimilating to them. They are not and will never be unified in the old sense, because they are inevitably the products of several interlocking histories and cultures, belonging at the same time to several 'homes' – and thus to no one, particular home.

Salman Rushdie, who should know, has remarked, 'having been borne across the world … they are translated men'. They are the product of a diasporic consciousness. They have come to terms with the fact that in the modern world identity is always an open, complex, unfinished game – always under construction. It moves into the future through a symbolic detour through the past, produces new subjects, who bear the traces of the specific histories, traditions and identities that not only formed them but enable them to produce themselves anew and differently. To quote Rushdie again from his *Imaginary Homelands*:

> *The Satanic Verses* celebrates hybridity, impurity, intermingling, the transformation that comes of new and unexpected combinations of human beings, cultures, ideas, politics, movies, songs. It rejoices in mongrelisation and fears the absolutism of the Pure. Melange, hotch-potch, a bit of this and that, is how newness enters the world. It is the great possibility that mass migration gives the world and I have tried to embrace it. *The Satanic Verses* is for change-by-fusion, change-by-co-joining. It is a love-song to our mongrel selves.

PART 3 NEOLIBERALISM

The great moving nowhere show

1998

WHAT IS THE political character of the Blair regime? Is New Labour a radically new response to the core political issues of our time? Is its perspective as broad in sweep, modern in outlook and coherent as Thatcherism's neoliberal project, only different – because it is breaking decisively with the legacy and logic of the Thatcher years? Or is it a series of pragmatic adjustments and adaptive moves to essentially Thatcherite terrain? Since taking office, New Labour has certainly been hyperactive, setting policy reviews in place here, legislating and innovating there. A careful audit of the achievements and failures of these early years remains to be made. But that is for a different occasion. Here, we want to stay with 'the big picture'. Where is New Labour really going? Does Mr Blair have a political project?

Thatcherism, from which Mr Blair has learned so much, certainly did have a project. Its aim was to transform the political landscape, irrevocably: to make us think in and speak its language as if there were no other. It had a strategy – an idea of where it wanted to get to and how to get there. Mrs Thatcher had no fondness for intellectuals: the word 'ideas' did not trip lightly off her tongue. Nevertheless, everything she did was animated by a social 'philosophy'. From a reductive reading of Adam Smith, she learned to see individuals as exclusively economic agents. From Hayek, she learned that the social good is impossible to define and that to try to harness markets to social objectives led down a one-way slippery slope to the nanny state, misguided social engineering, welfare dependence and moral degeneration – 'There is No Such Thing As Society'. From the monetarists she learned market fundamentalism: markets are 'good' and work mysteriously to the benefit of all; they are self-instituting and self-regulating entities;

market rationality is the only valid mode of social calculation, 'market forces must prevail!'

What is more, she armed herself with a decisive analysis of the points of historical change which had created the opening to Thatcherism. But she did not, like some versions of the 'Third Way', simply project the sociological trends on to the political screen. She never supposed Thatcherite subjects were already out there, fully formed, requiring only to be focus-grouped into position. Instead, she set out to produce new political subjects – Entrepreneurial Man – out of the mix of altruism and competitiveness of which ordinary mortals are composed. Above all she knew that, to achieve radical change, politics must be conducted like a war of position between adversaries. She clearly identified her enemies, remorselessly dividing the political field: Wets v Drys, Us v Them, those who are 'with us' v 'the enemy within'.

When *Marxism Today* first began to discuss Thatcherism as a 'project', smart-arsed journalists and Labour analysts joined forces to pour scorn on the idea – a thought altogether too concerted and 'continental' for the empiricist temper of British political culture. Geoff Mulgan (Director of Demos, former *MT* contributor and now in the Number 10 Policy Unit) advances a similar view elsewhere in this issue.[1] 'Meta-political' questions, he says, are irrelevant – a sign that the left intellectuals who ask them are hopelessly isolated from the 'real' business of government. They would be better employed, like Demos, thinking up concrete proposals which New Labour could put into effect.

Guilty British academics on the left are particularly vulnerable to this kind of gross anti-intellectualism. However, Mulgan's position seems disingenuous. Of course, policy innovation is essential to any political strategy – that is why Martin Jacques dreamed up the idea of Demos in the first place. There is lots of room for lateral thinking. But – Mr Blair's Rendezvous With Destiny notwithstanding – May 1997 was not the start of 'Year Zero'. All questions of perspective and strategy have not been 'solved'. As Decca Aitkenhead put it recently, the Blairites sometimes behave as if 'Number 10 is sorted for nuts and bolts; it's just not sure what sort of machine they add up to'. In fact, it's impossible to know how radical and innovative a concrete proposal is until you know which strategy it is attempting to put in place and the criteria against which its 'radicalism' is being assessed. Without a strategic framework, the 'concrete proposals' could be brilliant; or they could simply be off-the-wall – completely batty. In recent months. Demos has offered us plenty of both kinds.

In fact, seen in the context of New Labour's sustained hype and vaunting ambition over the past eighteen months, Mulgan's idea that nothing requires serious attention apart from pragmatic effectiveness is not only wrong but curiously 'off-message' and wholly out of synch with His Master's Voice. It was clear from the outset that Mr Blair saw himself in the Thatcherite mould and he has worked hard to model himself on her style of leadership. And with some success! Recent polls suggest the electorate is impressed with 'what they regard as the strong Thatcherite style', though they also seem unsure whether this is anything more than 'better gloss, more PR and spin' and, more worryingly, they doubt that New Labour 'will make a real difference and force a clean policy break with the Tory years'.[2] Mr Blair has also modelled his ambitions to make everything in Britain 'New' on Thatcherism's project of national self-renewal. Consequently, these days, no New Labour spokesperson opens his/her mouth, nor journalist reports the event, without reference to 'the Blair project'. It is New Labour, not the intellectuals, who put this 'meta-political' question on the agenda. It is Blair who talks of New Labour in apocalyptic terms – 'one of the great, radical, reforming governments of our history', 'to be nothing less than the model twenty-first century nation, a beacon to the world', 'becoming the natural party of government'. ('Natural parties of government' are those whose ideas lead on all fronts, carrying authority in every domain of life; whose philosophy of change has become the common sense of the age. In the old days we used to call them 'hegemonic'.) Mr Blair is definitely into 'the vision thing'.

New Labour's latest bid to give 'this vision thing' historic credibility and so to capture and define 'the big picture' is the 'Third Way'. This comes in several shapes and sizes. There is the intellectual's version of the 'Third Way' offered by Anthony Giddens, Mr Blair's most influential intellectual, which sketches out a number of significantly novel sociological shifts which seem to have major political consequences. Many of these one would be happy to agree with or to debate further.

After all, economic globalisation is a reality and has transformed the space of operations and the 'reach' of nation states and national economies. There is a new individualism abroad, due to the growing social complexity and diversity of modern life, which has undermined much of the old collectivism and the political programmes it underpinned. Many problems do present new challenges or assume new forms not well covered by the old political ideologies. We do need to broker a new relationship between markets and the public good, the individual and the community. These sociological shifts are part of the great historical rupture – the onset of late-late-modernity – which Thatcherism first mastered politically but certainly did not originate or set in motion. This is where *Marxism Today*'s 'New Times' analysis and its call for the reinvention of the left began, all those years ago. So much is indeed shared territory.

But when we move from the intellectual to New Labour's more political and strategic version of the 'Third Way', we are less on the terrain of political strategy and more, as Francis Wheen recently observed, in some 'vacant space between the Fourth Dimension and the Second Coming'. The 'Third Way' has been hyped as 'a new kind of politics'. Its central claim is the discovery of a mysterious middle course on every question between all the existing extremes. However, the closer one examines this, the more it looks, not like a way through the problems, but a soft-headed way around them. It speaks with forked, or at the very least garbled, tongue. It is advanced as a New International Model to which centre-left governments around the world are even now rallying. However, when it is not rapturously received, it suddenly becomes, not 'a Model', just a 'work in progress'. Can it be both heroic and tentative? It cannot make up its mind whether its aim is to capture 'the radical centre' or to modernise 'the centre left' (and should not therefore be surprised to find young voters placing its repositioning as clearly 'centre right'!). It claims to draw from the repertoires of both the new right and social democracy – but also to have transcended them – to be 'beyond right and left'. These shifting formulations are not quite what one would call a project with a clear political profile.

In so far as one can make out what it is claiming, does it offer a correct strategic perspective? The fact – of which the 'Third Way' makes a great deal – that many of the traditional solutions of the left seem historically exhausted, that its programme needed to be radically overhauled, and that there are new problems which outrun its analytic framework, does not mean that its principles have nothing to offer to the task of political renewal on the left. Welfare reform is only one of many areas where there is a continuing debate between two clearly competing models, drawing on, if not identical with, the two great traditions that have governed political life: the left-of-centre version, looking for new forms in which to promote social solidarity, interdependence and collective social provision against market inequality and instability; and the neoliberal, promoting low taxes, a competitive view of human nature, market provision and individualism. Can the 'tough decisions' on welfare which New Labour have been 'taking' for eighteen months really be 'beyond left and right'? Or is that a smoke-screen thrown up to evade the really hard questions of political principle which remain deeply unresolved.

One of the core reasons for the 'Third Way's semantic inexactitude – measured by the promiscuous proliferation of such troubling adverbs as 'between', 'above' and 'beyond' – is its efforts to be all-inclusive. It has no enemies. Everyone can belong. The 'Third Way' speaks as if there are no longer any conflicting interests which cannot be reconciled. It therefore envisages a 'politics without adversaries'. This suggests that, by some miracle of transcendence, the interests represented by, say, the ban on tobacco advertising and 'Formula One', the private car lobby and John Prescott's White Paper, an ethical foreign policy and the sale of arms to Indonesia, media diversity and the concentrated drive-to-global-power of Rupert Murdoch's media empire, have been effortlessly 'harmonised' on a Higher Plane, above politics. Whereas, it needs to be clearly said that a project to transform and modernise society in a radical direction, which does not disturb any existing interests, and has no enemies, is not a serious political enterprise.

The 'Third Way' is hot on the responsibilities of individuals, but those of business are passed over with a slippery evasiveness. 'Companies', Tony Blair argues in his Fabian pamphlet *The Third Way*, 'will devise ways to share with their staff the wealth their know-how creates'. Will they? The 'Third Way' does observe accelerating social inequality but refuses to acknowledge that there might be structural interests preventing our achieving a more equitable distribution of wealth and life chances. As Ross McKibbin recently remarked, although most people 'do believe that society should be based on some notion of fairness', they also believe 'that the rich and powerful can only be made to acknowledge this by political action'. The 'Third Way's discourse, however, is disconcertingly devoid of any sustained reference to power. Mr Blair is constantly directing us, instead, to 'values'. But when one asks, 'which values?', a rousing but platitudinous vagueness descends. He can be very eloquent about community, an inclusive society, with the strong supporting the weak, and the value of facing challenges together. The problem arises when this communitarian side of the Blair philosophy meets head-on the equally authentic, rocklike, modernising, targeting, moralising streak in 'Blairism'. In practice it is difficult to believe fervently in 'the politics of community' and at the same time to hold unshakably to the view that the task of government is 'to help individuals to help themselves', especially when the ways of implementing each so often point in diametrically opposed directions. Besides, as a timely *Guardian* editorial observed: 'What distinguishes governments of the centre left is not their values ... but their perennial dissatisfaction with what markets – necessary as they are – produce.'

It therefore seems most unlikely that the shifting indecisions and ambiguous formulations of the 'Third Way' offer us clear guidelines for assessing the underlying thrust of the Blair political project. For an answer to our original question, we will need to look at the Blair performance overall, sifting the strong tendencies from the ebb and flow of everyday governance, trying to disinter from its practice its underlying political logic, philosophy and strategic direction.

In the global context, New Labour has brought a sweeping interpretation of globalisation, which it regards as the single most important factor which has transformed our world, setting an impassable threshold between New Labour and Old, now and everything that went before. This is crucial because, in our view, it is its commitment to a certain definition of globalisation which provides the outer horizon, as well as a dubious legitimacy, to Mr Blair's whole political project.

New Labour understands globalisation in very simplistic terms – as a single, uncontradictory, uni-directional phenomenon, exhibiting the same features and producing the same inevitable outcomes everywhere. Despite Giddens's strictures, New Labour does deal with globalisation as if it is a self-regulating and implacable Force of Nature. It treats the global economy as being, in effect, like the weather. In his speech to the Labour Party conference. Mr Blair portrayed the global economy as moving so fast, its financial flows so gigantic and so speedy, the pace at which it has plunged a third of the world economy into crisis so rapid, that its operations are now effectively beyond the control of nation states and probably of regional and international agencies as well. He calls this, with a weary finality, 'the way of the world'.

His response is to 'manage change'. But it seems that what he really means is that we must 'manage ourselves to adapt to changes which we cannot otherwise control' – a similar sounding but substantively very different kettle of fish.

This accounts for the passivity of the Blair government, despite its pivotal role in Europe and leading position in the G7, etc, in the face of the current crisis in Asia, Russia and elsewhere. It continued until very late to reiterate the false reassurances that the Asian crisis would have little noticeable effect on Britain. It has shown a surprising lack of flexibility in the face of mounting evidence to the contrary. It seems content to reiterate the mantra: 'The goal of economic stability and stable inflation will never be abandoned or modified. New Labour is not for turning' – which sounds increasingly like a desperate struggle to win, not the present, but the last war.

It has signally failed to seize the advantage of the rapidly changing terms of macro-economic debate to offer early, effective or radical leadership to the international community, as one country after another deserts the neoliberal ship and moves towards thinking the unthinkable – that the unregulated movement of currency and capital, aided and abetted by de-terrestrialised corporate power and new technology, will, if left to the 'hidden hand' of macro-economic forces alone, bring the whole edifice crashing to the ground. His belated proposals for the reform of the IMF are far from radical. Paradoxically, it is the high priests of global neoliberalism – Jeffrey Sachs, Paul Krugman and George Soros – not Blair and Brown, who have led the retreat towards regulation.

New Labour appears to have been seduced by the neoliberal gospel that 'the global market' is an automatic and self-instituting principle, requiring no particular social, cultural, political or institutional framework. It can be 'applied' under any conditions, anywhere. New Labour therefore seems as bewildered as every neoliberal hot-gospeller that Japanese bankers don't actually behave like Wall Street bankers, and that if you dump 'the market' into a state-socialist society like Russia without transforming its political institutions or its culture – a much slower and more complex operation – it is likely to produce, not Adam Smith's natural barterers and truckers, but a capitalist mafia. As Andrew Marr shrewdly observed, 'It's the politics, stupid!'

Since globalisation is a fact of life to which There Is No Alternative, and national governments cannot hope to regulate or impose any order on its processes or effects, New Labour has accordingly largely withdrawn from the active management of the economy (in the long run, Keynes is dead!'). What it has done, instead, is to set about vigorously adapting society to the global economy's needs, tutoring its citizens to be self-sufficient and self-reliant in order to compete more successfully in the global marketplace. The framing strategy of New Labour's economic repertoire remains essentially the neoliberal one: the deregulation of markets, the wholesale refashioning of the public sector by the New Managerialism, the continued privatisation of public assets, low taxation, breaking the 'inhibitions' to market flexibility, institutionalising the culture of private provision and personal risk, and privileging in its moral discourse the values of self-sufficiency, competitiveness and entrepreneurial dynamism.

Economic Man or as s/he came to be called, The Enterprising Subject and the Sovereign Consumer, have supplanted the idea of the citizen and the public sphere. As the government's *Annual Report* boldly reminded us: 'People are not only citizens, they are also customers'. The government's most significant breaches in this neoliberal edifice have been the statutory minimum wage and the Working Time directive – commitments it would have been difficult for New Labour to have abandoned. It has, however, set the minimum wage at the lowest politically-negotiable level, excluding the sector most at risk to structural unemployment – young people between 18 and 21.

Giving the Bank of England its independence may have been a good idea. But only a touching faith in economic automatism can explain why this meant restricting its brief, effectively, to one dimension of economic policy only – inflation – with, in effect, only one tool of economic management – interest rates. It suggests that Labour has been quietly seduced by the neoliberal view that, as far as possible, the economy must be treated like a machine, obeying economic 'laws' without human intervention. In practice, what is gained in credibility by being able to say – 'The Government is not involved! Rising interest rates, an over-valued currency, falling order books and rising regional unemployment have nothing to do with us. They are unfortunate "facts of life" which folks must simply put up with. You can't buck global trends!' – is lost in terms of strategic control. Whether New Labour acknowledges this or not, its effect is automatically to prioritise meeting inflation targets over everything else. The irony is that it is precisely the whole structure of neoliberal, scientistic jiggery-pokery which is rapidly falling apart. Economies are not machines. Changes in one sector have knock-on consequences elsewhere. The hedge-funds equations which have kept the inflated bubble of futures, options and derivatives markets afloat are liquefying. The infamous monetarist 'natural rate of unemployment', which enabled banks and governments to calculate the necessary unemployment 'costs' for a given level of inflation, has fallen into disrepute. The Bank of England itself says that 'it cannot be directly measured and changes over time'. The Federal Reserve long ago sacrificed it on the altar of jobs and growth.

On the domestic front, the policy repertoire seems at first sight more diverse, but has tended to follow the same tendential groove. The main emphasis has been thrown on to the supply side of the equation. There have been many commendable social-democratic interventions. But its key watchwords – 'Education and Training, Training and Education' – are driven, in the last analysis, less by the commitment to opportunities for all in a more egalitarian society, and more in terms of supplying flexibility to the labour market and re-educating people to 'get on their bikes' when their jobs disappear as a result of some unpredictable glitch in the global market. New Labour does not and cannot have much of an industrial economic policy. But it can and does expend enormous moral energy seeking to change 'the culture' and produce new kinds of subjects, kitted out and defended against the cold winds that blow in from the global marketplace.

To this source also we must trace the remoralisation of the work ethic, and the restoration of that discredited and obscene Victorian utilitarian distinction between 'the deserving' and 'the undeserving' poor. The New Deal subsidises training and Mr Blunkett attacks class sizes and expands nursery places for lone parents willing to seek employment – very commendable, and about time too. New Labour will not, however, intervene to ensure that there are jobs, though its entire welfare reforms are riveted to work and paid employment. Since it must depend on the private sector to provide them, it can only morally exhort. Hence the paradox of Jack Straw holding parents exclusively responsible for their children's misdemeanours, while Welfare-to-Work insists that anyone who can move and wants to draw a benefit must leave their children, get up off their sick beds, overcome their disability, come back out of retirement and work. Not since the workhouse has labour been so fervently and single-mindedly valorised.

Social inequality, broadly defined, is one of the critical defining issues of national politics and a crucial test of the distinction between the Blair project and market fundamentalism. According to Giddens, in his book *The Third Way*: 'The gap between the highest paid and the lowest paid workers is greater than it has been for the last 50 years'; and, though 'the majority of workers are better off in real terms than 20 years ago, the poorest 10 per cent have seen their real incomes decline'. This is no aberration. It follows a period of the most intense 'marketisation'. It is what markets do – the kind of Will Hutton, 40/30/30 society which markets 'naturally' produce when left to themselves. What's more, the nature of poverty has changed, becoming more diverse, while its causes have multiplied. The term 'social exclusion' draws attention to these differences, and underlines the fact that income and economic factors are by no means the only reason different groups find themselves excluded from the mainstream of society. There is, however, considerable evasiveness, both in Giddens's argument and in New Labour's appropriation of it, around the question of how important the income/economic factor in 'social exclusion' is and what to do about it. Giddens's bald statement that 'exclusion is not about gradations of inequality' looks like a sentence in search of a 'not only' that went missing.

These issues are at the heart of New Labour's profound ambiguity and duplicity around welfare reform. After months of a Great Debate, and a disastrous and aborted effort to begin to put 'it' into effect, we are still really none the wiser about what Mr Blair really thinks or proposes to do about welfare. We do not know whether he proposes to transform the welfare state to meet its broader social purposes more effectively, or intends to go down in history as the politician with the 'courage' to wind up the welfare state as the basis of the social settlement between the 'haves' and the 'have-nots' which has kept twentieth-century capitalist societies relatively stable and free of social violence. 'Reform' is the weasel-word, the floating signifier, which masks this gaping absence.

He says welfare is not reaching those who are most in need. True: but it does not follow that 'targeting', as such, is the correct overall strategy. He says Britain, in a global economic context, cannot financially sustain it. But he does not make anything of the fact that the UK is about fifteenth in the world league table of social security spending. He treats the present level of wealth distribution as a Natural

Law rather than a political outcome. He believes welfare is bad for us, corrupting our morals and inducing us to commit crime. But the actual level of fraud is one of the most contested social statistics, and the Fraud Office systematically fails to produce the missing millions. There is as much evidence that the really poor, of whatever kind, can't live decently on the level of benefits they are offered, and that many are thereby driven to crime, as there is for the proposition that millions of people are making a 'lifestyle choice' to live on benefit in perpetuity. He promises the poor not social justice (that is a bridge too far) but 'social fairness'. But his actual image of the citizen is of the lonely individual, 'set free' of the state to face the hazards of the global weather alone, armed against incalculable risk, privately insured up to the hilt against every eventuality – birth, unemployment, disability, illness, retirement and death – like those lean urban 'survivors' on their mountain bikes who haunt our streets, their chocky bar, Evian water-bottle and change of trainers in their knapsacks. Man as 'poor, bare, fork'd animal', isolated and at bay before the elements.

Mr Blair represents his welfare reforms as a continuation of the spirit of Beveridge, but this is simply not the case. For Beveridge understood that welfare systems reflect and have profound effects on the wider social framework. He knew that the principle of 'social insurance' was not only efficient but a way of underwriting citizenship; that 'universalism', despite its costs, was essential to binding the richer sections of society into collective forms of welfare. He anticipated Galbraith's argument that the whole system would be in danger as soon as the rich could willingly exclude themselves from collective provision by buying themselves out. Why should they go on paying for a service they had ceased to use? This potential 'revolt of the elites' is, of course, the critical political issue in welfare reform. The establishment of a two-tiered system, with the richer sectors buying themselves into private provision, is what helps to fix in stone the political threshold against redistribution. It destroys the public interest in favour of private solutions dictated by wealth inequalities, and must drive what is then left in the residual 'public' sector to the bottom, perpetually in crisis and starved of investment, while propelling those who are left out to the margins.

This 'law' is already manifest in education – though New Labour systematically refuses to confront it. Buying the children out of public education and into the selective private system has become a habitual middle-class pastime, in which New Labour's own leaders have indulged as light-heartedly as any other ordinary, unreflective, Thatcherite, possessive individual. 'Targeting', 'selectivity', and 'means testing', which Mr Blair has surreptitiously slid into place as his great 'principles of reform', are destined, as surely as night follows day, to deepen already existing inequalities, to increase marginalisation and social exclusion, to divide society into two unbridgeable tiers and further fragment social integration and reciprocity. Hence the muffled confusion surrounding the Harriet Harman/Frank Field fiasco.[3] Mr Field bats with the best of New Labour in terms of self-righteous moralism about poverty and the desire to do to people things which are good for their souls. His Methodist spirit is riveted by the fantasy of the great Demon Fraud and the Feckless Work-shy. But he understood that the principles of contributory social insurance and 'universalism' had to be preserved, however modified their forms; that a network of voluntary agencies could only be introduced if regulated, underpinned and enforced by the state. He believed that benefits must provide, not a residual but a decent standard of life for those who qualify for them; and that the costs of transition from one form of delivering these principles to another had to be borne. These were the 'unthinkable' thoughts for which he was dismissed. The debate about how much, in what form, with what effects, therefore, remains to be had. Tiered universalism, combinations of public/private contributory solutions, etc, remain to be debated. There is work for Demos to do! But only after the principles of reform have been openly and thoroughly debated.

It is deeply characteristic of the whole style of the Blair project that Great Debates are announced which do not actually take place. Instead of a clear and open laying-out of the alternatives, we have a massive public relations and spinning exercise, and policy forums to speak over the heads of the much-abused 'experts and critics', direct to selectively chosen members of the Great British Public. There may be an open invitation to participate, to join the consultation. But this openness is effectively closed by Mr Blair's own already-settled conviction that he is Right – what Hugo Young called 'his unfreighted innocence, wide-eyed rationality and untroubled self- belief'. When in difficulties, the party faithful – about whom he is a less than devoted admirer – are summoned to hear the message, not to state their views. The Labour Party, as an organisation within which these profound matters of strategy may gain, through debate, some broader resonance in terms of the everyday lives and experiences of ordinary folks, and genuinely be modified or win consent, has been ruthlessly emasculated. A terrifying and obsequious uniformity of view has settled over the political scene, compounded by a powerful centralisation of political authority, with twenty-something Young Turks beaming out ill-will from ministerial backrooms, the whole caboodle under surveillance from Millbank and cemented in place by a low-flying authoritarianism.

The Labour benches have, with a few honourable exceptions, been the most bedazzled by the hope of preferment, the most obsequious of all. Critics, welcomed at the front door, are systematically discredited through innuendo, and spin-doctored at the back door as being trapped in a time warp, if not actually barking mad. Anyone who does not pass the loyalty test is labelled with the ritual hate-word, 'intellectual', gathered into one indiscriminate heap – those who called for the reinvention of the left while Mr Blair was still, metaphorically, in his political cradle lumped in with Trotskyist wreckers – and the whole shooting-match branded as 'Old Labour'. 'Bring me the head of Roy Hattersley!'

Against a majority of people on the left, *Marxism Today* argued that bringing the Labour Party into the late twentieth century and transforming many of its traditional habits and programmes were necessary, if traumatic, events. But the reduction of the party to a sound-box is quite another thing. It reveals, to borrow a phrase of Martin Kettle's, how far the demotic has triumphed over the democratic in the New Labour project. The attempt to govern by spin (through the management of appearances alone), where you 'gloss' because you cannot make your meaning clear; New Labour's systematic preference for media reality over sterner political realities; indeed, the constant hype about 'hard choices' coupled with the consistent refusal to make them – all are part of the same phenomenon. This is not a superficial 'style' we don't much like, but something that goes to the heart of the Blair project.

Despite all the promising talk about decentralisation and participation, the commitment to devolution and constitutional reform – which are significant – one gets the queasy feeling that New Labour increasingly finds the rituals of democratic practice tiresome, and in practice, if not formally, would be happy to move in the direction of a more 'direct', plebiscitary, referendum style of governance. The project is consistently more 'populist' than 'popular'. This is not the populism of Mrs Thatcher's neoliberal right, but it is a variant species of 'authoritarian populism' none the less – corporate and managerialist in its 'downward' leadership style and its moralising attitude to those to whom good is being done. It's also deeply manipulative in the way it represents the authority it poses as somehow 'empowering us' – another triumph for 'customer services'.

The same can be said of New Labour's sense of agency – of who exactly are the political subjects in whose image the Blair Revolution is made. Many of us responded to his election as leader of the Labour Party with the same optimism we greeted the nomination of Bill Clinton. Not because we agreed with everything he believed, or properly knew what it was he did believe, but because he was of the generation who had lived through the Thatcher-Reagan era, through the 1960s and the social and cultural revolutions of our time. We hoped he would respond – however much we might disagree in detail – with sensibilities informed by these late-modern experiences. How wrong we were. The Blair social project is 'modernising' but modern only to a very limited extent.

His key social constituency in the run up to the election was 'Middle England' – a profoundly traditionalist and backward-looking cultural investment. His discourse on the family, social values and diversity remains deeply conventional. Middle England commands some votes. But as a characterisation of New Labour's political subject, it is the repository of English traditionalism, irredeemably small-'c' conservative. As Jonathan Freedland recently reminded us, Middle England is a place of the mind, an imagined community, always located somewhere south or in the centre of the country, never north – though Mr Mandelson has recently put in a claim for Hartlepool Man. Middle England is peopled by skilled, clerical or supervisory grade home-owners, never manual workers or public sector professionals. It is committedly suburban, anti-city, family-centred, devoted to self-reliance and respectability. Its cultural icons, he argues, are 'Neighbourhood Watch, Gordon's Gin, Enid Blyton, Ford Mondeo, Hyacinth Bucket, *The Antiques Roadshow*, Nescafe Gold Blend, Acacia Avenue, Scouts and Brownies, Nigel Kennedy and the Salvation Army'. Its voice is the *Daily Mail*.

Since the election, we have heard less of 'Middle England' and more of 'The People'. This is the great body unknowns, the Essex Lads, the 'Babes', *hommes et filles moyen sensuels*. 'The People', Jonathan Freedland argues, are the imagined subject of phrases like the 'People's priorities', the Lottery as the 'People's money', the 'People's Princess'. The People are definitely not the 'working classes' or the 'underclasses' or the 'chattering classes' or manual workers or lone parents or black families or trade unionists or public sector workers or Labour Party rank-and-file members, come to that. Their desires must be flattered: 'wooed' rather than 'represented'. They are spoken to rather than speaking. When not watching GMTV or Sky Sport, they are to be found in focus groups. The People, Nick Sparrow remarks, 'are those who matter once every five years'. Their voice is *The Sun*.

Then there are The Businessmen. The longer New Labour governs, the more it cosies up to Business, reinventing itself in full-dress corporate disguise. Mr Blair is constantly to be seen in their company. Visually, he is exclusively associated with Success, a dedicated follower of celebrity, which is the modern form of the success story. He looks decidedly uncomfortable in the company of the poor. No doubt a Labour government needs support from the business community. But New Labour's relentless wooing of the new business nouveaux riches is nothing short of abject. Businessmen can do no wrong. Their logo adorns every Labour Party conference delegate's name-tag ('Serving the community nationwide' – courtesy of Somerfield supermarket). Their ads will soon be beamed into every classroom that is wired up to the National Grid for Learning. Their expertise is required on every public, regulatory or advisory body. They are the 'wealth creators', whose salaries are beyond control, dictated by some extra-terrestrially defined 'rate for the job': the big spenders, the off-shore investing 'patriots', the Mercedes-Benz and Don Giovanni crowd, with a finger in every share-option deal and a luxury pad in every global city. The fact that, comparatively speaking, they are set fair to also being the most poorly educated, philistine, anti-intellectual, short-termist and venal 'business class' in the western world does not seem to matter.

In an ill-advised attempt to appropriate the spirit of the new British cultural revival, there was, briefly, 'Cool Britannia'. But it was short-lived. The energy levels here proved too high, the swing too wild and unmanageable, the rhythms too loud, the fashion too see-through, the culture too 'multi-cultural', too full of clever creative folk, too subversive, too 'Black British' or 'Asian cross-over' or 'British hybrid' for New Labour's more sober, corporate-managerialist English style. This was definitively not the 'modernity' towards which Britain required to be 'modernised'.

Finally, in recent weeks, an 'enemy' has surfaced on New Labour's social stage. These are 'the intellectuals', or, as Mr Blair charmingly characterised them, the 'chattering classes'. Recently, he declared himself to have been 'never a partaker of the chattering classes'. Critics and whingers to the backbone, this lot 'pocket everything that they do like and then moan about the 10 things they don't like'. He clearly found it difficult to keep the tone of exasperation out of his voice. The 'sneer squad', as he dubbed them, occupy the forbidden zone of Radio 4, *The Guardian*, *The Observer*, *Newsnight*, *Channel 4 News*. They are outside the circle of influence, 'below the radar'. There is little doubt that the readers of *Marxism Today* belong firmly to the lower circles of this encampment.

It will inevitably be said that this account has been unfairly selective. What about all the good things New Labour has set in train – the peace deal in Northern Ireland, incorporating Human Rights into British legislation, the minimum wage, family tax credit, expanding nursery places, the school and hospital building programme, breaking the tide of Euro-scepticism, the move towards devolution, constitutional reform? Of course, these initiatives are welcome. They add up to a substantial claim on our support. There are many others which point in the right direction, which we should support, though their implementation may be controversial. These include some of the proposals for urban renewal, the efforts to reach through to some of the deep, underlying causes of social exclusion in communities, and the general commitment to improve standards in education – though whether letting Chris Woodhead, Thatcherism's chief Enforcer, loose to brow-beat schools and abuse teachers is the best approach to the latter objective one begs leave to doubt.

The momentous landslide victory of May 1997 was indeed an historic opportunity, inviting New Labour to the difficult task of facing up to the complexities of historical change and at the same time, offering an alternative political strategy, different from and breaking decisively with the neoliberal project, which was, internationally, the first – but cannot be forever the last. And they don't keep coming back, offering you a second chance. So in answering the big questions about the Blair project, one has had to be ruthlessly selective and go for the strategic choices, trying to identify the persistent tendencies: what seems to be the underlying framework of assumptions, the shaping 'philosophy'.

The picture is ambiguous. There are still counter-arguments to hear. New Labour remains in some ways an enigma, and Mr Blair, either despite of or because of his ceaseless efforts to talk a project into place, paradoxically appears both 'bold' and 'vacillating'. But having held one's breath and crossed one's fingers, it is necessary to speak it as it looks. New Labour, faced with a near-impossible historic task, has not fully confronted its challenge. Instead, it has been looking for easy – 'Third' – ways out, craftily triangulating all the troubling questions, trying to finesse the difficulties. It may therefore turn out to be a half-way decent Labour government, one which one would have been grateful to have in 'normal' circumstances. The times – and the task – however, are exceptional. And the higher the spin doctors pump up the balloon, the more firmly one becomes aware how much of it is hot air.

What we knew after Thatcher was that the new right could respond to the new historical conditions, though the results of its attempt to do so were an unmitigated disaster. But could the left? The left was certainly not in good shape when New Labour took office. However, the fact is that Mr Blair does not seem to have any deep political roots in its hopes and traditions. He is in some ways a modern man, at ease with some of the changes which now characterise our world. But, politically, he is essentially a post-Thatcherite figure, in the sense that the experience of Thatcherism was, it seems, his shaping and formative political experience.

So, try as he may to find an alternative ground on which to stand, he finds the imperatives of a soft Christian humanism more compelling; its cadences come to him more naturally than those of the centre left. He is an able and clever politician and has become a clever, even to some a charismatic, leader. Just now he is basking in the power a landslide majority has conferred on him. And, far from betraying his principles, he seems totally and honestly persuaded that what he is doing is right. He has and will continue to make many important adjustments to the legacy he inherited. There is also a genuine humanity which one would have been unwise to put any money on in Mrs Thatcher. They are similar figures, but they are not the same.

However, the difficult truth seems to be that the Blair project, in its overall analysis and key assumptions, is still essentially framed by and moving on terrain defined by Thatcherism. Mrs Thatcher had a project. Blair's historic project is adjusting Us to It. That touches half – the modernising part – of the task, as *Marxism Today* argued it.

But the other, more difficult, half – that of the left reinventing a genuinely modern response to the crisis of our times – has been largely abandoned. At the global and domestic levels, the broad parameters of the 'turn' which Thatcherism made have not been radically modified or reversed. The project of renewal thus remains roughly where it did when *Marxism Today* published its final issue. Mr Blair seems to have learned some of the words. But, sadly, he has forgotten the music.

Notes

1. Geoff Mulgan's piece in the special 1998 issue was entitled 'A Whinge and a Prayer', and was included as a dissenting voice.
2. *The Guardian*, 28 September 1998.
3. Frank Field was welfare reform minister in Blair's first government, working under Harriet Harman, who was Secretary of State for Social Security. The two clashed, and in a 1998 reshuffle both were removed from their posts.

New Labour's double-shuffle

2003

THE LABOUR ELECTION victory in 1997 took place at a moment of great political opportunity. Thatcherism had been decisively rejected by the electorate. But eighteen years of Thatcherite rule had radically altered the social, economic and political terrain in British society. There was therefore a fundamental choice of directions for the incoming government.

One was to offer an alternative radical strategy to Thatcherism, attuned to the shifts which had occurred in the 1970s and 1980s; with equal social and political depth, but based on radically different principles. Two basic calculations supported this view. What Thatcherism seemed to have ruled out was both another bout of Keynesian welfare-state social democracy, Wilsonian-style, and another instalment of old-style nationalisation. More significantly, Thatcherism had evolved not just an effective occupancy of power, but a broad hegemonic basis for its authority. This 'revolution' had deep philosophical foundations as well as an effective popular strategy. It was grounded in a radical remodelling of state and economy and the 'colonising' of civil society by a new neoliberal common-sense. Its effects were 'epochal' (i.e. defined a new political stage).

This was not likely to be reversed by a mere rotation of the electoral wheel of fortune. The historic opportunities for the left required bold, imaginative thinking and decisive action in the early stages of taking power, signalling a new direction. Critical to this was a 'transitional programme' – a few critical examples, popular but radical, like raising taxes to repair the destruction of the social fabric, a re-invention of the state education system and the reversal of the very unpopular privatisation of rail – to be introduced at once, chosen for their indicative significance.

As critics, we had concentrated on this Thatcherite reconstruction of the political/ideological terrain. On this, we were fundamentally right.

But we may have underestimated the degree to which all this was itself related to much deeper global shifts – the new post-industrial society, the struggle by capital to restore its 'right to manage', the 'globalisation' of the international economy (which was its way out of that impasse), the technological revolution and the rise of a new individualism and the hegemony of neoliberal free-market ideas. This was the sea-change which overtook the world in the 1970s. It still constitutes the 'horizon' which everybody – including the left – is required to address.

The other choice was, of course, to adapt to Thatcherite/neoliberal terrain. There were plenty of indications that this would be New Labour's preferred direction: Peter Mandelson's book, for example, and the revisionist ideas peddled in this triumphalist phase by the New Labour intelligentsia – 'differences between left and right are obsolete'; 'there is no alternative' (to neoliberal globalisation); 'we have no objection to people becoming filthy rich' – provided clear evidence of the kind of re-thinking in progress in inner New Labour circles.[1] Certainly one had no illusions about what 'taking power as New Labour and governing as New Labour' implied. Martin Jacques and I wrote an article for *The Observer* called 'Thatcherism With a Human Face?' on the Sunday before the 1997 election, which cast us irrevocably into outer political darkness. We knew that, once squandered, such a moment would be lost for many years, perhaps forever. We had a strong premonition that New Labour had already made strategic choices which put it irrevocably on the second track.

And so it turned out. In a profound sense, New Labour has adapted to neoliberal terrain – *but in a significant and distinctive way*. Its critics are still not sufficiently clear about what the nature of that adaptation is. Its novelty – if not in terms of what it consists of, then in how the elements are combined – is not well understood. Still, it took only a few weeks in 1997 for the basic direction to become crystal clear: the fatal decision to follow Conservative spending priorities and commitments, the sneering renunciation of redistribution ('tax and spend'), the demonisation of its critics ('Old Labour'), the new ethos of managerial authoritarianism ('We know that we are right'), the quasi-religious air of righteous conviction ('Either for us or against us'), and the reversal of the historic commitment to equality, universality and collective social provision.

The welfare state had been Labour's greatest achievement, then savaged and weakened under Mrs Thatcher. Its deconstruction was to be New Labour's historic mission. The two-tier society, corporate greed and the privatisation of need were inevitable corollaries. This was glossed positively as 'modernisation' – who could possibly be against it? The linguistic operation – generating a veritable flowering of Third Way waffle, double-talk, evasions and 'spin', depending on which audience was being addressed – was critical to the whole venture.

The prime minister's recent claims that New Labour's reforms of schools and hospitals (i.e. the re-introduction of selectivity and creeping privatisation) are 'firmly within Labour's historic battle for social justice', or that foundation hospitals are fully in line with the efforts of Nye Bevan to create a universal NHS which would de-commodify health care – that such hospitals are *really* designed to 'give power back to local communities' rather than to open the door to private investment – are only the most recent, blatant examples. The shamelessness of this widespread evasiveness – being economical with the truth as a principle of government – and the profound contempt for the electorate it implies, has gone far to corrupt the whole political culture. Cynicism and political apathy have inevitably followed. (New Labour 'spin' has it that falling electoral participation is a sign of mass contentment. But what is the point of voting, if the result is a New Labour administration which agrees with the Tories on fundamentals, only with bells on?)

New Labour does have a long-term strategy, 'a project': through what Antonio Gramsci called a process of 'transformism', the aim is to adapt social democracy from above into a particular variant of free-market neoliberalism. However, it remains fashionable to deny that anything like a project is at work here. Even the disenchanted cling desperately to the hope that English pragmatism will prevail. New Labour's reasoned critics – Roy Hattersley, Frank Dobson, Chris Smith, Bill Morris, even Polly Toynbee – remain 'loyal' (but to what?). They look hopefully for signs that New Labour will of its own accord – now that the second term is spinning out of control, perhaps in the third? – refashion itself into something different. The key thing to say about New Labour is that its so-called 'pragmatism' is the English face it is obliged to wear in order to 'govern' in one set of interests while maintaining electoral support in another. It isn't fundamentally pragmatic, any more than Thatcherism was – which doesn't mean that it isn't constantly making things up on the run. In relation to the NHS, Mrs Thatcher too was pragmatic in the short run ('The NHS is safe in our hands!'), but strategically an anti-pragmatist. As with the miners, she knew when to withdraw in order to fight again, more effectively, another day.

Pragmatism is the crafty, incremental implementation of a strategic programme – being flexible about the way you push it through, giving ground when the opposition is hot, tactically revising your formulations when necessary. (Having given us 'the enabling state' and the celebration of 'risk', the distinguished Third Way guru Anthony Giddens now effortlessly slips us on to 'the ensuring state' – as more businesses absolve themselves of their pensions obligations.) Pragmatism requires modestly shifting the emphases to catch the current political wind, saying what will keep traditional 'heartland' supporters happy ('It can come across a bit technocratic, a bit managerial' – the PM), whilst always returning to an inflexible ideological base-line ('the fundamental direction in which we are leading the country is correct' – the PM). Of course, there will be a thousand scams and devices dreamed up by New Labour's blue-skies policy-wonks, as 'government is re-invented' – for that is the mission of the policy-advisers-turned-civil-servants in the No.10 policy, strategy and innovation units, and the New Labour-inclined 'think-tanks' (the IPPR, Demos). But unerringly, at the strategic level, the project returns to its watch-words: 'wealth-creation', 'reform' and 'modernisation'.

There is a dominant strategy or logic at work here, and fundamentally it is neoliberal in character. Thus New Labour has worked – both domestically and globally (through the institutions of 'global governance' such as the IMF, the WTO, the World Bank, etc) – to set the corporate economy free, securing the conditions necessary for its effective operation at home and globally. It has renounced the attempts to graft wider social goals on to the corporate world. (Will Hutton's project of 'stake-holder power' lasted all of five minutes.) It has deregulated labour and other markets, maintained restrictive trade union legislation, and established relatively weak and compliant regulatory regimes. The rail regulator, for example, cuts train services and raises fares in order to make rail more 'efficient'; it mainly serves as the conduit for substantial public subsidies to inefficient private firms, taking the risk out of investment, but still cannot find a public alternative to the railways' fragmented structure. The new broadcasting regulator's main purpose seems to be to dismantle the barriers which currently prevent global interests like Murdoch from buying at will into and monopolising British press and media channels.

New Labour has spread far and wide the gospel of 'market fundamentalism' – markets and market criteria as the true measure of value. It has 'cosied up to business', favouring its interests in multiple public and private ways (from the Formula One cigarette advertising scandal onwards). The trend to inequality has grown exponentially during its administrations, escalating towards American proportions. 'The rich now have a bigger share of the nation's post-tax income than at any time under Mrs Thatcher' (Michael Meacher). It has protected corporate boardroom greed, and promoted business influence in shaping social agendas favourable to its interests at the heart of government (the connections of those advising the government on GM and environmental issues with pharmaceutical and bio-technology corporate interests have only just come to light). It has promoted the image of 'the businessman' and 'the entrepreneur' as *the* principal social role model, spreading the gospel of 'entrepreneurial values' ('efficiency', 'choice', 'selectivity') through the land. It has pursued a splendidly variable range of privatisations – sustaining the sell-off of critical public assets (transport, the London tube, air-traffic control, the postal services); forcing the public sector to 'mimic' the market in its internal operations, fatally blurring the public/private distinction (Public Finance Initiatives, public-private 'partnerships'); and stealthily opening doors for private investment in, and the corporate penetration of, parts of the public sector (the prison service, schools, the NHS). Every media debate as to whether the latest creeping privatisation is '*really* privatisation' is a form of trivial pursuit.

However, New Labour has adapted the fundamental neoliberal programme to suit its conditions of governance – that of a social democratic government trying to govern in a neoliberal direction while maintaining its traditional working-class and public-sector middle-class support, with all the compromises and confusions that entails. It has modified the classic anti-statist stance of American-style neoliberalism by a 're-invention of active government'. This is not a return to government as we have known it, but a revolution in 'governance'.[2] The term 'governance' is itself another shifty New Labour concept: not a synonym for 'government' but the signifier of 'a new process of governing, a changed condition of ordered rule', specifically designed to blur the difference between state and civil society.[3] As Paul Du Gay argues, this involves 'a new rationality of rule', in which 'political government has been re-structured in the name of an economizing logic'.

'Entrepreneurial governance', its advocates advise, promotes competition between service providers, favours the shift from bureaucracy to 'community', focuses not on inputs but on outcomes (delivery), redefines clients as consumers, decentralises authority through 'participatory management', and prefers market mechanisms to administrative ones.[4] Its neoliberal origins are hard to disguise. Far from breaking with neoliberalism, 'entrepreneurial governance' constitutes its continuation – but in a transformed way. 'To govern better the state is to govern less but more "entrepreneurially"' (Du Gay).

The entrenched New Labour orthodoxy is that only the private sector is 'efficient' in a measurable way. The public sector is, by definition, 'inefficient' and out of date, partly because it has social objectives beyond economic efficiency and value-for-money. It can only save itself by becoming more like the market. This is the true meaning of 'modernisation'. As Alan Finlayson argues, 'modernisation' is a loosely performative speech-act, in the sense that it 'acquires meaning and force only in the moment of its usage ... It is an "up" word, that makes things sound exciting, progressive and positive ... [Its] usage helps generate an appearance of structured and unified thinking ... It helps to render "natural" and un-contestable that which is not necessarily so'.[5]

Part of its purpose is to establish a permanent divide between new sheep and old goats. Public sector workers who oppose this drift are represented as immured in the past, seriously 'out of date' and therefore 'the enemy within'. They too must be 'modernised'. Of course, in fact they are grossly under-rewarded in relation to the private sector, and deeply excluded as partners in the drive to improve the services they actually deliver – the objects, but never the subjects, of 'reform'. The prime minister advised them to think of themselves more as 'social entrepreneurs'. Meanwhile, the whole concept of 'the public interest' and 'the public good' has collapsed. It too has been declared obsolete. New Labour's critics on the left or media commentators are too embarrassed to invoke it. The proposition that markets are the only measure of 'the social good' – advanced by Hayek, adopted by Mrs Thatcher and reinvented by New Labour – has been swallowed, hook, line and sinker. Marketisation is now installed in every sphere of government. This silent revolution in 'governance' seamlessly connects Thatcherism to New Labour. It is the code which underpins the 'jargon' which New Labour ministers spout in their sleep. It is uttered as 'truth' by New Labour's welfare intellectuals from the hallowed walls of places like the LSE.

The new managerialism

During the 1980s, sceptical critics used to ask how the analysis of Thatcherite ideology affected 'the real world'. One answer then – and it is now even more the case – is through the practices of management. Apparently simply a neutral social technology, 'The New Managerialism' is really the vehicle by means of which neoliberal ideas actually inform institutional practices. In New Labour's case, in the public sector, this is via the 'New Public Management' approach. This involves the marketisation of the state's governing and administrative practices, the transformation of public service individuals into 'entrepreneurial subjects' and the adaptation of the machinery of state to the 'mission' of 'entrepreneurial governance'. Central to this reconstruction of governance and the state is the enthusiastic adoption of a 'Public Choice' approach to the public sector. This 'shift[s] the balance of incentives [from input to delivery, and] … in Britain in the 1980s led to the contracting out of services, the spread of internal markets and outright privatisation' (*Making sense*, p111). It is the main source of the drive to reconstitute citizens as consumers.[6]

To its influence we now owe the boring repetition of 'choice' as one of the key 'modern' values in Tony Blair's discourse. Actually, there is no identified groundswell of public demand for more 'choice' in the abstract. Undoubtedly, many people would quite like to be able to choose a good secondary school for their children and an efficient hospital to be ill in, wherever they live and however rich or poor they may be – a quite different matter. However, repeating that 'choice' is a wide-spread demand is a way of making what is affirmed as a fact but is really only a prophecy, self-fulfilling, on the principle that 'those things which people can be made to believe is true will be "true" (i.e. "real") in their effects'. As the prime minister said, in a classic instance of Third Way gobble-de-gook, 'Choice enhances quality of provision for the poorest, helping to tackle inequalities while it also strengthens middle class commitment to collective provision'.[7] He added that the purpose of public service reform was 'to deliver in a modern, consumer-focused fashion'. As Catherine Needham rightly observed, 'ministers have begun to step back from the explicit language of consumerism and competition, while still continuing to endorse the principles behind them' (*Citizen-Consumers*, p25).

The New Public Management 'empowers' civil servants to abandon the principles of political impartiality and, like private-sector CEOs, 'take ownership' of their sectors, in a more 'agency-driven' style (the doctrine embodied in the famous 'Next Steps' document). It replaces professional judgement and control by the wholesale importation of micro-management practices of audit, inspection, monitoring, efficiency and value-for money, despite the fact that neither their public role nor their public interest objectives can be adequately reframed in this way. For this purpose, we require an army of managers, who know little of the content of their field, but everything about strategies of managerial control – and a regiment of consultants to advise clients how to 'creatively' fudge their monitors. More widely, it fosters the concerted drive to introduce corporate business leaders into every sector of public life in order to spread a climate favourable to 'entrepreneurialism'. As the private corporations and advisers on loan from business become more and more practically entrenched at the centre of government, and their representatives actively 'volunteered' at more local levels, so 'the corporate enterprise' itself becomes progressively *the new model of the state* ...

The state's 'educative' function combines intensive micro-management and centralisation of targets with more strategic interventions exercised 'culturally' and 'at a distance'. The latter is a neo-Foucauldian 'governmentality' approach – controlling behaviour and outcomes not by direct constraints but through the consent and 'freedom' of individuals (which may explain why neo-Foucauldians like Nikolas Rose are so favourably mesmerised by it). This approach does not require a mass conversion to entrepreneurial values (another error made by critics of our analysis in the 1980s). Instead, knowing that individuals can occupy various subject positions, the New Managerialism aims to reproduce all of us in the new position of practising 'entrepreneurial subjects', by fostering certain 'capacities' while down-grading others, shifting individual behaviour indirectly by altering the environment in which people work, and operationalising new values by 'modernising' old practices. You change what individuals do not by changing their minds but by changing their practices, and thus the 'culture'.

The wider point is to inculcate in the population at large a new *habitus* ('culture-change'): making into a new kind of common sense those habits and practices which the new 'free-market', consumer-focused conception of 'governance' requires. This approach is effective well outside the machinery of state. Slowly but surely, everybody – even if kicking and screaming to the end – becomes his/her own kind of 'manager'. The market and market criteria become entrenched as the *modus operandi* of 'governance' and institutional life. Media commentators and the press know no other language with which to address public issues. They may object to this or that piece of New Labour over-centralised 'managerialism', but seem unable to place the *logic* from which these arise. Democracy has long since faded as a practical ideal. Except in the banal form of 'liberal democracy', Tony Blair has not had a single thought on the subject over two terms in government. The general public seems to have swallowed this managerialist discourse whole.

The passing-off of market fundamentalism as 'the new common sense' has helped to drive home the critical lesson which underpins the 'reform' of the welfare state: the role of the state 'nowadays' is not to support the less fortunate or powerful in a society which 'naturally' produces huge inequalities of wealth, power and opportunity, but to help individuals themselves to provide for all their social needs – health, education, environmental, travel, housing, parenting, security in unemployment, pensions in old age, etc. Those who can – the new middle-class majority – must. The rest – the residuum – must be 'targeted', means-tested, and kept to a minimum of provision lest the burden threaten 'wealth creation'. This is what we used to call 'the one third/two thirds strategy', and is now referred to as 'the two-tier society'. New Labour, of course, says it cannot recognise the phenomenon. However, it is manifestly the lynchpin of public sector 'modernisation'. It sounds the death-knell to the old notion of 'the public realm', the social conception of the individual ('There is no such thing as society') and the basic social-democratic idea of collective provision.

A double regime

New Labour is therefore confusing in the signals it gives off, and difficult to characterise as a regime. It constantly speaks with forked tongue. It *combines* economic neoliberalism with a commitment to 'active government'. More significantly, its grim alignment with the broad global interests and values of corporate capital and power – the neoliberal project, which is in the *leading position* in its political repertoire – is paralleled by another, *subaltern* programme, of a more social-democratic kind, running alongside. This is what people invoke when they insist, defensively, that New Labour is not, after all, 'neoliberal'. The fact is that New Labour is a *hybrid* regime, composed of two strands. However, one strand – the neoliberal – is in the dominant position. The other strand – the social democratic – is subordinate. What's more, its hybrid character is not simply a static formation; it is the *process* which combines the two elements which matters. The process is 'transformist'. The latter always remains subordinate to and dependent on the former, and is *constantly being 'transformed' into* the former, dominant one.

How can we explain New Labour's double character? The political scientist Andrew Gamble long ago pointed out that left parties in government are often subject to contrary pulls – one towards realising their governmental programme, the other towards doing what is necessary to win electoral support and hold on to power. These frequently conflict. New Labour's subaltern programme is driven by the second of those imperatives. It is the necessary 'cost' of maintaining loyalty amongst its traditional supporters, whilst its governmental project favours a quite different set of interests. This is not necessarily just opportunistic calculation. Many Labour MPs have persuaded themselves that New Labour is still fundamentally attached to 'old' Labour values, which will somehow eventually reassert themselves; and the Blair government itself defends its massive departures from these old values by rhetorically 'spinning' its verbal continuity with them. It must therefore find space in its programme to address these subordinate pressures and constituencies – provided they are not allowed to derail the progress towards a more developed market state. Thus New Labour's 'balancing act', its two-step shuffle – and the way it has become mired in endless 'spin' in order to square the impossible circle.

There is another consideration. The full-blown neoliberal drive to the market state we saw in Thatcherism had its costs. Its brutalism antagonised many in society, including some of its original supporters. People thought neoliberalism 'red in tooth and claw' a step too far. Even many of Mrs T's most fervent converts eventually abandoned her for reasons of electoral calculation. But moving to the full blown market state via a subordinated social-democratic route has the advantage of addressing some of the problems of 'the residuals' and losers – those who are likely to benefit least from the neoliberal route. It also takes account of some of the 'costs' and the social upheaval which its 'transformism' will create. It is authentically a 'hegemonic' strategy, even though it may not be capable of producing a stable hegemonic outcome. It aims to win enough consent as it goes, and to build subordinate demands back into its dominant logic. Forging a plausible or pragmatic pathway from left to right, carrying a proportion of its old supporters with it on particular points, dividing and confusing the oppositions, and winning a measure of consent for the project, may serve to establish neoliberal society on firmer, less contested foundations. Certainly, the confusion which its double-headed strategy sows in its own ranks obscures the long-term objective and prevents a coherent and organised opposition from emerging. The social-democratic route to neoliberalism may turn out in the end to be what Lenin might have called 'the best shell' for global capitalism.

This subordinate part of the New Labour programme involves a certain measure of indirect taxation and redistribution, reforms like the minimum wage, family tax credits, inducements to return to work (the high visibility given to 'skills and training', however, is solidly in line with the neoliberal emphasis on 'the supply side'). To this we also owe, in the second term, the build up of concern about the delivery of public services, including a substantial injection of public funds into health and education. In a retrospective gloss, New Labour now suggests that the latter was always what it intended for its second term, but the evidence for this is not compelling. In its first term it systematically demonised the public sector and redistribution, and was consistently and unapologetically 'entrepreneurial'. Failing public services surfaced as an issue, unannounced and unanticipated, towards the end of the first term, around the time of the resignation of Peter Kilfoyle, when the disillusionment amongst New Labour's 'heartland' traditional supporters had reached fever pitch; it was clearly forced on to New Labour's political agenda from the outside.

Public service delivery in the second term is really the key to understanding how this hybrid New Labour regime functions. New Labour is committed to improving the delivery of public services. But its means of achieving this are impeccably 'new managerialist'. Redistribution, where it occurs, must be by stealth, lest a more vocal and organised constituency should develop around it. New Labour has set its stony face against enlisting public service workers and professionals in the enterprise. It refuses to countenance a return to a more full-blooded 'mixed' public/private regime (hence the unrelenting vendetta against Ken Livingstone about funding the tube). Instead, it has adopted the top-down managerialist approach of centralised control, supplemented by the rich panoply of 'the audit culture': the exponential expansion of public service managers over professionals at the coal face; unachievable targets; socially uninformative league tables; perpetual monitoring; moralistic 'shaming'; the merciless proliferation of pointless bureaucratic detail; the introduction of selectivity under the guise of 'diversity' (another piece of linguistic expropriation); vulgar hectoring by public sector ministers retrained in the new, 'bruiser school' of New Labour leadership (Prescott, Blunkett, Clarke, Reid); and the novel, contradictory strategy of 'tough love'.

In public service 'reform', how does the articulation of the subaltern 'social democratic' part of the repertoire with the dominant, neoliberal part operate? Every change in the public sector *must* be accompanied by a further tightening of the 'modernising' screw, as the unshakeable trade-off of a certain kind of 'reform'. The public think the aim here is 'better delivery'. The government knows that the price which must be paid for this is 'more modernisation'. Nothing – however good or necessary – is allowed to happen which is not accompanied by another dose of 'reform'. And the kind of 'reform' implied must meet the following criteria: (a) it must open the door to private investment or blur the public/private distinction; (b) it must meet market criteria of efficiency and value-for-money; (c) it must put managerial authority in command; (d) it must reform working practices in a less collective, more individualised direction; (e) it must stimulate competition and divide workers by introducing incentive pay schemes and undermining collective bargaining; (f) it must weaken the bargaining power of the unions; (g) it must reduce the size of the workforce and the cost of the service; (h) it must hold public sector pay in line well behind the private sector; (i) the service must be remodelled along 'two-tier' lines by introducing selectivity. In short, marketisation and privatisation, whether frontally or incrementally introduced, is what 'reform' now *means*. This type of 'modernisation' is the New Labour 'trade-off' for any kind of change.

Take the fire-fighters' dispute.[8] Of course, a modern fire service should function efficiently. Fire-fighters deserve to be well paid for the risks they take on our behalf, and in return should have their paramedical skills and professional levels enhanced. 'Spanish practices', where they exist, serve no useful social purpose. But New Labour is determined that they should not get a penny more unless and until they first submit to new forms of managerial control imposed from above, and at the cost of cuts in the labour force and the number of fire stations.

New Labour 'hybridisation' has its political antecedents. Its immediate ancestor is Clintonian triangulation. Clinton borrowed from the Democrats, borrowed from the Republicans, and moved the whole wagon-train further towards the market – a 'knight's move', or three-pronged shift, which was very influential in New Labour thinking in its early stages, and even more so when Clinton was able to bring off the much-envied prize of a second election victory. The essence of this 'transformism' game depends on pulling selectively, and in an ordered hierarchy, from opposing political repertoires, maintaining a double-address to their different 'publics', so that you can advance a 'radical' (sic) overall strategy of governance, on the one hand, while maintaining electoral support and securing a third term on the other. The subordinate agenda – redistribution, belated public investment, public service 'delivery', etc – has to do, essentially, with this second goal. That is the crucial 'double-shuffle' or 'triple-play' involved in the New Labour project. It delivers what Philip Bobbit calls 'the market state', or, more simply, a 'social democratic variant of neoliberalism' (in exactly the same way that Thatcherism delivered a 'neoliberal variant' of classic Conservatism). No prizes for identifying the common thread!

This is the principal reason why 'spin' is an essential and organic part of the New Labour project; it is not a surface excrescence, as many critics fondly suppose. 'Spin' has the obvious purpose of putting a favourable gloss on everything. It turns every argument, by a rhetorical sleight-of-hand, in New Labour's favour. It is a sign of the reduction of politics to public relations and the manipulation of public opinion. But 'spin' also has the much deeper function of 'squaring circles': re-presenting a broadly neoliberal project, favourable to the global interests of corporate capital and the rich, in such a way that it can mobilise the popular consent of Labour voters and supporters, the trades unions and the less-well-off in society. This sleight-of-hand can only be done by continuously *sliding* one agenda into or underneath another. The New Labour phenomenon of linguistic slippage is thus a function of its double-pronged mode of address. It spins the word 'reform', with its positive associations – the Reform Acts, the Factory Acts, the welfare state, etc – until it somehow becomes equivalent to its absolute opposite – marketisation! It masks the consistent shift of direction from public to private, by exploiting the vagaries of words like 'change' – or 'radical' – which can point in any direction (after all, even Mussolini made the trains run on time!). Choice, which is designed to introduce selectivity and the private sector, is represented as part of an anti-inequality strategy. 'Spin' mobilises a concept's positive resonances – and transfers this charge to a very different, usually contrary, idea.

Take the NHS. It remains 'free at the point of delivery' (actually, it isn't, but let that pass for a moment). Of course some public hospitals will now be built by private construction companies on PFI terms, whose real costs will only become clear two or three generations ahead, and some of its services will be delivered by private American or British pharmaceutical or health service companies to foundation hospitals which have been 'freed' to raise funds and compete for staff. Who cares that this is all at the expense of the general social provision of health care and the founding principle of universality, and will create a two-tier service? You foreground the pragmatic practicalities of 'delivery' in order to silence these other awkward questions about principle and purpose you would prefer not to have to answer. What 'delivery' presumes is that no-one any longer *cares* who owns, runs, controls or profits from, health-care, providing the possessively-individual consumer's personal need is satisfied. The reduction of the citizen to consumer, and the 'privatisation of need' at the centre of the market model, are thus the absolutely crucial but unspoken foundations to this strategy. New Labour not only banks on the fact that this shift has occurred, but is actively 'spinning' to bring it about. It is not a passive victim of sociological change but an active agent in its unravelling. If people think of themselves as having a stake in the NHS, then it matters to them who owns it, what principles inform its operation. But if they can be induced, by relentless 'spin', to think of the NHS only in the individualist terms of 'I need a better bed', or 'I need to move faster up the waiting list', then they won't mind who produces it or whether health becomes a lucrative site of private sector investment. It's simply one more 'market' response to consumer demand.

At the moment, the resistance to the New Labour project is coming mainly from the backwash of the invasion of Iraq and Blair's decision to commit Britain, wholesale and without qualification, as an ancillary support to the US drive to global hegemony. No account of the New Labour project would be complete without taking into account how its domestic programme fits into its global mission to push through a global neoliberal agenda and the dependency this has produced in the foreign policy and geopolitical domains. The account offered here is therefore incomplete. However, it does have a political purpose. The New Labour 'project' is a complex political initiative and we need to understand its complexities better than we do. The idea that it has simply, like Topsy, grown higgledy-piggledy by its own accord, is nonsense. Now that there are serious forces wishing to distance themselves from the overall goals, we need to build the different, particular points of opposition (the war, the US alliance, foundation hospitals, selectivity in education, private-public initiatives, the reconstruction of the NHS, the trade union opposition to privatisation, etc) into a more substantive and integrated critique, in order that a more concerted and coherent vision – and the political forces to make it popular and put it into effect – can emerge. The two years between now and the next election are just enough time to construct an alternative political project for/from the left. Failing this, beyond the election awaits a third installation of New Labour's double shuffle, or – Heaven forfend – IDS!

Notes

1. Peter Mandelson was one of the main architects of New Labour. He was co-author of *The Blair Revolution: Can New Labour Deliver?* Faber 1996; and *The Blair Revolution Revisited* (2nd ed), Politicos 2002.

2. See *Modernising Government White Paper*, HMSO 1999.
3. R. Rhodes, 'The New Governance: Governing without Government', *Political Studies* 44 1996.
4. David Osborne and Ted Gaebler, *Reinventing Government: How the Entrepreneurial Spirit is Transforming the Public Sector*, Addison Wesley 1992.
5. Alan Finlayson, *Making Sense of New Labour*, L&W 2003, p67.
6. For a critique, see Catherine Needham's pamphlet, *Citizen-Consumers*, Catalyst 2003.
7. Tony Blair, *The Courage of Our Convictions: why reform of the public services is the route to social justice*, Fabian Society 2002, p28.
8. The FBU were engaged in a bitter dispute with the Labour government from 2002 to 2003, which ended in a 16 per cent pay increase linked to imposed changes in working conditions. As a result of this the FBU disaffiliated from Labour in 2004. 'Spanish practices' refers to trade union practices – usually those that have developed over years of custom and practice – that give advantages to workers that are regarded as unjustifiable by management and, at times, broader publics.

The neoliberal revolution

2011

How do we make sense of our extraordinary political situation: the end of the debt-fuelled boom, the banking crisis of 2007-10, the defeat of New Labour and the rise to power of a Conservative-Liberal-Democratic Coalition? What sort of crisis is this? Is it a serious wobble in the trickle-down, win-win, end-of-boom-and-bust economic model which has dominated global capitalism? Does it presage business as usual, the deepening of present trends, or the mobilisation of social forces for a radical change of direction? Is this the start of a new conjuncture?

Gramsci argued that, though the economic must never be forgotten, conjunctural crises are never solely economic, or economically-determined 'in the last instance'. They arise when a number of contradictions at work in different key practices and sites come together – or 'con-join' – in the same moment and political space, and, as Althusser said, 'fuse in a ruptural unity'.[1] Analysis here focuses on crises and breaks, and the distinctive character of the 'historic settlements' which follow. The condensation of forces during a period of crisis, and the new social configurations which result, mark a new 'conjuncture'.

My argument is that the present situation *is* a crisis, another unresolved rupture of that conjuncture which we can define as 'the long march of the Neoliberal Revolution'. Each crisis since the 1970s has looked different, arising from specific historical circumstances. However, they also seem to share some consistent underlying features, to be connected in their general thrust and direction of travel. Paradoxically, opposed political regimes have all contributed in different ways to expanding this project.

The term 'neoliberal' is not a satisfactory one. Its reference to the shaping influence of capitalism on modern life sounds recidivist to contemporary ears. Intellectual critics say the term lumps together too many things to merit a single identity; it is reductive, sacrificing attention to internal complexities and geohistorical specificity. I sympathise with this critique. However, I think there are enough common features to warrant giving it a *provisional* conceptual identity, provided this is understood as a first approximation. Even Marx argued that analysis yields understanding at different levels of abstraction, and critical thought often begins with a 'chaotic' abstraction – though we then need to add 'further determinations' in order to 'reproduce the concrete in thought'. I would also argue that naming neoliberalism is *politically* necessary, to give resistance content, focus and a cutting edge.

Pragmatism may account in part for this scepticism about neoliberalism as a concept: English intellectuals often cannot see the practical efficacy of long-term, theoretical ideas. A discussion on, say, the principles behind capital punishment quickly degenerates into a debate on whether hanging, drawing or quartering best achieves the purpose. I recall that many refused to apply the term 'project' to Thatcherism and New Labour, though it was crystal clear that neither political formation had been instituted by sleep-walkers, driven by purely pragmatic imperatives. But in English common sense, pragmatism often rules.

The neoliberal model

What, then, are the leading ideas of the neoliberal model? We can only pull at one thread here. However anachronistic it may seem, neoliberalism is grounded in the 'free, possessive individual', with the state cast as tyrannical and oppressive. The welfare state, in particular, is the arch enemy of freedom. The state must never govern society, dictate to free individuals how to dispose of their private property, regulate a free-market economy or interfere with the God-given right to make profits and amass personal wealth. State-led 'social engineering' must never prevail over corporate and private interests. It must not intervene in the 'natural' mechanisms of the free market, or take as its objective the amelioration of free-market capitalism's propensity to create inequality. Harvey's book offers a useful guide.[2] Theodore, Peck and Brenner summarise it thus: 'Open, competitive and unregulated markets, liberated from state intervention and the actions of social collectivities, represent the optimal mechanism to socio-economic development … This is the response of a revived capitalism to "the crisis of Keynesian welfarism" in the 70s'.[3] (Capitalism's other response, incidentally, was to evade state intervention by 'going global'.)

According to the neoliberal narrative, the welfare state (propelled by working-class reaction to the depression of the 1930s and the popular mobilisation of World War II) mistakenly saw its task as intervening in the economy, redistributing wealth, universalising life-chances, attacking unemployment, protecting the socially vulnerable, ameliorating the condition of oppressed or marginalised groups and addressing social injustice. It tried to break the 'natural' (sic) link between social needs and the individual's capacity to pay. But its do-gooding, utopian sentimentality enervated the nation's moral fibre, and eroded personal responsibility and the over-riding duty of the poor to work. It imposed social purposes on an economy rooted in individual greed and self interest. State intervention must never compromise the right of private capital to 'grow the business', improve share value, pay dividends and reward its agents with enormous salaries, benefits and bonuses. The function of the liberal state should be limited to safeguarding the conditions in which profitable competition can be pursued without engendering Hobbes's 'war of all against all'.

Margaret Thatcher, well instructed by Keith Joseph, grasped intuitively Hayek's argument that the 'common good' either did not exist or could not be calculated: 'There is no such thing as society. There is only the individual and his (sic) family'. She also grasped Milton Friedman's lesson that 'only a crisis – actual or perceived – produces real change. When that crisis occurs the actions that are taken depend on the ideas that are around … our basic function [is] to develop alternatives to existing policies … until the politically impossible becomes politically inevitable'.[4] As the free-market think-tank, the Institute of Economic Affairs, observed during the rise of Thatcherism, 'the market is an idea whose time has come'. This could well be a Coalition vision-statement.

The welfare state had made deep inroads into private capital's territory. To roll back that post-war 'settlement' and restore the prerogatives of capital had been the ambition of its opponents ever since Churchill dreamt in the 1950s of starting 'a bonfire of controls'. The crisis of the late 1960s-1970s was neoliberalism's opportunity, and the Thatcher and Reagan regimes grabbed it with both hands.

Neoliberalism is also critical to contemporary geopolitics. Structural adjustment programmes have forced the 'developing world' to set market forces free, and open their economies to free trade and foreign investment, while promoting the 'liberal' virtues of elections, multi-party politics, the rule of law and 'good governance'. This was the prescription to bring about the 'liberal-democracy' that Francis Fukayama saw as marking the end of ideology and the fulfilment of the struggle for the good life. Western super-powers have consistently intervened globally to defend this model in recent decades.

It should be noted, of course, that neoliberalism has many variants. There are critical differences, for example, between American, British and European 'social market' versions; South East Asian state-supported growth and Chinese 'state capitalism'; Russia's oligarchic/kleptomaniac state; and the monetarist 'experiments' in Latin America. Neoliberalism is not *one* thing. It evolves and diversifies. Nevertheless, geopolitically, neoliberal ideas, policies and strategies are incrementally gaining ground, re-defining the political, social and economic model, governing the strategies and setting the pace.

As we have noted, neoliberalism's principal target in the UK has been the reformist social-democratic welfare state. Though this was a radically compromised formation, which depended on dynamic capitalist growth to create the wealth for redistribution, its full-employment objectives, welfare support systems, the NHS, and free comprehensive and higher education, transformed the lives of millions. In this model the state took over some key services (water, bus transport, the railways), but it was less successful in nationalising productive industry (cars, energy, mining).

The liberal heritage

Where do neoliberal ideas come from? Historically, they are rooted in the principles of 'classic' liberal economic and political theory. Here we can only outline the development of this body of ideas in summary, headline terms. Critical was the agrarian revolution, the expansion of markets (in land, labour, agriculture and commodities) and the rise of the first commercial-consumer society in eighteenth-century Britain. These arose on the back of successes in war, naval supremacy over continental rivals, the expansion of commerce, the conquest of India and a high point in the colonial slave plantation economies, which produced – often in conditions of un-free labour, violence and systematic degradation – commodities and profits for the metropolitan market: 'jewels in the crown', as the French called Saint-Domingue (Haiti) just before the Haitian Revolution.

Economically, its foundations lay in the rights of free men – 'masters of all they survey and captains of their souls' – to dispose of their property as they saw fit, to 'barter and truck', as Adam Smith put it, to make a profit and accumulate wealth, consulting only their own interests. Smith's *The Wealth of Nations* brilliantly 'codified' the economic model (using as an example no industrial enterprise larger than a pin factory!).

Marx once described this moment in the accumulation circuits of capital as 'the very Eden of the innate rights of man', the source of the lexicon of bourgeois ideas – freedom, equality, property and 'Bentham' (i.e. possessive individualism and self-interest):

> Freedom because both buyer and seller of a commodity ... are constrained only by their own free-will. They contract as free agents ... Equality because each enters into the relation with the other as with a simple owner of commodities and they exchange equivalent for equivalent. Property because each disposes of what is his own. And Bentham because each looks only to himself. The only force that brings them together and puts them in relation with each other is the selfishness, the gain and the private interests of each (*Capital*, 1, p112).

Political liberalism has its roots in the struggles of the rising classes associated with these developments to challenge, break and displace the tyranny of monarchical, aristocratic and landed power. Englishmen were born free: England was the true home of Liberty. This required the consent of free, propertied men to a limited form of state, and a leading position for them in society as well as wider political representation. Key moments were the Civil War; the execution of Charles I; the 'historic compromise' of the 'Glorious Revolution' of 1688; the successes of the rising mercantile classes in commerce and trade; and the loss of the American colonies, but then in consolation a Lockean-inspired Constitution for an American Republic of free propertied men. Then came 1789, the violence and excessive egalitarianism of the French Revolution, the successes of the Napoleonic Wars and the conservative reaction to civil unrest.

Industrialisation and the rise of manufacture followed in the nineteenth century: the 'disciplines' of waged labour, the factory system, the triumph of free trade, urbanisation and the industrial slum, as Britain became 'the workshop of the world'. Hobsbawm calls this triumph of the bourgeois classes, and of bourgeois ideas, modes of organisation, thought and value, 'The Age of Capital'. But radical currents that had awkwardly nestled beneath the commodious canopy of liberalism now began to chart another path: the Jacobin clubs, radicalism, the demonstrators of Peterloo, Chartism, the struggles over the franchise, cooperative and utopian communities, the early trade unions and friendly societies. This contradiction forced forward the 'age of reform' – struggles to extend the franchise; to impose limits on working hours, and on child and female labour; and for Catholic Emancipation, the abolition of slavery, repeal of the Combination Acts and the Corn Laws; but it also propelled the gradual disengagement from Liberalism of an independent working-class interest.

Later, family businesses became consolidated into joint-stock companies – the basis of a corporate capitalist economy – which came to dominate domestic and imperial economic expansion. This development underpinned Britain as centre of the largest, most far-flung empire on earth, and facilitated the triumph of a liberal imperial class – 'the lords of creation' – and their 'civilising' mission.

These developments over two centuries form the core of classical liberal political and economic thought on which neoliberalism now dreams again. But here also begin the antinomies and ambiguities of liberalism. Political ideas of 'liberty' became harnessed to economic ideas of the free market: one of liberalism's intersecting fault-lines which re-emerges with neoliberalism. As Edmund Burke ironically observed: 'It would be odd to see the Guinea captain [of a slave ship] attempting at the same instant to publish his proclamation of Liberty and to advertise its sale of slaves'. But this is precisely the 'splitting' that Liberalism practised: Progress, but simultaneously the need to contain any 'threat from below'; tolerance, reform, moderation and representative government for the English race, but colonial governmentality, discipline and authority for recalcitrant 'other' native peoples abroad; emancipation *and* subjugation; free men in London, slaves in the West Indies; freedom now for some, an unending apprenticeship to freedom for others; the universal language of 'mankind' vs the particularity of the discourse of women; a civilising 'mission' that harboured an untranscended gulf between the civilised and the barbarians; today, the 'soft' face of compassionate conservatism and The Big Society here, the hard edge of cuts, workfare and the gospel of self-reliance there.

Classic liberal ideas began to decline in the late nineteenth century. Dangerfield cited the suffragettes, the trade unions, reform of the House of Lords (an old aristocratic bastion) and the struggle for Irish independence as key triggers of the 'Strange Death of Liberal England'. In an increasingly plutocratic society, there was a growing coalescence between land and capital: industrialists sought respectability in their new country piles, while the old aristocratic and landed classes were pleased to travel to the City to invest, as the rate of profit from imperial trade soared. The new plutocratic classes took the world market as their oyster. But the sharpening competition with other states and the 'scramble' for imperial power led Lenin to describe imperialism as 'the highest stage of capitalism'.

Facing competition from Prussia and Japan, a New Liberalism emerged in Britain that embraced state intervention and 'the community' (as ever, a convenient half-way stop to class). The social insurance reforms of the Liberal Coalition of 1906-11 (Lloyd George and Churchill) laid down an early template for the welfare state. Later on, intervention against unemployment and the struggle against poverty – associated with Keynes and Beveridge – led the second phase. This is a history that Nick Clegg and the Lib Dems – grumpily clinging to the tail-coats of their Conservative Coalition allies – have conveniently forgotten or never understood.

The 1880s to the 1920s were a critical watershed that saw the rise of capitalist 'mass society': mass production, mass consumer markets, the market way of incorporating the masses into a subaltern position in the system, mass political parties and industrial unions, the mass media, mass culture, mass leisure, mass sport and entertainment, mass advertising, and new methods of marketing, testing and supplying the 'needs' of the masses and shaping demand – embryo forms of today's focus groups, life-style market segmentation, branding, personal relations consultancies, consumer services and the rest. The 'managerial revolution' – a new coalition of interests between share-holders and capital's senior managers – created not bourgeois entrepreneurs but the investor and executive classes of the giant multinational capitalist enterprises that now span the globe.

Neoliberalism, then, evolves. It borrows and appropriates extensively from classic liberal ideas; but each is given a further 'market' inflexion and conceptual revamp. Classic liberal principles have been radically transformed to make them applicable to a modern, global, post-industrial capitalism. In translating these ideas to different discursive forms and a different historical moment, neoliberalism performs a massive work of transcoding, while remaining in sight of the lexicon on which it draws. It is able do its dis-articulating and re-articulating work because these ideas have long been inscribed in social practices and institutions, and sedimented into the 'habitus' of everyday life, common sense and popular consciousness – 'traces without an inventory'.

Of course, transcoding can also be an opportunity for mystification. Thus Tory MP Jesse Norman, in *The Big Society*, quotes John Donne's wonderful affirmation of human inter-dependence: 'No man is an Island … Any man's death diminishes me because I am involved in mankind'. Norman then goes on to quote De Tocqueville, as if he and Donne were saying the same thing: 'The more [the state] stands in the place of associations, the more will individuals, losing the notion of combining together, require its assistance'. This is a mischievous conflation, which the editorial addition of the '[the state]' has greatly helped on its way.

Neoliberalism in the postwar period: Thatcherism and Blairism

How then has neoliberalism been nurtured, honed and developed across the post-war conjunctures? During the years that immediately followed the second word war there was a rare interlude – the 'Butskell' moment – of near-consensus on the basic shape of the welfare state and mixed economy. But as the post-war economy revived, and the US replaced the UK as the 'paradigm instance', internal tensions came increasingly to the surface. Changes in the class structure and the spread of affluence provoked a crisis of confidence on the left. 'Can Labour survive the coming of the telly, the washing machine, the fridge and the small car?' Gaitskell asked anxiously. In the 1960s, rock music, the new youth culture, the decline of deference, the liberating effect for women of the contraceptive pill, the counterculture and mind-expanding drugs – all were straws in the wind of trouble to come: 'resistance through rituals'. '1968' unleashed an avalanche of protest, dissent and disaffiliation: student occupations, participatory democracy, community politics, second-wave feminism, 'turn on, tune in and drop out', an ambivalent libertarianism; but also the cult of 'Che' Guevara, Vietnam, the IRA, industrial unrest, black power, the red brigades ... While all this was going on, in the mid-1970s, and as inflation soared, the IMF, useful for imposing structural adjustment programmes on Third World states, imposed one on the British Chancellor. And in the dim light of the three-day week Ted Heath declared the country ungovernable. The post-war 'settlement' had collapsed.

In 1979 Thatcherism launched its assault on society and the Keynesian state. But simultaneously it began a fundamental reconstruction of the socio-economic architecture with the first privatisations. (One-nation Tory Harold Macmillan called it 'selling off the family silver') Thatcherism thoroughly confused the left. Could it be not just another swing of the electoral pendulum but the start of a reconstruction of society along radically new, neoliberal lines?

Still, the old had to be destroyed before the new could take its place. Margaret Thatcher conspired in a ruthless war against the cabinet 'wets' and simultaneously plotted to break trade union power – 'the enemy within'. She impelled people towards new, individualised, competitive solutions: 'get on your bike', become self-employed or a share-holder, buy your council house, invest in the property-owning democracy. She coined a homespun equivalent for the key neoliberal ideas behind the sea-change she was imposing on society: value for money, managing your own budget, fiscal restraint, the money supply and the virtues of competition. There was anger, protest, resistance – but also a surge of populist support for the ruthless exercise of strong leadership.

Thatcherism mobilised widespread but unfocused anxiety about social change, engineering populist calls from 'below' to the state 'above' to save the country by imposing social order. This slide towards a 'law and order' society (see *Policing the Crisis*) was a key stage in the contradictory advance towards 'authoritarian populism'.[5]

One counter-intuitive feature was that, in the dark days of her electoral unpopularity, Thatcher brilliantly summoned to the rescue, not market rationality but an archaic British nationalism. The Falklands War allowed Thatcherism to play, when required, from two different ideological repertoires, with resonance in apparently opposing reservoirs of public sentiment: marching towards the future clad in the armour of the past. 'The market' was a modern, rational, efficient, practically-oriented discourse, inscribed in the everyday. Nationalist discourse, with its imperialist undertow (what Paul Gilroy calls its 'melancholia', the unrequited mourning for a lost object), was haunted by the fantasy of a late return to the flag, family values, national character, imperial glory and the spirit of Palmerstonian gunboat diplomacy.

Ideology is always contradictory. There is no single, integrated 'ruling ideology' – a mistake we repeat again now in failing to distinguish between conservative and neoliberal repertoires. Ideology works best by suturing together contradictory lines of argument and emotional investments – finding what Laclau called 'systems of equivalence' between them. Contradiction is its *metier*. Andrew Gamble characterised Thatcherism as combining 'free market'/'strong state'. Many believed this contradiction would be Thatcherism's undoing. But, though not logical, few strategies are so successful at winning consent as those which root themselves in the contradictory elements of common sense, popular life and consciousness. Even today, the market/free enterprise/private property discourse persists cheek by jowl with older conservative attachments to nation, racial homogeneity, Empire, tradition. 'Market forces' is good for restoring the power of capital and destroying the redistributivist illusion. But in moments of difficulty one can trust 'the Empire' to strike back. 'The people' will turn out to cheer the fleet returning to Plymouth from some South Atlantic speck of land; they will line the streets of Wootton Bassett to honour the returning dead from 'a war without end' in Afghanistan. (How many remembered this was Britain's *fourth* Afghan War?)

In the end Thatcherism was too socially destructive and ideologically extreme to triumph in its 'scorched earth' form. Even her cabinet fan-club knew it could not last. But it was a 'conviction moment' they will never forget. And today, once again, many yearn to return to it in some more consolidated, permanent and settled form.

Paradoxically, such a form was provided by Blair's hybrid, New Labour, which abandoned Labour's historic agenda and set about reconstructing social democracy as 'the best shell' for a New Labour variant of neoliberalism. Hybrid, because – borrowing the skills of triangulation (one idea from each end of the political spectrum to make a 'Third Way') from Clinton – it re-articulated social reform, free enterprise and the market. This conflation was the real source of New Labour 'spin' – not an irritating habit but a serious political strategy, a 'double shuffle'. New Labour repositioned itself from centre-left to centre-right. Covered by that weasel word, 'modernisation', the New Labour 'saints' remorselessly savaged 'Old' Labour. A substantial sector of Labour's 'heartland' left, never to return. But the 'middle ground', the pin-head on which all mainstream parties now compete to dance, became the privileged political destination.

New Labour believed that the old route to government was permanently barred. It was converted, Damascus-like, to neoliberalism and the market. And, buying in to the new managerial doctrine of public choice theory taught by the US Business Schools, New Labour finally understood that there was no need for the political hassle to privatise. You could simply burrow underneath the distinction between state and market. Out-sourcing, value-for-money and contract-contestability criteria opened one door after another through which private capital could slip into the public sector and hollow it out from within. This meant New Labour adopting market strategies, submitting to competitive disciplines, espousing entrepreneurial values and constructing new entrepreneurial subjects. Tony Giddens, a Third Way pioneer, is supposed to have told Blair that nothing could resist 'the unstoppable advance of market forces'. 'Marketisation' became the cutting-edge of New Labour's neoliberal project.

New Labour thus embraced 'managerial marketisation'. The economy was actively 'liberalised' (with disastrous consequence for the coming crisis), while society was boxed in by legislation, regulation, monitoring, surveillance and the ambiguous 'target' and 'control' cultures. It adopted 'light-touch' regulation. But its 'regulators' lacked teeth, political courage, leverage or an alternative social philosophy, and were often playing on both sides of the street. Harnessing social purposes to a free-wheeling private economy proved to be an exercise much like Tawney's 'trying to skin a tiger stripe by stripe'.

There were social problems requiring urgent attention, but what was most striking was New Labour's moralistically driven legislative zeal in its approach to them: ASBOs, community policing, widening surveillance, private policing and security firms, out-sourcing the round-up and expulsion of visa-less migrants, imprisonment of terrorist suspects without trial, and ultimately complicity with rendition and a 'cover-up' of involvement with torture. Despite the 'liberalism', punitive conceptions of punishment took hold: longer sentences, tougher prison regimes, harsher youth-offender disciplines. A new kind of liberal 'authoritarianism' turned out to be one of the jokers in New Labour's neoliberal pack. Michael Howard declared that 'prison works', implying that those who thought it didn't were 'bleeding-heart liberals'. Blair, certainly not one, espoused 'tough love'. (Later David Cameron invented 'muscular liberalism'.) This is certainly not the first time these two contradictory Janus-faces of Liberalism have been evident.

New Labour did initiate very important social reforms, including the minimum wage, shorter hospital waiting times, better health targets, attempts to reduce child poverty, the doubling of student numbers and (rather reluctantly) some equality and human rights legislation. But triangulation was its life-blood, its leading tendency. There was a continuous tension between a strident, Fabian, Benthamite tendency to regulate and manage and the ideology of the market, with its pressure for market access to areas of public life from which it had hitherto been excluded. Regulation was often the site of a struggle to resolve the contradiction between an enhanced role for the private sector and the need to demonstrate positive outcomes. But there was a strong impulse towards getting rid of the excrescences of the 'nanny state', in areas such as planning and health and safety regulations, and towards 'flexibility' in labour markets.

What was distinctively neoliberal about New Labour's strategies? The private funding of New Labour's flagship achievements via the Public Finance Initiative left future generations in hock for thirty years to re-pay the debt at exorbitant interest rates. Yet 'public-private partnership' became a required condition of all public contracts. Contracting out, competitive tendering and 'contestability' opened up the state to capital. Private contractors were better placed to cut costs and shed staff, even at the expense of service quality. The rising archipelago of private companies providing public services for profit was spectacular. Consultants floated in and out to 'educate' the public sphere in the ways of corporate business. Senior public servants joined the Boards of their private suppliers through 'the revolving door'.

Emptied out from inside, the ethos of public service underwent an irreversible 'culture change'. The habits and assumptions of the private sector became embedded in the state.

Neoliberal discourse promoted two discursive figures – the 'taxpayer' (hard-working man, over-taxed to fund the welfare 'scrounger') and the 'customer' (fortunate housewife, 'free' to exercise limited choice in the market-place, for whom the 'choice agenda' and personalised delivery were specifically designed). No-one ever thinks either could also be a citizen who needs or relies on public services.

The prevailing market discourse is, of course, a matter of ideological representation – a point that Doreen Massey develops in her article in this issue.[6] Actual markets do not work that way. They do not work mysteriously by themselves, or 'clear' at their optimum point. Only by bracketing-out the relative wealth of buyer and seller can they be called 'fair'. No 'hidden hand' guarantees the common good. Markets often require the external power of state and law to establish and regulate them. But the discourse provides subjects with a 'lived' 'imaginary relation' to their real conditions of existence. This does not mean that markets are simply manufactured fictions. Indeed, they are only too real! They are 'false' because they offer partial explanations as an account of whole processes. But it is worth remembering that 'those things which we believe to be true are "real" in their consequences'.

Globally, New Labour agreed that 'developing countries' must be exposed to the bracing winds of Free Trade and foreign investment. The main purpose of global governance was to protect markets and investments and maintain the conditions for the successful pursuit of global capitalist enterprise. This required a major commitment to a new geopolitical order, military expenditure, and the construction of a ring of client states and dictators, many of whom routinely used repression, violence, imprisonment and torture; and, if necessary, direct military intervention – though naturally in humanitarian disguise.

The Blair experiment ended unexpectedly – the result of long subservience to US foreign policy goals. The 'special relationship' guaranteed the UK a role as geopolitical junior partner and a place in the global sun. It stood 'shoulder to shoulder' against the rise of Islamic fundamentalism. George Bush, supported by the neoconservative lobby, led Blair into armed intervention and regime change in Iraq. Blair's moralism was compromised by his specious logic, dissembling, secret agreements of which everyone was kept in ignorance, sexed-up documents and flawed intelligence. His reputation has never recovered.

Gordon Brown, who followed, did not fundamentally alter New Labour's neoliberal inclinations. Never a paid-up 'Third Way' proselytiser, his manse background, high moral seriousness and early Labour formation stood in the way. The positive side of New Labour's 'double shuffle' became identified with him: public investment, limiting third-world debt and child poverty. But 'redistribution by stealth' failed to build a political constituency or a principled defence of the welfare state.

Besides, Brown admired the dynamism of American free-enterprise capitalism. He fell for the profoundly mistaken belief that Labour had somehow ended the cycle of 'boom and bust'. He did not heed the signs that the boom could not last forever – the uncontrollable property market, the swelling private and public debt, the dubious risk-taking devices invented by ambitious young traders, the unregulated predations of the hedge-fund and private equity sectors, the scandal of banks selling sub-prime mortgages worth more than many borrowers' total annual income, the enhancement of share values, the astronomic executive salaries and bonuses, banking's shift to risk-taking investment activities. These were all signs a sophisticated economic technician like Brown should not have missed. In the crisis Brown's international leadership was impressive, but it was all too late. Neoliberal hubris had done its damage. By the time of the election (which Brown should have called a year before), it was clear Labour would lose. It did.

The coalition variant

A Conservative-Liberal Democratic coalition was fully in line with the dominant political logic of realignment. In the spirit of the times, Cameron, with Blair as his role model, signalled his determination to reposition the Tories as a 'compassionate conservative party', though this has turned out to be a something of a chimera.

At the same time, many underestimated how deeply being out of office and power had divided the Lib-Dem soul and misjudged the self-deception, hypocrisy and lack of principle of which the Lib-Dem leadership was capable. Coalition now set the neoliberal-

THE NEOLIBERAL REVOLUTION

inclined *Orange Book* supporters, who favoured an alliance with the Conservatives, against the 'progressives', including former social democrats, who leaned towards Labour. A deal – its detail now forgotten – was stitched up, in which the social liberals were trounced, and Cameron and Clegg 'kissed hands' in the No. 10 rose garden (the former looking like the cat that had swallowed the cream). The Lib Dems thus provided the Cameron leadership with the 'fig leaf' it needed – while the banking crisis gave the 'alibi'. The Coalition government seized the opportunity to launch the most radical, far-reaching and irreversible social revolution since the war.

Coalition policy often seems incompetent, with failures to think things through or join things up. But, from another angle, it is arguably the best prepared, most wide-ranging, radical and ambitious of the three regimes which since the 1970s have been maturing the neoliberal project. The Conservatives had for some time been devoting themselves to preparing for office – not in policy detail but in terms of how policy could be used in power to legislate into effect a new political 'settlement'. They had convinced themselves that deep, fast cuts would have to be made to satisfy the bond markets and international assessors. But could the crisis be used, as Friedman had suggested, to 'produce real change'?

The legislative avalanche began immediately and has not let up. It begins negatively ('the mess the previous government left us') but ends positively, in embracing radical structural reform as the solution. Ideology is in the driving seat, though vigorously denied. The front-bench ideologues – Osborne, Lansley, Gove, Maude, Duncan Smith, Pickles, Hunt – are saturated in neoliberal ideas and determined to give them legislative effect. As *One Flew over the Cuckoo's Nest* put it, 'The crazies are in charge of the asylum'. They are single-minded about the irreversible transformation of society, ruthless about the means, and in denial about the 'fall-out'. Osborne – smirking, clever, cynical, 'the smiler with the knife' – wields the chopper with zeal. Cameron – relaxed, plausible, charming, confident, a silver-spooned patrician, 'a smooth man' – 'fronts' the Coalition TV show. This crew long ago accepted Schumpeter's adage that there is no alternative to 'creative destruction'. They have given themselves, through legislative manoeuvring, an uninterrupted five years to accomplish this task.

Its wide-ranging character must be judged in terms of the operational breadth of the institutions and practices they aim to 'reform', their boldness in siphoning state-funding to the private sector, and the number of constituencies they are prepared to confront. Reform and choice – words already hijacked by New Labour – are the master narrative. They may be Conservatives but this is *not* a 'conserving' regime (it is a bemused Labour which is toying with the 'blue-Labour' conservative alternative now). Tories and Lib Dems monotonously repeat the dissembling mantras of their press and public relations people: 'we are clearing up the mess inherited from the previous government'. But the neoliberal engine is at full throttle.

We cannot deal with the cuts in any detail here. They have only just started and there is much more to come. Instead we limit ourselves to tracking the neoliberal logic behind the strategy.

First, targeted constituencies – i.e. anyone associated with, relying or dependent on the state and public services. For the rich, the recession never happened. For the public sector, however, there will be massive redundancies, a wage freeze, pay running well behind the rate of inflation, pensions which will not survive in their present form, rising retirement ages. Support for the less well off and the vulnerable will be whittled away, and welfare dependency broken. Benefits will be capped, workfare will be enforced. The old must sell homes to pay for care; working parents must buy child care; and invalidity benefit recipients must find work. Sure Start, the schools refurbishment programme and Independent Maintenance Grants are on hold. Wealthy parents can buy children an Oxbridge education, but many other students will go into life-long debt to get a degree. You cannot make £20 billion savings in the NHS without affecting front-line, clinical and nursing services. Andrew Lansley, however, 'does not recognise that figure'. Similarly, though everybody else knew most universities would charge the maximum £9000 tuition fees, David 'Two-Brain' Willetts doesn't recognise that figure. Saying that square pegs fit into round holes has become a front-bench speciality.

Women stand where many of these savage lines intersect. As Beatrix Campbell reminds us, cutting the state means minimising the arena in which women can find a voice, allies, social as well as material support; and in which their concerns can be recognised. It means reducing the resources society collectively allocates to children, to making children a shared responsibility, and to the general 'labour' of care and love.

Second, there is privatisation – returning public and state services to private capital, re-drawing the social architecture. Privatisation comes in three sizes: (1) straight sell-off of public assets; (2) contracting out to private companies for profit; (3) two-step privatisation 'by stealth', where it is represented as an unintended consequence. Some examples: in criminal justice, contracts for running prisons are being auctioned off, and in true neoliberal fashion Ken Clarke says he cannot see any difference in principle whether prisons are publicly or privately owned; in health care, the private sector is already a massive, profit-making presence, having cherry-picked for profit medical services that hospitals can no longer afford to provide; while in the most far-reaching, top-down NHS reorganisation, GPs, grouped into private consortia (part of whose profits they retain), will take charge of the £60 billion health budget. Since few GPs know how or have time to run complex budgets, they will 'naturally' turn to the private health companies, who are circling the NHS like sharks waiting to feed. Primary Care Trusts, which represented a public interest in the funding process, are being scrapped. In the general spirit of 'competition', hospitals must remove the 'cap' on the number of private patients they treat.

Third, the lure of 'localism'. In line with David Cameron's Big Society, 'free schools' (funded from the public purse – Gove's revenge) will 'empower' parents and devolve power to 'the people'. But parents – beset as they are by pressing domestic and care responsibilities, and lacking the capacity to run schools, assess good teaching, define balanced curricula, remember much science or the new maths, or speak a foreign language, while regarding history as boring, and not having read serious novel since GCSE – will have to turn to the private education sector to manage schools and define the school's 'vision'. Could the two-step logic be clearer?

Fourth, phoney populism: pitching 'communities' against local democracy. Eric Pickles intends to wean councils permanently off the central grant system. Meanwhile, social housing is at a standstill, housing benefits will be cut and council rents allowed to rise to commercial levels in urban centres. Many will move to cheaper rentals, losing networks of friends, child support, family, school friends and school places. Parents must find alternative employment locally – if there is any – or allow extra travelling time. Jobseekers' allowances will be capped. As the private housing lobby spokesperson said, 'we are looking forward to a bonanza'. Since the early days of Thatcher we have not seen such a ferocious onslaught on the fabric of civil society, relationships and social life.

Fifth, cutting down to size state involvement in quality of life. Amenities like libraries, parks, swimming baths, sports facilities, youth clubs, community centres will either be privatised or disappear. Either unpaid volunteers will 'step up to the plate' or doors will close. In truth, the aim is not – in the jargon of '1968' from which the promiscuous Cameron is not ashamed to borrow – to 'shift power to the people', but to undermine the structures of local democracy. The left, which feels positively about volunteering, community involvement and participation – and who doesn't? – finds itself once again triangulated into uncertainty. The concept of the 'Big Society' is so empty that universities have been obliged to put it at the top of their research agenda on pain of a cut in funding – presumably so that politicians can discover what on earth it means: a shabby, cavalier, duplicitous interference in freedom of thought.

What is intended is a permanent revolution. Can society be permanently reconstructed along these lines? Is neoliberalism hegemonic?

The protests are growing. Weighty professional voices are ranged against structural reforms, and the speed and scale of cuts in a fragile economy. There are pauses, rethinks and u-turns. There may be more. If the Lib-Dem 'wheeze' of delivering cuts in government and campaigning against them at the next election fails to persuade, they face the prospect of an electoral wipe-out. The Coalition may fall apart, though at an election the Conservatives might get the majority they failed to muster last time. What happens next is not pregiven.

Hegemony is a tricky concept and provokes muddled thinking. No project achieves 'hegemony' as a completed project. It is a process, not a state of being. No victories are permanent or final. Hegemony has constantly to be 'worked on', maintained, renewed, revised. Excluded social forces, whose consent has not been won, whose interests have not been taken into account, form the basis of counter-movements, resistance, alternative strategies and visions ... and the struggle over a hegemonic system starts anew. They constitute what Raymond Williams called 'the emergent' – and the reason why history is never closed but maintains an open horizon towards the future.

However, in ambition, depth, degree of break with the past, variety of sites being colonised, impact on common sense and shift in the social architecture, neoliberalism does constitute a *hegemonic project*. Today, popular thinking and the systems of calculation in daily life offer very little friction to the passage of its ideas. Delivery may be more difficult: new and old contradictions still haunt the edifice, in the very process of its reconstruction. Still, in terms of laying foundations and staging the future on favourable ground, the neoliberal project is several stages further on. To traduce a phrase of Marx's: 'well grubbed, old mole'. Alas!

Notes

1. Louis Althusser, 'Contradiction and Over-determination', in *For Marx*, Penguin 1969.
2. David Harvey, *A Brief History of Neoliberalism*, OUP 2007.
3. Nik Theodore, Jamie Peck and Neil Brenner, 'Neoliberal Urbanism: Cities and the Rule of Markets', in Sophie Watson and Gary Bridge (eds), *The New Blackwell Companion to the City*, Wiley 2011, p15.
4. Friedrich Hayek, Preface, 1982 edition *Capitalism and Freedom* (first published 1962.
5. See Stuart Hall, Chas Critcher, Tony Jefferson, John Clarke and Brian Roberts, *Policing the Crisis: 'Mugging', the State and Law and Order*, Macmillan 1978.
6. Doreen Massey, 'Re-imagining the political field', *Soundings* 48, 2011.

AFTERWORD:

Stuart Hall as a political intellectual

Michael Rustin

THERE IS, OF course, something slightly anomalous about gathering a collection of Stuart Hall's work under the title of 'Political Writings'. This is because, while the essays in this collection are certainly 'political' in their topics and concerns, so was virtually everything that Hall wrote.[1] With *Universities and Left Review*, the Campaign for Nuclear Disarmament, the early *New Left Review*, *Marxism Today*, *Soundings* and the *Kilburn Manifesto*, and in other such contexts throughout his life, Hall worked with political friends and comrades to make many political interventions. But each of the major areas of his work – for example his decisive contribution to the invention and development of the field of Cultural Studies, his work in redefining the sociology curriculum at the Open University, his contributions to the understanding of race and ethnicity, and his major role in the establishment of two institutions devoted to the arts of ethnically diverse and diasporic communities, the Institute of International Visual Arts (Iniva) and Autograph ABP – were also 'political' in his own broad understanding of this term. One of the main purposes of his writing from its beginnings was to extend the meaning of 'the political' outwards, in doing so drawing on intellectual resources and interests which others might not recognise as 'political' at all.

Stuart Hall describes himself as having been compelled to see the world in 'political' ways almost from his early childhood. Being identified within his Jamaican middle class home as the darkest of his parents' three children was, he has said, his first formative experience, since in that colour-coded world to be the darkest was by no means to be perceived as the most favoured. Thus one could say that Hall felt marginal from his very beginnings, a sense of himself which was further enhanced by his arrival in Oxford at the age of 18, as a Rhodes Scholar, in the still culturally conservative England of 1951. He found himself drawn, in Oxford, to students who shared his dissident and radical feelings, many of them, like him, having come from abroad to study. He has described how he became aware of himself as a 'West Indian' (not merely a Jamaican) only after he came to England. The 'Caribbean Marxism' of Eric Williams and C.L.R. James, and their understanding from this perspective of the nature of imperialism, was important in his early intellectual formation.

Hall became a member of a leftist political group in Oxford that was already at odds with 'official' Labour Party politics. But, although there were Communist Party members in his group of friends and political associates at this time, dissidence from Marxist orthodoxy arrived at its moment of crisis in 1956 with the Soviet invasion of Hungary, when many left the Communist Party. 1956 was also the year of Suez, which was understood by Hall and many others as Britain's disastrous reversion to its old assumptions of colonial superiority and imperial entitlement, after an apparent shift of attitude within the Conservative Party after the war. He continued to occupy this position of dissent both from the imperial mind-set of the British governing class, and from the dogmatism and authoritarianism of the Soviet system, throughout his life, with the intellectual fights on two fronts which this always entailed. The emergence of the Campaign for Nuclear Disarmament, and its rejection of both the contending Cold War alliances, in which Hall played a prominent role as one of its foremost speechmakers and intellectuals, enabled him to find that his own commitments were shared by a whole new generation of activists and campaigners.

In his later life, Hall began to write in more personal terms about his experiences as a black West Indian permanently resident and working in Britain, and the continuing partial sense of estrangement from the majority society to which this gave rise. This ongoing sense of vulnerability remained with him, notwithstanding the fact that he was himself a significant public figure, not least through his broadcasting, most often for the Open University, and that he was widely respected for the originality and engagingness of his work.[2]

Hall described the expansions of the definition of politics as one of the main commitments of the first New Left, at a conference in

1997 which was called by a new generation of Oxford postgraduates
to examine its contribution. Here is what he said about this:

> I think that there then was, and always will be, a space for radical
> politics which is neither Stalinist nor social democratic. Somewhere
> between the old forms of social democracy and the old forms of
> Stalinism is the space in which a new politics and a new socialist
> agenda can be constructed ... The New Left contributed to – though
> in no way completed – an expansion of the definition of what politics
> is about. It helped to transform that narrow, confined, institution-
> ally limited notion of 'the political'. I think it only just began that
> important job.[3]

Hall's group of Oxford University friends became one of the strands
which came together as the first New Left in Britain, from 1956. The
foundation of *Universities and Left Review* (from which two of the
chapters of this book has been selected) and of the Universities and
Left Review Club and the Partisan Coffee House in London were
formative moments in this development. Film makers, dramatists,
artists and intellectuals of all sorts became involved in this early movement, which was an exceptional moment of political rebirth. In parallel
with this development was the conversion of the dissident Communist
Party journal, *The Reasoner*, into the *New Reasoner*, following many
prominent resignations from the party. Hall's dialogue with Marxist
perspectives significantly took place through this relationship, not least
with the historian Edward Thompson, who was the *New Reasoner*'s
most charismatic figure.

New intellectual resources

It is a notable fact that few of the formative figures of the New
Left were political scientists by intellectual formation, still less
'professional politicians'. They sought to bring to politics perspectives and ways of understanding which came from fields that were
broader than was traditional for politics as it had come to develop
in contemporary liberal societies. Three of its most influential
founding figures, Raymond Williams, Richard Hoggart and Stuart
Hall, had their first intellectual home in English literature, and all

of them made use of its critical methods and moral sensibilities to understand broader social and cultural fields. Charles Taylor, a co-editor of *Universities and Left Review*, was a Hegelian philosopher, and a critic of positivist approaches to social science. Another leading figure, Edward Thompson, was a historian, although one of a decidedly literary disposition, as was Raphael Samuel, who, like Thompson, was committed to a genre of history which gave primary importance to the experience and imagination of ordinary people. For these writers, influenced as most of them were by Marxist ways of thinking, politics meant much more than was captured by the categories of conventional political science.

Hall and his colleagues were indeed receptive to insights from many sources. One early influence on him was the literary criticism of F.R. Leavis, who insisted, against what he saw as a complacent upper class culture, that the moral dilemmas and possibilities of an entire society were captured in the work of its best imaginative writers. Hall, who studied English literature at Oxford, adapted the *Scrutiny* school's critical methods to show that popular as well as high cultural forms should be valued and subject to discrimination.[4] Richard Hoggart's classic *The Uses of Literacy*, which described the life of a working-class community as a 'lived culture', no less full of meaning and values than more specialised and rarefied cultural productions, was exemplary in this respect. Theoretically fundamental for Hall was Raymond Williams's understanding of societies as essentially constituted by the meanings assigned to them by individuals and groups, in particular as these were defined by their locations in structures and cultures of class. Thus the study of popular culture in Hall's work, from his 1964 book *The Popular Arts* (co-authored with Paddy Whannel) to the many works of description and interpretation undertaken by him and his colleagues at the Centre for Contemporary Cultural Studies, became an important 'lens' through which a society and its politics could be understood, and one of the spaces within which its implicit politics could be challenged. Indeed, one of the central contributions of Hall and the New Left to political thinking lay in the importance it attached to the dimension of culture and meaning.[5]

In the 1970s, Hall and his colleagues absorbed the approach of the sociological school of symbolic interactionism in the United States. This had become a resource for the 'new criminology' and its sympathetic reinterpretations of the meaning of 'deviancy', of which the National Deviancy Symposium became the container in Britain. The 'European' perspectives of semiotics and structuralism also became resources for Hall's analysis of mass communications including television. While liberal media took pride in their commitment to open-mindedness and balance, and their avoidance of overt political bias, Hall and his students were able to show the ways in which agendas were nevertheless set by invisible and unrecognised conventions, whose effect was to confine debate within safe limits, and deny a hearing to disruptive and 'illegitimate' kinds of dissent. Hall's article in this collection, 'A world at one with itself', exemplifies this insight. This was not so much a matter of explicit political bias – this of course happens, but Hall was rarely interested in stating the obvious – but rather of a structure of representation which was powerful because it was not quite what it seemed or claimed to be. The ideas and approaches of psychoanalysis were also found to be of value, especially to the understanding of differences of gender, ethnicity and identity, which became more salient in Hall's later writing.

Hall was Professor of Sociology at the Open University for seventeen years, beginning in 1979 when he left the Birmingham Centre for Contemporary Cultural Studies. Although he did not see himself as a conventional sociologist, he nevertheless engaged deeply with this field, which became open in the 1970s and 1980s to new theoretical perspectives. Several of Hall's significant early papers engaged with sociological debates, for example his interventions in debates about class and class consciousness. In 'A sense of classlessness' (1958), reprinted in this volume, Hall took note of changes which were taking place in the consciousness of social class at that time in Britain. He observed a weakening of working-class identity, in particular, and the emergence of less limited ideas of the self among working people. The growing significance of 'mass consumption' in contemporary society, and the opportunities which this afforded for self-expression and choice, were an element of this. Hall was tentative in his interpretation of these changes. He did not claim that the working class was disappearing, or was becoming 'bourgeoisified'. Nor did he believe that the Labour Party, as some of its intellectuals and leaders such as Anthony Crosland and Hugh Gaitskell advocated, ought to abandon its working-class identification. The potentialities of this new sense of classlessness were still, he thought, uncertain and open. A little later, the most perceptive sociologists of class of that time, John Goldthorpe and David

Lockwood advanced a comparable view.[6] The distinction they drew between 'expressive' and 'instrumental' collectivism allowed for the possibility that a weakening of the cultures of class solidarity might be taking place, rather as Hall had suggested, but that there might also be a countervailing increase in 'economistic' class militancy. This proved to be the case in the 1970s, although the militancy of this period was pursued as much to maintain wage differentials within the working class as to struggle against capital. Hall's argument, which became formative for his later political perspective, was that socialists, and the Labour Party in particular, could not assume that class structures and their traditional solidarities could just be called up on demand by politicians. One had to understand the situation of working people as they themselves saw it, and not rest on assumptions about their traditional loyalties. Hall's argument in 'A sense of classlessness' was vigorously disputed in the pages of *Universities and Left Review*, by Edward Thompson, and, less vehemently, by Raphael Samuel. Both suggested that the manifestations of a more classless sensibility to which Hall had drawn attention were actually superficial. They might, they argued, have some purchase in the metropolis, but the ideas of self-help and individualism had precedents in the nineteenth century, and in any case had little relevance to the cultures of the working class in northern industrial Britain. Hall made a spirited reply to these criticisms in 'The big swipe' in *Universities and Left Review*.[7] One can already see in these exchanges the seeds of political divisions which in a few years were to fracture the first new left.

Hall identified another new dimension of social change in a long review article in *Universities and Left Review*, 'Absolute beginnings', which anticipated some of most influential later writing of Hall and the Centre for Contemporary Cultural Studies.[8] Writing from his experience as a teacher in a south London secondary modern school, Hall wrote about the emergence of a spirited and lively youth culture, which appeared to him quite fresh. He observed that even well-meaning teachers in the contemporary school system had little capacity to engage with these young people. Here was another kind of 'emancipation' which Hall recognised to be taking place, in his prescient way. He again took note of the standard 'sociological' description of this development, in young people's enhanced purchasing power, and their thus constituting a new commercial market. His own emphasis, however, was on its challenging and creative significance for the dominant culture. This recognition of differences and divisions of generation gave rise to another area of disagreement with standard left-wing perspectives.

Before long, the study of youth cultures as sites of resistance to the dominant way of life became one of the most influential areas of work by Hall and the Centre for Contemporary Cultural Studies. Their collective volume, *Resistance through Rituals*, examined different instances of cultural diversity and dissidence, interpreted by their authors as the expressions of different forms of relationship to the dominant class structure.[9] Hall himself wrote a fine article (not included in that book), 'The hippies: an American moment', which interpreted the complex ways in which this subculture had both taken issue with conventional American norms and beliefs, yet had drawn on 'other' traditions (American Indian and Eastern) to fashion a counterculture in opposition to the mainstream.[10] The theoretical chapters of *Resistance through Rituals* began to examine the issues involved in understanding the latent politics of these developments, drawing from the newly translated work of Gramsci and his ideas of cultural hegemony and conflict. In fact the political implications of this generational awakening had already become visible, in the large following for the Campaign for Nuclear Disarmament from the late 1950s, and in the student protests and emergent counter-cultures which came to their climax in the late 1960s. For young people coming to university from families with little formal education, the study of youth cultures, and popular cultures more generally, became a point of entry into academic work which linked with their own experience, and challenged the condescensions of class which had hitherto dominated the academy. These issues of generational difference are now acquiring a new kind of relevance, as we have seen a vast increase in the numbers of young people entering university compared with the 1960s, but a decline in the opportunities for creative and rewarding work available to them.

Marx and Marxism

Whilst Hall's political thinking took account of these many different disciplinary perspectives, he sought always also to 'articulate' them into an integrated although subtle understanding of the larger social system. ('Articulation' was one of his favourite theoretical terms.) This holistic perspective, concerned always with the possibilities for the betterment of society, involved him a lifelong engagement with the intellectual tradition of Marx.

Here is how Hall reflected on his original political formation, in 1992:

> I entered cultural studies from the New Left, and the New Left always regarded Marxism as a problem, as trouble, as danger, not as a solution. Why? It had nothing to do with theoretical questions as such or in isolation. It had to do with the fact that my own (and its own) political formation occurred in a moment historically very much like the one we are in now – which I am astonished so few people have addressed – the moment of disintegration of a certain kind of Marxism. In fact the first British New Left emerged in 1956 at the moment of the disintegration of an entire historical/political project.[11]

This process of course had several subsequent vicissitudes, with various hopes of revival of European Communism then ending in its total collapse. Hall's interrogations of this tradition coexisted with a repeated rejection of its dogmatic formulations. And as one can see from several essays in this volume, he engaged in never-ending skirmishes with its guardians of orthodoxy, and with their echo in the weak Labourist belief that political loyalties could be simply assigned to classes as unproblematic labels.

He understood that 'totalising' chains of connection between the parts and whole of a society were frequently placed under great intellectual strain. Too strong a pull from the end of what Althusser termed specific 'levels and instances', and the idea of a holistic coherence and interdependency was at risk of disappearing from sight.[12] But at the other end of the scale, too strong an insistence on the idea of a unified social system, and complexities could be simplified to the point where no understanding could be gained.[13] Particulars, such as the attributes of youth cultures, or of a protest movement, or of work in the arts, mattered in themselves, since it was in the specific spaces of a social system that creative possibilities emerged.

The central issue at stake in the engagement with Marx by Hall and the New Left was set out in this canonical formulation from Marx's *Preface to the Critique of Political Economy*:

In the social production which men carry on they enter into definite relations that are indispensable and independent of their will; these relations of production correspond to a definite stage of development of their material forces of production. The sum total of these relations of production constitutes the economic structure of society – the real foundation, on which rises a legal and political superstructure and to which correspond definite forms of social consciousness. The mode of production in material life determines the social, political and intellectual life processes in general. It is not the consciousness of men that determines their being, but, on the contrary, their social being that determines their consciousness.[14]

This model or metaphor of 'base and superstructure' was one with which the main figures of the New Left, including Raymond Williams, Edward Thompson, Hall himself, and in its second phase, Perry Anderson, took issue.[15] The decisive place which these writers, including Hall, sought to assign to the place of consciousness, meaning and culture, and, linked with this, to autonomous polit-ical action, could scarcely be reconciled with this materialist thesis. Williams's critique of the base and superstructure model was crucial to this debate, especially in the field of Cultural Studies.[16] The problem was to retain the essential idea of capital's pervasive power within the entire social system, yet also to recognise the essential role played by subjective meaning and political agency. There was also the need to understand the specific attributes of contemporary capitalism, in particular its apparent stability and durability, given that in the period during which these debates took place its supercession or overthrow seemed extremely unlikely. The key resources for this work, within the Marxist tradition, were found to lie in the writings of Antonio Gramsci and Louis Althusser, many of which were newly translated in English during the 1970s.

Gramsci had identified the different forms of domination practised by the ruling classes of 'western' and 'eastern societies', and the different problems which these presented for subordinate social classes. The dense networks of civil society in liberal western societies, and the fact that ruling class domination was achieved most of the time through the management of consent rather than by violence, rendered the 1789 or 1917 models of revolutionary seizure of power at the centre unworkable and inappropriate. (Gramsci had learned a hard lesson from the failure of Italian Communist insurgency in the 1920s, and the rise of fascism, which had led to his spending the remainder of his life after 1926 in Mussolini's prisons.) Thus Gramsci made the distinction between the 'war of manoeuvre' and the 'war of position', the latter being the necessary mode of struggle within relatively stable liberal societies.

Gramsci had recognised that the ruling class exercised its power not through the domination of a single class, but more often through assembling alliances or 'blocs' of classes and class fractions. Differences and divisions of religious and regional affiliation and subdivisions among class fractions were significant in the constitution of such blocs, which had to be seen as feats of political leadership. Resistance had also to be conceived in strategic terms, and not imagined as the outcome of an inevitable process which must eventually bring the working class to power. Hall had found Gramsci's essay on Americanism and Fordism particularly instructive, in so far as it recognised the part which modern social organisation – including mass production and consumption – were beginning to play in a society which was elsewhere semi-feudal in its social relations. It was from Gramsci's analysis of this development in the 1920s that the concept of 'Fordism' was evolved in the 1970s to explain the mature operation of post-war capitalism, curiously enough at the very time when the Fordist model in the West was itself soon to fail. Hall and his colleagues on the journal *Marxism Today*, from which we republish several articles, were greatly influenced by these Gramscian ideas. *Marxism Today* was part of a broader 'Eurocommunist' tendency in the 1980s, which followed the Italian Communist Party's lead in trying to develop a more democratic form of communism, better suited to Western European political life than actual existing socialism in the Eastern bloc. Gramsci's reflections on the differences between the revolutionary potentialities of different social systems at different moments led him to begin to develop the concept of conjuncture which was further developed in Hall's political thinking and became essential to it. Social formations and their modes of class domination differ from one another, and even where these differences can be accounted for, there remains an element of the uncertain and contingent in political action.

For example, Lenin's political success in the 1917 revolution had to be explained as a consequence of intersecting causal factors rather than as the working-out of the inevitable laws of historical materialism.[17]

These causes included Lenin's genius for decisive leadership, the defeat of the Tsarist armies in the Great War, even, one might add, the fact of the German High Command having transported Lenin to the Finland Station in a sealed train in order that he might effect the revolutionary destruction of their enemy. Trotsky's 'law of combined and uneven development' better explained the condition of possibility of an urban revolution in an agrarian country than the orthodox Marxist view which saw revolution as the inevitable crisis of a mature capitalism.

Hall agreed with a formulation in the work of Marx which he most admired, *The 18th Brumaire of Louis Bonaparte*.[18]

> Men make their own history, but they do not make it as they please; they do not make it under self-selected circumstances, but under circumstances existing already, given and transmitted from the past.

It is this co-existence of determination with an uncertain element of freedom that gives meaning to the idea of conjuncture. In that text, Marx wrote as a historian of the near-present, and this was Hall's preferred method of political writing too.

In a related way Althusser's contribution to Marxist theory was also found valuable by Hall, although he had more disagreements with Althusser's ideas than with Gramsci's. Althusser made use of ideas similar to those of American functionalist sociology in his understanding of the role of sub-systems in the organisation of modern capitalism. His identification of the role of the 'ideological state apparatuses' provided a resource for analysing the roles of culture, education and the mass media in the system of domination.[19] His idea of 'interpellation', and his adaptation of Lacan's understanding of the role of language in the formation of identity, provided a means for bringing cultural analysis down to the micro-level of identities and the role of unconscious socialisation in maintaining consent. The ideas of the 'condensation' and 'displacement' of meanings between one signifier and other, derived ultimately from Freud via Lacan, added a further dimension to the 'mechanisms' by which ideologies functioned as instruments of power. The story which Hall and his co-authors told in *Policing the Crisis*, of the ways in which symbolic equations were made between popular fears of quite specific kinds of street crime and more widely-felt anxieties about social disorder and breakdown, deployed this form of explanation. Althusser's theory of 'overdetermination' was valuable in the understanding of how, at a particular historical moment (the May Events of Paris 1968 were an example), different 'instances' of social conflict could become superimposed upon one another. In this way a local confrontation might become the catalyst for the expression of much wider grievances, sometimes revealing unexpected fractures in the social order.

One could observe that such opportunities had been seized by one's political adversaries. The argument of *Policing the Crisis* was that 'mugging' had been exploited by the political right as just such a moment of cascading disruption. Its larger thesis was that this crisis (of high inflation, widespread strike action, and other social disorders) had brought the collapse of the 'corporatist' settlement through which relations between capital, labour, and the state had been managed during the 1970s. This collapse gave the opportunity for the New Right to impose Thatcherism as a counter-revolutionary solution to the contradictions of the British welfare state. *Policing the Crisis*, which follows through a chain of effects which began with the reporting of street crimes, is insufficiently recognised to be an exceptional work of political analysis. It anticipated the future shape and direction of Thatcherism a year before the election in which Thatcher came to power.

We can see in this volume how many theoretical resources Hall drew upon to analyse political developments in Britain. He pointed to the new potentialities of a changing society, and argued for a political recognition of these, including by the Labour Party.[20] He developed a critique of that party's habits of thought, trapped as it was by its acceptance of constitutional forms and the routines of politics understood mainly as marketing. While these methods might sometimes bring it a Parliamentary majority, what was mostly absent (as we have noted, he saw Ken Livingstone's GLC as one exception) was the ideological and organisational mobilisation needed to maintain momentum once office had been achieved. In the unequal struggle of forces which followed whenever Labour took power, the drive for change was usually defeated.

Hall's most influential and memorable political essays, for example 'The great moving right show' and its sequels, make use of a Gramscian understanding of political strategy to analyse the purposes and methods of the right. These essays, with reference to a specific political conjuncture, describe how a counter-revolution was achieved,

bringing about a defeat for the left and social democracy. The New
Left had identified the elements of a new politics – renewing a radical
culture, joining up new and old kinds of social resistance, identifying
emergent cultural potentials – and had made some connections
between them in theory and practice. But in both the 1960s and 1970s
these radical hopes and aspirations were disappointed and stifled as
the Labour governments which had partially embodied them failed to
win control of their environment.

By contrast, Hall showed how Thatcherism was able to construct an
effective hegemonic project, gathering rather than losing momentum
as it retained office. Its achievement was to bring together many
different currents and movements of reactionary feeling and intention,
for example the *Black Papers'* attack on progressive education, the
religiously-motivated and anti-feminist defence of the 'the right to life',
the censorious demand for 'decency' in the media, calls for respect for
military traditions ('the Falklands factor'), and the evocation of the
fear of crime and immigration (the moral panic around 'mugging'
was the starting-point of the systemic analysis set out in *Policing the
Crisis*). Thatcherism succeeded in articulating many strands into a
contradictory but nevertheless politically effective coherence. It was
able to be at the same time authoritarian – with the central state as
its enforcer, sweeping away intermediary resistances to its power in
local government, the professions, and the unions – and populist –
mobilising 'the people' against what it represented as the patronising
attitudes of the social-democratic state. It was able to be individualist,
in its advocacy of the virtues of competition and the free market, yet
also to advocate the 'traditional' values, of nation, family, race and
empire. Hall's understanding of Thatcherite populism was influenced
by Chantal Mouffe and Ernesto Laclau's writing, which described
the discursive processes through which political identifications were
achieved by the force of political action, and were not merely the
reflections of people's 'objective' class positions.[21]

In articles published on 'New Times' in *Marxism Today* in the
1980s, Hall, Martin Jacques and others went on to attack the
assumptions of 'Old Labour', arguing that the political initiative could
not be recaptured for the left by mere evocations of the past.[22] Their
idea was that the popular aspirations which had been emerging over
recent decades, for greater individual autonomy, higher qualities of
social provision, and a non-authoritarian approach by the state to the

people, might be the basis for a new progressive movement to challenge Thatcherism. What actually happened, however, after the election of Tony Blair as leader in 1994, was the emergence of the 'New Labour' project of renewal, the main aim of which was to break the pattern of electoral defeat that Labour had suffered for nearly two decades.

Marxism Today, in which the theory and critique of Thatcherism had been largely developed, ceased publication in 1991. Committed to continuing the political analysis and argument he had been conducting all his life, Hall then joined with Doreen Massey and Michael Rustin in 1995 to found a new journal, *Soundings*. This, from its opening editorial, placed itself firmly in the tradition of the first New Left: it was inclusive and questioning, and was committed to a much broader conception of the political than the conventional definitions allowed. Hall contributed actively to *Soundings* until he died, writing about many issues – race and legacy of the *Empire Windrush*, international relations after 9-11, the European idea – with the range and connectedness that had always characterised his work.

It was in *Soundings* that Hall took full measure of New Labour. He had initially welcomed some aspects of its project, particularly Blair's willingness to challenge Labour traditionalism and tribalism. Whatever the content of Blair's proposed reforms to the Labour Party, which were centralising and exclusionary in their intentions and effects, Hall welcomed the open and democratic means by which they were at first pursued, and admired Blair's abilities as a political performer – as he had once regretfully acknowledged Thatcher's. He also saw no point in defending a 'Clause 4' of the Labour Party Constitution, which no longer embodied any substantive purpose, and he had no nostalgia for the old days of the trade union block vote, on whoever's side it may have been cast. However, he was critical of the emptiness of the New Labour programme, and its failure to make any significant challenge to the decaying post-Thatcherite regime. This was to become a major theme for Hall, and for *Soundings*.

In 'Parties on the verge of a nervous breakdown', Hall noted New Labour's failure to think through what a feasible alternative to the hegemony of individualism and the market might be.[23] But he set out the basis of his major critique of New Labour's project in his article 'New Labour's double shuffle', written in 2003, which analysed Labour's huge 1997 victory (its Parliamentary majority was 179) as a catastrophically lost opportunity to bring about real change.[24] Hall saw

New Labour in government as a hybrid system, whose dominant logic was a neoliberal subordination to markets and corporate power, while it retained a subordinate 'social-democratic' logic whose necessary aim was to retain support from Labour's traditional supporters. This was the strategy which Gramsci described as 'transformism' – the reprocessing of a reforming set of goals and values (in this case social-democratic) within a pre-existing (in this case neoliberal) framework, providing a semblance but not the reality of change. Especially illuminating in Hall's account was the idea that the ambiguity of the New Labour project was part of its essence.

The analysis of neoliberalism from then on remained the main focus of Hall's political writings, as well as being a key theme for *Soundings*. The Gramscian mode of thought which had been deployed in the analysis of both Thatcherism and New Labour became increasingly important following the financial crisis of 2007-2008. Hall noted that neoliberalism had persisted in its course, giving no ground in the face of its massive economic crisis. In 'The neoliberal revolution', he analysed the pervasive power of this system, arguing that what was intended was the permanent reconstruction of society on neoliberal lines.[25] With his colleagues, Hall went on to deepen this analysis, first in a series of *Soundings* articles written between 2009 and 2011, later published together as *The Neoliberal Crisis*, and then in a series of essays published as *After Neoliberalism? The Kilburn Manifesto*.[26] After Hall died in 2014, *Soundings* initiated a further 'programmatic' stage of this argument, *Soundings Futures: Alternatives to Neoliberalism*, to which he would have contributed had he lived longer, together with Doreen Massey, our friend and co-founding editor of *Soundings*, who died in March 2016.

This volume of *Political Writings* is not being published merely as an archive of his work. The essays do show his development as a political writer, and illuminate fifty years of British political history. But at a time when politics has become an alienated activity, and much academic study has retreated into its own instrumental specialisations, they do much more than this. They provide an example of how it is possible to bring the capabilities of an intellectual and an educator to bear on thinking about politics, and in doing so to redefine politics. We believe the scale of Hall's achievement will become even more evident as further volumes of his work are collected together and republished. We hope that his writing will provide inspiration for a new generation.

We will give the final words to Hall himself. Reflecting on the New Left, in a discussion in 1987, he said:

> … To be a socialist now is to be a socialist with questions: it is to be a socialist in the understanding that to be a socialist is also to be a feminist, and that feminism interrogates socialism in a profound way. It is also, for me, to be black, which interrogates thought in the categories and in relation to the experience of 'the West' in very profound ways. In that sense our political commitments are bound to be provisional or contingent in ways in which they have not customarily been. That is how I try to think the space in which the socialist project could be renewed: taking the pressure of the irreversible movements in contemporary society, and indeed around the world, towards greater diversity, greater openness, greater choice, and therefore in some senses, greater fragmentation. But it's not only fragmentation as loss. There are also gains …[27]

Notes

1. My co-editors discuss the selection criteria in the introduction to this book.
2. Documents of this early period of Hall's life are John Akomfrah's film installation, *The Unfinished Conversation*, and its single-screen version *The Stuart Hall Project*, and the first volume of Hall's memoirs.
3. Stuart Hall, in Stuart Hall, Raphael Samuel and Charles Taylor, 'Then and Now: A Re-evaluation of the New Left', in Oxford University Socialist Discussion Group (eds), *Out of Apathy: Voices of the New Left Thirty Years On*, Verso 1989, pp150-1.
4. He began a doctoral thesis on the novels of Henry James.
5. Dennis Dworkin describes this development in *Cultural Marxism in Post-War Britain*, Duke University Press 1997.
6. J.K. Goldthorpe, D. Lockwood, F. Bechofer, and J. Platt, *The Affluent Worker in the Class Structure*, Cambridge University Press 1969.
7. Stuart Hall, 'The big swipe: some comments on the "classlessness Controversy"', *Universities and Left Review* 7, 1959 (not published in this collection).
8. Stuart Hall, 'Absolute beginnings: reflections on the secondary modern generation', *Universities and Left Review* 7, 1959 (not published in this collection).
9. Hall and Jefferson (eds), *Resistance through Rituals: Youth Subcultures in Post-War Britain*, Hutchinson 1976.

10. Stuart Hall, 'The hippies: an American moment', in J. Nagel (ed), *Student power*, Merlin 1969.

11. Stuart Hall, 'Cultural Studies and its Theoretical Legacies', in L. Grossberg, C. Nelson and P. Treichler (eds), *Cultural Studies*, Routledge 1992, p279.

12. He saw this as a risk in the academic establishment of Cultural Studies, in which its original 'political' purpose could be lost.

13. He perhaps came nearest to a 'post-modern' repudiation of holistic coherence in the *New Times* project of *Marxism Today* in the 1980s, and in his own essay on that subject (reprinted in this issue). So damaging was his critique of traditional socialist formulae, in the midst of eighteen years of Tory government and defeats for the left, that it was hard to see the grounds within it for a positive alternative politics.

14. Karl Marx, Preface, *Contribution to the Critique of Political Economy*, 1959, p1.

15. Edward Thompson's *The Making of the English Working Class* asserted the causal primacy of consciousness over structure in the formation of classes. Perry Anderson, in *Passages from Antiquity to Feudalism*, described the crucial role of the church as the bearer of the West's dynamic cultural heritage, thus acknowledging the force of Max Weber's critique of Marx's account of capitalism's origins. Raymond Williams's work is a prolonged demonstration of the causal powers located in the production of cultures.

16. R. Williams, 'Base and Superstructure in Marxist Cultural Theory', *New Left Review*, 1/82. November-December 1973.

17. For more on this see introduction, pp2–3.

18. Karl Marx, *The 18th Brumaire of Louis Bonaparte*, Lawrence & Wishart 1954.

19. See Louis Althusser, *Lenin and Philosophy and other Essays,* New Left Books 1971.

20. At times Hall took an active role in trying to influence the Labour Party, for example in the early 1960s in the production during Labour Party Conferences of memorable overnight newsletters distributed each morning to the delegates

21. But while Hall learned from the post-Marxist critique of Laclau and Mouffe's *Hegemony and Socialist Strategy* (Verso 1976), he did not follow them all in the way in their critiques of marxism.

22. Stuart Hall and Martin Jacques, *New Times: The Changing Face of Politics in the 1990s*, Lawrence and Wishart 1989.

23. Stuart Hall, 'Parties on the verge of a nervous breakdown', *Soundings* 1, 1995.

24. Stuart Hall, 'New Labour's Double Shuffle', *Soundings* 24, 2003, reprinted in this volume.

25. Stuart Hall, 'The neoliberal revolution', *Soundings* 48, 2011, reprinted in this volume.

26. Sally Davison and Katharine Harris (eds), *The neoliberal revolution*, Lawrence & Wishart 2015; Stuart Hall, Doreen Massey and Michael Rustin (eds), *After Neoliberalism: The Kilburn Manifesto*, Lawrence & Wishart 2015.
27. Stuart Hall, 'Then and Now', p155.

Notes on historical figures

Aneurin Bevan (1897-1960): an impressively fiery tribune of the people, organised by the particular popular politics of the South Wales industrial working class and intimately attached to the Labour Party. Represented Ebbw Vale as MP for over thirty years. Minister of Health from 1945-1951, overseeing the founding of the National Health Service. Fierce opponent of Eden's Suez intervention in 1956. A year later he shocked a good many of his followers by renouncing unilateral nuclear disarmament.

Rhodes Boyson (1925-2012): brought up in a Labour household, becoming a Methodist lay-preacher and a school-teacher. A man of uncompromisingly old-fashioned views – which he proclaimed with brio – persuaded by the moral virtues of the market, the wisdom of caning in schools, and the evils of homosexuality. Gravitated from Labour to Conservative, becoming a Tory MP in 1974, and remaining so until 1997. His *Black Papers in Education* (1977 and later) represented a powerful assault on comprehensive schooling and on anything which went under the banner of 'progressive'. He was part of the popular undertow of the politics identified by Hall in 'The great moving right show'.

George Brown (1914-1985): senior Labour politician in the 1960s. Of working-class origins, trade unionism providing him with a route through public life. A foot soldier in the making of the postwar settlement, first mentored by Ernest Bevin. MP from 1945. He represented the right-wing of the Labour Party, and after his active public career came to a premature end, he quietly joined the newly formed Social Democratic Party.

Rab Butler (1902-1982): the principal ideological and political architect of the Conservative commitment to the postwar settlement. Overseer of the great reforming Education Act of 1944, and thereafter Chancellor of the Exchequer, Home Secretary and Foreign Secretary. Outmanoeuvred for the job of Prime Minister in 1957 and in 1963.

James Callaghan (1912-2005): Labour Prime Minister from 1976 to 1979, losing the election of 1979 to Margaret Thatcher, after government policies on public sector pay had resulted in the Winter of Discontent. Presided over the beginning of the dramatic undoing of Labour's 'forward march'. Initiator of the 'great debate' on education. In his years as prime minister one could see his political authority evaporating day by day. Over his political career he gravitated further and further to the right of the party.

Kenneth Clarke (1940-): a beneficiary of the postwar settlement, joining the Conservatives as a student at Cambridge. Regarded as possessing a reforming and liberal instinct, but followed the prevailing political winds as a presence in Tory politics. Chancellor of the Exchequer 1993 to 1997 under John Major, and before that Home Secretary. Remained pro-Europe when his party begin to drift to a Eurosceptic position. In 2003 he opposed the invasion of Iraq. Stood for leadership of the Conservatives in 1997, 2001 and 2005, regarding himself as ever-more an independent Tory after each defeat. Relishes his own 'outspokenness'.

Robin Cook (1946-2005): an MP of the Labour left, who espoused a number of progressive causes, and was a parliamentarian of standing. MP from 1974 until his death. A tentative supporter of constitutional reform. Foreign Secretary under Tony Blair, but then effectively demoted. Famously resigned his posts in 2003 in protest over the war with Iraq.

Anthony Crosland (1918-1977): the most conspicuous intellectual of Labour modernisation at the end of the 1950s, arguing against both Labour traditionalism and inherited notions of socialism. This represented a very different species of 'modernisation' from that represented by the New Left of the same years. See especially *The Future of Socialism* (1956). The intellectual face of Hugh Gaitskell's Labour revisionism, he first entered parliament in 1950. A Labour MP and cabinet minister.

Anthony Eden (1897-1977): in the 1930s seen as the quintessential young, dashing, reform-minded Conservative. Foreign Secretary in 1938 but resigned in protest against appeasement, thereby usefully allying himself with Churchill. Emerged alongside Harold Macmillan as a 'natural' leader to follow Churchill, becoming Prime Minister in 1955. With his decision to invade Egypt the following year, his political reputation all but collapsed and Macmillan and Butler worked to remove him from office. He resigned in January 1957, leaving the Tories – it seemed – in a perilous state.

Hugh Gaitskell (1906-1963): the arch-political moderniser of the Labour Party at the end of the 1950s, espousing a social democracy underwritten by a faith in the 'politics of opportunity'. Consciously active on the right of the Labour Party. Endeavoured to move the party away from its historic commitments to Labour socialism, and its close relations to the trade union movement, pursuing this as leader of Labour from 1955 until his death in 1963. In fighting to jettison the party's commitment to the socialisation of the means of production (Clause 4), and in his steadfast and militant rejection of unilateral nuclear disarmament, he was constantly in the sights of the New Left.

Peter Griffiths (1928-2013): Conservative politician involved in the notorious 1964 general election campaign in Smethwick in the West Midlands, during which the slogan 'If you want a nigger for a neighbour, vote Liberal or Labour' appeared. Griffiths won the seat from the sitting Labour MP, shadow foreign secretary Patrick Gordon Walker. The visit of Malcolm X also brought global attention to the constituency.

Jo Grimond (1913-1993): a Liberal politician and MP for Orkney and Shetland between 1950 and 1983. Led the party between 1956 and 1967 and in 1976. A supporter of Scottish home rule and an opponent of the UK's nuclear arsenal, he moved the party leftwards during his leadership.

Lord Hailsham (Quintin Hogg) (1907-2001): Conservative politician, writer and orator. A major Conservative ideologue, formed within the cultures of high Toryism, and born into an aristocratic back ground. In 1938 stood as MP and won in a by-election for the Conservatives, as a supporter of appeasement (his opponent was Patrick Gordon Walker). At the time of the Suez crisis he was First Lord of the Admiralty, and during his long career later served as Lord Chancellor under Margaret Thatcher. On the moralistic end of Conservative politics, Hall et al note in *Policing the Crisis* that Selsdon Park released Hailsham into a 'renewed burst of moral energy'.

Roy Hattersley (1932-): prominent Labour politician and writer, MP for Birmingham Sparkbrook between 1963 and 1997. Deputy leader to Neil Kinnock between 1983 and 1992, and involved in attempts to 'modernise' the party and oppose the Militant Tendency. A Yorkshireman associated with the right of the party, he later became a strong critic of New Labour, from a position to their left.

Edward Heath (1916-2005): influential Conservative politician, MP for Bexley between 1950 and 2001 and Prime Minister between 1970 and 1974. Prior to the 1970 election, in a shadow cabinet 'secret conclave' at Selsdon Park, Heath articulated a British take on Nixon's law and order strategy and free market agenda, described by Hall et al in *Policing the Crisis* as a 'nebulous package of popular fears and stereotypes'. The significant and well-organised industrial unrest during the Heath government led to a U-turn on his free-market agenda, as he faced concerted opposition to the Industrial Relations Act of 1971, and in 1972 and 1974 two successful miners' strikes.

Derick Heathcoat-Amory (1899-1981): a justifiably forgotten Tory, impeccably traditional in every facet of his life. A strangely phantasmatic distillation of old-school England, all the more curious as he could never see who he was historically. Harold Macmillan's Chancellor of the Exchequer from 1958 to 1960. A keen sailor, best known for having his yacht brought up the Thames to collect him after his budget speeches.

Roy Jenkins (1920-2003): first elected a Labour MP in 1948, and a major figure in the Labour governments after 1964. A great liberalising Home Secretary, overseeing (among other measures) the decriminalisation of homosexuality and the relaxation of abortion law, but on other issues on the right of the party. A strong pro-European, becoming President of the European Commission in 1977. One of the Labour right-wing 'gang of four' who in January 1981 defected from Labour to form the Council of Social Democracy (CSD) which soon changed its name to the Social Democratic Party. Hall described the gang as 'little Caesars' (Caesarism refers to the rise of a leader or other compromise-broker from above, in a situation where two political blocs are at stalemate). Jenkins later (briefly) became the party's first leader, winning a seat in a 1982 by-election in Glasgow Hillhead (which he lost in 1987). In June 1981 the SDP formed an alliance with the Liberal Party and in 1988 the two parties merged, adopting the name Liberal Democrats in 1989.

Keith Joseph (1918-1994): Conservative MP from 1956 to 1987, and a minister under Macmillan, Home, Heath and Thatcher. An intellectual mentor of Margaret Thatcher and a neoliberal ideologue, strongly influenced by the ideas of Milton Friedman. After the electoral defeat of Heath in 1974 worked with Thatcher to establish the Centre for Policy Studies, a think tank promoting free-market conservatism, and wrote its inaugural pamphlet. Shared Thatcher's combination of free market ideas and regressive positions on race and family, and as Education Secretary was strongly critical of the foundational module in the Open University Social Sciences Foundation Course, which Hall was involved in.

Harold Macmillan (1894-1986): Conservative Prime Minister from 1957 to 1963. Helped shape a Conservative politics in line with the post-war consensus (later dismantled by Thatcher). A keen advocate of the Suez invasion and vehement critic of Nasser, he speedily reversed this commitment once he understood the depth of Washington's outrage. He was known as 'Supermac', and 'you've never had it so good' was his catchphrase.

John Major (1943-): son of a circus performer from Brixton, rising unspectacularly to become Conservative Prime Minister after Margaret Thatcher was knifed by her erstwhile acolytes. Won the 1992 general election, but his government was defined by sleaze, infighting over Europe and economic disarray, particularly after the exit from the Exchange Rate Mechanism on Black Wednesday. Given to flights of fancy about 'maids cycling through the mist', cricket and warm beer, his attempt to re-assert traditional values through a 'back to basics' campaign foundered quickly due to the (unwise) attention it brought to the private lives of his backbenchers and ministers. Presciently described the Eurosceptic wing of his party as 'bastards'.

Angus Maude (1912-1993): Conservative politician and writer, dreamer of a crystalline, uncompromising vision of Conservatism. Directed the Conservative Political Centre from 1951 to 1955. A key figure in Margaret Thatcher's campaign for the leadership in 1975, became Paymaster General in 1979, a post he held until his resignation in 1981.

Richard Nixon (1913-1994): Republican President of the United States from 1969 to 1974. In his 1969 election campaign popularised the term 'silent majority', by means of which he summoned the idea of a conservative middle America whose voice had been lost among the vociferousness of the liberals, hippies and anti-war campaigners of the 1960s. He also deployed a strong 'law and order' rhetoric, again as a way of detaching traditional voters from liberalism. Hall saw this as influencing Edward Heath at his Selsdon Park pre-election conference in 1970. Nixon's election represented a return to conservatism after a more liberal decade. He was forced to resign in 1974, however, as a result of the Watergate scandal. Spiro Agnew was Nixon's Vice President from 1969-1973, but had already been forced to resign because of being charged with criminal tax evasion. Nixon was therefore replaced as president by Agnew's replacement as Vice President – Gerald Ford.

David Owen (1938-): a doctor of medicine, first elected as a Labour MP in 1966, and a minister in the 1974-9 Labour government. One of the 'gang of four' in 1981 (for more information see Roy Jenkins entry), and SDP party leader from 1983-7, retaining his seat as an SDP and then independent MP until 1992. Owen opposed the 1988 merger with the Liberals and continued as leader of the rump SDP until it closed down (apart from a few branches) in 1990. He was made a peer by John Major in 1992.

Cecil Parkinson (1931-2016): Conservative MP between 1970 and 1992. A devoted Thatcherite who resigned from office on the same day as Thatcher. A member of the Falklands war cabinet, and, as Conservative Party chair, architect of the party's 1983 election victory. Appointed Secretary of State for Trade and Industry but forced to resign in October 1983 when the pregnancy of his personal secretary Sara Keays became public knowledge. Influenced by Pinochet's experiment with introducing neoliberalism in Chile in the 1970s, he argued that, under authoritarian conditions, 'Chile could impose a policy and a speed of application in that policy which just isn't possible in this country'.

James Prior (1927-): a Conservative MP from 1959 to 1987 and a minister in the Heath government of 1970-74. Served as a minister under Margaret Thatcher, but was regarded by her as a 'wet'. He resigned from government in 1984.

Nicholas Ridley (1929-1993): Conservative MP from 1959 to 1992. After Edward Heath abandoned the Selsdon Park programme formed the Selsdon Group to keep its spirit alive. Served as a minister and cabinet member throughout almost the entire period of Margaret Thatcher's cabinet but was forced to resign a few months before her, as a result of ill-advised remarks about Europe and Germany.

Bill Rodgers (1928-): first elected as a Labour MP in a 1962 by-election, minister in the Labour government of 1974-9. Joined the 'gang of four' in 1981 (for more information see Roy Jenkins entry). Lost his seat in the 1983 general election, made a peer in 1992.

Arthur Scargill (1938-): left school to become a coal miner in 1953, President of the Yorkshire Miners from 1973, president of the NUM from 1981 to 2002. Played a key role in the miners' strikes of 1972 and 1974, which are regarded as having significantly contributed to the demise of the Heath government. Played an important role in NUM support for the Grunwick strikers from 1976 to 1978. As NUM President in the 1984-5 miners' strike, his strategic leadership came under criticism from a number of quarters, particularly for his decision not to organise a national strike ballot. Hall shared much of this criticism, but was clear that it was the Labour Party leadership that was most to be criticised for failure of leadership during the strike.

Norman Tebbit (1931-): Conservative MP 1970-1992. A leading right-wing ideologue and anti-union campaigner, and successor in 1981 to Jim Prior as employment secretary, in which role he adopted a much more hawkish attitude to the unions. Remained in Margaret Thatcher's cabinet until 1987, when he left government in order to look after his wife who had been injured in the 1984 Brighton hotel bombing. In 1990 he proposed what became known as the Tebbit test – when he argued that 'a large number of Britain's Asian population fail to pass the cricket test': 'Which side do they cheer for? It's an interesting test'.

Shirley Williams (1930-): first elected as a Labour MP in 1964, and a minister in the 1974-9 Labour government, but lost her seat in the 1979 general election. A member of the 'gang of four' in 1981 (for more information see Roy Jenkins entry), she won a seat for the SDP in a by-election later that year, losing it again in 1983. In 1993 she became a life peer.

Harold Wilson (1916-1995): Labour MP 1945-1983, cabinet member 1947-51, Labour leader 1963-76, Prime Minister 1964-70 and 1974-76. Regarded in his early career as a left-winger, Wilson as prime minister was a centrist and pragmatist. In 1963 he made a famous party conference speech calling for a new Britain to be forged in the 'white heat' of the scientific revolution – thereby inaugurating a long tradition within the Labour Party of modernisation as a substitute for socialism.

Index

United States 22, 26, 33, 41, 43, 59, 102, 111, 115, 118, 126, 149, 159, 168, 239, 256-7, 315, 321-2, 324, 330, 342
and Cuban missiles crisis 70-84 passim
Universities and Left Review (ULR) 118, 120, 121, 124, 126, 129, 130, 131, 135, 137, 336, 338, 339, 341
ULR Club 129, 130
Uses of Literacy 29, 40, 44, 121, 339

Vietnam 89, 107, 111-2, 149, 325
Violence 107, 109, 111, 112, 113, 114, 115, 116, 117, 159, 160, 170, 329

Wallerstein, Immanuel 275
Walvin, James 142
War of position/war of manoeuvre 12, 137, 219, 237, 264, 267, 284, 345
Welfare state 18, 20, 21, 43, 50, 59, 95, 120, 136, 152, 218, 225, 227-8, 229, 230-1, 243, 292-3, 302-3, 309, 318-9, 320, 323, 347
Westergaard, John 92
Whannell, Paddy 123, 131, 339
Willetts, David 332,
Williams, Eric 337,
Williams, Raymond 30, 37, 39, 41, 61, 105, 118, 120, 123, 128, 279-81, 334, 338, 344, 339
Williams, Shirley 193, 195, 360
Wilson, Harold 98, 99, 100, 101, 110, 132, 163, 176, 360
Wright Mills, Charles 40-1, 126, 135
Working class 20, 28, 29, 30-1, 32, 35, 36, 37, 38, 39, 40, 41, 42, 47-8, 50, 54, 56, 59, 64-6, 124, 148, 149, 151, 176, 178, 183, 214-5, 250, 339; *see also* labour movement

Youth/young people 49, 50, 86, 131, 134, 148, 152, 154-5, 233, 234, 260, 299, 341-2